Index to Periodical Articles by and about Blacks: 1983

Compiled by the staff of the
Hallie Q. Brown Memorial Library
Central State University, Wilberforce, Ohio

G. K. Hall & Co.
70 Lincoln Street, Boston, Massachusetts 02111

This publication is printed on permanent/durable acid-free paper.

INTRODUCTION

The *Index to Periodical Articles By and About Blacks* is an index to Afro-American periodicals of general and scholarly interest. Author and subject entries are interfiled into a single alphabet. Sublistings for creative works and reviews may be found, arranged by title, under their respective subject headings. Filing variations may appear from one edition to another because of the computer-based compilation of data.

The subject heading authority is *Library of Congress Subject Headings,* ninth edition, although more current or specialized sources may also be consulted. The subject heading Afro-Americans and those beginning with Afro-American appear rarely, owing to the limited scope of this index. Under the heading First Facts are found entries relative to events that break patterns of race and sex discrimination. These articles are also indexed by author and subject.

All Black American periodicals are considered for indexing. Others which include a significant number of articles about the Black experience may also be considered.

Suggestions for additional titles may be directed to the Indexing Project, Hallie Q. Brown Memorial Library, Central State University, Wilberforce, Ohio 45384.

NOTES ON USING THE INDEX

ARRANGEMENT: In this edition the authors, subjects, and references are filed in dictionary format. Because the data is compiled by computer, certain variations may appear.

CREATIVE WORKS: These are indexed under the author's name. In addition, the titles are listed under one of the following headings:

> Dramas
> Musical Compositions
> Novels
> Poems
> Short Stories

REVIEWS: These are indexed under the name of the author of the work being reviewed, under the name of the author of the review, and under one of the following headings:

> Book Reviews
> Drama Reviews
> Motion Picture Reviews
> Music Reviews
> Record Reviews

SUBJECT POLICY: Generally, the subject Afro-Americans and subjects starting with the word Afro-American are not used, due to the specialized scope of the *Index.*

ABBREVIATIONS: There are very few abbreviations in this edition. Months of the year are limited to the first three letters.

CITATION FORMAT:

> Author Entries—(including authors of reviews)
>
> (a) author in bold-face type
> (b) article title. (c) added information.

(d) journal title in italics. (e) journal volume number and page
    numbers
(f) month and year of publication

Subject Entries—(including subjects of obituaries and authors of
works being reviewed)

(a) subject term in bold-face type
(b) article title. (c) added information.
(d) author(s) (unless there is no author).
(e) journal title in italics. (f) journal volume number and page
    numbers
(g) month and year of publication

Added information includes the following:

        Abridgement
        Abstract
        Anonymous
        Bibliography
        Book Review
        Department
        Drama
        Drama Review
        Editorial
        Excerpt
        First Facts
        Interview
        Motion Picture Review
        Musical Composition
        Music Review
        Notes
        Novel
        Record Review
        Short Story
        Symposium
        Tables Translation

LIST OF PERIODICALS INDEXED

about . . . time
Afro-Americans in New York Life and History

Black American Literature Forum

Black Art, An International Quarterly

Black Books Bulletin

The Black Collegian

Black Enterprise

Black Law Journal

Black Male/Female Relationships

The Black Perspective in Music

The Black Scholar

The Black Sociologist

CAAS Newsletter

CLA Journal

The Crisis

Ebony

Encore American & Worldwide News

Essence

Freedomways

Howard Law Journal

Interracial Books for Children Bulletin (Selective Indexing)

Jet (Selective Indexing)

Journal of African Civilizations

Journal of Black Psychology

Journal of Black Studies

Journal of Negro Education

Journal of Negro History

Journal of Religious Thought

Journal of the National Medical Association

Negro Educational Review

Negro History Bulletin

Phylon

Research in African Literatures

Review of Black Political Economy

Umoja

The Urban League Review

The Western Journal of Black Studies

ADDRESSES OF PERIODICALS INDEXED

about . . . time
About . . . Time Magazine, Inc.
30 Genesee Street
Rochester, New York 14611

AFRO-AMERICANS IN NEW YORK
LIFE AND HISTORY
Afro-American Historical Association
of the Niagara Frontier, Inc.
P.O. Box 1663
Hertle Station
Buffalo, New York 14216

BLACK AMERICAN
LITERATURE FORUM
Statesman Towers West, 1005
Indiana State University
Terre Haute, Indiana 47809

BLACK ART AN
INTERNATIONAL QUARTERLY
Black Art, Ltd
137-55 Southgate Street
Jamaica, New York 11413

BLACK BOOKS BULLETIN
Institute of Positive Education
7524 South Cottage Grove Avenue
Chicago, Illinois 60619

THE BLACK COLLEGIAN
1240 South Broad Street
New Orleans, Louisiana 70125

BLACK ENTERPRISE
Earl Graves Publishing
    Company, Inc.
P.O. Box 5500
Bergenfield, New Jersey 07621

BLACK LAW JOURNAL
University of California at
    Los Angeles
School of Law
Room 2125
Los Angeles, California 90024

BLACK MALE/FEMALE
RELATIONSHIPS
Black Think Tank
1801 Bush Street
Suite 118
San Francisco, California 94109

THE BLACK PERSPECTIVE
IN MUSIC
The Foundation for Research in the
    Afro-American
    Creative Arts, Inc.
Post Office Drawer I
Cambria Heights, New York 11411

THE BLACK SCHOLAR
Black World Foundation, Inc.
Box 908
Sausalito, California 94965

THE BLACK SOCIOLOGIST
Department 8010
Transaction Periodicals Consortium
Rutgers University
New Brunswick, New Jersey 08903

CAAS NEWSLETTER
University of California
Center for Afro-American Studies
3111 Campbell Hall
Los Angeles, California 90024

ADDRESSES OF PERIODICALS INDEXED

CLA JOURNAL
College Language Association
c/o Cason L. Hill, Editor
Morehouse College
Atlanta, Georgia 30314

THE CRISIS
186 Remsen Street
Brooklyn, New York 11201

EBONY
Johnson Publishing Company
820 South Michigan Avenue
Chicago, Illinois 60605

ENCORE AMERICAN &
WORLDWIDE NEWS
Tanner Publications Company, Inc.
2 Penn Plaza
Suite 1500
New York, New York 10001

ESSENCE
P.O. Box 2989
Boulder, Colorado 80302

FREEDOMWAYS
Freedomways Associates, Inc.
799 Broadway
New York, New York 10003-6849

HOWARD LAW JOURNAL
Howard University
School of Law
2900 Van Ness Street, N.W.
Washington, D.C. 20008

INTERRACIAL BOOKS FOR
CHILDREN BULLETIN
(Selective Indexing)
1841 Broadway
New York, New York 10023

JET (Selective Indexing)
Johnson Publishing Company
820 South Michigan Avenue
Chicago, Illinois 60605

JOURNAL OF AFRICAN
CIVILIZATIONS
Transaction Periodicals
Consortium
Rutgers University
New Brunswick, New Jersey 08903

JOURNAL OF BLACK
PSYCHOLOGY
Association of Black Psychologists
P.O. Box 2929
Washington, D.C. 20013

JOURNAL OF BLACK STUDIES
Sage Publications, Inc.
275 South Beverly Drive
Beverly Hills, California 90212

JOURNAL OF NEGRO
EDUCATION
Bureau of Educational Research
P.O. Box 311
Howard University
Washington, D.C. 20059

JOURNAL OF NEGRO HISTORY
Association for the Study of
   Afro-American
   Life and History
1401 14th Street, N.W.
Washington, D.C. 20005

JOURNAL OF RELIGIOUS
THOUGHT
Howard University
Divinity School
1240 Randolph Street, N.E.
Washington, D.C. 20017

JOURNAL OF THE NATIONAL
MEDICAL ASSOCIATION
25 Van Zant Street
East Norwalk, Connecticut 06855

NEGRO EDUCATIONAL
REVIEW
P.O. Box 2895
General Mail Center
Jacksonville, Florida 32203

NEGRO HISTORY BULLETIN
Association for the Study of
   Afro-American
   Life and History
1401 14th Street, N.W.
Washington, D.C. 20005

PHYLON
Atlanta University
Atlanta, Georgia 30314

RESEARCH IN AFRICAN
LITERATURES
University of Texas Press
P.O. Box 7819
Austin, Texas 78712

REVIEW OF BLACK POLITICAL
ECONOMY
Transaction Periodicals Consortium
Rutgers University
New Brunswick, N.J. 08903

UMOJA
Campus Box 294
University of Colorado at Boulder
Boulder, Colorado 80309

THE URBAN LEAGUE REVIEW
Transaction Periodicals Consortium
Rutgers University
New Brunswick, N.J. 08903

THE WESTERN JOURNAL OF
BLACK STUDIES
Washington State University Press
Pullman, Washington 99164

A.F.T.

See American Federation Of Teachers

A.I.D.S.

See Acquired Immune Deficiency Syndrome

A.N.C.

See African National Congress

A.S.A.A.L.H.

See Association For The Study Of
Afro-American Life And History

A.U.D.E.L.C.O.

See Audience Development Committee, Inc.

Abolitionists

Frederick Douglass: Agitator For Liberty, Justice,
Equality And Afro-American Uplift. Illustrated.
Frederick Douglass (Jr.) Jefferson. *about. . . time.*
11: 8-11+ (Feb 83)

Academic Achievement

Functional Language, Socialization, And Academic
Achievement. Notes. Richard L. Wright. *Journal of
Negro Education.* 52: 3-14 (Winter 83)

Reading, Dialect, And The Low-Achieving Black
College Student. Notes. Carole F. Stice. *Negro
Educational Review.* 34: 84-87 (Apr 83)

Salute To Black Scholars: Bringing Scholarships
And Students Together. Illustrated. Elizabeth
Knight. *about. . . time.* 11: 12-13 (Jun 83)

Academic Dissertations

See Dissertations, Academic

Academy Awards (Motion Pictures)

Gossett Wins An Oscar; Urges Hollywood To Use
More Blacks In Movies. Illustrated. *Jet.* 64: 60 (2
May 83)

Accad, Evelyne

L'Influence De La Littérature Française Sur Le
Roman Arabe. Book review. *Research in African
Literatures.* 14: 203-207 (Summer 83)

Achebe, Chinua—Criticism And Interpretation

No Longer At Ease: Chinua Achebe's "Heart Of
Whiteness". Notes. Philip Rogers. *Research in
African Literatures.* 14: 165-183 (Summer 83)

Achievement, Academic

See Academic Achievement

Acquired Immune Deficiency Syndrome

Plagued By AIDS Scare. Tables. David J. Dent.
Black Enterprise. 14: 24 (Dec 83)

What (And Why) You Should Know About. . .
AIDS. Eric Copage. *Essence.* 14: 51 (Jul 83)

Actors And Actresses

An Actor Trades Pounds For Jobs! Illustrated. Ruth
Dolores Manuel. *Essence.* 14: 116 (Nov 83)

Billy Dee Williams: The Serious Side Of A Sex
Symbol. Illustrated. Charles L. Sanders. *Ebony.* 38:
126-128+ (Jun 83)

Clifton Davis: How Marriage And Ministry
Changed Him. Illustrated. Trudy S. Moore. *Jet.* 65:
54-57 (12 Sep 83)

The Dream Guys Of 'Dreamgirls'. Illustrated.
Ebony. 38: 74-76+ (Apr 83)

Eddie Murphy: An Incredible Leap To
Superstardom. Illustrated. Walter Leavy. *Ebony.*
38: 35-36+ (Oct 83)

From Ragtime To Realtime: A Profile Of Howard
Rollins. Illustrated. Crystal V. Rhodes. *Black
Collegian.* 14: 134-135+ (Sep-Oct 83)

Gossett Wins An Oscar; Urges Hollywood To Use
More Blacks In Movies. Illustrated. *Jet.* 64: 60 (2
May 83)

Harry Belafonte: Daughter Pays Father's Day Tribute To Her Famous Father. Illustrated. Robert E. Johnson. *Jet.* 64: 58-61 (20 Jun 83)

James Bond's Movie, Never Say Never Again, Features Black Actor Bernie Casey. Illustrated. Aldore Collier. *Jet.* 65: 56-57+ (21 Nov 83)

Jennifer Beals: Sultry Student Strikes Stardom In 'Flashdance'. Illustrated. *Jet.* 64: 60-63 (6 Jun 83)

Louis Gossett, Natalie Cole Tell Of Changes In Their Lives. Illustrated. *Jet.* 64: 60-63 (23 May 83)

Marla Gibbs. Illustrated. Craig W. Reid. *Essence.* 13: 15 (Mar 83)

Mr. T Among Stars In Hottest New TV Show. Illustrated. *Jet.* 64: 54-56 (28 Mar 83)

New Faces In Hollywood. Illustrated. *Ebony.* 38: 62-64+ (Apr 83)

Robert Guillaume: Behind The Scenes With TV's 'Benson'. Illustrated. Aldore Collier. *Ebony.* 39: 133-134+ (Nov 83)

Shari And Harry. Illustrated. Michele Wallace. *Essence.* 14: 82-83 (Aug 83)

Showstopper: Darnell Williams. Illustrated. Ruth Dolores Manuel. *Essence.* 14: 35 (Nov 83)

Showstopper: Kim Fields. Illustrated. Craig Reid. *Essence.* 14: 47 (Aug 83)

To Liberate Black Actors. Clayton Riley. *Freedomways.* 23: No. 4: 236-239 (83)

The Year Of The Black Male In Films. Illustrated. Aldore D. Collier. *Ebony.* 38: 168+ (Aug 83)

See Also Children As Actors

Actresses

See Actors And Actresses

Adams, Hunter Havelin (III)

African Observers Of The Universe: The Sirius Question. Illustrated, notes, tables. *Journal of African Civilizations.* 05: 27-46 (Apr-Nov 83)

New Light On The Dogon And Sirius. Notes. *Journal of African Civilizations.* 05: 47-49 (Apr-Nov 83)

Adams, Lenny (about)

What Happens When. . . The Active Career In Sports Is Over? Illustrated. Willis Anderson. *about. . . time.* 11: 14-19 (Jan 83)

Adams, Milton S.

Management Of Attention Deficit Disorders. Notes. *National Medical Association Journal.* 75: 187-189 (Feb 83)

Addison, Linda D.

Built To Last! Illustrated, tables. *Essence.* 14: 35 (Dec 83)

Ade, King Sunny (about)

The New King Of Swing. Illustrated. Frank Dexter Brown. *Black Enterprise.* 13: 42 (Jun 83)

Adedeji, Joel

Nationalism And The Nigerian National Theatre. Book review. Ebun Clark. *Research in African Literatures.* 14: 107-108 (Spring 83)

Adekunle, Ademakinwa (joint author)

See Oluwole, Soji F.

Administrative Law—Underdeveloped Areas

Administrative Law And Development: The American 'Model' Evaluated. Notes. Paul H. Brietzke. *Howard Law Journal.* 26: No. 2: 645-698 (83)

Administrative Law—United States

Administrative Law And Development: The American 'Model' Evaluated. Notes. Paul H. Brietzke. *Howard Law Journal.* 26: No. 2: 645-698 (83)

Admirals

Admiral Hacker Takes Command. Illustrated. *Ebony.* 38: 74+ (Feb 83)

Adoff, Arnold

All The Colors Of The Race. Book review. Kate Shackford. *Interracial Books for Children.* 14: No. 1: 35 (83)

Adolescence

Caste: The Blight Of Adolescence. Editorial. Harry Bloch. *National Medical Association Journal.* 75: 457-458 (May 83)

Adolescent Boys

A Manchild Of The '80s. Illustrated. Peter Bailey and Moneta (Jr.) Sleet. *Ebony.* 38: 68+ (Aug 83)

Adolescent Mothers

Contraceptive Practices Of Teenage Mothers. Tables, notes. Anita C. Washington and others. *National Medical Association Journal.* 75: 1059-1063 (Nov 83)

Adolescent Psychology

Psychopolitical Orientations Of White And Black Youth: A Test Of Five Models. Tables, notes. Samuel Long. *Journal of Black Studies.* 13: 439-456 (Jun 83)

Adolescents

See Youth

Adopted Children

See Children, Adopted

Advertising Campaigns

Marketing: Social Conscience. Illustrated. Iders Marsh. *Black Enterprise.* 13: 39-41 (Jan 83)

Advertising—Lawyers

Attorney's Expanding Right To Advertise Under The First Amendment. Notes. Audrey Shields. *Howard Law Journal.* 26: No. 1: 281-304 (83)

Advertising—Vocational Guidance

Advertising: An Ad-Venture. Illustrated. Monique Clesca. *Essence.* 14: 32 (Jul 83)

Aged

The Passing Of Wisdom (A Reflection On The Meaning Of Cynthia Fitzpatrick's Life). Illustrated. David A. Anderson. *about. . . time.* 11: 24-25 (Apr 83)

Problems Of Black High-Risk Elderly. Notes, tables. Morgan W. F. Dickerson. *Journal of Black Studies.* 14: 251-260 (Dec 83)

    See Also Alcohol And The Aged

Aged—Care And Hygiene

Preventive Issues And The Black Elderly: A Biopsychosocial Perspective. Notes, tables. Orlando B. Lightfoot. *National Medical Association Journal.* 75: 957-963 (Oct 83)

Aged—Medical Care

Access Of The Black Urban Elderly To Medical Care. Tables, notes. Jacquelyn H. Wolf and others. *National Medical Association Journal.* 75: 41-46 (Jan 83)

Aging—Research

Aging Research, Black Americans, And The National Institute On Aging. Daniel D. Cowell. *National Medical Association Journal.* 75: 99 + (Jan 83)

Agriculture—Egypt—Origins

An Ancient Harvest On The Nile. Tables. Fred Wendorf and others. *Journal of African Civilizations.* 05: 58-64 (Apr-Nov 83)

Air Force

    See United States. Air Force

Air National Guard

    See United States—Air National Guard

Air Pilots

America's Black Flying Clubs. Illustrated. Roger Witherspoon. *Black Enterprise.* 13: 75 + (Mar 83)

    See Also Women Air Pilots

Ajagbe, H. A. and Daramola, J. O.

Fibro-Osseous Lesions Of The Jaw: A Review Of 133 Cases From Nigeria. Illustrated, notes. *National Medical Association Journal.* 75: 593-598 (Jun 83)

Akan Poetry—History And Criticism

To Praise Or Not To Praise The King: The Akan Apae In The Context Of Referential Poetry. Notes. Kwesi Yankah. *Research in African Literatures.* 14: 381-400 (Fall 83)

Akan Writing

    See Writing, Akan

Akhtar, Abbasi J.

A Healthful Approach To Death And Dying. Editorial, Notes. *National Medical Association Journal.* 75: 350 (Apr 83)

Akpan, Monday B.

European Imperialism In Liberia: The Scramble And Partition - 1882-1914. Notes. *Negro History Bulletin.* 46: 93-94 (Oct-Dec 83)

Alabama—Governors—Racial Attitudes

Has Gov. George Wallace Really Changed? Interview, Illustrated. George C. Wallace and Charles L. Sanders. *Ebony.* 38: 44-46 + (Sep 83)

Aladj, Mary

Black History Month Specials. Illustrated. *about. . . time.* 11: 22-23 (Feb 83)

Alakoye, Imogunla

Love Poem. Poem. *Essence.* 13: 16 (Feb 83)

Albany, New York—History

Three Dark Centuries Around Albany: A Survey Of Black Life In New York's Capital City Area Before World War I. Notes, tables. Thomas J. Davis. *Afro-Americans in New York Life and History.* 07: 7-23 (Jan 83)

Albee, Edward—Criticism And Interpretation

"Pow!" "Snap!" "Pouf!": The Modes Of Communication In Who's Afraid Of Virgina Woolf? Notes. Dan Ducker. *CLA Journal.* 26: 465-477 (Jun 83)

Albrecht, Otto E.

Marian Anderson: A Catalog Of The Collection At University Of Pennsylvania Library. Book review. Janet L. Sims-Wood. *The Black Perspective in Music.* 11: 221-222 (Fall 83)

Alcohol And The Aged

Alcoholism In The Elderly: An Analysis Of 50 Patients. Tables, notes. Lawrence Blum and Fred Rosner. *National Medical Association Journal.* 75: 489-495 (May 83)

Alcohol And Women

Blues In A Bottle. Illustrated. Doris Jean Austin. *Essence.* 14: 88-89 + (Aug 83)

Alcoholic Beverages

Spirited Summer Drinks. Illustrated. Eunice Fried. *Black Enterprise.* 13: 66 (Jul 83)

    See Also Beer
    Wine And Wine Making

Aldrich, T. E. (joint author)

    See Torres, C. G.

Alexander, Adele Logan

Booker T. Washington: The Wizard Of Tuskegee, 1901-1915. Book review. *Crisis.* 90: 32 (Dec 83)

Private Consequences Of A Public Controversy. . . Grandmother, Grandfather, W.E.B. Du Bois And Booker T. Washington. Illustrated. *Crisis.* 90: 8-11 (Feb 83)

Alexander, George A.

Geographical Aspects Of Cancer In Tanzania. Tables, illustrated, notes. *National Medical Association Journal.* 75: 797-804 (Aug 83)

Radiotherapy In Tanzania. Illustrated, tables. *National Medical Association Journal.* 75: 289-295 (Mar 83)

Alexander, Jan

Strategy Sessions For Corporate Success.
Illustrated. *Black Enterprise*. 14: 61-62+ (Aug 83)

Alexander, Kelly M. (Sr.)

The Keynote. . . "Take Up This Crusade".
Illustrated. *Crisis*. 90: 16-18 (Aug-Sep 83)

Alexander, Nanine

Stow It: Get More Room From Less Space.
Illustrated. *Black Enterprise*. 13: 70-71 (Apr 83)

Alexander, T. M. (Jr.) (about)

Alexander Dies At 51. Connie Green. *Black Enterprise*. 14: 22 (Aug 83)

Alexis, Gail

All The Way Home. Poem. *Black American Literature Forum*. 17: 153 (Winter 83)

Athlete. Poem. *Black American Literature Forum*. 17: 153 (Winter 83)

For Robin H, Upon Seven Years Of Motherhood, At Age 21. Poem. *Black American Literature Forum*. 17: 152 (Winter 83)

Talking Horse. Poem. *Black American Literature Forum*. 17: 152 (Winter 83)

Alfaro, Lizandro Chavez

The Cut Of The Vest. Short story. *Black Scholar*. 14: 58-71 (Mar-Apr 83)

Alford, Beverly

The $100 Bet I Won By Losing Weight. Illustrated. *Essence*. 14: 130 (Jun 83)

Ali, Veronica (about)

Muhammad Ali's Wife Veronica Turns Horse Hobby Into Blue Ribbons. Illustrated. Aldore Collier and Isaac Sutton. *Jet*. 65: 22-25 (19 Sep 83)

Alien Labor

Constitutional Law-State Requirement That Peace Officers Be American Citizens Is Not Unconstitutional. Notes. Jeffery Beard. *Howard Law Journal*. 26: No. 1: 327-344 (83)

Undocumented Workers: In Search Of A Profile. Notes. Madeline L. Morris. *The Urban League Review*. 07: 91-99 (Summer 83)

See Also Children Of Alien Laborers

Alimentary Canal—Cancer

Synchronous Cancers Of The Gastrointestinal Tract: Results, Diagnosis, And Treatment. Tables, notes. Earl Belle Smith. *National Medical Association Journal*. 75: 311-313 (Mar 83)

Allen, Aubrey (about)

Voulez-Vous Un Big Mac? Illustrated. Wendell Gault. *Black Enterprise*. 14: 39 (Dec 83)

Allen, Bonnie

Bobbi Humphrey Toots Her Own Flute. Illustrated. *Essence*. 13: 66-68 (Mar 83)

Eddie Murphy: Black Humor With An Edge. Illustrated. *Essence*. 13: 12 (Jan 83)

Of Men And Money. Illustrated. *Essence*. 14: 89+ (Jun 83)

The Price We Paid For 'Giving It Up'.. *Essence*. 13: 61-62+ (Feb 83)

To Know Him Is To Love Him. Illustrated. *Essence*. 14: 58-60 (Nov 83)

Allen, Charles E. (about)

Charles Allen's Declaration Of Independence. Illustrated, tables. Lloyd Gite. *Black Enterprise*. 13: 113-114+ (Jun 83)

Allen, Eloise (about)

Woman At The Helm Of Philadelphia Presbytery. Illustrated. Marilyn Marshall. *Ebony*. 38: 51-52+ (Jul 83)

Allen, Marcus (about)

Marcus Allen: Raider Running Back May Be The Best Ever In The NFL. Illustrated. *Ebony*. 39: 143-144+ (Nov 83)

Alleyne, Reginald H. (Jr.)

Foreword [To Volume 8 Number 3].. *Black Law Journal*. 08: 370-372 (Winter 83)

Allowances, Children's

See Children's Allowances

Alston, Carrie (about)

Essense Women: Carrie Alston. Illustrated. Leslie Gourse. *Essence*. 13: 22 (Apr 83)

Amas Repertory, Inc.

Rosetta LeNoire: The Lady And Her Theatre. Notes. Linda Kerr Norflett. *Black American Literature Forum*. 17: 69-72 (Summer 83)

Ambassadors

Black Ambassadors Feted By Boston TransAfrica. Illustrated. D. Michael Cheers. *Jet*. 63: 36-39 (28 Feb 83)

Sydnor To Serve As U.S. Ambassador To Mauritius. Illustrated. *Jet*. 63: 4 (7 Mar 83)

Terence Todman Sworn In As Ambassador To Denmark. Illustrated. *Jet*. 65: 5 (24 Oct 83)

Amber Hues Cosmetiques

How This Sister Turned A Winning Bid Into A Gold Mine! Illustrated. Lloyd Gite. *Essence*. 14: 31 (Jul 83)

Amegbleame, S. Agbeko

Mister Tameklor, Suivi De Francis Le Parisien Par Le Happy Star Concert Band De Lome- (Togo). Book review. *Research in African Literatures*. 14: 114-116 (Spring 83)

Amela, Amelavi E.

Colloque Sur Litérature Et Esthétique Négro-Africanes. Book review. *Research in African Literatures*. 14: 560-564 (Winter 83)

American Black Achievement Awards, Fourth, 1982

Debbie Allen, Michael Warren Host American Black Achievement Awards Annual TV Show. Illustrated. *Jet*. 63: 54-57+ (28 Feb 83)

A Tribute To Black Excellence. Illustrated. *Ebony.* 38: 42-44+ (Apr 83)

American College Theatre Festival

A Slender Thread Of Hope: The Kennedy Center Black Theatre Project. Notes. Winona L. Fletcher. *Black American Literature Forum.* 17: 65-68 (Summer 83)

American Federation Of Teachers

CIBC Responds To Charges. Editorial. *Interracial Books for Children.* 14: No. 1: 3+ (83)

American Muslim Mission, St. Petersburg, Florida

Prayers And Profits. Illustrated. Curtis G. Bunn. *Black Enterprise.* 14: 28 (Dec 83)

American Revolution

See United States—History—Revolution, 1775-1783

Americans In Haiti—History

Emigration Of Black Americans To Haiti, 1821-1863. Leon D. Pamphile. *Crisis.* 90: 43-44 (Nov 83)

Amputees

Selma Amputee-Burn Victim Is Married To Hometown Policeman. Illustrated. Harmon Perry. *Jet.* 63: 22-25 (24 Jan 83)

Amsterdam News (Newspaper)

NY Paper In Trouble. Illustrated. Jill Nelson. *Black Enterprise.* 13: 20 (May 83)

Amusement Parks

Disney Epcot Center: A Family Experience. Illustrated. James Ruffin. *Black Enterprise.* 13: 105-106+ (Feb 83)

Anderson, Bernard E.

Economic Recovery And Black Employment. Illustrated. *Black Enterprise.* 13: 29 (Jul 83)

The Employment Challenge: A Job For Every Worker. Illustrated. *Black Enterprise.* 13: 24 (Jan 83)

Anderson, David A.

The Passing Of Wisdom (A Reflection On The Meaning Of Cynthia Fitzpatrick's Life). Illustrated. *about. . . time.* 11: 24-25 (Apr 83)

Anderson, Jervis

This Was Harlem: A Cultural Portrait, 1900-1950. Book review. Estelle W. Taylor. *Journal of Negro Education.* 52: 178-182 (Spring 83)

This Was Harlem: A Cultural Portrait, 1900-1950. Book review. James H. Randall. *Journal of Negro History.* 68: 105-107 (Winter 83)

Anderson, Marion

Bombs Or Bread: Black Unemployment And The Pentagon Budget. Tables. *Black Scholar.* 14: 2-11 (Jan-Feb 83)

Anderson, Robert (about)

From Slavery To Achievement: Keep On A Goin'. Illustrated. Robert L. (Jr.) Harris. *Black Collegian.* 13: 142-147 (Feb-Mar 83)

Anderson, Sheila (about)

New Faces In Hollywood. Illustrated. *Ebony.* 38: 62-64+ (Apr 83)

Anderson, WIlliam H. (Jr.) and Williams, BIshetta Merritt

TV And The Black Child: What Black Children Say About The Shows They Watch. Notes, tables. *Journal of Black Psychology.* 09: 27-42 (Feb 83)

Anderson, Willis

Victims Of Unemployment: Coping With Stress. Illustrated. *about. . . time.* 11: 10-13+ (Mar 83)

What Happens When. . . The Active Career In Sports Is Over? Illustrated. *about. . . time.* 11: 14-19 (Jan 83)

Anemia

Hypothyroidism Causing Macrocytic Anemia Unresponsive To B_{12} And Folate. Notes. Edward G. Sims. *National Medical Association Journal.* 75: 429-431 (Apr 83)

See Also Sickle Cell Anemia

Angelou, Maya (about)

Maya Angelou: The Heart Of The Woman. Illustrated. Stephanie Stokes Oliver. *Essence.* 14: 112-114+ (May 83)

The Heart Of A Woman. Book review. Maria K. Mootry Ikerionwu. *Phylon.* 44: 86-87 (Mar 83)

To A Man. Poem, Illustrated. *Ebony.* 38: 50 (Feb 83)

Where We Belong, A Duet. Poem, Illustrated. *Ebony.* 38: 46 (Feb 83)

Angelou, Maya—Criticism And Interpretation

Displacement And Autobiographical Style In Maya Angelou's The Heart Of A Woman. Notes. Carol E. Neubauer. *Black American Literature Forum.* 17: 123-129 (Fall 83)

Anger

Black Women's Anger. Illustrated. Audre Lorde. *Essence.* 14: 90-92+ (Oct 83)

Angola

See Also Missionaries—Angola

Anthony, Earl

Essence Women: Catherine Smallwood-Murchison. Illustrated. *Essence.* 14: 62 (Oct 83)

Anti-Nuclear Movement

Dialogues Of The World Assembly For Peace And Life, Against Nuclear War - Prague, Czechoslovakia June 21-26, 1983.. *Black Scholar.* 14: 44-46 (Nov-Dec 83)

The Exchange Of Experiences And Ideas Of Peace Movements In Support Of Disarmament.. *Black Scholar.* 14: 49-50 (Nov-Dec 83)

The Nuclear Controversy: The Black Point Of View. Illustrated. Garland Thompson. *Black Enterprise*. 13: 215-216+ (Jun 83)

Nuclear Policy, Social Justice, And The Third World. Tables. Robert Chrisman. *Black Scholar*. 14: 26-43 (Nov-Dec 83)

Antiques As An Investment

Turning Heirlooms Into Cash. J. Gregory Clemons. *Black Enterprise*. 14: 137-138 (Oct 83)

Antisemitism

Chronological, Cognitive And Political Effects In The Study Of Interminority Group Prejudice. Notes, tables. Ronald Tadao Tsukashima. *Phylon*. 44: 217-231 (Sep 83)

Apartheid

See South Africa—Race Relations

Apollo Theater, New York (City)

Stars To Shine At The Apollo. Illustrated. Ken Jones. *Black Enterprise*. 14: 18 (Sep 83)

Apostle, Richard A.

The Anatomy Of Racial Attitudes. Book review. Keith A. Winsell. *Phylon*. 44: 246-248 (Sep 83)

Appalachian Region, Southern

See Also Education—Appalachian Region, Southern

Apportionment (Election Law)

The Three Rs Revisited: Redistricting, Race And Representation In North Carolina. Notes, tables. Beeman C. Patterson. *Phylon*. 44: 232-243 (Sep 83)

Arab-Jewish Relations

See Jewish-Arab Relations

Arabs In Palestine

See Palestinian Arabs—Israel

Archer, Chalmers (Jr.)

Real Education Equity: A One-System Approach. Editorial. *Journal of Negro Education*. 52: 375-377 (Fall 83)

Architects

Black Architects: Shapers Of Urban America. Illustrated. Frank (III) White. *Ebony*. 38: 62-64+ (Jul 83)

Armatrading, Joan (about)

Joan Armatrading. Illustrated. Eric Copage. *Essence*. 14: 51 (Dec 83)

Armed Forces

See United States. Air Force
United States—Air National Guard
United States—Armed Forces
United States. Navy

Armstead, J. Holmes (Jr.)

Third World Legal Studies-1982: Law In Alternative Strategies Of Rural Development. Book review. *Black Law Journal*. 08: 459-461 (Winter 83)

Armstrong, Denise Carreathers (about)

Two Women In Houston Turn Their Dreams Of Owning A Bookstore Into A Successful Reality. Illustrated. Lloyd Gite. *Essence*. 13: 32+ (Mar 83)

Armstrong, Don

Detroit Fighters Build On Rich Historic Tradition. Illustrated. *Crisis*. 90: 28-29 (Apr 83)

The Importance Of Politics And Prayer. Illustrated. *Crisis*. 90: 30 (Apr 83)

A Man For All Sessions. Illustrated. *Crisis*. 90: 32 (Apr 83)

Odetta-A Citzen Of the World. Illustrated. *Crisis*. 90: 51-52 (Jun-Jul 83)

"Who Can We Turn To For Justice?" Illustrated. *Crisis*. 90: 20-21 (Nov 83)

Armstrong, Earl M.

Therapy Of Tuberculosis. Tables, notes. *National Medical Association Journal*. 75: 714-716+ (Jul 83)

Armstrong, George (about)

Armstrong Gets Personnel Position At White House.. *Jet*. 64: 6 (5 Sep 83)

Arnez, Nancy L.

Papa Babe's Stamp Collection. Book review. *Crisis*. 90: 50 (Aug-Sep 83)

Arnold, Stephen

Preface To A History Of Cameroon Literature In English. Notes. *Research in African Literatures*. 14: 498-515 (Winter 83)

Arnott, Ann

When Your Office Is At Home. Illustrated. *Black Enterprise*. 14: 132 (Oct 83)

Arnott, Nancy

Sis Diets. . . Brother Does Too! Illustrated. *Essence*. 14: 128 (Dec 83)

Arrest

A Case Of Anonymity. Illustrated. Jill Nelson. *Black Enterprise*. 13: 26 (Mar 83)

Arrest (Police Methods)

Accountability Of Law Enforcement Officers In The Use Of Deadly Force. Notes. Robert Berkley Harper. *Howard Law Journal*. 26: No. 1: 119-151 (83)

Art—Collectors And Collecting

Collecting Pre-Columbian Art. Illustrated. Barbara Kai. *Black Enterprise*. 13: 108+ (Feb 83)

Art—Exhibitions

A Checklist Of Afro-American Art Exhibits In The State Of New York, 1913 - 1983. Lynn Moody Igoe. *Afro-Americans in New York Life and History*. 07: 59-70 (Jul 83)

A Voice Of The People. Illustrated. Edwin B. Lake. *Black Enterprise*. 13: 42 (Jun 83)

The Work Of Four Creative Expressions In Crocheting, Drawing, Sewing And Furniture. Illustrated. *about. . . time*. 11: 18-20 (May 83)

Art In Literature

The Plastic Arts Motif In Roots. Notes. Carol P. Marsh. *CLA Journal*. 26: 325-333 (Mar 83)

Art In Universities And Colleges

The Visual Arts In Black Colleges: From Benign Neglect To Progress. Notes. Harold G. Cureau. *Negro Educational Review*. 34: 27-36 (Jan 83)

Art—Study And Teaching

The Visual Arts In Black Colleges: From Benign Neglect To Progress. Notes. Harold G. Cureau. *Negro Educational Review*. 34: 27-36 (Jan 83)

Artisans

Development Of Culture By Black Artisans. Notes. Sharon F. Patton. *Negro History Bulletin*. 46: 43-45 (Apr-Jun 83)

Artists

John A. Kendrick: A Salute. Illustrated. Jeff Donaldson. *Black Collegian*. 13: 130-131 (Feb-Mar 83)

See Also Women Artists

Arts

The Politics Of Black Arts. Woodie (Jr.) King. *Black American Literature Forum*. 17: 30 (Spring 83)

Asante, Kariamu (joint author)

See Asante, Molefi

Asante, Molefi and Asante, Kariamu

Great Zimbabwe: An Ancient African City-State. Illustrated. *Journal of African Civilizations*. 05: 84-91 (Apr-Nov 83)

Asante, Molefi Kete

The Ideological Significance Of Afrocentricity In Intercultural Communication. Notes, bibliography. *Journal of Black Studies*. 14: 3-19 (Sep 83)

Asbestosis

Asbestosis And The Serratus Anterior Muscle. Tables, illustrated. James D. Collins and others. *National Medical Association Journal*. 75: 296-300 (Mar 83)

Asbury, Charles A.

Roots Of Soul. Book review. *Journal of Negro Education*. 52: 176-177 (Spring 83)

Ashayeri, Ebrahim and others

Internal Mammary Implantation: The Need For Revival Of A Simple Technique. Illustrated, tables, notes. *National Medical Association Journal*. 75: 137-142

Ashe, Arthur (about)

Professor Arthur Ashe: Tennis' Class Act Moves Into The Classroom. Illustrated. *Ebony*. 38: 79-80+ (Jul 83)

Askin, Steve

The Hidden Power Of Pension Funds. Illustrated. *Black Enterprise*. 13: 35-37 (Jan 83)

Mary Hatwood Futrell: Top Teacher. Illustrated. *Black Enterprise*. 14: 124-126+ (Oct 83)

Wage Secrecy At IBM.. *Black Enterprise*. 13: 24 (Apr 83)

Washington's Successor.. *Black Enterprise*. 14: 19 (Nov 83)

Association For The Study Of Afro-American Life And History

ASALH Sixty-Eighth Anniversary 1983 Convention Program.. *Negro History Bulletin*. 46: 53-59 (Apr-Jun 83)

Resolutions Adopted By The Membership 68th Annual Meeting, Detroit Michigan. Illustrated. *Negro History Bulletin*. 46: 79-81 (Jul-Sep 83)

The Sixty-Sixth Annual Meeting. Notes. Donnie D. Bellamy. *Journal of Negro History*. 68: 54-58 (Winter 83)

Associations, Institutions, Etc.

Collective Goods And Black Interest Groups. Notes, tables. Dianne M. Pinderhughes. *Review of Black Political Economy*. 12: 219-236 (Winter 83)

Our Organizations Can Be Vehicles For Change. Illustrated. Earl G. Graves. *Black Enterprise*. 14: 11 (Dec 83)

Associations, Institutions, Etc.—Finance

Grant Master In A Flash. Constance García-Barrio. *Essence*. 14: 16 (Aug 83)

Asthma

An Analysis Of Skin Prick Test Reactions On Asthmatics In Lagos. Tables, notes. E. O. Bandele and others. *National Medical Association Journal*. 75: 511-514 (May 83)

The Bronchial Challenge Test: A New Direction In Asthmatic Management. Tables, notes. Calvin Dixon. *National Medical Association Journal*. 75: 199-204 (Feb 83)

Astronauts

Bluford, Nation Ready For Space Shuttle's Launch. Illustrated. *Jet*. 64: 21 (22 Aug 83)

Guy Bluford: Black Astronaut Makes First Space Mission. First facts, illustrated. Clarence Waldron. *Jet*. 64: 20-22+ (5 Sep 83)

Lt. Col. Guion S. Bluford Jr. Takes. . . A Historic Step Into Space. Illustrated. Walter Leavy. *Ebony*. 39: 162-164+ (Nov 83)

Astronomy—Africa

African Observers Of The Universe: The Sirius Question. Illustrated, notes, tables. Hunter Havelin (III) Adams. *Journal of African Civilizations*. 05: 27-46 (Apr-Nov 83)

New Light On The Dogon And Sirius. Notes. Hunter Havelin (III) Adams. *Journal of African Civilizations*. 05: 47-49 (Apr-Nov 83)

Astronomy—Kenya

Namoratunga: The First Archaeoastronomical Evidence In Sub-Saharan Africa. Illustrated, tables, notes. B. M. Lynch and L. H. Robbins. *Journal of African Civilizations*. 05: 51-56 (Apr-Nov 83)

Athletes

Black Athletes—Are There Any Winners? Illustrated. Louie Robinson. *Crisis*. 90: 6-7 (May 83)

The Challenge To Black Supremacy In Sports. Illustrated. *Ebony*. 38: 49-50+ (Aug 83)

Champions On And Off The Field. James M. Blount. *about. . . time*. 11: 4 (Jan 83)

The Impact Of Rule 48 Upon The Black Student Athlete: A Comment. Notes, tables. Alexander (Jr.) Williams. *Journal of Negro Education*. 52: 362-373 (Summer 83)

Jesse Owens' Olympic Triumph Over Time And Hitlerism. Illustrated. Lerone (Jr.) Bennett. *Ebony*. 39: 140+ (Dec 83)

The New Bidding Game In Sports. Illustrated. Nelson George. *Black Enterprise*. 13: 28-32 (Jan 83)

The Runningest, Jumpingest Athlete In The World. Illustrated. Walter Leavy. *Ebony*. 38: 139-140+ (Sep 83)

We Need To Educate Our Athletes! Illustrated. Lloyd V. Hackley. *Black Collegian*. 13: 35-37 (Apr-May 83)

What Happens When. . . The Active Career In Sports Is Over? Illustrated. Willis Anderson. *about. . . time*. 11: 14-19 (Jan 83)

See Also Football Players
    Gymnasts
    Jockeys

Athletes—Religious Life

Born-Again Stars. Illustrated. Aldore Collier. *Ebony*. 39: 51-52+ (Dec 83)

Athletes, Women

The Black Female Athlete - Past And Present. Illustrated. Bessie Stockard. *Crisis*. 90: 16-18 (May 83)

Essence Women: Diana Valdes Owens. Illustrated. Ken Smikle. *Essence*. 13: 29-30 (Mar 83)

'Playing' Your Way Through College. Illustrated. Knolly Moses. *Essence*. 14: 52 (Aug 83)

See Also Women Tennis Players

Athletics

See Also Boxing
    Weight Lifting

Atkins, Sam O.

Urological Emergency Admissions To A Community Hospital: A Review. Tables, notes. *National Medical Association Journal*. 75: 557-559 (Jun 83)

Atkinson, Donald R. (joint author)

See Morten, George

Atlanta

See Also Medical Colleges—Georgia—Atlanta

Atomic Weapons And Disarmament

The Arms Race, How To Stop And Reverse It.. *Black Scholar*. 14: 48-49 (Nov-Dec 83)

Dialogues Of The World Assembly For Peace And Life, Against Nuclear War - Prague, Czechoslovakia June 21-26, 1983.. *Black Scholar*. 14: 44-46 (Nov-Dec 83)

European Security And Disarmament.. *Black Scholar*. 14: 46-48 (Nov-Dec 83)

The Role Of The United Nations For Peace And Disarmament.. *Black Scholar*. 14: 50-52 (Nov-Dec 83)

See Also Anti-Nuclear Movement

Atomic Weapons And Disarmament—Economic Aspects

Economic Aspects Of The Arms And Of Disarmament.. *Black Scholar*. 14: 53-55 (Nov-Dec 83)

Attention

Management Of Attention Deficit Disorders. Notes. Milton S. Adams. *National Medical Association Journal*. 75: 187-189 (Feb 83)

Attorney And Client

Leis V. Flynt - Yet Another Perspective. Notes. Carlton Bailey. *Black Law Journal*. 08: 95-126 (Spring 83)

Attorneys

See Lawyers

Aubrey, Denise (about)

Breakthrough Under The Big Top. Illustrated. *Ebony*. 39: 69-70+ (Dec 83)

Audience Development Committee, Inc.

AUDELCO, An Organization Of Theatre True Believers. Illustrated. A. Peter Bailey. *Black Collegian*. 13: 140 (Feb-Mar 83)

The First Ten Years Of AUDELCO. Vivian Robinson. *Black American Literature Forum*. 17: 79-81 (Summer 83)

Audiences, Theater

See Theater Audiences

Austin, Doris Jean

Blues In A Bottle. Illustrated. *Essence*. 14: 88-89+ (Aug 83)

Think. . . For Yourself. Illustrated. *Essence*. 14: 150 (May 83)

Authors

See Also Women Authors

Authors, Brazilian

An Artist's Identity Versus The Social Role Of The Writer: The Case For Joaquim Maria Machado De Assis. Notes. Maria Luisa Nunes. *CLA Journal*. 27: 187-196 (Dec 83)

Authorship

In Their Own Write. Illustrated. Claudia Tate and others. *Essence*. 14: 24+ (Oct 83)

Autobiography

Displacement And Autobiographical Style In Maya Angelou's The Heart Of A Woman. Notes. Carol E. Neubauer. *Black American Literature Forum.* 17: 123-129 (Fall 83)

Vision And Revision In The Autobiographies Of Frederick Douglass. Notes. Thomas De Pieto. *CLA Journal.* 26: 384-396 (Jun 83)

Automobile Industry And Trade—Law And Legislation

Auto Trade Policy: What It Means For African-Americans. Notes. Emory West. *The Urban League Review.* 07: 100-112 (Summer 83)

Automobile Industry And Trade—Vocational Guidance

Back To The Drawing Board. Illustrated. Thomas McCarroll. *Black Enterprise.* 13: 75-76+ (Feb 83)

Automobile Racing Drivers

See Also Women Automobile Racing Drivers

Automobiles

Making The Best Deal For New Wheels. Illustrated. Dennis A. Williams. *Black Enterprise.* 14: 81-82+ (Nov 83)

Putting The Squeeze On Four-Wheel Lemons. J. Gregory Clemons. *Black Enterprise.* 14: 90 (Nov 83)

Automobiles—Equipment And Supplies

Traveling Music. Michael George. *Black Enterprise.* 14: 86+ (Nov 83)

Automobiles—Maintenance And Repair

On The Road Again. Jacqueline Paris Chitanvis. *Black Enterprise.* 14: 89 (Nov 83)

Automobiles—Museums

Archives For Auto Buffs. Illustrated. Jay Koblenz. *Black Enterprise.* 14: 87-88 (Nov 83)

Automobiles, Rental

Riding In Style. Illustrated. Elaine Gregg. *Black Enterprise.* 14: 91-92 (Nov 83)

Automobiles—Safety Appliances

Why You Should Buckle Up Baby. Illustrated. Barbara E. Tucker. *Essence.* 14: 120+ (Jul 83)

Azuonye, Chukwuma

Stability And Change In The Performances Of Ohafia Igbo Singers Of tales. Tables, bibliography, notes. *Research in African Literatures.* 14: 332-380 (Fall 83)

Babatunde, Obba (about)

The Dream Guys Of 'Dreamgirls'. Illustrated. *Ebony.* 38: 74-76+ (Apr 83)

Bachik, Michael and others

Idiopathic Hypertrophic Subaortic Stenosis And Acute Myocardial Infarction: An Uncommon Association. Tables, illustrated. *National Medical Association Journal.* 75: 305-309 (Mar 83)

Backache

Body Alive: Quick Relief For Back Pain. Illustrated. D. Baloti Lawrence. *Essence.* 14: 129 (May 83)

How To Live With A Bad Back. Illustrated. *Ebony.* 39: 96+ (Nov 83)

Badi, Gary

A Mother's Day Message. Poem. *about. . . time.* 11: 24 (May 83)

Pennsiveness. Poem. *about. . . time.* 11: 17 (Mar 83)

That Undying Spirit. Poem. *about. . . time.* 11: 17 (Mar 83)

Bahamas—Economic Conditions

The Bahamas: A Decade Of Independence. Illustrated. Thad Martin. *Ebony.* 38: 117-118+ (Apr 83)

Bailey, A. Peter

AUDELCO, An Organization Of Theatre True Believers. Illustrated. *Black Collegian.* 13: 140 (Feb-Mar 83)

Can Harlem Be Saved? Illustrated. *Ebony.* 38: 80-82+ (Jan 83)

A Look At. . . The Contemporary Black Theatre Movement. Illustrated. *Crisis.* 90: 22-25 (Feb 83)

A Look At The Contemporary Black Theatre Movement. Notes. *Black American Literature Forum.* 17: 19-21 (Spring 83)

The Magic Of Technical Theatre. Illustrated. *Black Collegian.* 14: 75+ (Sep-Oct 83)

Whatever Happened To Black Toys? Illustrated. *Ebony.* 39: 39-40+ (Nov 83)

Bailey, Carlton

Leis V. Flynt - Yet Another Perspective. Notes. *Black Law Journal.* 08: 95-126 (Spring 83)

Bailey, Chauncey

The Overground Railroad. Illustrated. *Crisis.* 90: 6-9+ (Nov 83)

Bailey, Peter and Sleet, Moneta (Jr.)

A Manchild Of The '80s. Illustrated. *Ebony.* 38: 68+ (Aug 83)

Baker, Alvis

The Bottomless Pit. Book review. Leroy Mobley. *Crisis.* 90: 50 (Aug-Sep 83)

Baker, Evelyn Marie (about)

Black Woman Judge Is Named To Missouri Court. First facts. *Jet.* 64: 30 (2 May 83)

Baker, F. M. and Moynihan, Barbara

Emergency Service Nursing Staff: A Survey Of Knowledge, Attitudes, And Concerns. Tables, notes. *National Medical Association Journal.* 75: 417-421 (Apr 83)

Baker, Houston A. (Jr.)

From DuBois To Van Vechten: The Early New Negro Literature, 1903-1926. Book review. *Research in African Literatures*. 14: 554-560 (Winter 83)

Loss/Angel-Less/Blue. Poem. *Black American Literature Forum*. 17: 174 (Winter 83)

Baldness

How Young Men Cope With Baldness. Illustrated. Frank (III) White. *Ebony*. 38: 54+ (Jun 83)

Balkum, Sylvia Louise

Alone. Poem. *about. . . time*. 11: 24 (Jun 83)

He Looked At Me. Poem. *about. . . time*. 11: 24 (Jun 83)

I Am. Poem. *about. . . time*. 11: 24 (Jun 83)

I Like Me. Poem. *about. . . time*. 11: 24 (Jun 83)

My Best Friend. Poem. *about. . . time*. 11: 24 (Jun 83)

My Side. Poem. *about. . . time*. 11: 24 (Jun 83)

The Phone Call. Poem. *about. . . time*. 11: 24 (Jun 83)

Some Days. Poem. *about. . . time*. 11: 24 (Jun 83)

The Tryouts. Poem. *about. . . time*. 11: 24 (Jun 83)

Ball, Joanne

Fighting For Economic Parity.. *Black Enterprise*. 14: 50 (Nov 83)

Balliett, Whitney

Jelly Roll, Jabbo & Fats: 19 Portraits In Jazz. Book review. George L. Starks. *The Black Perspective in Music*. 11: 215-218 (Fall 83)

Baltodano, Monica (about)

Sandino's Daughters. Excerpt, Illustrated. Margaret Randall. *Black Scholar*. 14: 48-57 (Mar-Apr 83)

Bamgbose, Ayo

Education In Indigenous Languages: The West African Model Of Language Education. Notes. *Journal of Negro Education*. 52: 57-64 (Winter 83)

Band (Music)

An Oral History: The Great Lakes Experience. Illustrated, notes. Samuel Floyd. *The Black Perspective in Music*. 11: 41-61 (Spring 83)

Bandele, E. O. and others

An Analysis Of Skin Prick Test Reactions On Asthmatics In Lagos. Tables, notes. *National Medical Association Journal*. 75: 511-514 (May 83)

Bandsmen

Cab Calloway: After 50 Years In Show Business The Hi-De-Ho Man Is Still Going Strong. Illustrated. Herschel Johnson. *Ebony*. 38: 66-67+ (Feb 83)

In Retrospect: Alfred Jack Thomas: Performer, Composer, Educator. Notes. James Nathan Jones. *The Black Perspective in Music*. 11: 62-75 (Spring 83)

The New King Of Swing. Illustrated. Frank Dexter Brown. *Black Enterprise*. 13: 42 (Jun 83)

Bane, Michael

Who's Who In Rock. Book review. Doris Evans McGinty. *The Black Perspective in Music*. 11: 212-214 (Fall 83)

Banfield, Beryle and Wilson, Geraldine L.

The Black Experience Through White Eyes- The Same Old Story Once Again. Illustrated, tables. *Interracial Books for Children*. 14: No. 5: 4-13 (83)

Jake And Honeybunch Go To Heaven. Book review. *Interracial Books for Children*. 14: No. 1: 32-33 (83)

Banham, Martin

A Critical View On Wole Soyinka's The Lion And The Jewel. Book review. Robert M. Wren. *Research in African Literatures*. 14: 110-111 (Spring 83)

Bankruptcy

Bankruptcy: Is It The Answer To Your Money Problems? Phil W. Petrie. *Essence*. 14: 24+ (Jun 83)

Banks And Banking

In The Interest Of Survival: Bank Overview. Tables. William D. Bradford. *Black Enterprise*. 13: 103-104+ (Jun 83)

Banks And Banking—Florida—Miami

No Checks; Cash Only. Valerie J. Hill. *Black Enterprise*. 13: 22 (Apr 83)

Banks And Banking—Michigan—Detroit

Charles Allen's Declaration Of Independence. Illustrated, tables. Lloyd Gite. *Black Enterprise*. 13: 113-114+ (Jun 83)

Banks, Barbara (about)

Essence Women: Barbara Banks. Illustrated. Curtia James. *Essence*. 13: 20+ (Jan 83)

Banks, C. Tillery

Untitled. Poem. *Essence*. 14: 88 (Oct 83)

Banks, Samuel L.

Role Model Blacks: Known But Little Known. Book review. *Journal of Negro Education*. 52: 87-89 (Winter 83)

Banks, Shirley (about)

Taking Care Of Business. Illustrated. Lloyd Gite. *Essence*. 13: 28 (Jan 83)

Banks, W. Curtis and others

Delayed Gratification In Black: A Critical Review. Notes, tables. *Journal of Black Psychology*. 09: 43-56 (Feb 83)

Banneker-Douglass Museum Of Afro-American Life And History

A State Recalls Its Heritage: A Museum For Maryland. Illustrated. Carroll (Jr.) Greene. *Crisis*. 90: 12+ (Feb 83)

Bar Associations—Indiana—Indianapolis

The Marion County Lawyers CLub: 1932 And The Black Lawyer. Notes. J. Clay (Jr.) Smith. *Black Law Journal.* 08: 170-176 (Fall 83)

Baraka, Amina

Confirmation: An Anthology Of African American Women. Book review. Carole E. Gregory. *Freedomways.* 23: No. 4: 287-289 (83)

Baraka, Amiri (about)

The Concealed Dependence Upon White Culture In Baraka's 1969 Aesthetic. Notes. Elizabeth Hadley Freydberg. *Black American Literature Forum.* 17: 27-29 (Spring 83)

Confirmation: An Anthology Of African American Women. Book review. Carole E. Gregory. *Freedomways.* 23: No. 4: 287-289 (83)

The Descent Of Charlie Fuller Into Pulitzerland And The Need For African-American Institutions.. *Black American Literature Forum.* 17: 51-54 (Summer 83)

Baraka, Amiri—Criticism And Interpretation

The Dramatic Structure Of Dutchman. Illustrated, notes. Andrzej Ceynowa. *Black American Literature Forum.* 17: 15-18 (Spring 83)

Barbados—Description And Travel

Barbados Happenings. Illustrated. *Essence.* 13: 118-119+ (Apr 83)

Barbecue Cookery

How To Make Your Barbecue Sizzlin' Good. Illustrated. Curtia James. *Essence.* 14: 95+ (Jul 83)

Bards And Bardism

The Nanga Bards Of Tanzania: Are They Epic Artists? Illustrated, tables, notes. M. Mulukozi. *Research in African Literatures.* 14: 283-311 (Fall 83)

Bardwell, Chris

Tips For Preparing For An Interview.. *Black Collegian.* 13: 85 (Feb-Mar 83)

Barnes-Harden, Alene

For Dark Women And Others. Book review. *Journal of Black Studies.* 14: 261-262 (Dec 83)

Barnett, Marguerite Ross

The New Federalism And The Unfinished Civil Rights Agenda. Notes. *Black Law Journal.* 08: 375-386 (Winter 83)

Barnett, Wayne (about)

Riding High At Seventeen. Illustrated. Marilyn Marshall. *Ebony.* 38: 60-61+ (May 83)

Barrett, Nancy S.

Perspectives On Unemployment And Policy. Notes. *Review of Black Political Economy.* 12: 55-61 (Spring 83)

Barth, John—Criticism And Interpretation

Facing The Abyss: The Floating Opera And End Of The Road. Notes. Ben Satterfield. *CLA Journal.* 26: 341-352 (Mar 83)

Bartter, Frederic C. (1914-1983) (about)

In Memoriam Frederic C. Bartter, MD 1914-1983. Melvin E. Jenkins. *National Medical Association Journal.* 75: 1111 (Nov 83)

Baseball Hall Of Fame, Cooperstown, New York

Marichal, Robinson In Hall 9 Black Players Fall Short. Illustrated. *Jet.* 63: 53 (31 Jan 83)

Baseball Players

Baseball's Greatest 'Thief'. Illustrated. Walter Leavy. *Ebony.* 38: 135-136+ (Jun 83)

Reggie Jackson Admits Second Love Is For His 50 Cars. Illustrated. Norman O. Unger. *Jet.* 63: 46-49 (17 Jan 83)

Willie Stargell: The Rare Combination Of Athlete And Humanitarian. Illustrated. Madeline Sulaiman. *about... time.* 11: 8-11 (Jan 83)

Basheer, Talik Aboul

1983 March Reflections. Illustrated. *about... time.* 11: 20-21 (Oct 83)

Bashfulness

How To Overcome Shyness. Dennis E. Hensley and Wista Johnson. *Essence.* 14: 71+ (Aug 83)

Basketball Players

Terry Cummings: Basketball's Million-Dollar Minister. Illustrated. Marilyn Marshall. *Ebony.* 38: 42-44 (Feb 83)

Bass de Martinez, Bernice

Perspectives In Multicultural Education. Book review. Geneva Gay. *Journal of Negro Education.* 52: 461-463 (Fall 83)

Bass, George Houston

Theatre And The Afro-American Rite Of Being. Notes. *Black American Literature Forum.* 17: 60-64 (Summer 83)

Basset, Lawrence W.

Mammography, Thremography And Ultrasound In Breast Cancer Detection. Book review. Cornelius W. Merrick. *National Medical Association Journal.* 75: 1023 (Oct 83)

Bastien, Rochelle T. (joint author)

See Myers, Hector F.

Bates, Timothy

The Impact Of Multinational Corporations On Power Relations In South Africa. Notes. *Review of Black Political Economy.* 12: 133-143 (Winter 83)

The Potential For Black Business: A Comment. Notes. *Review of Black Political Economy.* 12: 237-240 (Winter 83)

Bates, Valery Y. R.

Computer Graphics: Blending Art With Science. Illustrated. *Black Collegian.* 14: 82-83+ (Nov-Dec 83)

Bathing Suits

Sunsational Beachwear. Illustrated. Eunice W. Johnson. *Ebony.* 38: 70-72+ (Jan 83)

Battestini, Simon P. X.

Le Vieux Nègre Et La Médaille De Ferdinand
Oyono. Book review. *Research in African
Literatures*. 14: 237-238 (Summer 83)

Battiste, Luther (III) (about)

Two Blacks Win Seats On S. Carolina City
Council. First facts, Illustrated. *Jet*. 64: 4 (25 Apr
83)

Baugh, E. Lorraine and Shorter, Beryl Elyese

The National Black Nurses' Association. Illustrated.
Black Collegian. 13: 62 (Apr-May 83)

Bayton, James A. (joint author)

    See Hendricks, Leo E.

Beals, Jennifer (about)

Jennifer Beals: Sultry Student Strikes Stardom In
'Flashdance'. Illustrated. *Jet*. 64: 60-63 (6 Jun 83)

Beard, Jeffery

Constitutional Law-State Requirement That Peace
Officers Be American Citizens Is Not
Unconstitutional. Notes. *Howard Law Journal*. 26:
No. 1: 327-344 (83)

Beard, Linda Susan

A Century Of South African Short Stories. Book
review. *Research in African Literatures*. 14:
219-222 (Summer 83)

Modern South African Stories. Book review.
Research in African Literatures. 14: 219-222
(Summer 83)

Bearden, Romare (about)

A Voice Of The People. Illustrated. Edwin B.
Lake. *Black Enterprise*. 13: 42 (Jun 83)

Beaubien, Michael

Aid For Poor Kids.. *Black Enterprise*. 13: 20 (Apr
83)

Beaulieu, Lovell

Black History On Display. Illustrated. *Black
Enterprise*. 14: 28 (Oct 83)

Beaumont, Jennifer

African News Agency Opens.. *Black Enterprise*.
14: 18 (Aug 83)

Beauty Contestants

Vanessa Williams: New Miss America Wants
Character, Not Color To Count. Illustrated. *Jet*. 65:
12-16+ (10 Oct 83)

Beauty Contests

Here She Is. . . Miss America. Illustrated. Lynn
Norment. *Ebony*. 39: 132-134+ (Dec 83)

Beauty, Personal

Hairstyles 1983. Illustrated. *Ebony*. 38: 100-102+
(Jan 83)

How To Have Kissable Lips. Illustrated. *Essence*.
14: 74-77 (Nov 83)

Put Your Best Self Forward. Illustrated. Mikki
Garth-Taylor and Paula S. White. *Essence*. 13:
69+ (Jan 83)

Putting Your Best Face Forward. Illustrated.
Essence. 14: 83-85 (Sep 83)

Speaking of Lips: Luscious, Voluptuous Lips. . .
Are In. Illustrated. Alfred (Jr.) Fornay. *Ebony*. 38:
94-96+ (Jan 83)

Spring Radiance. Illustrated. Alfred (Jr.) Fornay.
Ebony. 38: 146-148+ (Apr 83)

    See Also Hairdressing

Beavers, Herm

A Picture Of Bird. Poem. *Black American
Literature Forum*. 17: 154 (Winter 83)

Untitled. Poem. *Black American Literature Forum*.
17: 154 (Winter 83)

Beckham, Barry

The Black Student's Guide To Colleges. Book
review. Elza Dinwiddie. *Black Enterprise*. 13: 23
(Feb 83)

Bedau, Hugo Adam

Witness To A Persecution: The Death Penalty And
The Dawson Five. Notes. *Black Law Journal*. 08:
7-28 (Spring 83)

Beer

A Woman's Guide To Beer. Illustrated. Dolly
Calhoun. *Essence*. 14: 114 (Jun 83)

Beezer, Bruce

North Carolina's Rationale For Mandating Separate
Schools: A Legal History. Notes. *Journal of Negro
Education*. 52: 213-226 (Summer 83)

Beier, Ulli (about)

"Border Operators": Black Orpheus And The
Genesis Of Modern African Art And Literature.
Notes. Peter Benson. *Research in African
Literatures*. 14: 431-473 (Winter 83)

Beir, Ulli

Yoruba Myths. Book review. Oludare Olajubu.
Research in African Literatures. 14: 538-543
(Winter 83)

Beker, J. Christiaan

The Challenge Of Paul's Apocalyptic Gospel For
The Church Today.. *Journal of Religious Thought*.
40: 9-15 (Spring-Summer 83)

Belafonte-Harper, Shari (about)

Harry Belafonte: Daughter Pays Father's Day
Tribute To Her Famous Father. Illustrated. Robert
E. Johnson. *Jet*. 64: 58-61 (20 Jun 83)

Belafonte Harry (about)

Harry Belafonte: Daughter Pays Father's Day
Tribute To Her Famous Father. Illustrated. Robert
E. Johnson. *Jet*. 64: 58-61 (20 Jun 83)

Shari And Harry. Illustrated. Michele Wallace.
Essence. 14: 82-83 (Aug 83)

Belafonte-Harper, Shari (about)

Shari And Harry. Illustrated. Michele Wallace.
Essence. 14: 82-83 (Aug 83)

Bell, Carl C.

Simultaneous Treatment Of Hypertension And Opiate Withdrawal Using An α_2-Adrenergic Agonist.. *National Medical Association Journal.* 75: 89-93 (Jan 83)

Bell, Carl C. and Palmer, John

Survey Of The Demographic Characteristics Of Patients Requiring Restraints In A Psychiatric Emergency Service. Tables, notes. *National Medical Association Journal.* 75: 981-987 (Oct 83)

Bell, Derrick

Shades Of Brown: New Perspectives On School Desegregation. Book review. W. Edwin Derrick. *Journal of Negro Education.* 52: 177-178 (Spring 83)

Time For The Teachers: Putting Educators Back Into The Brown Remedy. Notes. *Journal of Negro Education.* 52: 290-301 (Summer 83)

Bell, Derrick A. (Jr.)

Race, Racism And American Law. Book review, Notes. William Payne. *Black Law Journal.* 08: 361-366 (Fall 83)

Bell, Terrel and Jones, Hughes

An Interview With The Secretary Of Education: Terrell Bell. Interview, Illustrated. *Black Collegian.* 13: 51-53 (Apr-May 83)

Bellamy, Donnie D.

The Sixty-Sixth Annual Meeting. Notes. *Journal of Negro History.* 68: 54-58 (Winter 83)

Bemba, S.

Bio-Bibliographie Des Ecrivains Congolais: Belles Lettres - Littérature. Book review. Daniel Whitman. *Research in African Literatures.* 14: 215-216 (Summer 83)

Ben-Amos, Dan

Introduction [To volume 14 Number 3, 1983]. Notes. *Research in African Literatures.* 14: 277-282 (Fall 83)

Benedict, Gary C. and Gerardi, Robert J.

Desegregation In Milwaukee: Attitudes May Be A Factor. Notes, tables. *Negro Educational Review.* 34: 20-26 (Jan 83)

Benjamin, Playthell

Will Jazz Survive? Thoughts On The State Of The Great American Art.. *Freedomways.* 23: No. 4: 212-225 (83)

Bennett, Lerone (Jr.)

Chronicles Of Black Courage. Illustrated. *Ebony.* 38: 147-148+ (Oct 83)

Chronicles Of Black Courage (Part III): Father Of Black History Changed Vision Of Black America. Illustrated. *Ebony.* 38: 31-32+ (Feb 83)

Chronicles Of Black Courage (Part IV). Illustrated. *Ebony.* 38: 131-134 (Sep 83)

Jesse Owens' Olympic Triumph Over Time And Hitlerism. Illustrated. *Ebony.* 39: 140+ (Dec 83)

We Still Have A Dream. Illustrated. *Ebony.* 39: 152-153+ (Nov 83)

Benson, George (about)

George Benson: Move To Hawaii Helps Him Survive Crises. Illustrated. Robert E. Johnson and Isaac Sutton. *Jet.* 63: 58-62+ (21 Feb 83)

Benson, Peter

"Border Operators": Black Orpheus And The Genesis Of Modern African Art And Literature. Notes. *Research in African Literatures.* 14: 431-473 (Winter 83)

Bentley, Charles Edwin (1859-1926) (about)

Prevention Began Early: Charles Edwin Bentley, DDS 1859-1926. Clifton O. Dummett. *National Medical Association Journal.* 75: 1235-1236 (Dec 83)

Berea College

Blacks In Appalachian America: Reflections On Biracial Education And Unionism. Notes. William H. Turner. *Phylon.* 44: 198-208 (Sep 83)

Berendt, Joachim E.

The Jazz Book: From Ragtime To Fusion And Beyond. Book review. George L. Starks. *The Black Perspective in Music.* 11: 215-218 (Fall 83)

Bergman, Walter (about)

FBI Liable In Freedom Rider Attack. Illustrated. *Jet.* 64: 7 (20 Jun 83)

Berlowits, Marvin J.

The United States Educational System: Marxist Approaches. Book review. Lanthin D. (Jr.) Camblin. *Journal of Black Studies.* 14: 102-103 (Sep 83)

Bermuda—Description And Travel

Bermuda: More Than A Honeymoon Haven. Illustrated. Ben F. Carruthers. *Black Enterprise.* 14: 72-73 (Sep 83)

Berry, Faith

Langston Hughes: Before And Beyond Harlem. Book review. Nieda Spigner. *Freedomways.* 23: No. 4: 285-286 (83)

Berry, Graham

The Pride And Passion - Introduction To Black History. Illustrated. *Negro History Bulletin.* 46: 47-50 (Apr-Jun 83)

Berry, Jay R.

The Achievement Of William Demby. Notes. *CLA Journal.* 26: 434-451 (Jun 83)

Berry, Leonidas H.

I Wouldn't Take Nothin For My Journey: Two Centuries Of An Afro American Minister's Family. Book review. Larry Murphy. *National Medical Association Journal.* 75: 1232-1234 (Dec 83)

A Physician Becomes An Historian. Illustrated. *Negro History Bulletin.* 46: 22-23 (Jan-Mar 83)

Berry, Mary Frances

Turning Back The Clock On Women And Minority Rights: The Regan Record. Illustrated. *Negro History Bulletin.* 46: 82-84 (Jul-Sep 83)

Best, Yvette (joint author)

See Lee, Clarence M.

Betances, Samuel and Copeland, Virginia

Racism No Longer Denied. Notes. *Interracial Books for Children.* 14: No. 1: 24 (83)

A Better Chance, Inc.

A Better Chance. Illustrated. Lynn Norment. *Ebony.* 38: 46+ (Jun 83)

Better, Shirley

Black Women And Homeownership: The Financial Challenge Of The '80s. Tables, notes. *Black Scholar.* 14: 38-45 (Sep-Oct 83)

Bevien, Janice

Sandino's Daughters: Testimonies Of Nicaraguan Women In Struggle. Book review. *Black Scholar.* 14: 74-75 (Mar-Apr 83)

Bialick, Stephanie

Weekend Getaways For You And Your Man. Illustrated. *Essence.* 13: 36+ (Feb 83)

Bianchi, Antoinette (about)

In The Chips! Illustrated. Knolly Moses. *Essence.* 14: 30 (Aug 83)

Bible. N.T. James—Criticism, Interpretation, Etc.

Partiality And God's Law: An Exegesis Of James 2:1-13. Notes. Cain H. Felder. *Journal of Religious Thought.* 39: 51-69 (Fall-Winter 83)

Biesele, Megan

Namibia: Land And Peoples, Myths And Fables. Book review. *Research in African Literatures.* 14: 405-407 (Fall 83)

Biestman, Karen Williams

Abolitionism And Wooden Nutmegs: Repealing The Gag Rule. Notes. *Black Law Journal.* 08: 408-416 (Winter 83)

Biggers, Samuel L. (joint author)

See Byrd, Sharon E.

Bilingual Education

See Education, Bilingual

Bill Of Rights (United States)

See United States. Constitution. 1st-10th Amendments

Birmingham, Alabama

See Also Voting—Alabama—Birmingham

Birmingham, Alabama—Officials And Employees

The Impact Of Black Political Participation On Public Sector Employment And Representation On Municipal Boards And Commissions. Notes, tables. Huey L. Perry. *Review of Black Political Economy.* 12: 203-217 (Winter 83)

Bishop, David W.

The Consent Decree Between The University Of North Carolina System And The U. S. Department Of Education, 1981-82. Notes. *Journal of Negro Education.* 52: 350-361 (Summer 83)

Bishop, Norma

A Nigerian Version Of A Greek Classic: Soyinka's Transformation Of The Bacchae. Notes. *Research in African Literatures.* 14: 68-80 (Spring 83)

Bjornson, Richard

Journal Of African And Comparative Literature. Book review. *Research in African Literatures.* 14: 119-121 (Spring 83)

Black Alternative Conference, 1980

A Black Lawyer's Response To The Fairmont Papers. Notes. J. Clay (Jr.) Smith. *Howard Law Journal.* 26: No. 1: 195-225 (83)

Black Collegian (Periodical)

Breaking Out Of The Ghetto. Editorial. *Black Collegian.* 13: 10 (Feb-Mar 83)

A Year Of Awards, Achievements And Changes. Editorial, Illustrated. *Black Collegian.* 14: 14+ (Sep-Oct 83)

Black English

Black Children. Jack L. Daniel. *Interracial Books for Children.* 14: No. 7: 8 (83)

Language And Liberation. Notes. Geneva Smitherman. *Journal of Negro Education.* 52: 15-23 (Winter 83)

A Survey OF Bidialectal Language Arts Programs In The United States. Notes, tables. Orlando L. Taylor and others. *Journal of Negro Education.* 52: 35-45 (Winter 83)

See Also Gullah Dialect

Black History Month

Black Historical Scholarship And The Black Historian. Notes. *Negro History Bulletin.* 46: 38-40 (Apr-Jun 83)

Black History Month. James M. Blount. *about. . . time.* 11: 4 (Feb 83)

Black History Month Specials. Illustrated. Mary Aladj. *about. . . time.* 11: 22-23 (Feb 83)

Why Black History Month? Illustrated. Benjamin L. Hooks. *Crisis.* 90: 4 (Feb 83)

Black Muslims

The Black Muslim Movement And The American Constitutional System. Tables, notes. Oliver (Jr.) Jones. *Journal of Black Studies.* 13: 417-437 (Jun 83)

Black Nationalism

Make The Past Serve The Present: Strategies For Black Liberation. Notes. Oba Simba T'Shaka. *Black Scholar.* 14: 21-37 (Jan-Feb 83)

Black Orpheus (Periodical)

"Border Operators": Black Orpheus And The Genesis Of Modern African Art And Literature. Notes. Peter Benson. *Research in African Literatures*. 14: 431-473 (Winter 83)

Black Unemployed Youth Movement

Boycotting For Jobs. Illustrated. David J. Dent. *Black Enterprise*. 13: 28 (Mar 83)

Black United Front

See National Black United Front

Black Women's History Conference, 1983

A Black Women's History Conference. Shirley B. Cathie and Willa Blackshear. *Crisis*. 90: 56-57 (Jun-Jul 83)

Blacks—Canada—Bibliography

Revisiting Black Canada: Notes On Recent Literature. Jason H. Silverman. *Journal of Negro History*. 68: 93-94 (Winter 83)

Blacks—France—Race Identity

Brown France Vs. Black Africa: The Tide Turned In 1932. Notes. Martin Steins. *Research in African Literatures*. 14: 474-497 (Winter 83)

Blacks—Puerto Rico

The Black Presence In Puerto Rico. Juan Hernandez-Cruz. *Interracial Books for Children*. 14: No. 1: 23-24 (83)

Blackshear, Willa (joint author)

See Cathie, Shirley B.

Blackwell, James

Mainstreaming Outsiders: The Production Of Black Professionals. Book review. Darryl Paulson. *Journal of Negro History*. 68: 99-101 (Winter 83)

Blackwell, Unita (about)

Her Honor, The Mayor. Illustrated. Julie Chenault. *Essence*. 14: 14+ (Jul 83)

Blair, Billie (about)

Billie Blair: Model Close-Up. Illustrated. *Essence*. 14: 74 (Oct 83)

Blair, Dorothy S.

African Literature In French: A History Of Creative Writing In French From West And Equatorial Africa. Book review. Keith Q. Warner. *Research in African Literatures*. 14: 202-203 (Summer 83)

Blake, Eubie (1883-1983) (about)

Farewell To Ragtime's Apostle Of Happiness. Illustrated. Lynn Norment. *Ebony*. 38: 27-28+ (May 83)

Blindness

Woman Regains Sight, Sees Her Husband For First Time. Illustrated. D. Michael Cheers. *Jet*. 65: 20-24 (28 Nov 83)

Bloch, Harry

Caste: The Blight Of Adolescence. Editorial. *National Medical Association Journal*. 75: 457-458 (May 83)

Blockade

The International Law Of Maritime Blockade-A Measure Of Naval Economic Interdiction. Notes. Thomas David Jones. *Howard Law Journal*. 26: No. 2: 759-779 (83)

Blood Pressure, High

See Hypertension

Blount, Carolyne S.

The Black College Experience: A Viable Choice For Students. Illustrated. *about. . . time*. 11: 10-11 (Jun 83)

An Evaluation Of Black Family Life. Editorial. *about. . . time*. 11: 4 (Sep 83)

Test Your Family Values. Illustrated. *about. . . time*. 11: 8-9 (Sep 83)

The Unemployment Dilemma. Editorial. *about. . . time*. 11: 4+ (Mar 83)
DeLain, Martha A.
Hostutler, John D.

Blount, James M.

Black History Month.. *about. . . time*. 11: 4 (Feb 83)

Champions On And Off The Field.. *about. . . time*. 11: 4 (Jan 83)

A Commitment And Sacrifice To Goals.. *about. . . time*. 11: 4 (Apr 83)

Dr. Kenneth B. Clark: Fighter For Educational Opportunity. Interview, Illustrated. *about. . . time*. 11: 14-15+ (May 83)

An Educational Dilemma.. *about. . . time*. 11: 4 (May 83)

The Fate Of America's Cities.. *about. . . time*. 11: 4 (Jul 83)

Understanding The Political Process.. *about. . . time*. 11: 4 (Oct 83)

Bluestone, Barry

Deindustrialization And Unemployment In America. Tables, Notes. *Review of Black Political Economy*. 12: 27-42 (Spring 83)

Bluford, Guion (about)

Bluford, Nation Ready For Space Shuttle's Launch. Illustrated. *Jet*. 64: 21 (22 Aug 83)

Careers Behind The Launchpad. Illustrated. *Black Enterprise*. 13: 59-60+ (Feb 83)

Guy Bluford: Black Astronaut Makes First Space Mission. First facts, illustrated. Clarence Waldron. *Jet*. 64: 20-22+ (5 Sep 83)

Lt. Col. Guion S. Bluford Jr. Takes. . . A Historic Step Into Space. Illustrated. Walter Leavy. *Ebony*. 39: 162-164+ (Nov 83)

Blum, Lawrence and Rosner, Fred

Alcoholism In The Elderly: An Analysis Of 50 Patients. Tables, notes. *National Medical Association Journal*. 75: 489-495 (May 83)

Boards Of Education

See School Boards

Boateng, Felix

African Traditional Education: A Method Of
Disseminating Cultural Values. Notes. *Journal of
Black Studies*. 13: 321-336 (Mar 83)

Boats And Boating—Africa—History

Traditional African Watercraft: A New Look.
Illustrated, tables, notes. Stewart C. Malloy.
Journal of African Civilizations. 05: 163-176
(Apr-Nov 83)

Bodnar, John

Lives Of Their Own: Blacks, Italians, And Poles In
Pittsburgh, 1900-1960. Book review. Clayborne
Carson. *Journal of Negro History*. 68: 98-99
(Winter 83)

Bogle, Donald

A Familiar Plot (A Look At The History Of Blacks
In American Movies). Illustrated. *Crisis*. 90: 14-19
(Jan 83)

Bohana, Donald T. (about)

Bohana Bets On Insurance. Illustrated. Derek T.
Dingle. *Black Enterprise*. 14: 24+ (Nov 83)

Bombings—Texas—Dallas

The Social Ecology Of Bomb Threats: Dallas,
Texas. Notes, tables. Daniel E. Georges-Abeyie.
Journal of Black Studies. 13: 305-320 (Mar 83)

Bond, Julian (about)

The Private Side Of Julian Bond. Illustrated.
Stephanie Stokes Oliver. *Essence*. 14: 103-104+
(Nov 83)

What's Next? Illustrated. *Negro History Bulletin*.
46: 72-73+ (Jul-Sep 83)

Book Censorship

See Censorship

Book Reviews

African Language Literatures: An Introduction To
The Literary History Of Sub-Saharan Africa. By
Albert S. Gérard. Reviewed by Vladimír Klíma.
Research in African Literatures. 14: 200-202
(Summer 83)

African Literature In French: A History Of Creative
Writing In French From West And Equatorial
Africa. By Dorothy S. Blair. Reviewed by Keith Q.
Warner. *Research in African Literatures*. 14:
202-203 (Summer 83)

African Writing Today. Reviewed by Thomas R.
Knipp. *Research in African Literatures*. 14:
116-119 (Spring 83)

The Afro-American Novel Since 1960. By Peter
Bruck and Wolfgang Karrer. Reviewed by Joe
Weixlmann. *Black American Literature Forum*. 17:
134-136 (Fall 83)

Ain't I A Woman: Black Woman And Feminism.
By Bell Hooks. Reviewed by Beverly Guy-Sheftall.
Phylon. 44: 84-85 (Mar 83)

Ain't I A Woman: Black Woman And Feminism.
By Bell Hooks. Reviewed by Maria K. Mootry
Ikerionwu. *Phylon*. 44: 85-86 (Mar 83)

Ain't I A Woman: Black Women And Feminism.
By Bell Hooks. Reviewed by Barbara Smith. *Black
Scholar*. 14: 38-45 (Jan-Feb 83)

Ain't I A Woman: Black Women And Feminism.
By Bell Hooks. Reviewed by Dorothy
Randall-Tsuruta. *Black Scholar*. 14: 46-52 (Jan-Feb
83)

Aké: The Years Of Childhood. By Wole Soyinka.
Reviewed by Carole Bovoso. *Essence*. 13: 20 (Mar
83)

Ake, The Years Of Childhood. By Wole Soyinka.
Reviewed by James Gibbs. *Research in African
Literatures*. 14: 98-102 (Spring 83)

Al-Drama Al-Afriqia. By Ali Shalash. Reviewed by
Kole Omotoso. *Research in African Literatures*. 14:
108-110 (Spring 83)

All About Success For The Black Woman. By
Naomi Sims. Reviewed by Elza Teresa Dinwiddie.
Black Enterprise. 13: 31 (Jun 83)

All The Colors Of The Race. By Arnold Adoff.
Reviewed by Kate Shackford. *Interracial Books for
Children*. 14: No. 1: 35 (83)

America's Public Schools In Transition: Future
Trends And Issues. By T. M. Stinnett and K. T.
Henson. Reviewed by Wilfred A. Johnson. *Journal
of Negro Education*. 52: 459-461 (Fall 83)

American Popular Culture: A Guide To Information
Sources. By Larry N. Landrum. Reviewed by Doris
Evans McGinty. *The Black Perspective in Music*.
11: 212-214 (Fall 83)

American Women In Jazz: 1900 To The Present.
By Sally Placksin. Reviewed by D. Antoinette
Handy. *The Black Perspective in Music*. 11: 83-85
(Spring 83)

The Anatomy Of Racial Attitudes. By Richard A.
Apostle and Charles Y. Glock and Thomas Piazza
and Marijean Suelzle. Reviewed by Keith A.
Winsell. *Phylon*. 44: 246-248 (Sep 83)

The Antioch-Suite Jazz. By Abba Elethea.
Reviewed by Tom Dent. *Freedomways*. 23: No. 01:
42-49 (83)

Arna Bontemps-Langston Hughes: Letters
1925-1967. By Charles H. Nichols. Reviewed by
Maria K. Mootry-Ikerionwu. *CLA Journal*. 27:
226-228 (Dec 83)

The Art Of Slave Narrative: Original Essays In
Criticism And Theory. By John Sekora and Darwin
T. Turner. Reviewed by Henry-Louis (Jr.) Gates.
Black American Literature Forum. 17: 131-134
(Fall 83)

Art Tatum: A Guide To His Recorded Music. By
Arnold Laubich and Ray Spencer. Reviewed by
James Remel Burden. *The Black Perspective in
Music*. 11: 86-88 (Spring 83)

Baba Of Karo: A Woman Of The Muslim Hausa.
By Mary F. Smith. Reviewed by Margaret M.
Knipp. *Research in African Literatures*. 14:
407-409 (Fall 83)

Becoming A Lawyer: A Humanistic Perspective On Legal Education And Professionalism. By Elizabeth Dvorkiu and Jack Himmelstein and Howard Lesnick. Reviewed by Elana Yancey. *Black Law Journal*. 08: 164-166 (Spring 83)

The Belle Of Ashby Street: Helen Douglas Mankin And Georgia Politics. By Lorrain Nelson Spritzer. Reviewed by Margaret L. Dwight. *Journal of Negro History*. 68: 102-104 (Winter 83)

Betting It All Together. By Mike Fields. Reviewed by Paula S. White. *Essence*. 14: 48 (Nov 83)

Between Black And White: Race, Politics, And The Free Colored In Jamaica. By Gad J. Heuman. Reviewed by Glenn O. Phillips. *Afro-Americans in New York Life and History*. 07: 73-74 (Jul 83)

Bibliography Of Black Music Volume 3: Geographical Studies. By Dominique-Rene DeLerma. Reviewed by Doris Evans McGinty. *The Black Perspective in Music*. 11: 79-82 (Spring 83)

Big Sixteen. By Mary Calhoun and Trina Schart-Hyman. Reviewed by Geraldine L. Wilson. *Interracial Books for Children*. 14: No. 5: 25 (83)

Bio-Bibliographie Des Ecrivains Congolais: Belles Lettres - Littérature. By L. P. Mamonsono and S. Bemba. Reviewed by Daniel Whitman. *Research in African Literatures*. 14: 215-216 (Summer 83)

Biographical Dictionary Of Afro-American And African Musicians. By Eileen Southern. Reviewed by Doris Evans McGinty. *The Black Perspective in Music*. 11: 79-82 (Spring 83)

Black Americans And The Missionary Movement In Africa. By Sylvia M. Jacobs. Reviewed by L. B. J. Machobane. *Journal of Negro History*. 68: 118-119 (Winter 83)

Black Athletes In The United States: A Bibliography Of Books, Articles, Autobiographies, And Biographies On Black Professional Athletes In The United States, 1800-1981. By Lenwood G. Davis and Belinda S. Daniels. Reviewed by Harry Edwards. *Crisis*. 90: 30-31 (May 83)

Black Liberation In Kentucky: Emancipation And Freedom. By Victor B. Howard. Reviewed by Thomas J. Davis. *Negro History Bulletin*. 46: 85 (Jul-Sep 83)

Black Life In Corporate America: Swimming In The Mainstream. By George Davis and Glegg Watson. Reviewed by Elza Teresa Dinwiddie. *Black Enterprise*. 13: 27+ (Jun 83)

Black Life In Corporate America: Swimming In The Mainstream. By George Davis and Glegg Watson. Reviewed by Gerald C. Horne. *Freedomways*. 23: No. 01: 51-54 (83)

Black Life In Corporate America: Swimming In The Mainstream. By George Davis and Glegg Watson. Reviewed by J. Alvin Wakefield. *The Urban League Review*. 07: 113-115 (Summer 83)

The Black Manager: Making It In The Corporate World. By Floyd Dickens and Jacqueline Dickens. Reviewed by Elza Terera Dinwiddie. *Black Enterprise*. 13: 30 (Jun 83)

Black Music In America: A Bibliography. By JoAnn Skowronski. Reviewed by Dominique-Rene DeLerma. *Negro History Bulletin*. 46: 85-86 (Jul-Sep 83)

Black Music In America: A Bibliography. By JoAnn Skowronski. Reviewed by Lucius R. Wyatt. *The Black Perspective in Music*. 11: 219-220 (Fall 83)

A Black Odyssey: John Lewis Waller And The Promise Of American Life, 1878-1900. By Randall Bennett Woods. Reviewed by G. W. Reid. *Journal of Negro History*. 68: 119-120 (Winter 83)

Black Pentecostalism: Southern Religion In An Urban World. By Arthur E. Paris. Reviewed by Robert E. Moran. *Journal of Negro History*. 68: 122-124 (Winter 83)

The Black Student's Guide To Colleges. By Barry Beckham. Reviewed by Elza Dinwiddie. *Black Enterprise*. 13: 23 (Feb 83)

Black Students In Higher Education: Conditions And Experiences In The 1970's. By Gail E. Thomas. Reviewed by Vanneise A. Collins. *Afro-Americans in New York Life and History*. 07: 70-71 (Jan 83)

Black Theatre: Present Condition. By Woodie (Jr.) King. Reviewed by Owen Dodson. *Black American Literature Forum*. 17: 94-95 (Summer 83)

Black Violence: Political Impact Of The 1960s Riots. By James W. Button. Reviewed by Herman (Jr.) George. *Afro-Americans in New York Life and History*. 07: 72-73 (Jul 83)

Black-White Contact In Schools: Its Social And Academic Effects. By Martin Patchen. Reviewed by Paul-Albert Emoungu. *Journal of Negro Education*. 52: 182-184 (Spring 83)

The Black Woman's Career Guide. By Beatryce Nivens. Reviewed by Elza Teresa Dinwiddie. *Black Enterprise*. 13: 30-31 (Jun 83)

The Black Woman's Career Guide. By Beatryce Nivens. Reviewed by Carole Bovoso. *Essence*. 13: 20 (Mar 83)

Black Women Writers At Work. By Claudia Tate. Reviewed by Carole E. Gregory. *Freedomways*. 23: No. 4: 287-289 (83)

Booker T. Washington: The Wizard Of Tuskegee, 1901-1915. By Louis R. Harlan. Reviewed by Adele Logan Alexander. *Crisis*. 90: 32 (Dec 83)

Books In Print South Africa 1980/Suid Afrikaanse Boeke Tans In Druk. Reviewed by G. E. Gorman. *Research in African Literatures*. 14: 266-268 (Summer 83)

The Bottomless Pit. By Alvis Baker. Reviewed by Leroy Mobley. *Crisis*. 90: 50 (Aug-Sep 83)

The Brandeis/Frankfurter Connection. By Bruce Allen Murphy. Reviewed by Irving Ferman. *Howard Law Journal*. 26: No. 1: 345-358 (83)

But Some Of Us Are Brave. By Gloria T. Hull and Patricia Bell Scott and Barbara Smith. Reviewed by Hortense D. Lloyd. *Negro Educational Review*. 34: 45-46 (Jan 83)

Canto Nero. By Giampiero Cane. Reviewed by Dominique-Rene DeLerma. *The Black Perspective in Music*. 11: 78-79 (Spring 83)

Carl Schurz: A Biography. By Hans L. Trefousse. Reviewed by Daniel C. Vogt. *Journal of Negro History*. 68: 124-125 (Winter 83)

A Case Of Black And White: Northern Volunteers And The Southern Freedom Summers, 1964-65. By Mary Aickin Rothschild. Reviewed by Gerald Horne. *Journal of Negro History*. 68: 107-109 (Winter 83)

A Century Of South African Short Stories. By Jean Marquard. Reviewed by Linda Susan Beard. *Research in African Literatures*. 14: 219-222 (Summer 83)

Change Of Territory. By Melvin Dixon. Reviewed by Adam David Miller. *Black American Literature Forum*. 17: 179-180 (Winter 83)

Children's Fiction About Africa In English. By Nancy J. Schmidt. Reviewed by Osayimwense Osa. *Research in African Literatures*. 14: 257-261 (Summer 83)

Circle Of Fire. By William H. Hooks. Reviewed by Lyla Hoffman. *Interracial Books for Children*. 14: No. 5: 25 (83)

Colloque Sur Litérature Et Esthétique Négro-Africanes. Reviewed by Amelavi E. Amela. *Research in African Literatures*. 14: 560-564 (Winter 83)

The Color Purple. By Alice Walker. Reviewed by Dorothy Randall-Tsuruta. *Black Scholar*. 14: 54-55 (Summer 83)

The Color Purple. By Alice Walker. Reviewed by Chester A. (Sr.) Higgins. *Crisis*. 90: 49 (Jun-Jul 83)

The Color Purple. By Alice Walker. Reviewed by Maryemma Graham. *Freedomways*. 23: No. 4: 278-280 (83)

The Color Purple: A Moral Tale. By Alice Walker. Reviewed by Ernece B. Kelley. *CLA Journal*. 27: 91-96 (Sep 83)

Commonwealth Children's Literature. Reviewed by Nancy J. Schmidt. *Research in African Literatures*. 14: 255-257 (Summer 83)

Community Politics And Educational Change: Ten School Systems Under Court Order. By Charles V. Willie and Susan L. Greenblatt. Reviewed by George L. Mims. *Journal of Black Studies*. 13: 375-376 (Mar 83)

Confirmation: An Anthology Of African American Women. By Amiri Baraka and Amina Baraka. Reviewed by Carole E. Gregory. *Freedomways*. 23: No. 4: 287-289 (83)

Conversations: Some People, Some Place, Some Time-South Africa. By Avril Herber. *Research in African Literatures*. 14: 252-253 (Summer 83)

Corporate Crime. By Marshall B. Clinard and Peter C. Yeager. Reviewed by Walter L. (III) Gordon. *Black Law Journal*. 08: 152-159 (Spring 83)

Count On Your Fingers African Style. By Claudia Zaslavsky and Jerry Pinkney. Reviewed by Jane Califf. *Interracial Books for Children*. 14: No. 5: 27 (83)

Critical Perspectives On Wole Soyinka. By James Gibbs. Reviewed by T. V. Prakash. *Research in African Literatures*. 14: 102-107 (Spring 83)

A Critical View On Elechi Amadi's. By Alastair Niven. Reviewed by Robert M. Wren. *Research in African Literatures*. 14: 110-111 (Spring 83)

A Critical View On John Pepper Clark's Selected Poems. By Kirsten Holst Petersen. Reviewed by Robert M. Wren. *Research in African Literatures*. 14: 110-112 (Spring 83)

A Critical View On Wole Soyinka's The Lion And The Jewel. By Martin Banham. Reviewed by Robert M. Wren. *Research in African Literatures*. 14: 110-111 (Spring 83)

Decolonizing Theology: A Caribbean Perspective. By Noel Leo Erskine. Reviewed by John B. Eubanks. *Journal of Religious Thought*. 39: 70-71 (Fall-Winter 83)

A Dictionary Of Africanisms: Contributions Of Sub-Saharan Africa To The English Language. By Gerard M. Dalgish. Reviewed by David F. Dorsey. *Phylon*. 44: 88-90 (Mar 83)

A Dictionary of Africanisms: Contributions Of Sub-Saharan Africa To The English Language. By Gerard M. Dalgish. Reviewed by Baruch Elimelech. *CAAS Newsletter*. 07: 13+ (May 83)

Dictionary Of American Negro Biography. By Rayford W. Logan and Michael R. Winston. *Crisis*. 90: 58 (Feb 83)

Dictionary Of American Negro Biography. By Rayford W. Logan and Michael R. Winston. Reviewed by Eunice Shaed Newton. *Journal of Negro Education*. 52: 454-455 (Fall 83)

Die Funktion Englischsprachiger Westafrikanischer Literatur: Eine Studie Zur Gesellschaftlichen Bedeutung Des Romans In Nigeria. By Günter Trenz. Reviewed by Eckhard Breitinger. *Research in African Literatures*. 14: 212-215 (Summer 83)

The Dilemma Of Access: Minorities In Two Year Colleges. By Michael A. Olivas. Reviewed by Obra V. Hackett. *Journal of Negro History*. 68: 130-131 (Winter 83)

Doris Lessing: The Problem Of Alienation And The Form Of The Novel. By Rotraut Spiegel. Reviewed by Roberta Rubenstein. *Research in African Literatures*. 14: 242-244 (Summer 83)

Double Dilemma: Minorities And Women In Science Education. By Jane B. Kahle. Reviewed by Julia V. Clark. *Journal of Negro Education*. 52: 85-87 (Winter 83)

Echos Du Commonwealth. Reviewed by Angelita Reyes. *Research in African Literatures*. 14: 123-126 (Spring 83)

Effective School Desegregation: Equity, Quality, And Feasibility. By Willis D. Hawley. Reviewed by Muriel Moore. *Journal of Black Studies*. 13: 371-375 (Mar 83)

Emancipation Féminine Et Roman Africain. By Arlette Chemain-Degrange. Reviewed by Charlotte Bruner. *Research in African Literatures*. 14: 209-212 (Summer 83)

An Empire For The Masses: The French Popular Image Of Africa, 1870-1900. By William H. Schneider. Reviewed by Sylvia M. Jacobs. *Journal of Negro History*. 68: 116-117 (Winter 83)

Encyclopedia Of Black America. By W. Augustus Low and Virgil A. Clift. Reviewed by Doris Evans McGinty. *The Black Perspective in Music*. 11: 79-82 (Spring 83)

Ethnic Relations In America. By Lance Liebman. Reviewed by David A. Gerber. *Afro-Americans in New York Life and History*. 07: 75-76 (Jul 83)

Ethnocultural Processes And National Problems In The Modern World. By I. R. Grigulevich and S. Ya Kozlov and H. Campbell Creighton. Reviewed by Alonzo T. Stephens. *Journal of Negro History*. 68: 128-129 (Winter 83)

European And African Stereotypes In Twentieth-Century Fiction. By Sarah L. Milbury-Steen. Reviewed by G. D. Killam. *Research in African Literatures*. 14: 225-228 (Summer 83)

Exits And Entrances. By Naomi Long Madgett. Reviewed by Tom Dent. *Freedomways*. 23: No. 01: 42-49 (83)

Faulkner: The House Divided. By Eric J. Sundquist. Reviewed by Elizabeth J. Higgens. *CLA Journal*. 27: 97-101 (Sep 83)

The FBI And Martin Luther King, Jr. By David J. Garrow. Reviewed by Gerald C. Horne. *Freedomways*. 23: No. 4: 290-294 (83)

Female Immigrants To The United States: Caribbean, Latin American, And African Experience. By Delores M. Mortimer and Roy S. Bryce-Laporte. Reviewed by Marcus E. Jones. *Phylon*. 44: 245-246 (Sep 83)

Fifteen Black American Composers: A Bibliography Of Their Works. By Alice Tischler and Carol Tomasic. Reviewed by Lucius R. Wyatt. *The Black Perspective in Music*. 11: 219-220 (Fall 83)

Flash Of The Spirit: African And Afro-American Art And Philosophy. By Robert Farris Thompsom. Reviewed by Beth Brown. *CLA Journal*. 27: 230-234 (Dec 83)

Folk Music And Modern Sound. By William Ferris and Mary L. Hart. Reviewed by Doris Evans McGinty. *The Black Perspective in Music*. 11: 212-214 (Fall 83)

For Dark Women And Others. By Satiafa. Reviewed by Alene Barnes-Harden. *Journal of Black Studies*. 14: 261-262 (Dec 83)

Forsaking All Others. By Jimmy Breslin. Reviewed by Chester A. (Sr.) Higgens. *Crisis*. 90: 36 (Apr 83)

The Free Black In Urban America: 1800-1850. By Leonard P. Curry. Reviewed by Janice Sumler-Lewis. *Black Law Journal*. 08: 162-163 (Spring 83)

The Free Black In Urban America, 1800-1850. By Leonard P. Curry. Reviewed by James O. Horton. *Afro-Americans in New York Life and History*. 07: 63-70 (Jan 83)

From DuBois To Van Vechten: The Early New Negro Literature, 1903-1926. By Chidi Ikonné. Reviewed by Houston A. (Jr.) Baker. *Research in African Literatures*. 14: 554-560 (Winter 83)

From The Old South To The New: Essays On The Transitional South. By Walter J. (Jr.) Fraser and Winfred B. (Jr.) Moore. Reviewed by H. Leon (Sr.) Prather. *Journal of Negro History*. 68: 120-122 (Winter 83)

Garveyism As A Religious Movement: The Institutionalization Of A Black Civil Religion. By Randall K. Burkett. Reviewed by Otey M. Scruggs. *Afro-Americans in New York Life and History*. 07: 71-72 (Jul 83)

Gifts Of Power: The Writings Or Rebecca Jackson. By Jean McMahon Humez. Reviewed by Henry Justin Ferry. *Journal of Religious Thought*. 39: 71-72 (Fall-Winter 83)

God Made Alaska For The Indians: Selected Essays. By Ishamel Reed. Reviewed by Jerome Klinkowitz. *Black American Literature Forum*. 17: 137-139 (Fall 83)

The Heart Of A Woman. By Maya Angelou. Reviewed by Maria K. Mootry Ikerionwu. *Phylon*. 44: 86-87 (Mar 83)

Helping With Literature. By D. E. K. Krampah. Reviewed by Chikwenye Okonjo Ogunyemi. *Research in African Literatures*. 14: 254-255 (Summer 83)

Heremakhonon. By Maryse Conde. Reviewed by Carole Bovoso. *Essence*. 13: 19 (Apr 83)

The Hero As A Villain. By J. P. Clark. Reviewed by Robert M. Wren. *Research in African Literatures*. 14: 112-113 (Spring 83)

Hit Hard. By David Williams. Reviewed by Chester A. (Sr.) Higgens. *Crisis*. 90: 44-47 (Nov 83)

Honey, I Love. By Eloise Greenfield and Byron Morris. Reviewed by Nieda Spigner. *Freedomways*. 23: No. 01: 55-56 (83)

I Wouldn't Take Nothin For My Journey: Two Centuries Of An Afro American Minister's Family. By Leonidas H. Berry. Reviewed by Larry Murphy. *National Medical Association Journal*. 75: 1232-1234 (Dec 83)

The Illustrated Encyclopedia Of Black Music. By Jon Futrell and Chris GillSt. Pierre Roger and Clive Richardson and Chris Trengove and Bob Fisher and Bill Sheehy and Lindsay Wesker. Reviewed by Doris Evans McGinty. *The Black Perspective in Music*. 11: 212-214 (Fall 83)

Imaginaire, Langage-Identité Culturelle, Négritude. By Jacqueline Leiner. Reviewed by Martin Steins. *Research in African Literatures*. 14: 553-554 (Winter 83)

In The Eye Of The Beholder: Contemporary Issues In Stereotyping. By Arthur G. Miller. Reviewed by Barbara D. Lyles. *Journal of Negro Education*. 52: 83-85 (Winter 83)

Integration And Disintegration In East Africa. By Christian P. Potholm and Richard A. Fredland. Reviewed by Frank M. Chiteji. *Review of Black Political Economy*. 12: 243-245 (Winter 83)

Introduction À L' Étude Du Roman Nœgro-Africain De Langue Française: Problemes Culturels Et Littèraires. By Jean-Pierre Makouta-M'Boukou. Reviewed by Jonathan Ngaté. *Research in African Literatures*. 14: 207-209 (Summer 83)

Introduction To Black Studies. By Mulana Karenga. Reviewed by Kuumba Na Kazi. *Black Collegian*. 13: 139 (Dec-Jan 83)

An Introduction To The Writings Of Ngugi. By G. D. Killam. Reviewed by Govind Narain Sharma. *Research in African Literatures*. 14: 238-242 (Summer 83)

The IQ Game: A Methodological Inquiry Into The Heredity-Environment Controversy. By Howard F. Taylor. Reviewed by Sandra E. Taylor. *Phylon*. 44: 244-245 (Sep 83)

Jake And Honeybunch Go To Heaven. By Margot Zemach. Reviewed by Beryle Banfield. *Interracial Books for Children*. 14: No. 1: 32-33 (83)

The Jazz Book: From Ragtime To Fusion And Beyond. By Joachim E. Berendt. Reviewed by George L. Starks. *The Black Perspective in Music*. 11: 215-218 (Fall 83)

Jazz Masters/Art Tatum. By Jed Distler. Reviewed by James Remel Burden. *The Black Perspective in Music*. 11: 86-88 (Spring 83)

Jazz Piano: A Jazz History. By Billy Taylor. Reviewed by George L. Starks. *The Black Perspective in Music*. 11: 215-218 (Fall 83)

The Jazz Tradition. By Martin Williams. Reviewed by George L. Starks. *The Black Perspective in Music*. 11: 215-218 (Fall 83)

Jazzforschung/Jazz Research. Reviewed by Lewis Porter. *The Black Perspective in Music*. 11: 85-86 (Spring 83)

Jelly Roll, Jabbo & Fats: 19 Portraits In Jazz. By Whitney Balliett. Reviewed by George L. Starks. *The Black Perspective in Music*. 11: 215-218 (Fall 83)

Journal Of African And Comparative Literature. Reviewed by Richard Bjornson. *Research in African Literatures*. 14: 119-121 (Spring 83)

Just Schools: The Ideal Of Racial Equality In American Education. By David L. Kirp. Reviewed by Peter Sola. *Journal of Negro Education*. 52: 457-459 (Fall 83)

Kaiso! The Trinidad Calypso. By Keith Q. Warner. Reviewed by Wilson Harris. *Research in African Literatures*. 14: 417-421 (Fall 83)

Kipling And Conrad: The Colonial Fiction. By John A. McClure. Reviewed by Martin Tucker. *Research in African Literatures*. 14: 228-232 (Summer 83)

L'Influence De La Littérature Française Sur Le Roman Arabe. By Kawsar Abdel Salam El Beheiry. Reviewed by Evelyne Accad. *Research in African Literatures*. 14: 203-207 (Summer 83)

Langston Hughes: Before And Beyond Harlem. By Faith Berry. Reviewed by Nieda Spigner. *Freedomways*. 23: No. 4: 285-286 (83)

Lawyers V. Educators: Black Colleges And Desegregation In Public Higher Education. By Jean L. Preer. Reviewed by Yvette Chancellor. *Black Law Journal*. 08: 160-161 (Spring 83)

Le Harlem De Chester Himes. By Ambroise Kom. Reviewed by Edward F. Taylor. *CLA Journal*. 27: 224-225 (Dec 83)

Le Thèâtre Noir Aux États-Unis. By Geneviève Fabre. Reviewed by Andrzej Ceynowa. *Black American Literature Forum*. 17: 95-96 (Summer 83)

Le Vieux Nègre Et La Médaille De Ferdinand Oyono. By M. F. Minyono-Nkodo. Reviewed by Simon P. X. Battestini. *Research in African Literatures*. 14: 237-238 (Summer 83)

Leipolot 100. By Merwe Scholtz. Reviewed by Ampie Coetzee. *Research in African Literatures*. 14: 248-251 (Summer 83)

Let's Write A Novel. By Es'kia Mphahlele. Reviewed by Johnny Masilela. *Research in African Literatures*. 14: 253-254 (Summer 83)

Let The Trumpet Sound: The Life Of Martin Luther King, Jr.. By Stephen B. Oates. Reviewed by Gereald C. Horne. *Freedomways*. 23: No. 4: 290-294 (83)

The Life And Poems Of A Cuban Slave: Juan Francisco Manzano, 1797-1854. By Edward J. Mullen. Reviewed by Ian I. Smart. *Research in African Literatures*. 14: 414-417 (Fall 83)

Lift Every Voice And Sing: A Collection Of Afro-American Spirituals And Other Songs. By Irene V. Jackson. Reviewed by Carl G. (Jr.) Harris. *The Black Perspective in Music*. 11: 82-83 (Spring 83)

The Literary Half-Yearly. Reviewed by Kalu Ogbaa. *Research in African Literatures*. 14: 126-128 (Spring 83)

Literatur Und Geschichte In Afrika: Darstellung Der Vorkolonialen Und Kultur Afrikas In Der English-Und Frazosischsprachig. en Fiktionalen Afrikanischen Literatur. By Karl Heinz Jansen. Reviewed by Barbara Ischinger. *Research in African Literatures*. 14: 545-549 (Winter 83)

Literature And Ideology In Haiti, 1915-1961. By J. Michael Dash. Reviewed by Andrew Salkey. *Research in African Literatures*. 14: 564-566 (Winter 83)

The Literature Of Jazz: A Critical Guide. By Donald Kennington and Danny L. Read. Reviewed by George L. Starks. *The Black Perspective in Music*. 11: 215-218 (Fall 83)

Live And Off-Color: News Biz. By Bob Teague. Reviewed by Gerald C. Horne. *Freedomways*. 23: No. 01: 51-54 (83)

Lives Of Their Own: Blacks, Italians, And Poles In Pittsburgh, 1900-1960. By John Bodnar and Roger Simon and Michael P. Weber. Reviewed by Clayborne Carson. *Journal of Negro History*. 68: 98-99 (Winter 83)

The Longest War: Israel In Lebanon. By Jacobo Timerman. Reviewed by Jane Power. *Freedomways*. 23: No. 3: 202-205 (83)

Mainstreaming Outsiders: The Production Of Black Professionals. By James Blackwell. Reviewed by Darryl Paulson. *Journal of Negro History*. 68: 99-101 (Winter 83)

Mammography, Thremography And Ultrasound In Breast Cancer Detection. By Lawrence W. Basset and Richard H. Gold. Reviewed by Cornelius W. Merrick. *National Medical Association Journal*. 75: 1023 (Oct 83)

Marian Anderson: A Catalog Of The Collection At University Of Pennsylvania Library. By Neda M. Westlake and Otto E. Albrecht. Reviewed by Janet L. Sims-Wood. *The Black Perspective in Music*. 11: 221-222 (Fall 83)

Marked By Fire. By Joyce Carol Thomas. Reviewed by Geraldine L. Wilson. *Freedomways*. 23: No. 4: 289-290 (83)

Markets And Minorities. By Thomas Sowell. Reviewed by Bernadette P. Chachere. *Review of Black Political Economy*. 12: 163-177 (Winter 83)

Marva Collins' Way. By Marva Collins and Civia Tamarkin. Reviewed by Carole Bovoso. *Essence*. 13: 19 (Jan 83)

Migrations Of The Heart. By Martia Golden. Reviewed by Gerald D. Kendrick. *CLA Journal*. 26: 362-363 (Mar 83)

Minority Aging: Sociological And Social Psychological Issues. By Ron C. Manuel. Reviewed by Jacob U. Gordon. *Journal of Negro History*. 68: 110-111 (Winter 83)

Mister Tameklor, Suivi De Francis Le Parisien Par Le Happy Star Concert Band De Lome- (Togo). By Nobel Akam Et Alain Richard. Reviewed by S. Agbeko Amegbleame. *Research in African Literatures*. 14: 114-116 (Spring 83)

Modern South African Stories. By Stephen Gray. Reviewed by Linda Susan Beard. *Research in African Literatures*. 14: 219-222 (Summer 83)

The Mojo Hands Call/I Must Go. By Sterling D. Plumpp. Reviewed by Doris Davenport. *Black American Literature Forum*. 17: 177-179 (Winter 83)

Mother Of The Blues: A Study Of Ma Rainey. By Sandra R. Lieb. Reviewed by D. Antoinette Handy. *The Black Perspective in Music*. 11: 83-85 (Spring 83)

Music, Printed And Manuscript, In The James Weldon Johnson Memorial Collection Of Negro Arts And Letters: An Annotated Catalog. By Rae Linda Brown. Reviewed by Arena L. Stevens. *Journal of Negro History*. 68: 101-102 (Winter 83)

Music, Printed And Manuscript, In The James Weldon Johnson Memorial Collection Of Negro Arts And Letters: An Annotated Catalog. By Rae Linda Brown. Reviewed by Janet L. Sims-Wood. *The Black Perspective in Music*. 11: 221-222 (Fall 83)

My Mama Needs Me. By Mildred Pitts Walter. Reviewed by Geraldine L. Wilson. *Interracial Books for Children*. 14: No. 5: 26-27 (83)

The N.A.A.C.P. Crusade Against Lynching, 1909-1950. By Robert L. Zangrando. Reviewed by A. Wade Smith. *Phylon*. 44: 169 (Jun 83)

Namibia: Land And Peoples, Myths And Fables. By Jan Knappert. Reviewed by Megan Biesele. *Research in African Literatures*. 14: 405-407 (Fall 83)

Narratives: Poems In The Tradition Of Black Women. By Cheryl Clarke. Reviewed by Doris Davenport. *Black American Literature Forum*. 17: 177-179 (Winter 83)

Nationalism And The Nigerian National Theatre. By Joel Adedeji. Reviewed by Ebun Clark. *Research in African Literatures*. 14: 107-108 (Spring 83)

Natural Birth: Poems. By Toi Derricotte. Reviewed by Joe Weixlmann. *Black American Literature Forum*. 17: 180-182 (Winter 83)

The Negro Almanac: A Reference Work On The Afro-American. By Harry A. Polski and James Williams. Reviewed by Earle H. West. *Journal of Negro Education*. 52: 455-457 (Fall 83)

New Testament Apocalyptic. By Paul S. Minear. Reviewed by Cain H. Felder. *Journal of Religious Thought*. 39: 72-73 (Fall-Winter 83)

Ngugi Wa Thiong'o. By Clifford B. Robson. Reviewed by Govind Narain Sharma. *Research in African Literatures*. 14: 238-242 (Summer 83)

The Notorious Triangle, Rhode Island And The African Slave Trade, 1700-1807. By Jay Coughtry. Reviewed by John E. Fleming. *Journal of Negro History*. 68: 113-114 (Winter 83)

Opera Wonyosi. By Wole Soyinka. Reviewed by A. Rasheed Yesufu. *Journal of Black Studies*. 13: 496-499 (Jun 83)

Our Nig, Or Sketches From The Life Of A Free Black In A Two-Story House, North. By Harriet Wilson. Reviewed by Cassandra Byers Harvin. *Essence*. 13: 20 (Feb 83)

Papa Babe's Stamp Collection. By Gladys Turner. Reviewed by Nancy L. Arnez. *Crisis*. 90: 50 (Aug-Sep 83)

A Paul Robeson Research Guide: A Selected Annotated Bibliography. By Lenwood G. Davis. Reviewed by Lucius R. Wyatt. *The Black Perspective in Music*. 11: 219-220 (Fall 83)

Perspectives In Multicultural Education. By William E. Sims and Bernice Bass de Martinez. Reviewed by Geneva Gay. *Journal of Negro Education*. 52: 461-463 (Fall 83)

Perspectives On South African Fiction. By Sarah Christie and Geoffrey Hutchings and Don Maclennan. Reviewed by Stephen Gray. *Research in African Literatures*. 14: 216-218 (Summer 83)

A Piller Of Fire To Follow: American Indian Dramas, 1808-1859. By Priscilla F. Sears. Reviewed by Ola B. Criss. *Phylon*. 44: 90-91 (Mar 83)

Political Process And The Development Of Black Insurgency 1930-1970. By Doug McAdam. Reviewed by Ally Faye Mack. *Journal of Negro History*. 68: 127-128 (Winter 83)

The Politics Of Law: A Progressive Critique. By David Kairys. Reviewed by Meredith L. Caliman. *Black Law Journal*. 08: 462-463 (Winter 83)

The Politics Of Race In New York: The Struggle For Black Suffrage In The Civil War. By Phyllis F. Field. Reviewed by Charles T. Haley. *Journal of Negro History*. 68: 125-126 (Winter 83)

Popular Culture And American Life: Selected Topics In The Study Of American Popular Culture. By Martin Laforse and James A. Drake. Reviewed by Doris Evans McGinty. *The Black Perspective in Music*. 11: 212-214 (Fall 83)

Praisesong For The Widow. By Paule Marshall. Reviewed by John Oliver Killens. *Crisis*. 90: 49-50 (Aug-Sep 83)

Praisesong For The Widow. By Paule Marshall. Reviewed by Carole Bovoso. *Essence*. 13: 19 (Apr 83)

Preisgedichte Und Verse Aus Südwestafrika-Namibia. By Peter Sulzer. Reviewed by Dieter Riemenschneider. *Research in African Literatures*. 14: 412-413 (Fall 83)

Race, Racism And American Law. By Derrick A. (Jr.) Bell. Reviewed by William Payne. *Black Law Journal*. 08: 361-366 (Fall 83)

Raising The Bottom Line: Business Leadership In A Changing Society. By Carlton E. Spitzer. Reviewed by Elza Teresa Dinwiddie. *Black Enterprise*. 13: 30 (Jun 83)

Reflections Of An African Nationalist. By T. O. Dosumu-Johnson. Reviewed by Sulayman S. Nyang. *Phylon*. 44: 164-168 (Jun 83)

The Relational Self Ethics And Therapy From A Black Church Perspective. By Archie (Jr.) Smith. Reviewed by John B. Eubanks. *Journal of Religious Thought*. 40: 73-74 (Spring-Summer 83)

Role Model Blacks: Known But Little Known. By Carroll L. Miller. Reviewed by Samuel L. Banks. *Journal of Negro Education*. 52: 87-89 (Winter 83)

Roots Of Soul. By Alfred B. Pasteur and Ivory L. Toldson. Reviewed by Charles A. Asbury. *Journal of Negro Education*. 52: 176-177 (Spring 83)

The Ruling Race: A History Of American Slaveholders. By James Oakes. Reviewed by Joseph P. Reidy. *Journal of Negro History*. 68: 95-97 (Winter 83)

Saints, Slaves And Blacks: The Changing Place Of Black People Within Mormonism. By Newell G. Bringhurst. Reviewed by Gordon D. Morgan. *Journal of Negro History*. 68: 111-112 (Winter 83)

Sandino's Daughters: Testimonies Of Nicaraguan Women In Struggle. By Margaret Randall and Lynda Yanz. Reviewed by Janice Bevien. *Black Scholar*. 14: 74-75 (Mar-Apr 83)

Sassafrass, Cypress And Indigo. By Ntozake Shange. Reviewed by Kuumba Na Kazi. *Black Collegian*. 13: 132+ (Feb-Mar 83)

Science, Myth, Reality: The Black Family In One-Half Century Of Research. By Eleanor Engram. Reviewed by Dorothy Linder. *Phylon*. 44: 87-88 (Mar 83)

Season Of Hunger/Cry Of Rain. By E. Ethelbert Miller. Reviewed by Tom Dent. *Freedomways*. 23: No. 01: 42-49 (83)

Seasons Of Hunger/Cry Of Rain. By E. Ethlbert Miller. Reviewed by Lateifa Ramona L. Hyman. *Black American Literature Forum*. 17: 182 (Winter 83)

Senefer And Hatshepsut. By Beatrice Lumpkin. Reviewed by Claudia Zaslavsky. *Freedomways*. 23: No. 4: 294-296 (83)

Shades Of Brown: New Perspectives On School Desegregation. By Derrick Bell. Reviewed by W. Edwin Derrick. *Journal of Negro Education*. 52: 177-178 (Spring 83)

Shadow. By Marcia Brown. Reviewed by Geraldine Wilson. *Interracial Books for Children*. 14: No. 1: 33-34 (83)

Shadow And Substance: Afro-American Experience In Contemporary Children's Fiction. By Rudine Sims. Reviewed by Charlotte K. Brooks. *Black American Literature Forum*. 17: 136-137 (Fall 83)

Shadow & Substance: Afro-American Experience In Contemporary Children's Fiction. By Rudine Sims. Reviewed by Minnie Finch. *Journal of Negro Education*. 52: 184-185 (Spring 83)

Shakespeare's Sonnets. By Kenneth Muir. Reviewed by Carol P. Marsh. *CLA Journal*. 26: 478-479 (Jun 83)

Slavery And Social Death: A Comparative Study. By Orlando Patterson. Reviewed by Howard Ross. *Phylon*. 44: 332-333 (Dec 83)

Slaves No More: Letters From Liberia, 1833-1869. By Bell I. Wiley. Reviewed by Jason H. Silverman. *Negro History Bulletin*. 46: 105 (Oct-Dec 83)

Socio-Political Aspects Of The Palaver In Some African Countries. Reviewed by Corinne Kratz. *Research in African Literatures*. 14: 409-412 (Fall 83)

Songs From My Father's Pockets. By Llewellyn Ivory Giles. Reviewed by Adam David Miller. *Black American Literature Forum*. 17: 179-180 (Winter 83)

The Struggle That Must Be. By Harry Edwards. Reviewed by Manning Carlyle Peterson. *Journal of Black Studies*. 14: 99-102 (Sep 83)

Studies In 20th Century Literature. Reviewed by Arthur Flannigan. *Research in African Literatures*. 14: 121-123 (Spring 83)

Sweet Whispers Brother Rush. By Virginia Hamilton. Reviewed by Geraldine Wilson. *Interracial Books for Children*. 14: No. 1: 32 (83)

Teacher/Student Work Manual: A Model Evaluating Traditional U.S. History Textbooks. By Mack Bernard Morant. Reviewed by Henry E. Hankerson. *Journal of Negro Education*. 52: 89-90 (Winter 83)

The Terrible Twos. By Ishmael Reed. Reviewed by Henry Louis (Jr.) Gates. *Black Enterprise*. 13: 16 (Apr 83)

The Terrible Twos. By Ishmael Reed. Reviewed by Carole Bovoso. *Essence*. 13: 19 (Jan 83)

Thalassemia: Recent Advances In Detection And Treatment. Reviewed by Oswaldo L. Castro. *National Medical Association Journal.* 75: 1023+ (Oct 83)

The Things They Say Behind Your Back: Stereotypes And The Myths Behind Them. By William H. Helmreich. Reviewed by Keith A. Winsell. *Phylon.* 44: 246-248 (Sep 83)

Third World Legal Studies-1982: Law In Alternative Strategies Of Rural Development. Reviewed by J. Holmes (Jr.) Armstead. *Black Law Journal.* 08: 459-461 (Winter 83)

This Was Harlem: A Cultural Portrait, 1900-1950. By Jervis Anderson. Reviewed by Estelle W. Taylor. *Journal of Negro Education.* 52: 178-182 (Spring 83)

This Was Harlem: A Cultural Portrait, 1900-1950. By Jervis Anderson. Reviewed by James H. Randall. *Journal of Negro History.* 68: 105-107 (Winter 83)

Tic Tac Toe And Other Three-In-A-Row Games From Ancient Egypt To The Modern Computer. By Claudia Zaslavsky. Reviewed by Marian Borenstein. *Freedomways.* 23: No. 01: 54-55 (83)

Towards The Decolonization Of African Literature. By Chinweizu and Onwuchekwa Jemie and Ihechukwu Madubuike. Reviewed by Gerald Moore. *Research in African Literatures.* 14: 549-553 (Winter 83)

Towards The Mountain: An Autobiography. By Alan Paton. Reviewed by Martin Rubin. *Research in African Literatures.* 14: 261-266 (Summer 83)

The Transforming Image: A Study Of Shelley's Major Poetry. By Jean Hall. Reviewed by Elizabeth J. Higgins. *CLA Journal.* 27: 228-230 (Dec 83)

The Trickster In West Africa: A Study Of Mythic Irony And Sacred Delight. By Robert D. Pelton. Reviewed by Richard K. Priebe. *Research in African Literatures.* 14: 401-405 (Fall 83)

Twelve African Writers. By Gerald Moore. Reviewed by A. A. Roscoe. *Research in African Literatures.* 14: 232-236 (Summer 83)

Un Fusil Dans La Main, Un Poème Dans La Poche. By Emmanuel Dongala. Reviewed by Thelma Ravell-Pinto. *Journal of Black Studies.* 13: 369-371 (Mar 83)

The United States Educational System: Marxist Approaches. By Marvin J. Berlowits and Frank E. (Jr.) Cahpman. Reviewed by Lanthin D. (Jr.) Camblin. *Journal of Black Studies.* 14: 102-103 (Sep 83)

Walter Hines Page And The World's Work, 1900-1913. By Robert J. Rusnak. Reviewed by Roger D. Launius. *Journal of Negro History.* 68: 104-105 (Winter 83)

War And Race: The Black Officer In The American Military, 1915-1941. By Gerald W. Patton. Reviewed by Phillip McGuire. *Journal of Negro History.* 68: 114-116 (Winter 83)

Waves & License. By Stephen Todd Booker. Reviewed by Doris Davenport. *Black American Literature Forum.* 17: 177-179 (Winter 83)

White Supremacy: A Comparative Study In American And South African History. By George Frederickson. Reviewed by Vincent P. Franklin. *Phylon.* 44: 160-163 (Jun 83)

Who's Who In Rock. By Michael Bane. Reviewed by Doris Evans McGinty. *The Black Perspective in Music.* 11: 212-214 (Fall 83)

With Fire. By Mariah Britton. Reviewed by June Jordan. *Freedomways.* 23: No. 01: 50 (83)

The Women Of Brewster Place. By Naylor Gloria. Reviewed by Loyle Hairston. *Freedomways.* 23: No. 4: 282-285 (83)

Women, Race And Class. By Angela Y. Davis. Reviewed by Sandra Virginia Gonsalves. *Journal of Negro History.* 68: 109-110 (Winter 83)

Writers In Exile: The Creative Use Of Home In Modern Literature. By Andrew Gurr. Reviewed by Gareth Griffiths. *Research in African Literatures.* 14: 222-225 (Summer 83)

The Writing Of Peter Abrahams. By Kolawole Ogungbesan. Reviewed by Clive Leeman. *Research in African Literatures.* 14: 245-248 (Summer 83)

Yoruba Myths. By Ulli Beir. Reviewed by Oludare Olajubu. *Research in African Literatures.* 14: 538-543 (Winter 83)

Youngblood. By John Oliver Killens. Reviewed by Lance Jeffers. *Black Scholar.* 14: 49-50 (Sep-Oct 83)

Youngblood. By John Oliver Killens. Reviewed by Elizabeth Nunez-Harrell. *Crisis.* 90: 42-43 (Oct 83)

Zami - A New Spelling Of My Name. By Audre Lorde. Reviewed by Gloria I. Joseph. *Black Scholar.* 14: 48-49 (Sep-Oct 83)

Zami: A New Spelling Of My Name. By Audre Lorde. Reviewed by Carole Bovoso. *Essence.* 13: 20 (Mar 83)

Zami: A Spelling Of My Name. By Audre Lorde. Reviewed by Kuumba Na Kazi. *Black Collegian.* 13: 68 (Apr-May 83)

Zionism In The Age Of The Dictators: A Reappraisal. By Lenni Brenner. Reviewed by William Loren Katz. *Freedomways.* 23: No. 3: 199-202 (83)

Booker, Martin

Engineering Options. Illustrated. *Black Collegian.* 13: 32-34+ (Dec-Jan 83)

Booker, Simeon

Invitation To Invade Black Nation Called 'Gunboat Diplomacy'. Illustrated. *Jet.* 65: 8-9+ (14 Nov 83)

President Reagan Praises King, Signs Holiday Bill. Illustrated. *Jet.* 65: 4-7 (21 Nov 83)

Vice President Bush Says He'll Continue To 'Plug' For GOP Among Blacks. Illustrated. *Jet.* 64: 16-17 (22 Aug 83)

Booker, Stephen Todd

Waves & License. Book review. Doris Davenport. *Black American Literature Forum.* 17: 177-179 (Winter 83)

The Centrifugal Force Of Orez. Poem. *Black American Literature Forum*. 17: 171 (Winter 83)

Booksellers And Bookselling

Where To Find: Black Books By Mail. Marcia McNair. *Essence*. 14: 54 (Jul 83)

Boots And Shoes

Winter-Proofing Your Boots. Sandra Jackson-Opoku. *Essence*. 14: 40 (Nov 83)

Borders, James

The CEO Survey On Affirmative Action: Has Corporate America Abandoned Affirmative Action?. *Black Collegian*. 13: 30+ (Feb-Mar 83)

Is Affirmative Action In Trouble? An Analysis Of Recent Developments. Illustrated. *Black Collegian*. 13: 36+ (Feb-Mar 83)

Trends In High Technology.. *Black Collegian*. 14: 100-104+ (Sep-Oct 83)
Rouselle, William
Toffler, Alvin

Borenstein, Marian

Tic Tac Toe And Other Three-In-A-Row Games From Ancient Egypt To The Modern Computer. Book review. *Freedomways*. 23: No. 01: 54-55 (83)

Bostick, Herman F. (joint author)

See Brierre, Jean

Boston, Taquiena and Katz, Vera J.

Witnesses To A Possibility: The Black Theater Movement In Wasington, D. C., 1968-1976. Illustrated, notes. *Black American Literature Forum*. 17: 22-26 (Spring 83)

Boston TransAfrica

Black Ambassadors Feted By Boston TransAfrica. Illustrated. D. Michael Cheers. *Jet*. 63: 36-39 (28 Feb 83)

Botwin, Carol and Fine, Jerome L.

Any Man Won't Do!. *Essence*. 13: 74-75+ (Feb 83)

Bovoso, Carole

Aké: The Years Of Childhood. Book review. *Essence*. 13: 20 (Mar 83)

The Black Woman's Career Guide. Book review. *Essence*. 13: 20 (Mar 83)

Heremakhonon. Book review. *Essence*. 13: 19 (Apr 83)

Marva Collins' Way. Book review. *Essence*. 13: 19 (Jan 83)

Praisesong For The Widow. Book review. *Essence*. 3: 19 (Apr 83)

The Terrible Twos. Book review. *Essence*. 13: 19 (Jan 83)

Zami: A New Spelling Of My Name. Book review. *Essence*. 13: 20 (Mar 83)

Bowser, Benjamin P. (about)

On Reconsidering Park, Johnson, DuBois, Frazier And Reid: Reply To Benjamin Bowser's "The Contribution Of Blacks To Sociological Knowledge.". Notes. Jerry G. Watts. *Phylon*. 44: 273-291 (Dec 83)

Boxers

Aaron Pryor: His Own Boss Inside And Outside The Ring. Illustrated. Walter Leavy. *Ebony*. 38: 35-36+ (May 83)

Detroit Fighters Build On Rich Historic Tradition. Illustrated. Don Armstrong. *Crisis*. 90: 28-29 (Apr 83)

Joe Louis-Model For The Physician. Illustrated. *Crisis*. 90: 22-23 (Apr 83)

Sugar Ray Leonard Replaces Boxing With Family, TV Show And New $2 Million Home. Illustrated. Norman O. Unger. *Jet*. 65: 20-23 (14 Nov 83)

Boxing

$4 Million Makes Foes Of Friends. Illustrated. Norman O. Unger. *Jet*. 63: 46-48 (14 Mar 83)

Boycott

Jesse Jackson: The Leader Of PUSH Urges Boycotts For Dollar Power. Interview, Illustrated. Jesse L. Jackson and Sid Cassese. *Essence*. 14: 14+ (Jun 83)

Boycott—South Africa

Boycotting Apartheid. Tables. Frank Dexter Brown. *Black Enterprise*. 14: 26 (Dec 83)

Boyd, Frederick V.

Outlook For Black Economic Development. Illustrated. *Black Enterprise*. 13: 247-248+ (Jun 83)

Boyer, Horace Clarence

Charles Albert Tindley: Progenitor Of Black-American Gospel Music. Illustrated, tables, notes. *The Black Perspective in Music*. 11: 103-132 (Fall 83)

Boyer, Jill Witherspoon

But I Say. Poem. *Essence*. 14: 140 (Dec 83)

Boys

See Also Adolescent Boys
Youth

Bradfield, Larry D.

Beyond Mimetic Exhaustion: The Reflex And Bone Structure Experiment. Notes. *Black American Literature Forum*. 17: 120-123 (Fall 83)

Bradford, Ernest

Towards A View Of The Influence Of Religion On Black Literature. Notes. *CLA Journal*. 27: 18-29 (Sep 83)

Bradford, William D.

In The Interest Of Survival: Bank Overview. Tables. *Black Enterprise*. 13: 103-104+ (Jun 83)

Bradley, Ed (about)

Ed Bradley At Ease. Illustrated. Michele Wallace. *Essence*. 14: 66-67 (Nov 83)

Bradley, Ethel (about)

L.A. Mayor's Wife Says She Is Prisoner In Posh Mansion; Never Sees Him. Illustrated. *Jet*. 65: 22-24 (26 Dec 83)

Bradley, Melvin L. (about)

Bradley Gets Upgraded Position On Reagan Staff. Illustrated. *Jet*. 63: 4 (21 Feb 83)

Bradley, Thomas (about)

Bradley Got Major Backing In Calif. Governor's Race. Illustrated. *Jet*. 64: 8 (21 Mar 83)

Brandy

The Warming Glow Of Cognac. Illustrated. Eunice Fried. *Black Enterprise*. 13: 60 (Jan 83)

Branson, Herman E. and others

Use Of Activated Partial Thromboplastin Time To Monitor Coumarin Anticoagulation. Tables, notes. *National Medical Association Journal*. 75: 61-64 (Jan 83)

Branton, Wiley A.

Little Rock Revisited: Desegregation To Resegregation. Notes. *Journal of Negro Education*. 52: 250-269 (Summer 83)

Braxton, Dwight (about)

$4 Million Makes Foes Of Friends. Illustrated. Norman O. Unger. *Jet*. 63: 46-48 (14 Mar 83)

Bray, Rosemary L.

Can Women And Men Be Friends? Illustrated. *Essence*. 14: 71-72 + (Jul 83)

Ready Or Not, Here Comes The Computer Future.. *Essence*. 14: 99-100 + (Oct 83)

Unemployment: How To Bounce Back.. *Essence*. 14: 121-122 + (Jun 83)

Brazilian Authors

See Authors, Brazilian

Brazziel, William F.

Baccalaureate College Of Origin Of Black Doctorate Recipients. Notes, tables. *Journal of Negro Education*. 52: 102-109 (Spring 83)

Breast—Tumors

Fibroadenoma Of The Female Breast: A Critical Clinical Assessment. Tables, notes. Claude H. (Jr.) Organ and Brian C. Organ. *National Medical Association Journal*. 75: 701-704 (Jul 83)

Breitinger, Eckhard

Die Funktion Englischsprachiger Westafrikanischer Literatur: Eine Studie Zur Gesellschaftlichen Bedeutung Des Romans In Nigeria. Book review. *Research in African Literatures*. 14: 212-215 (Summer 83)

Brenner, Lenni

Zionism In The Age Of The Dictators: A Reappraisal. Book review. William Loren Katz. *Freedomways*. 23: No. 3: 199-202 (83)

Breslau, Naomi (joint author)

See Wolf, Jacquelyn H.

Breslin, Jimmy

Forsaking All Others. Book review. Chester A. (Sr.) Higgins. *Crisis*. 90: 36 (Apr 83)

Brewer, Thomas H. (Sr.) (about)

Black Doctor Killed Under "Suspicious Circumstances". Illustrated. *Crisis*. 90: 23 (Apr 83)

Brewster-Walker, Sandi (about)

Essence Women: Sandi Brewster-Walker. Illustrated. Sid Cassese. *Essence*. 13: 22 + (Apr 83)

Bricktop

See Smith, Ada Beatrice Queen Victoria Louise Virginia

Bridges, Todd (about)

Todd Bridges And Janet Jackson: The Problems Of Teen-Age Stars. Illustrated. Aldore Collier. *Ebony*. 38: 58-59 + (Feb 83)

Bridgewater, Shirlene Evans (about)

Two Women In Houston Turn Their Dreams Of Owning A Bookstore Into A Successful Reality. Illustrated. Lloyd Gite. *Essence*. 13: 32 + (Mar 83)

Brien, Mimi

Life Insurance: What's Right For You.. *Essence*. 13: 52 + (Apr 83)

Brierre, Jean and Bostick, Herman F.

Poetic Encounters: An Interview With Jean F. Brierre. Notes. *CLA Journal*. 26: 277-287 (Mar 83)

Brietzke, Paul H.

Administrative Law And Development: The American 'Model' Evaluated. Notes. *Howard Law Journal*. 26: No. 2: 645-698 (83)

Brimmer, Andrew F.

Behind The Eight Ball In The Wholesale Industry. Illustrated. *Black Enterprise*. 13: 35 (Apr 83)

Blacks In The Stock Market.. *Black Enterprise*. 14: 41-42 (Oct 83)

The Economic Outlook For Blacks In 1983. Illustrated. *Black Enterprise*. 13: 37 (Feb 83)

Income And Taxes. Illustrated. *Black Enterprise*. 14: 43-44 (Dec 83)

Sources Of Income For Blacks Vs. Whites. Tables. *Black Enterprise*. 14: 33 (Aug 83)

Bringhurst, Newell G.

Saints, Slaves And Blacks: The Changing Place Of Black People Within Mormonism. Book review. Gordon D. Morgan. *Journal of Negro History*. 68: 111-112 (Winter 83)

British Virgin Islands—Description And Travel

The Unexpected Pleasures Of A Quiet Island. Illustrated. Frank Dexter Brown. *Black Enterprise*. 13: 66 + (May 83)

Britton, Gwyneth and Lumpkin, Margaret

Basal Readers: Paltry Progress Pervades. Tables, notes. *Interracial Books for Children.* 14: No. 6: 4-7 (83)

Britton, Mariah

With Fire. Book review. June Jordan. *Freedomways.* 23: No. 01: 50 (83)

A Wellness Has Spoken. Poem. *Essence.* 14: 89 (Oct 83)

Brock, William (about)

The Critical Choice: Facing The Contradictions Of Life In America. Editorial. *Black Collegian.* 13: 14 (Apr-May 83)

Brody, Jane

Talking To Your Doctor. Illustrated. *Essence.* 14: 38 + (Jun 83)

Brooklyn, New York

See Also Public Schools—New York (State)—Brooklyn—History

Brooklyn, New York—History

Did Brooklyn (N.Y.) Blacks Have Unusual Control Over Their Schools? Period I: 1815-1845. Notes. Robert J. Swan. *Afro-Americans in New York Life and History.* 07: 25-46 (Jul 83)

Brooks, A. Russell

The CLA Journal As A Mirror Of Changing Ethnic And Academic Perspectives. Notes. *CLA Journal.* 26: 265-276 (Mar 83)

Brooks, Charlotte K.

Shadow And Substance: Afro-American Experience In Contemporary Children's Fiction. Book review. *Black American Literature Forum.* 17: 136-137 (Fall 83)

Brooks, Gwendolyn

Telephone Conversations. Poem. *Black American Literature Forum.* 17: 148 (Winter 83)

Weaponed Woman. Poem. *Essence.* 14: 147 (Oct 83)

Brothers And Sisters

'She Hit Me First!': How To Combat Sibling Rivalry. Valerie Wilson Wesley. *Essence.* 14: 138 (Oct 83)

Sister, Sister. Illustrated. Julie Chenault. *Essence.* 14: 13-14 (May 83)

Brown, Beth

Flash Of The Spirit: African And Afro-American Art And Philosophy. Book review. *CLA Journal.* 27: 230-234 (Dec 83)

Brown, Frank and Muigai, Waithira

Court-Ordered School Desegregation: One Community's Attitude. Notes. *Journal of Black Studies.* 13: 355-368 (Mar 83)

Brown, Frank Dexter

The Activist Black Press.. *Black Enterprise.* 13: 38 (Jun 83)

Boycotting Apartheid. Tables. *Black Enterprise.* 14: 26 (Dec 83)

Jesse Jackson's Push For Power. Illustrated. *Black Enterprise.* 14: 44-46 + (Nov 83)

The New King Of Swing. Illustrated. *Black Enterprise.* 13: 42 (Jun 83)

States Versus Apartheid. Illustrated. *Black Enterprise.* 13: 22 (Apr 83)

The Unexpected Pleasures Of A Quiet Island. Illustrated. *Black Enterprise.* 13: 66 + (May 83) Sutton, Chuck

Brown, Lee P.

Report From Houston. . . Community Involvement Is Key To Future Success. Illustrated. *Crisis.* 90: 38-39 (Feb 83)

Brown, Mae Watts

Essence Women: Jewell Thompson. Illustrated. *Essence.* 13: 20 (Jan 83)

Brown, Mai

Essence Women: Suzan D. Johnson. Illustrated. *Essence.* 14: 42 (Sep 83)

Brown, Marcia

Shadow. Book review. Geraldine Wilson. *Interracial Books for Children.* 14: No. 1: 33-34 (83)

Brown, Rae Linda

Music, Printed And Manuscript, In The James Weldon Johnson Memorial Collection Of Negro Arts And Letters: An Annotated Catalog. Book review. Arena L. Stevens. *Journal of Negro History.* 68: 101-102 (Winter 83)

Music, Printed And Manuscript, In The James Weldon Johnson Memorial Collection Of Negro Arts And Letters: An Annotated Catalog. Book review. Janet L. Sims-Wood. *The Black Perspective in Music.* 11: 221-222 (Fall 83)

Brown, Richard K. J. (joint author)

See Collins, James D.

Brown, Wesley

"This Culture Fosters The View That Men Are Supposed To Leave Children, Not Assume Responsibility For Them". Illustrated. *Essence.* 14: 22 (Jun 83)

Brown, William A.

Concepts Of God In Africa. Notes. *Journal of Religious Thought.* 39: 5-16 (Fall-Winter 83)

My South African Odyssey. Illustrated. *The Black Perspective in Music.* 11: 3-21 (Spring 83)

Bruck, Peter

The Afro-American Novel Since 1960. Book review. Joe Weixlmann. *Black American Literature Forum.* 17: 134-136 (Fall 83)

Bruner, Charlotte

Emancipation Féminine Et Roman Africain. Book review. *Research in African Literatures.* 14: 209-212 (Summer 83)

Brutus, Dennis (about)

Dennis Brutus Fights Deportation. Illustrated. *Black Scholar*. 14: 72 (Mar-Apr 83)

Bryce-Laporte, Roy S.

Female Immigrants To The United States: Caribbean, Latin American, And African Experience. Book review. Marcus E. Jones. *Phylon*. 44: 245-246 (Sep 83)

Buckner, Alfreda Y.

The Era Of Diminished Expectations.. *Crisis*. 90: 33 (Apr 83)

Budget—United States

An Act of War. William Clay. *about. . . time*. 11: 8 (May 83)

Bombs Or Bread: Black Unemployment And The Pentagon Budget. Tables. Marion Anderson. *Black Scholar*. 14: 2-11 (Jan-Feb 83)

The Federal Budget And You. Illustrated. Bebe . Moore Campbell. *Black Enterprise*. 14: 48-50 + (Oct 83)

Federal Budget: Charles B. Rangel (D. N. Y.). Illustrated. Bebe Moore Campbell. *Black Enterprise*. 14: 56 (Oct 83)

Federal Budget: Harold E. Ford (D. Tenn.). Illustrated. Bebe Moore Campbell. *Black Enterprise*. 14: 54 (Oct 83)

Buffets (Cookery)

Brunch For A Bunch. Illustrated. *Essence*. 14: 102-103 + (Aug 83)

Building And Loan Associations

Vaulting To Better Times: Savings And Loans Overview. Tables. *Black Enterprise*. 13: 119-120 + (Jun 83)

Building And Loan Associations—Directories

Savings And Loans. Tables. *Black Enterprise*. 13: 125-126 (Jun 83)

Building And Loan Associations—Ohio —Cincinnati

Pauline Strayhorne Is Major Federal's Prime Asset. Illustrated, tables. Sharron Kornegay. *Black Enterprise*. 13: 129-130 + (Jun 83)

Bullock, Celeste

Essense Women: Mary Hatwood Futrell. Illustrated. *Essence*. 14: 38 (Nov 83)

Bunn, Curtis G.

Prayers And Profits. Illustrated. *Black Enterprise*. 14: 28 (Dec 83)

Burden, James Remel

Art Tatum: A Guide To His Recorded Music. Book review. *The Black Perspective in Music*. 11: 86-88 (Spring 83)

Jazz Masters/Art Tatum. Book review. *The Black Perspective in Music*. 11: 86-88 (Spring 83)

Burger King Corporation

Burger King Hosts Minority Students In Nation's Capital. Illustrated. *Jet*. 64: 6-8 (8 Aug 83)

$500 Million Trade Agreement Signed By PUSH And Burger King. Illustrated. *Jet*. 64: 26-29 (9 May 83)

Burkett, Randall K.

Garveyism As A Religious Movement: The Institutionalization Of A Black Civil Religion. Book review. Otey M. Scruggs. *Afro-Americans in New York Life and History*. 07: 71-72 (Jul 83)

Burns, Augustus Marion (III) (joint author)

See Otto, John Solomon

Bush, Ann Marie and Mitchell, Louis D.

Jean Toomer: A Cubist Poet. Illustrated, notes. *Black American Literature Forum*. 17: 106-108 (Fall 83)

Bush, George (about)

Vice President Bush Says He'll Continue To 'Plug' For GOP Among Blacks. Illustrated. Simeon Booker. *Jet*. 64: 16-17 (22 Aug 83)

Business

The Potential For Black Business: A Comment. Notes. Timothy Bates. *Review of Black Political Economy*. 12: 237-240 (Winter 83)

A Response To Timothy Bates' Comment. Notes. Don Markwalder. *Review of Black Political Economy*. 12: 241-242 (Winter 83)

Business Enterprises

Building A New Tradition. Tables. *Black Enterprise*. 13: 68-69 + (Jun 83)

House Work. Illustrated. Udayan Gupta. *Black Enterprise*. 13: 59-60 + (Apr 83)

Joint Ventures And Mergers: Keys To Black Business Development. Illustrated. Bebe Moore Campbell. *Black Enterprise*. 13: 19 (Jan 83)

The Top 100 Black Businesses. Tables. *Black Enterprise*. 13: 79 + (Jun 83)

See Also International Business Enterprises Minority Business Enterprises Partnership

Business Enterprises—Maryland—Bethesda

Maxima's 8a Dilemma. Illustrated. Harold J. Logan. *Black Enterprise*. 13: 42-45 (Jan 83)

Business Enterprises—Maryland—Kensington

MRTS's Cellular Ploy. Illustrated. *Black Enterprise*. 13: 194 (Jun 83)

Business Enterprises—Minnesota—Minneapolis

Everything For The Office, Inc. Illustrated. Marc Hequet. *Black Enterprise*. 14: 95-96 (Dec 83)

Business Enterprises—New York (State) —Rochester

Prescription FOr Success. Illustrated. Adolph Dupree. *about. . . time*. 11: 14-16 (Aug 83)

Business Enterprises, Women-Owned

See Women-Owned Business Enterprises

Business Etiquette

Winning At Office Politics. Illustrated. Bea Keith. *Essence*. 14: 79-80 + (Sep 83)

Business Executives

See Executives

Business—History

Yesterday (1929) In The Crisis. . . Exploitation Or Cooperation? Tables. William C. Matney. *Crisis.* 90: 20-22 (Dec 83)

Business Report Writing

The Write Stuff. Frank Emerson. *Black Enterprise.* 14: 73-74 + (Nov 83)

Business—Social Aspects

See Industry—Social Aspects

Business Travel

How To Make Traveling For Business A Breeze. Sandra Jackson-Opoku. *Essence.* 13: 42 + (Mar 83)

Mixing Business With Pleasure. Illustrated. Sylvia Rackow. *Black Enterprise.* 14: 84 (Aug 83)

Businessmen—California—Los Angeles

Bohana Bets On Insurance. Illustrated. Derek T. Dingle. *Black Enterprise.* 14: 24 + (Nov 83)

Businessmen—Illinois—Chicago

The House That Willie Built. Illustrated, tables. Ron Harris. *Black Enterprise.* 13: 90-92 + (Jun 83)

Butcher, Goler Teal

Southern African Issues In United States Courts. Notes. *Howard Law Journal.* 26: No. 2: 601-643 (83)

Testimony Before The House Foreign Affairs Subcommitties On Africa And International Economic Policy And Trade U.S. House Of Representatives. Notes. *Howard Law Journal.* 26: No. 1: 153-193 (83)

Butler, Elbert (about)

What Happens When. . . The Active Career In Sports Is Over? Illustrated. Willis Anderson. *about. . . time.* 11: 14-19 (Jan 83)

Button, James W.

Black Violence: Political Impact Of The 1960s Riots. Book review. Herman (Jr.) George. *Afro-Americans in New York Life and History.* 07: 72-73 (Jul 83)

Butts, June Dobbs (about)

Dr. June Dobbs Butts: How Did A Nice Lady Like Her Get To Be An Expert On Sex? Illustrated. Charles L. Sanders. *Ebony.* 38: 143-144 + (May 83)

Byrd, Sharon E. and others

The Radiographic Evaluation Of Infections Of The Spine. Illustrated, notes. *National Medical Association Journal.* 75: 969-977 (Oct 83)

C.I.B.C.

See Council On Interracial Books For Children

C.I.C.

See Committee On Institutional Cooperation

C.L.A.

See College Language Association

Cable Television—Vocational Guidance

What's Ahead In Cable TV. Monique Clesca. *Essence.* 14: 20 (Nov 83)

Cabrera, Lydia (about)

Folklore And The Creative Artist: Lydia Cabrera And Zora Neale Hurston. Notes. Miriam DeCosta Willis. *CLA Journal.* 27: 81-90 (Sep 83)

Caesar, Shirley (about)

Gospel Star Shirley Caesar Weds Bishop In Durham, N.C. Illustrated. *Jet.* 64: 13 (18 Jul 83)

Cahpman, Frank E. (Jr.)

The United States Educational System: Marxist Approaches. Book review. Lanthin D. (Jr.) Camblin. *Journal of Black Studies.* 14: 102-103 (Sep 83)

Calhoun, Dolly and Moses, Tony

A Closet Case. Illustrated. *Essence.* 13: 127-128 (Mar 83)

Tex-Mex With Soul: The Best Little Caterers In Texas. Illustrated. *Essence.* 14: 102-103 + (May 83)

A Woman's Guide To Beer. Illustrated. *Essence.* 14: 114 (Jun 83)

Calhoun, Dolly and Moses, Tony

Decorating With Your Fashion Favorites. Illustrated. *Essence.* 14: 119 (May 83)

Making Old Stuff New (For Under $100). Illustrated. *Essence.* 14: 117 (Jun 83)

New Ways To Dress Up Windows. Illustrated. *Essence.* 14: 111 (Aug 83)

Calhoun, Mary

Big Sixteen. Book review. Geraldine L. Wilson. *Interracial Books for Children.* 14: No. 5: 25 (83)

Califf, Jane

Count On Your Fingers African Style. Book review. *Interracial Books for Children.* 14: No. 5: 27 (83)

California

See Also Elections—California—Campaign Funds
Legislators—United States—California
Searches And Seizures—California

California Task Force On Civil Rights

Race Attacks On The Rise. Frederick F. Smith. *Black Enterprise.* 13: 40 (Jun 83)

Caliman, Meredith L.

The Politics Of Law: A Progressive Critique. Book review. *Black Law Journal.* 08: 462-463 (Winter 83)

Callaghan, Cedric

Black Theater In South Africa (Links With The United States Of America?). Notes. *Black American Literature Forum.* 17: 82-83 (Summer 83)

Calloway, Cab (about)

Cab Calloway: After 50 Years In Show Business
The Hi-De-Ho Man Is Still Going Strong.
Illustrated. Herschel Johnson. *Ebony.* 38: 66-67 +
(Feb 83)

**Camaroonian Literature (English)—History And
Criticism**

Preface To A History Of Cameroon Literature In
English. Notes. Stephen Arnold. *Research in
African Literatures.* 14: 498-515 (Winter 83)

Camblin, Lanthin D. (Jr.)

The United States Educational System: Marxist
Approaches. Book review. *Journal of Black
Studies.* 14: 102-103 (Sep 83)

Cameron, Bruce F. and others

Evaluation Of Clinical Severity In Sickle Cell
Disease. Tables, notes. *National Medical
Association Journal.* 75: 483-487 (May 83)

Camp, Retha

Essence Women: Valerie Shaw. Illustrated.
Essence. 13: 25 (Jan 83)

Campaign Funds

The Business Of Getting Elected. Illustrated. S. Lee
Hilliard. *Black Enterprise.* 14: 57-58 + (Nov 83)

Campbell, Bebe Moore

Apartheid's Ally: Reagan's Southern Africa Policy.
Illustrated. *Black Enterprise.* 13: 29 (Apr 83)

Blacks And Social Security Reform. Illustrated.
Black Enterprise. 13: 25 (May 83)

Democratic Presidential Hopefuls.. *Black
Enterprise.* 14: 35 (Oct 83)

Fair Housing Bills Proposed.. *Black Enterprise.* 14:
31 (Nov 83)

The Federal Budget And You. Illustrated. *Black
Enterprise.* 14: 48-50 + (Oct 83)

Federal Budget: Charles B. Rangel (D. N. Y.).
Illustrated. *Black Enterprise.* 14: 56 (Oct 83)

Federal Budget: Harold E. Ford (D. Tenn.).
Illustrated. *Black Enterprise.* 14: 54 (Oct 83)

Five Cents Gas Tax Promises Business
Opportunities For Blacks. Illustrated. *Black
Enterprise.* 13: 21 (Jul 83)

Joint Ventures And Mergers: Keys To Black
Business Development. Illustrated. *Black
Enterprise.* 13: 19 (Jan 83)

Medicare Switches To Prospective Payment Plan.
Illustrated. *Black Enterprise.* 14: 37 (Dec 83)

Religion And The Single Mother. Illustrated.
Essence. 14: 152 (Dec 83)

Supreme Court Challenge: Laying Off Affirmative
Action. Illustrated. *Black Enterprise.* 13: 31 (Feb
83)

A Tale Of Two Marches. Illustrated. *Black
Enterprise.* 14: 27 (Aug 83)

Voting Rights: The Symbol And The Substance..
Black Enterprise. 14: 25 (Sep 83)

Who's Supporting The Kids? Women And Children
Left Behind. Illustrated. *Essence.* 14: 75 + (Jul 83)

Campbell, Bebe Moore and Lee, Elliott D.

Beyond The Ballot Box. Illustrated. *Black
Enterprise.* 13: 40-42 + (Mar 83)

Campbell, Norm and others

Graduate School: Minority Admissions Recruitment
Network: Taking Care Of Business.. *Black
Collegian.* 14: 128-131 (Nov-Dec 83)

Camper, Diane

Black And The Supreme Court.. *Black Enterprise.*
13: 48 (Mar 83)

Camping

Camping. Illustrated. Catherine Kerr. *Black
Enterprise.* 13: 260-262 (Jun 83)

Camps

How To Choose A Summer Camp. Joan Hopewell.
Essence. 13: 124 + (Apr 83)

Canady, Alexa (about)

Neurosurgery: Two Black Women Surgeons Are
Pioneers In Highly Specialized Medical Field.
Illustrated. Marilyn Marshall. *Ebony.* 38: 72-74 +
(Sep 83)

Cancer

The Black Enterprise Guide To Good Health.
Illustrated. Sandra R. Gregg. *Black Enterprise.* 13:
39-43 (May 83)

Occupational Cancer In The Black Population: The
Health Effects Of Job Discrimination. Notes.
David Michaels. *National Medical Association
Journal.* 75: 1014-1018 (Oct 83)

See Also Alimentary Canal—Cancer
Lungs—Cancer
Stomach—Cancer
Thyroid—Cancer

Cancer—Tanzania

Geographical Aspects Of Cancer In Tanzania.
Tables, illustrated, notes. George A. Alexander.
National Medical Association Journal. 75: 797-804
(Aug 83)

Cane, Giampiero

Canto Nero. Book review. Dominique-Rene
DeLerma. *The Black Perspective in Music.* 11:
78-79 (Spring 83)

Canson, Virna (about)

Virna Canson: Fighting Fire With Fire. Illustrated.
Elizabeth Fernandez. *Crisis.* 90: 26 + (Jun-Jul 83)

Capital Punishment

Cruel And Unusual Punishment. Jill Nelson. *Black
Enterprise.* 13: 53 + (May 83)

Execution By Injection. Illustrated. Fatima Shaik.
Black Enterprise. 13: 25 (Mar 83)

An Eye For An Eye. Edmund Newton. *Black
Enterprise.* 13: 52 + (May 83)

See Also Executions And
Executioners—Colorado—Denver

Capital Punishment—Georgia

Witness To A Persecution: The Death Penalty And
The Dawson Five. Notes. Hugo Adam Bedau.
Black Law Journal. 08: 7-28 (Spring 83)

Capitalism And Islam

See Islam And Capitalism

Caple, Brenda A. (joint author)

See Johnson, Wilfred A.

Caracci, Giovanni and others

Phencyclidine In An East Harlem Psychiatric
Population. Tables, notes. *National Medical
Association Journal.* 75: 869-874 (Sep 83)

Cardiacs

The Man Who Has Lived Ten Years With Someone
Else's Heart. Illustrated. Frank (III) White. *Ebony.*
38: 90 + (Sep 83)

Careers

See Occupations

Carew, Topper (about)

Lights! Camera! Action! Illustrated. S. Lee Hilliard
and Nelson George. *Black Enterprise.* 14: 48-50 +
(Dec 83)

Caribbean Area

Caribbean Sea Circle: A Brass Ring For 40,000
Years. Illustrated. Adolph Dupree. *about. . . time.*
11: 13-21 + (Dec 83)

Caribbean Area—Description And Travel

Afternoon Tea: An Island Tradition. Jessica Harris.
Black Enterprise. 13: 72 + (May 83)

Antiquing In The Caribbean. Illustrated. Jessica
Harris. *Black Enterprise.* 13: 78-79 (May 83)

Off-season Bargains; On-season Fun. Illustrated.
Marcia Wallace. *Black Enterprise.* 13: 82 + (May
83)

A Tale Of Three Islands. Illustrated. Sandra
Jackson-Opoku. *Essence.* 13: 41-42 + (Apr 83)

Three Isles Of Diversity. Illustrated. Sandra
Jackson-Opoku. *Essence.* 14: 38 + (Oct 83)

Caribbean Cookery

See Cookery, Caribbean

Caribbean Literature—History And Criticism

Women In Caribbean Literature: The African
Presence. Notes. Loeta S. Lawrence. *Phylon.* 44:
1-10 (Mar 83)

Carotid Artery—Surgery

Clinical Experience With Carotid Stump Pressure
And EEG Monitoring To Determine Shunt
Placement During Carotid Endarterectomy. Tables,
notes. William P. (Jr.) Sweezer and others.
National Medical Association Journal. 75: 583-587
(Jun 83)

Carr, Carson (Jr.)

Internships Offer Valuable Work Experience.
Illustrated. *Black Collegian.* 13: 118 + (Feb-Mar
83)

Carruthers, Ben F.

Bermuda: More Than A Honeymoon Haven.
Illustrated. *Black Enterprise.* 14: 72-73 (Sep 83)

Cruising Into The Sun. Illustrated. *Black
Enterprise.* 14: 119 (Dec 83)

Carson, Clayborne

Lives Of Their Own: Blacks, Italians, And Poles In
Pittsburgh, 1900-1960. Book review. *Journal of
Negro History.* 68: 98-99 (Winter 83)

Carter, Carmen

What The ERA Means To Us. Illustrated. *Essence.*
13: 1154 (Mar 83)

Carter, James H.

Sociocultural Factors In The Psychiatric Assessment
Of Black Patients: A Case Study. Notes. *National
Medical Association Journal.* 75: 817-820 (Aug 83)

Carthan, Eddie J. (about)

The Ordeal Of Eddie James Carthan And The Fight
For Democratic Rights. Frank Chapman.
Freedomways. 23: No. 01: 10-13 (83)

Cartright, Lenora T. (about)

Essence Women! Lenora T. Cartright. Illustrated.
Angela Kinamore. *Essence.* 14: 40 (Sep 83)

Casey, Bernie (about)

James Bond's Movie, Never Say Never Again,
Features Black Actor Bernie Casey. Illustrated.
Aldore Collier. *Jet.* 65: 56-57 + (21 Nov 83)

Cassese, Sid

Essence Women: Sandi Brewster-Walker.
Illustrated. *Essence.* 13: 22 + (Apr 83)

See Jackson, Jesse L.

Castro, Oswaldo L.

Thalassemia: Recent Advances In Detection And
Treatment. Book review. *National Medical
Association Journal.* 75: 1023 + (Oct 83)

See Haddy, Theresa B.

Caterers And Catering

Tex-Mex With Soul: The Best Little Caterers In
Texas. Illustrated. Dolly Calhoun. *Essence.* 14:
102-103 + (May 83)

Cathie, Shirley B. and Blackshear, Willa

A Black Women's History Conference.. *Crisis.* 90:
56-57 (Jun-Jul 83)

Cazenaye, Noel A.

"A Woman's Place": The Attitudes Of
Middle-Class Black Men. Notes, tables. *Phylon.*
44: 12-32 (Mar 83)

Celebrities

Celebrities And Their Unusual Pets. Illustrated.
Ebony. 39: 52 + (Nov 83)

Sister, Sister. Illustrated. Julie Chenault. *Essence.*
14: 13-14 (May 83)

See Also Children Of Celebrities

Censorship

Blacks Fight TV Censoring. Illustrated. Chuck Sutton. *Black Enterprise*. 13: 25-26 (Mar 83)

Jake- And Library Issues Of Selection. Editorial. *Interracial Books for Children*. 14: No. 5: 3 (83)

Stop The Banning Of Books. Illustrated. Bethany L. Spotts. *Essence*. 13: 122 (Jan 83)

Central State University (Ohio)

The Struggle To Save A Black School: An Interview With Central State President Newsom. Interview, Illustrated. Lionel Newsom and William Rouselle. *Black Collegian*. 13: 38+ (Apr-May 83)

Centre de Documentation des Humaines, Wahran, Algeria

C.D.S.H., Centre De Documentation Des Sciences Humaines, Algeria. Anne Lippert. *Research in African Literatures*. 14: 193-195 (Summer 83)

Cephalosporin

Cephalosporins: Recent Developments. Notes. Ashir Kumar. *National Medical Association Journal*. 75: 218-223 (Feb 83)

Cesarean Section

Cesarean Section: A Seven-Year Study. Tables, notes. Leroy R. Weekes. *National Medical Association Journal*. 75: 465-476 (May 83)

Ceynowa, Andrzej

Black Theaters And Theater Organizations In America, 1961-1982: A Research List.. *Black American Literature Forum*. 17: 84-93 (Summer 83)

The Dramatic Structure Of Dutchman. Illustrated, notes. *Black American Literature Forum*. 17: 15-18 (Spring 83)

Le Thèâtre Noir Aux États-Unis. Book review. *Black American Literature Forum*. 17: 95-96 (Summer 83)

Chachere, Bernadette P.

Markets And Minorities. Book review. *Review of Black Political Economy*. 12: 163-177 (Winter 83)

Chambers, Donald C. (joint author)

See Miller, Joseph M.

Chancellor, Yvette

Lawyers V. Educators: Black Colleges And Desegregation In Public Higher Education. Book review. *Black Law Journal*. 08: 160-161 (Spring 83)

Change Of Sex

Sex Change Brings Man Love, Happiness. Illustrated. Trudy S. Moore and James Mitchell. *Jet*. 65: 28-32 (10 Oct 83)

Change, Social

See Social Change

Chapman, Frank

The Ordeal Of Eddie James Carthan And The Fight For Democratic Rights.. *Freedomways*. 23: No. 01: 10-13 (83)

Characters And Characteristics In Children's Literature

The Black Experience Through White Eyes- The Same Old Story Once Again. Illustrated, tables. Beryle Banfield and Geraldine L. Wilson. *Interracial Books for Children*. 14: No. 5: 4-13 (83)

Children's Literature On Puerto Rican Themes- Part I: The Messages Of Fiction. Illustrated. Sonia Nieto. *Interracial Books for Children*. 14: No. 1: 6-9 (83)

Jake- And Library Issues Of Selection. Editorial. *Interracial Books for Children*. 14: No. 5: 3 (83)

See Also Puerto Ricans In Children's Literature

Characters And Characteristics In Literature

Faulkner's Image Of Blacks In Go Down, Moses. Notes. Dorothy L. Denniston. *Phylon*. 44: 33-43 (Mar 83)

Shakespeare's Paulina: Characterization And Craftsmanship In the Winter's Tale. Notes. Myles Hurd. *CLA Journal*. 26: 303-310 (Mar 83)

See Also Women In Literature

Characters And Characteristics In Moving -Pictures

A Familiar Plot (A Look At The History Of Blacks In American Movies). Illustrated. Donald Bogle. *Crisis*. 90: 14-19 (Jan 83)

Hollywood's Racism Affects Our Black African Brothers, Too. Benjamin L. Hooks. *Crisis*. 90: 5 (Jan 83)

The Year Of The Black Male In Films. Illustrated. Aldore D. Collier. *Ebony*. 38: 168+ (Aug 83)

Charlotte, North Carolina—Economic Conditions

The Changing Profile Of Charlotte. Illustrated. David D. Porter and Rosalyn Gist Porter. *Black Enterprise*. 13: 178-180+ (Jun 83)

Chartism

William Cuffay: London's Black Chartist. Notes. Norbert J. Gossman. *Phylon*. 44: 56-65 (Mar 83)

Chassie, Marilyn B. (joint author)

See Handler, Diana S.

Chastain, Sherry

From Praises To Raises.. *Essence*. 14: 32 (Jun 83)

Chatelain, Heli (about)

Héli Chatelain: Pioneer Of A National Language And Literature For Angola. Notes. Gerald Moser. *Research in African Literatures*. 14: 516-537 (Winter 83)

Chavkin, Allen

Wordsworth's Secular Imagination And "Spots In Time". Notes. *CLA Journal*. 26: 452-464 (Jun 83)

Chawla, Kiran and others

Renal Angiomyolipoma With Retroperitoneal Adenopathy. Illustrated. *National Medical Association Journal*. 75: 431-434 (Apr 83)

Cheers, D. Michael

Alleged Irregularities: Blacks Turn Out In Record Numbers For Miss. Primary Vote. Illustrated. *Jet*. 64: 12-14 (22 Aug 83)

Black Ambassadors Feted By Boston TransAfrica. Illustrated. *Jet*. 63: 36-39 (28 Feb 83)

Black Skiers-Push Youths Toward '88 Winter Olympics. Illustrated. *Jet*. 64: 46-48+ (18 Apr 83)

Boy, 4, Gets VD After Sex Attack By Miss. White Man. Illustrated. *Jet*. 64: 6-7 (29 Aug 83)

Democratic Party Leaders To Stick By Washington Despite Byrne Write-In. Illustrated. *Jet*. 64: 6-8 (4 Apr 83)

Dianne Durham: Going For The Gold In '84 Olympics. Illustrated. *Ebony*. 38: 52-54+ (Sep 83)

Fla. Interracial Couple Loses Custody Battle. Illustrated. *Jet*. 64: 36-38 (28 Mar 83)

Gary's Dianne Durham Is Top U.S. Female Gymnast. Illustrated. *Jet*. 64: 46-50 (27 Jun 83)

Preacher Wages 30-Year Fight To Clear Name Of Rape Charge Against Him. Illustrated. *Jet*. 63: 14-16 (7 Mar 83)

White N.Y. Suburbanite Lives With Poor Family To Study The 'Other Side'. Illustrated. *Jet*. 63: 30-33 (31 Jan 83)

Why Aren't There More Blacks In Foreign Service? Illustrated. *Ebony*. 38: 89-90+ (May 83)

Woman Regains Sight, Sees Her Husband For First Time. Illustrated. *Jet*. 65: 20-24 (28 Nov 83)

World's Most Unusual Twins: One Is Black, The Other Is White. Illustrated. *Jet*. 65: 21-24 (12 Dec 83)

Cheers, D. Michael and Waldron, Clarence

The Unemployed Tell What Should Be Done About Their Plight. Illustrated. *Jet*. 63: 12-15 (07 Feb 83)

Chemain-Degrange, Arlette

Emancipation Féminine Et Roman Africain. Book review. Charlotte Bruner. *Research in African Literatures*. 14: 209-212 (Summer 83)

Chenault, Julie

Her Honor, The Mayor. Illustrated. *Essence*. 14: 14+ (Jul 83)

Sister, Sister. Illustrated. *Essence*. 14: 13-14 (May 83)

Chicago

Chicago's 150th Birthday; Mayor Lights Up Plaza, Hosts Dinner For VIPs. Illustrated. *Jet*. 65: 14-16+ (3 Oct 83)

See Also Elections—Illinois—Chicago
Hospitals—Illinois—Chicago

Chicago Business Hall Of Fame

Publisher Johnson Among 10 Enshrined In Chicago Business Hall Of Fame. Illustrated. *Jet*. 65: 6-8 (31 Oct 83)

Chicago—Mayors

Harold Washington Wins Hot Race To Become First Black Mayor Of Chicago. Illustrated, first facts. *Jet*. 64: 4-6+ (2 May 83)

Mayor Harold Washington: Changing Of The Guard In Chicago. Illustrated. Lynn Norment. *Ebony*. 38: 27-30+ (Jul 83)

Chicago—Politics And Government

Democratic Party Leaders To Stick By Washington Despite Byrne Write-In. Illustrated. D. Michael Cheers. *Jet*. 64: 6-8 (4 Apr 83)

Harold Washington: Makes Bold Bid To Become Chicago's First Black Mayor. Illustrated. Robert E. Johnson. *Jet*. 64: 12-16+ (21 Mar 83)

Kennedy Leads Democrats To Back Washington As Mayor Byrne Quits Race. Illustrated. Clarence Waldron. *Jet*. 64: 6-8 (11 Apr 83)

Race And The 1983 Chicago Election. Illustrated. Edward (III) Thompson. *Crisis*. 90: 14-15 (Oct 83)

Rumbling In Chicago. Illustrated. Melody M. McDowell. *Black Enterprise*. 14: 19 (Nov 83)

Unity Banquet Draws 5,500: Washington Supporters Told Beware Of 'False Security'. Illustrated. *Jet*. 64: 6-8 (18 Apr 83)

Washington Upsets Foes To Win Democratic Bid In Chicago Mayoral Race. Illustrated. Robert E. Johnson. *Jet*. 63: 6-7+ (14 Mar 83)

Chickens

See Also Cookery (Chicken)

Chiefs Of Police

See Police Chiefs

Child Abuse

Boy, 4, Gets VD After Sex Attack By Miss. White Man. Illustrated. D. Michael Cheers. *Jet*. 64: 6-7 (29 Aug 83)

Sexual Exploitation Of Children: A Call To Action. Editorial, Notes. Arthur T. Davidson. *National Medical Association Journal*. 75: 925-927 (Oct 83)

Child And Parent

See Parent And Child

Child Health Services

Assessing The Quality Of Care Provided To Pediatric Patients By Emergency Room Physicians. Tables, notes. Laura Wachsman and Alice Faye Singleton. *National Medical Association Journal*. 75: 31-35 (Jan 83)

Children And Federal Health Care Cuts. Sara Rosenbaum and Judith Weitz. *Freedomways*. 23: No. 01: 17-22 (83)

Child Welfare

Essence Women: Dorothy Pitman Hughes. Illustrated. Joy Duckett. *Essence*. 13: 22 (Feb 83)

Children

Cost Cutting For Parents. Valerie Wilson Wesley. *Essence*. 14: 22+ (Jul 83)

See Also Education Of Children
Sports For Children

Children, Abnormal And Backward

See Handicapped Children

Children, Adopted

Black Twins Search And Find Their White Mother After 34 Years. Illustrated. Clarence Waldron. *Jet*. 64: 24-30 (6 Jun 83)

Twins Find Mother After 34 Years. Illustrated. Clarence Waldron. *Ebony*. 38: 95-96+ (Sep 83)

Children And Adults

The Social Success Of Black Youth: The Impact Of Significant Others. Notes. Barbara J. Shade. *Journal of Black Studies*. 14: 137-150 (Dec 83)

Children As Actors

Emmanuel Lewis: Star Of TV Commercials To Debut In TV Series. Illustrated. Trudy S. Moore. *Jet*. 64: 60-64 (22 Aug 83)

Todd Bridges And Janet Jackson: The Problems Of Teen-Age Stars. Illustrated. Aldore Collier. *Ebony*. 38: 58-59+ (Feb 83)

Children—Care And Hygiene

Aid For Poor Kids. Michael Beaubien. *Black Enterprise*. 13: 20 (Apr 83)

Why You Should Buckle Up Baby. Illustrated. Barbara E. Tucker. *Essence*. 14: 120+ (Jul 83)

See Also Physical Fitness For Children

Children, Custody Of

See Custody Of Children

Children—Diseases

Management Of Attention Deficit Disorders. Notes. Milton S. Adams. *National Medical Association Journal*. 75: 187-189 (Feb 83)

Children, Exceptional

See Exceptional Children

Children—Management

Should Children Believe In Santa Claus? Wista Johnson. *Essence*. 14: 124+ (Dec 83)

Teaching Your Kids The Financial Facts Of Life. Illustrated. Pamela Douglas. *Black Enterprise*. 14: 106-108+ (Oct 83)

Turning Tykes On To Dow Jones. Udayan Gupta. *Black Enterprise*. 14: 112 (Oct 83)

You Can Raise Well-Disciplined Kids. Illustrated. Kay Kuzma. *Essence*. 13: 132 (Mar 83)

Children Of Alien Laborers—Education

Plyer V. Doe - Education And Illegal Alien Children. Notes. Ruth Jones. *Black Law Journal*. 08: 132-137 (Spring 83)

Children Of Celebrities

Whatever Happened To Bernice King? Illustrated. *Ebony*. 38: 160+ (Oct 83)

Children—Preparation For Medical Care

Preparing Your Child For A Hospital Stay. Constance Garcia-Barrio. *Essence*. 14: 136 (Oct 83)

Children—Religious Life

Religion And The Single Mother. Illustrated. Bebe Moore Campbell. *Essence*. 14: 152 (Dec 83)

Children's Allowances

I Taught My Children To Manage Money. Illustrated. Joanette Pete James. *Essence*. 14: 136+ (Jun 83)

Teaching Your Kids The ABC's Of Dollars And Cents. Illustrated. Pamela Douglas. *Black Enterprise*. 13: 205-206+ (Jun 83)

Children's Literature

Books For Equity. Bibliography. *Interracial Books for Children*. 14: No. 7: 27-29 (83)

Children's Literature On Puerto Rican Themes- Part I: The Messages Of Fiction. Illustrated. Sonia Nieto. *Interracial Books for Children*. 14: No. 1: 6-9 (83)

Children's Literature On Puerto Rican Themes- Part II: Non-fiction. Illustrated. Sonia Nieto. *Interracial Books for Children*. 14: No. 1: 10-12+ (83)

A Decade Of Progress? Byron Williams. *Interracial Books for Children*. 14: No. 1: 4-5 (83)

See Also Characters And Characteristics In Children's Literature

Childrens Periodicals

Ebony Jr! Celebrates Its Tenth Anniversary With Special May Issue. First facts, Illustrated. *Jet*. 64: 14+ (9 May 83)

Childs, Barbara A.

Once A Man Twice A Child. Poem. *about. . . time*. 11: 22 (Sep 83)

Chinweizu

Towards The Decolonization Of African Literature. Book review. Gerald Moore. *Research in African Literatures*. 14: 549-553 (Winter 83)

Chinyelu, Mamadi

The Voice Of One Crying In The Wilderness: Constructing The African Mass Communication Pyramid. Notes, tables. *Black Law Journal*. 08: 285-291 (Fall 83)

Chisholm Shirley

Racism And Anti-Feminism.. *Black Scholar*. 14: 2-7 (Sep-Oct 83)

Chitanvis, Jacqueline Paris

On The Road Again.. *Black Enterprise*. 14: 89 (Nov 83)

Chiteji, Frank M.

Integration And Disintegration In East Africa. Book review. *Review of Black Political Economy*. 12: 243-245 (Winter 83)

Chocolate

See Also Cookery (Chocolate)

Chrisman, Robert

Nicaragua: The Path To Peace. Editorial. *Black Scholar*. 14: 1 (Mar-Apr 83)

Nuclear Policy, Social Justice, And The Third World. Tables. *Black Scholar*. 14: 26-43 (Nov-Dec 83)

The Role Of Mass Media In U. S. Imperialism.. *Black Scholar*. 14: 13-17 (Summer 83)
Cunningham, Mirna

Christian, E. (joint author)

See Cameron, Bruce F.

Christian Haitian Outreach

Essence Women: Eleanor Workman. Illustrated. Kitty Oliver. *Essence*. 14: 54 (Dec 83)

Christianity And Other Religions

African Cults And Christian Churches In Trinidad: The Spiritual Baptist Case. Notes. Stephen D. Glazier. *Journal of Religious Thought*. 39: 17-25 (Fall-Winter 83)

Paul's Reinterpretation Of Jewish Apocalypticism: A Faculty Response To J. Christian Beker. Notes. Cain H. Felder. *Journal of Religious Thought*. 40: 18-22 (Spring-Summer 83)

Christianity And Politics

The Importance Of Politics And Prayer. Illustrated. Don Armstrong. *Crisis*. 90: 30 (Apr 83)

Christianity—Philosophy

The Challenge Of Paul's Apocalyptic Gospel For The Church Today. J. Christiaan Beker. *Journal of Religious Thought*. 40: 9-15 (Spring-Summer 83)

Paul's Apocalyptic In The Key Of Beker: A Student Response. Notes. Frank E. (Jr.) Drumwright. *Journal of Religious Thought*. 40: 16-17 (Spring-Summer 83)

Christie, Sarah

Perspectives On South African Fiction. Book review. Stephen Gray. *Research in African Literatures*. 14: 216-218 (Summer 83)

Christmas

Celebrities See Christmas As Something Special Too At Kwanza Celebration. Illustrated. *Jet*. 65: 56-58 (26 Dec 83)

The New Soul Christmas. Illustrated. Frank (III) White. *Ebony*. 39: 29-30+ (Dec 83)

Christmas Cookery

The Holiday Feast. Illustrated. Charla L. Draper. *Ebony*. 39: 100-102+ (Dec 83)

Holiday Gifts From The Kitchen. Illustrated. Charla L. Draper. *Ebony*. 39: 113-114+ (Nov 83)

When Christmas Dinner Is At Your House. Illustrated. *Essence*. 14: 96-97 (Dec 83)

Chromatographic Analysis

Measurement Of Glycosylated Hemoglobins In Black Diabetic Patients: A Note Of Caution. Illustrated, notes. Michael M. Lederman and others. *National Medical Association Journal*. 75: 353-355 (Apr 83)

Chrysler Corporation

Rebuilding America: Strong Spirits And Common Sense. Illustrated. Lee Iacocca. *Black Collegian*. 14: 90+ (Sep-Oct 83)

Church And Race Relations

"The Civil Rights Movement And The Black Church: A Conservative Or Militant Force". Notes. W. Sherman Jackson. *Negro History Bulletin*. 46: 41-42 (Apr-Jun 83)

Church Property—Taxation

No Tax Breaks For Racism. Illustrated. Dennis Williams. *Black Enterprise*. 14: 17 (Sep 83)

Churches, City

See City Churches

Churches—New York (State)—Rochester

Marking New Pages Of History (Memorial A.M.E. Zion Church: "The Mortgage Burning"). Illustrated. Alean Rush. *about. . . time*. 11: 20-21 (Jan 83)

Cincinnati, Ohio

See Also Community Development, Urban—Ohio—Cincinnati

Circus Performers

Breakthrough Under The Big Top. Illustrated. *Ebony*. 39: 69-70+ (Dec 83)

Cities And Towns

Ten Cities That Work For Blacks. Illustrated. R. G. Collazo. *Black Enterprise*. 13: 32-37+ (Jul 83)

Cities And Towns, Ancient—Zimbabwe

Great Zimbabwe: An Ancient African City-State. Illustrated. Molefi Asante and Kariamu Asante. *Journal of African Civilizations*. 05: 84-91 (Apr-Nov 83)

City And Town Life

Sources Of Variability In Rates Of Black Home Ownership In 1900. Notes, tables. Steven Mintz. *Phylon*. 44: 312-331 (Dec 83)

City Churches

Urban Black Churches: Conservators Of Value And Sustainers Of Community. Notes. Lawrence N. Jones. *Journal of Religious Thought*. 39: 41-50 (Fall-Winter 83)

City Councilmen—South Carolina—Columbia City

Two Blacks Win Seats On S. Carolina City Council. First facts, Illustrated. *Jet*. 64: 4 (25 Apr 83)

Civil Disobedience

See Government, Resistance To

Civil Rights

Civil Rights In The Third Wave. Alvin Toffler. *The Urban League Review*. 08: 14-20 (Winter 83)

Is Israel On The Road To Nazism? Israel Shahak. *Freedomways*. 23: No. 3: 153-164 (83)

See Also Due Process Of Law—United States Equality Before The Law

Searches And Seizures

Civil Rights Commission

See United States—Civil Rights Commission

Civil Rights Movement

"Struggle On!". Illustrated. Benjamin L. Hooks. *Crisis*. 90: 22-24 (Aug-Sep 83)

Civil Rights—United States

Civil Rights Challenges For The 1980's. Illustrated. Paul A. Fisher and Ralph G. Neas. *about. . . time*. 11: 10-13 + (May 83)

Civil Rights Enforcement Activity Of The Department Of Justice. Notes. Jack Greenberg. *Black Law Journal*. 08: 60-67 (Spring 83)

"The Civil Rights Movement And The Black Church: A Conservative Or Militant Force". Notes. W. Sherman Jackson. *Negro History Bulletin*. 46: 41-42 (Apr-Jun 83)

Civil Rights: Where Are We Now? Editorial. *Black Enterprise*. 14: 38-39 + (Aug 83)

A Color-Conscious Constitution: The One Pervading Purpose Redux. Notes. Kenneth S. Tollett and others. *Journal of Negro Education*. 52: 189-212 (Summer 83)

The Constitution And The Black American. R. Grann Lloyd. *Negro Educational Review*. 34: 2-3 (Jan 83)

The Keynote. . . "Take Up This Crusade". Illustrated. Kelly M. (Sr.) Alexander. *Crisis*. 90: 16-18 (Aug-Sep 83)

NAACP Civil Rights Report. . . President Ronald Reagan-The First Two Years. Althea T. L. Simmons. *Crisis*. 90: 30-33 (Jan 83)

The New Federalism And The Unfinished Civil Rights Agenda. Notes. Marguerite Ross Barnett. *Black Law Journal*. 08: 375-386 (Winter 83)

Profile Of Black America - A Grim Picture. Benjamin L. Hooks. *Crisis*. 90: 4 (Dec 83)

Reagan Civil Rights: The First Twenty Months. Notes. *Black Law Journal*. 08: 68-94 (Spring 83)

Students On Civil Rights Progress: It's An Era Of Challenge For Them. Illustrated. Elizabeth Knight. *about. . . time*. 11: 16-18 (Nov 83)

Turning Back The Clock On Women And Minority Rights: The Regan Record. Illustrated. Mary Frances Berry. *Negro History Bulletin*. 46: 82-84 (Jul-Sep 83)

"We Are Going To Enforce The Law.". Illustrated. Chester A. (Sr.) Higgins. *Crisis*. 90: 50-52 + (Feb 83)

Civil Rights Workers

FBI Liable In Freedom Rider Attack. Illustrated. *Jet*. 64: 7 (20 Jun 83)

The Keepers Of The King Dream 15 Years Later. Illustrated. *Ebony*. 38: 31-32 + (Apr 83)

Civil Service

The Disappearing Civil Servant. Illustrated. Isaiah Poole. *Black Enterprise*. 13: 91-92 + (Feb 83)

Civil Service—United States

The Advantages Of Working For The Federal Government. Reginald Felton. *Black Collegian*. 13: 72 + (Apr-May 83)

Civilization

See Also Culture

CLA Journal

The CLA Journal As A Mirror Of Changing Ethnic And Academic Perspectives. Notes. A. Russell Brooks. *CLA Journal*. 26: 265-276 (Mar 83)

Claiborne, Theresa (about)

Air Force Graduates First Black Woman Pilot. Illustrated, first facts. *Ebony*. 38: 46 + (Jan 83)

Clark, Ebun

Nationalism And The Nigerian National Theatre. Book review. *Research in African Literatures*. 14: 107-108 (Spring 83)

Clark, J. P.

The Hero As A Villain. Book review. Robert M. Wren. *Research in African Literatures*. 14: 112-113 (Spring 83)

Clark, Julia V.

Double Dilemma: Minorities And Women In Science Education. Book review. *Journal of Negro Education*. 52: 85-87 (Winter 83)

Clark, Kenneth B. (about)

Dr. Kenneth B. Clark: Fighter For Educational Opportunity. Interview, Illustrated. James M. Blount. *about. . . time*. 11: 14-15 + (May 83)

Clark, Michael

Authorial Displacement In Herman Melville's "The Piazza". Notes. *CLA Journal*. 27: 69-80 (Sep 83)

Clark, Ronald (joint author)

See Walton, Hanes (Jr.)

Clarke, Cheryl

Narratives: Poems In The Tradition Of Black Women. Book review. Doris Davenport. *Black American Literature Forum*. 17: 177-179 (Winter 83)

Clarke, Doris

How To Plan A Productive Summer. Illustrated. *Black Collegian*. 13: 27-28 + (Dec-Jan 83)

Clarke, John Henrik

Bibliographical Guide [To Black Scientists]. Bibliography. *Journal of African Civilizations*. 05: 295-302 (Apr-Nov 83)

Lewis Latimer-Bringer Of The Light. Illustrated, notes. *Journal of African Civilizations*. 05: 229-237 (Apr-Nov 83)

Classes, Social

See Social Classes

Clay, William

An Act of War.. *about. . . time*. 11: 8 (May 83)

"Coalition Of Conscience". Illustrated. *about. . . time*. 11: 23 (Oct 83)

Freedom From Want.. *about. . . time.* 11: 8 (Jul 83)

Proposition 13 And 1/2 (A No-Taxation Fantasy).. *about. . . time.* 11: 37 (Nov 83)

The Shame Of Unemployment? Illustrated. *about. . . time.* 11: 8 (Mar 83)

Clay, William and Roberts, Lillian

Addressing Unemployment Problems: A Jobs Bill Is Needed From The Federal Government. Illustrated. *about. . . time.* 11: 12-13 (Jan 83)

Clayton, Janet

Going For The Gold. Illustrated. *Black Enterprise.* 13: 65-66+ (Apr 83)

Clements, William M.

For Lincoln Perry. Poem. *Black American Literature Forum.* 17: 174 (Winter 83)

Clemons, J. Gregory

Putting The Squeeze On Four-Wheel Lemons.. *Black Enterprise.* 14: 90 (Nov 83)

Turning Heirlooms Into Cash.. *Black Enterprise.* 14: 137-138 (Oct 83)

Clergy

Clifton Davis: How Marriage And Ministry Changed Him. Illustrated. Trudy S. Moore. *Jet.* 65: 54-57 (12 Sep 83)

The Importance Of Politics And Prayer. Illustrated. Don Armstrong. *Crisis.* 90: 30 (Apr 83)

Joseph Robert Love, 1839-1914: West Indian Extraordinary. Notes. Joy Lumsden. *Afro-Americans in New York Life and History.* 07: 25-39 (Jan 83)

Man Of God And Gun. Illustrated. Raymond Lang. *Ebony.* 38: 102-104 (Sep 83)

Miles Mark Fisher: Minister, Historian And Cultural Philosopher. Illustrated, notes. Lenwood G. Davis. *Negro History Bulletin.* 46: 19-21 (Jan-Mar 83)

Ministers As Apocalyptic Advocates For The Poor. Jesse L. Jackson. *Journal of Religious Thought.* 40: 23-28 (Spring-Summer 83)

The Preacher For These Days. D. E. King. *Journal of Religious Thought.* 40: 29-33 (Spring-Summer 83)

Preacher Wages 30-Year Fight To Clear Name Of Rape Charge Against Him. Illustrated. D. Michael Cheers. *Jet.* 63: 14-16 (7 Mar 83)

School Of Religion For Men Behind Bars. Illustrated. Frank (III) White. *Ebony.* 38: 154+ (Apr 83)

Terry Cummings: Basketball's Million-Dollar Minister. Illustrated. Marilyn Marshall. *Ebony.* 38: 42-44 (Feb 83)

See Also Women Clergy

Clesca, Monique

Advertising: An Ad-Venture. Illustrated. *Essence.* 14: 32 (Jul 83)

What's Ahead In Cable TV.. *Essence.* 14: 20 (Nov 83)

Clift, Virgil A.

Encyclopedia Of Black America. Book review. Doris Evans McGinty. *The Black Perspective in Music.* 11: 79-82 (Spring 83)

Clifton, Lucille

Listen Children. Poem. *Essence.* 14: 88 (Oct 83)

Clinard, Marshall B.

Corporate Crime. Book review, Notes. Walter L. (III) Gordon. *Black Law Journal.* 08: 152-159 (Spring 83)

Clinical Medicine

See Medicine, Clinical

Clothing And Dress

See Also Fashion

Coaches (Athletics)

See Also Football Coaches

Coast Guard Academy

See United States. Coast Guard Academy

Cobb, Charles E.

Namibian Independence Stands On Its Own; South Africa's Murderous Raid Deplored.. *Crisis.* 90: 34 (Jan 83)

Packing Of Rights Body Reagan's "Most Severe Attack".. *Crisis.* 90: 5 (Oct 83)

"The People Have Spoken".. *Crisis.* 90: 28 (Nov 83)

Cobb, Vandell (joint author)

See Sanders, Charles

Cocaine Habit

Cocaine! A Deadly Blow. Illustrated. Jill Nelson Ricks. *Essence.* 14: 54-55+ (Sep 83)

Coetzee, Ampie

Leipolt 100. Book review. *Research in African Literatures.* 14: 248-251 (Summer 83)

Cofield, Milton L.

Dream. Poem. *about. . . time.* 11: 22 (Sep 83)

Cohia, John (about)

A Black Chief's Inspiring Saga. Illustrated. William Loren Katz. *Crisis.* 90: 38-39 (Apr 83)

Coiffure

See Hairdressing

Cole, Beverly P.

The State Of Education For Black Americans.. *Crisis.* 90: 42-45 (May 83)

Cole, Natalie (about)

Louis Gossett, Natalie Cole Tell Of Changes In Their Lives. Illustrated. *Jet.* 64: 60-63 (23 May 83)

Natalie Cole. Illustrated. Jack Slater. *Essence.* 14: 86-87+ (Oct 83)

Coleman, Arthur H. (joint author)

See Davidson, Arthur T.

Coleman, James W. and Gabbin, Joanne Veal

The Legacy Of George E. Kent. Notes. *Black American Literature Forum.* 17: 143-147 (Winter 83)

Coleman, Wanda

El Hajj Malik El-Shabazz. Poem. *Black American Literature Forum.* 17: 175 (Winter 83)

Ethiopian In The Fuel Supplies. Poem. *Black American Literature Forum.* 17: 176 (Winter 83)

Collazo, R. G.

Closing Down On Crime. Illustrated. *Black Enterprise.* 13: 39-41 + (Apr 83)

Ten Cities That Work For Blacks. Illustrated. *Black Enterprise.* 13: 32-37 + (Jul 83)

Collazo, Roberto G.

Wellness: The Happy Art Of Living Well.. *Essence.* 13: 49 + (Jan 83)

College, Choice Of

The Black College Experience: A Viable Choice For Students. Illustrated. Carolyne S. Blount. *about. . . time.* 11: 10-11 (Jun 83)

College Graduates

The Class Of '83. Illustrated. *Ebony.* 38: 154-156 + (Aug 83)

College Graduates—Employment

Avoiding After-College Panic. Curtia James. *Essence.* 14: 20 + (Aug 83)

Standing On The Front Line: The Class Of '83 Faces A Tight Job Market. Editorial. *Black Collegian.* 13: 14 (Apr-May 83)

College Integration

Three-Fifths Of A Professor, Too? R. Grann Lloyd. *Negro Educational Review.* 34: 50-51 (Apr 83)

College Integration—North Carolina

The Consent Decree Between The University Of North Carolina System And The U. S. Department Of Education, 1981-82. Notes. David W. Bishop. *Journal of Negro Education.* 52: 350-361 (Summer 83)

Hocutt: Genesis Of Brown. Notes. Gilbert Ware. *Journal of Negro Education.* 52: 227-233 (Summer 83)

College Language Association

The CLA Journal As A Mirror Of Changing Ethnic And Academic Perspectives. Notes. A. Russell Brooks. *CLA Journal.* 26: 265-276 (Mar 83)

The College Language Association And The Profession Of Languages And Literature. Notes. Eleanor Q. Tignor. *CLA Journal.* 26: 367-383 (Jun 83)

College-Level Examinations

Real Life 101: What You've Learned In Life May Be Worth College Credits. Constance García-Barrio. *Essence.* 14: 36 (Jul 83)

College Presidents

Dr. Robert Green Named New President of UDC.. *Jet.* 64: 30 (15 Aug 83)

Dr Wright Lassitar Jr. New Bishop College Prexy. Illustrated. *Jet.* 64: 24 (8 Aug 83)

A Nation At Risk: A Black Perspective On American Education: An Interview With Norman Francis. Interview, Illustrated. Norman Francis and William Rouselle. *Black Collegian.* 14: 69-72 (Nov-Dec 83)

The President Is A Colonel. Illustrated. Kendall Wilson. *Black Collegian.* 13: 46 (Apr-May 83)

The President That Time Forgot. Marvin Leon Lake. *Negro History Bulletin.* 46: 51-52 (Apr-Jun 83)

Satcher Inaugurated Meharry's Eighth President. Illustrated. *National Medical Association Journal.* 75: 210 + (Feb 83)

Sullivan Inaugurated As First President Of Morehouse School Of Medicine. Illustrated. Virgie S. Heffernan. *National Medical Association Journal.* 75: 826 + (Aug 83)

See Also Women College Presidents

College Sports

Athletic Performance In Exchange For An Education - A Contract Unfulfilled. Illustrated. Harry Edwards. *Crisis.* 90: 10-14 (May 83)

The Black Athlete In Big-Time Intercollegiate Sports, 1941-1968. Notes. Donald Spivey. *Phylon.* 44: 116-125 (Jun 83)

Debate Grows Over Rule 48. Robert McNatt. *Black Enterprise.* 13: 18 (May 83)

The Impact Of Rule 48 Upon The Black Student Athlete: A Comment. Notes, tables. Alexander (Jr.) Williams. *Journal of Negro Education.* 52: 362-373 (Summer 83)

See Football

College Students

The Antebellum "Talented Thousandth": Black College Students At Oberlin Before The Civil War. Notes, tables. Ellen N. Lawson and Marlene Merrill. *Journal of Negro Education.* 52: 142-155 (Spring 83)

A Family Affair At West Point. Illustrated. Pamela Noel. *Ebony.* 39: 45-46 + (Nov 83)

Maximizing Youth: With A Canteen Full Of Skills, Plans, Aspirations And Hope. Illustrated. Madeline Sulaiman. *about. . . time.* 11: 14-18 (Jun 83)

A Message To Black College Students. Illustrated. Stevie Wonder. *Black Collegian.* 13: 24-25 (Dec-Jan 83)

Reading, Dialect, And The Low-Achieving Black College Student. Notes. Carole F. Stice. *Negro Educational Review.* 34: 84-87 (Apr 83)

Students On Civil Rights Progress: It's An Era Of Challenge For Them. Illustrated. Elizabeth Knight. *about. . . time.* 11: 16-18 (Nov 83)

See Also Women College Students

College Students—Employment

How Placement Copes When Recruiters Don't Come. Illustrated. Yvette Franklin and William Rouselle. *Black Collegian*. 13: 20 + (Apr-May 83)

College Students—Health And Hygiene

Life Stress, Health, And Blood Pressure In Black College Students. Notes, tables. Hector F. Myers and others. *Journal of Black Psychology*. 09: 1-25 (Feb 83)

Colleges

See Universities And Colleges

Collier, Aldore

Born-Again Stars. Illustrated. *Ebony*. 39: 51-52 + (Dec 83)

James Bond's Movie, Never Say Never Again, Features Black Actor Bernie Casey. Illustrated. *Jet*. 65: 56-57 + (21 Nov 83)

Leona Mitchell: An All-American Opera Star. Illustrated. *Ebony*. 38: 37-38 + (Sep 83)

Robert Guillaume: Behind The Scenes With TV's 'Benson'. Illustrated. *Ebony*. 39: 133-134 + (Nov 83)

Todd Bridges And Janet Jackson: The Problems Of Teen-Age Stars. Illustrated. *Ebony*. 38: 58-59 + (Feb 83)

TV's New Season: What's Ahead For Blacks? Illustrated. *Ebony*. 38: 58 + (Oct 83)

Whatever Happened To The Nicholas Brothers? Illustrated. *Ebony*. 38: 103-104 + (May 83)

Collier, Aldore and Sutton, Isaac

Muhammad Ali's Wife Veronica Turns Horse Hobby Into Blue Ribbons. Illustrated. *Jet*. 65: 22-25 (19 Sep 83)

Collier, Aldore D.

Bill Cosby, Sammy Davis: First Time To Headline Club Date Together. Illustrated. *Jet*. 63: 58-62 (7 Mar 83)

Celebrate 10th Season Of 'The Jeffersons'. Illustrated. *Jet*. 65: 58-61 (3 Oct 83)

Rick James Talks About Life With Fast Women And Hot Cars. Illustrated. *Jet*. 65: 58-61 (26 Sep 83)

Taste Of Honey Sees Success In The New Year. Illustrated. *Jet*. 63: 60-62 (3 Jan 83)

The Year Of The Black Male In Films. Illustrated. *Ebony*. 38: 168 + (Aug 83)

Collins, James D. and others

Asbestosis And The Serratus Anterior Muscle. Tables, illustrated. *National Medical Association Journal*. 75: 296-300 (Mar 83)

Collins, Marva

Marva Collins' Way. Book review. Carole Bovoso. *Essence*. 13: 19 (Jan 83)

Collins, Vanneise A.

Black Students In Higher Education: Conditions And Experiences In The 1970's. Book review. *Afro-Americans in New York Life and History*. 07: 70-71 (Jan 83)

Colon-Muniz, Anaida

AV Materials On Puerto Rican Themes: What Are The Messages.. *Interracial Books for Children*. 14: No. 1: 25-27 (83)

Columbia, Missouri

See Also Police Chiefs—Missouri—Columbia

Columbus, Ohio

See Also Construction
Industry—Ohio—Columbus

Comedians

Bill Cosby Tells Why He Is Tough On His Children. Illustrated. *Jet*. 64: 60-63 (30 May 83)

Eddie Murphy: An Incredible Leap To Superstardom. Illustrated. Walter Leavy. *Ebony*. 38: 35-36 + (Oct 83)

Eddie Murphy: Black Humor With An Edge. Illustrated. Bonnie Allen. *Essence*. 13: 12 (Jan 83)

Eddie Murphy: Will Movie Hit Create Problems For Controversial Comic? Illustrated. Walter Leavy. *Ebony*. 38: 88 + (Apr 83)

Flip Wilson Brings 'Geraldine' Back As Answer To 'Tootsie'. Illustrated. *Jet*. 64: 58-61 (9 May 83)

Flip Wilson Says Family More Important Than Fame. Illustrated. *Jet*. 64: 61 (28 Aug 83)

Pryor Forms Production Co. Signs $40Mil. Film Pact With Columbia Pictures. Illustrated. *Jet*. 64: 54-55 (6 Jun 83)

Richard Pryor's Movie Company Releases First Film, 'Here And Now'. Illustrated. *Jet*. 65: 56-58 (28 Nov 83)

Richard Pryor: 'Superman III' And Hollywood's New $40 Million Man. Illustrated. *Jet*. 64: 60-63 (11 Jul 83)

Comer, James P.

Single-Parent Black Families.. *Crisis*. 90: 42-47 (Dec 83)

Committee On Institutional Cooperation

Graduate School: CIC Fellowships. John A. (Jr.) McCluskey. *Black Collegian*. 14: 124-127 (Nov-Dec 83)

Commodores (Singing Group)

Lionel Richie Tells Why He Really Quit The Commodores. Illustrated. *Jet*. 63: 36-38 (21 Feb 83)

Communication

Cooperative Communication Strategies: Observations In A Black Community. Notes, bibliography. Thurmon Garner. *Journal of Black Studies*. 14: 233-250 (Dec 83)

See Also Mass Media
Telecommunication

Communication In Literature

"Pow!" "Snap!" "Pouf!": The Modes Of Communication In Who's Afraid Of Virgina Woolf? Notes. Dan Ducker. *CLA Journal*. 26: 465-477 (Jun 83)

Communication, International

Global Telecommunications: Transborder Data Flow And The Role For Blacks. Tables, notes. Marc L. Randolph and Robert E. Wade. *The Urban League Review*. 08: 55-67 (Winter 83)

Community Development—New York (State) —Rochester

Community Action Works. Illustrated. Madeline Sulaiman. *about. . . time*. 11: 14-19 (Jul 83)

Community Development, Urban—Ohio —Cincinnati

The Rebirth Of Avondale. Illustrated. Britt Robson. *Black Enterprise*. 13: 35 (Jun 83)

Commuters

Essence Women: Jewell Thompson. Illustrated. Mae Watts Brown. *Essence*. 13: 20 (Jan 83)

Companies

See Partnership

Composers

Charles Albert Tindley: Progenitor Of Black-American Gospel Music. Illustrated, tables, notes. Horace Clarence Boyer. *The Black Perspective in Music*. 11: 103-132 (Fall 83)

Conversation With. . . Alvin Singleton, Composer. Interview, Illustrated. Alvin Singleton and Lucius Wyatt. *The Black Perspective in Music*. 11: 178-189 (Fall 83)

Kashif: A Musical Inventor For The '80s. Illustrated. Kalamu Ya Salaam. *Black Collegian*. 14: 118+ (Sep-Oct 83)

Computer-Assisted Instruction

Can Computers Close The Educational Equity Gap? Notes. James P. Johnson. *The Urban League Review*. 08: 21-25 (Winter 83)

Computer Graphics

Computer Graphics: Blending Art With Science. Illustrated. Valery Y. R. Bates. *Black Collegian*. 14: 82-83+ (Nov-Dec 83)

Computer Industry

Harnessing The Information Explosion. Illustrated. Hal J. Logan. *Black Enterprise*. 13: 223-224+ (Jun 83)

Computer Industry—Vocational Guidance

Built To Last! Illustrated, tables. Linda D. Addison. *Essence*. 14: 35 (Dec 83)

Keeping Pace In The Computer Age. Illustrated. Phil W. Petrie. *Black Enterprise*. 13: 46-50+ (Feb 83)

Computer Terminals

Video Terminals And Your Health. James Harney. *Essence*. 14: 50 (Oct 83)

Computers

What Effects Will Computer Technology Have On You? Bill Pitts. *The Urban League Review*. 08: 68-76 (Winter 83)

Computers—Study And Teaching

A Little Computer Literacy Goes A Long Way. Carole E. Gregory. *Black Collegian*. 14: 77-78+ (Nov-Dec 83)

Conable, Barber A. (Jr.)

Social Security Reform: What Has Been Accomplished?. *about. . . time*. 11: 22 (Apr 83)

Conboy, Neil and Hatch, James V.

An Index Of Proper Nouns For "The Place Of The Negro In The Evolution Of The American THeatre, 1767 To 1940," A Dissertation By Fannin Saffore Belcher, Jr. (Yale University, 1945).. *Black American Literature Forum*. 17: 38-47 (Spring 83)

Concerts

Jazz Great Ella Fitzgerald Performs In-Flight Concert. Illustrated. Clarence Waldron. *Jet*. 63: 62+ (31 Jan 83)

Concerts—Jerusalem

Gospel Goes To The Holy Land. Illustrated. Charles Sanders and Vandell Cobb. *Ebony*. 39: 36-38+ (Dec 83)

Conde, Maryse

Heremakhonon. Book review. Carole Bovoso. *Essence*. 13: 19 (Apr 83)

Conductors (Music)

Isaiah Jackson - A Leader In The Classic Sense. Illustrated. Sarah D. Kash. *Crisis*. 90: 36-38 (Dec 83)

Confession (Law)—United States

Confessions-Evidence Obtained Pursuant To An Illegal Arrest Is Inadmissible At Trial Taylor Vs Alabama. Notes. Debra D. Palmer. *Black Law Journal*. 08: 348-360 (Fall 83)

Congress

See United States. Congress—Freedom Of Debate

Congress Of Afrikan People

Make The Past Serve The Present: Strategies For Black Liberation. Notes. Oba Simba T'Shaka. *Black Scholar*. 14: 21-37 (Jan-Feb 83)

Congressmen

See Legislators—United States

Conklin, Pam

Big Sky's The Limit. Illustrated. *Black Enterprise*. 13: 46-48 (Jan 83)

Conservatism

A Black Lawyer's Response To The Fairmont Papers. Notes. J. Clay (Jr.) Smith. *Howard Law Journal*. 26: No. 1: 195-225 (83)

CIBC Responds To Charges. Editorial. *Interracial Books for Children*. 14: No. 1: 3+ (83)

Sowell's Knowledge And Decisions: Can Black Conservatism Establish Its Intellectual Credibility? Notes. Alex Willingham. *Review of Black Political Economy*. 12: 179-187 (Winter 83)

Constitutions

See Also United States. Constitution

Construction Industry—Ohio—Columbus

Garland Lands Nigeria Deal. Illustrated. Jill Nelson. *Black Enterprise*. 13: 25 (Feb 83)

Consumer Cooperatives

Essence Women: Jewell Thompson. Illustrated. Mae Watts Brown. *Essence*. 13: 20 (Jan 83)

Consumer Credit

All About Credit.. *Essence*. 14: 78-79 + (Jun 83)

Cash Or Charge? Illustrated. Frank Emerson. *Black Enterprise*. 14: 97-98 + (Dec 83)

Consumer Education

Cheap Chic. Illustrated. Pamela Noel. *Ebony*. 38: 58-59 + (Sep 83)

Consumers—Research

Black Enterprise Readers Rate The Consumer And Professional Services. Connie Green. *Black Enterprise*. 14: 73-74 (Aug 83)

Contraceptives

See Also Oral Contraceptives

Contracts, Public

See Public Contracts

Control Data Corporation

A New Role For Corporations: Linking Technology To Socioeconomic Development. William C. Norris. *The Urban League Review*. 08: 88-94 (Winter 83)

Cook, Thelma Upperman

Preparing For The On-Campus Interview.. *Black Collegian*. 14: 86 + (Nov-Dec 83)

Cooke, Lloyd M.

NACME Works For Engineering Students. Illustrated. *Black Collegian*. 13: 38 + (Dec-Jan 83)

Cookery

A Black-Native American Harvest. Illustrated. Curtia James. *Essence*. 14: 87-88 (Nov 83)

Casserole Cuisine. Illustrated. Charla L. Draper. *Ebony*. 38: 100-102 + (Oct 83)

Creole Cookin'! Illustrated. *Ebony*. 38: 90-92 + (Feb 83)

Fix Food Fast. Venezuela Newborn. *Essence*. 14: 106 + (May 83)

Good And Cheap. Illustrated. Venezuela Newborn and Curtia James. *Essence*. 14: 103-105 + (Jun 83)

His Turn To Cook. Illustrated. Charla L. Draper. *Ebony*. 38: 119-120 + (Aug 83)

New Year's Peas & Rice—Why? Connie Von Hundertmark. *Essence*. 14: 51 (Dec 83)

No Time To Cook? These Quick And Tasty Recipes Will Make Every Meal This Month A Joy. Venezuela Newborn. *Essence*. 13: 113-114 + (Mar 83)

Score With This Chili Bowl Menu. Illustrated. *about. . . time*. 11: 23 (Apr 83)

Simply Salads. Illustrated. Charla L. Draper. *Ebony*. 38: 114-116 + (Jun 83)

Star-Studded Dishes. Illustrated. Curtia James. *Essence*. 13: 95 + (Feb 83)

Summer Cookin'. Illustrated. Charla L. Draper. *Ebony*. 38: 92-94 + (Jul 83)

Tex-Mex With Soul: The Ultimate Chili Recipe. Illustrated. *Essence*. 14: 101 (May 83)

The Traditional New Year. Illustrated. *Ebony*. 38: 88-90 + (Jan 83)

What A Catch: Canned Seafood Staples. Illustrated. *about. . . time*. 11: 21 (Mar 83)

When All Else Fails. . . Substitute! Madeline Sulaiman. *about. . . time*. 11: 22-23 (Mar 83)

See Also Barbecue Cookery
Caterers And Catering
Christmas Cookery

Cookery, American—Texas

Tex-Mex With Soul: The Best Little Caterers In Texas. Illustrated. Dolly Calhoun. *Essence*. 14: 102-103 + (May 83)

Cookery, Caribbean

A Bajan Buffet. Illustrated. Curtia James. *Essence*. 13: 104-105 (Apr 83)

Dining Caribbean: From Callaloo Soup To Coconut Bread. Illustrated. Marcia Wallace. *Black Enterprise*. 13: 70 + (May 83)

Cookery (Chicken)

The Joy Of Chicken. Illustrated. Curtia James. *Essence*. 14: 93-94 + (Sep 83)

Cookery (Chocolate)

Chocolate Temptations. Illustrated. Charla L. Draper. *Ebony*. 38: 109-110 + (Sep 83)

Cookery (Fish)

Catch Of The Day. Illustrated. *Essence*. 14: 115-117 + (Oct 83)

Fish Stories. Illustrated. Charla L. Draper. *Ebony*. 38: 100-102 + (Apr 83)

Cookery, Jamaican

Jamaican Recipes. Illustrated. *about. . . time*. 11: 24 (Dec 83)

Cookery (Potatoes)

Stuffed Spuds Offer Filling And Delicious Ways To Enjoy Potatoes As A Main Course. Illustrated. *Essence*. 13: 102 (Feb 83)

Cookery (Vegetables)

Vegetable Variety. Illustrated. Charla L. Draper. *Ebony*. 38: 118-120 + (May 83)

Cookery, Wok

See Wok Cookery

Coombs, Orde

Black Men And White Women 13 Years Later. Illustrated. *Essence*. 14: 80-82+ (May 83)

Cooper, Grace C.

Oral Tradition In African Societies. Bibliography, notes. *Negro History Bulletin*. 46: 101-103 (Oct-Dec 83)

Cooper, Richard

Is The United States Entering A Period Of Retrogression In Public Health? Editorial, Tables, notes. *National Medical Association Journal*. 75: 741-744 (Aug 83)

Cooper, W. and others

1963-A Rochester Perspective. Illustrated. *about. . . time*. 11: 21-23 (Oct 83)

Cooper, Walter

Aspire To Excellence: Don't Let Others Limit Your Ambition. Illustrated. *about. . . time*. 11: 4 (Jun 83)

Cooperative Housing

See Housing, Cooperative

Cooperatives, Consumer

See Consumer Cooperatives

Copage, Eric

Essense Man: Franklin Thomas. Illustrated. *Essence*. 14: 40 (Nov 83)

Joan Armatrading. Illustrated. *Essence*. 14: 51 (Dec 83)

What (And Why) You Should Know About. . . AIDS.. *Essence*. 14: 51 (Jul 83)

Copeland, Virginia (joint author)

See Betances, Samuel

Coppin, Fanny Jackson (1837-193) (about)

From Slavery To Achievement: Keep On A Goin'. Illustrated. Robert L. (Jr.) Harris. *Black Collegian*. 13: 142-147 (Feb-Mar 83)

Cordell, LaDoris Hazzard (about)

Profiles: LaDoris Hazzard Cordell. Portrait. Julie E. Hall. *Black Law Journal*. 08: 150-151 (Spring 83)

Cornelius, Janet

"We Slipped And Learned To Read:" Slave Accounts Of The Literacy Process, 1830-1865. Notes, tables. *Phylon*. 44: 171-186 (Sep 83)

Cornelius, Samuel J. (about)

Food Stamp Administrator Named Aide To Head Of Department Of Agriculture. First facts, Illustrated. *Jet*. 63: 4 (7 Feb 83)

Coronary Heart Disease—Surgery

Coronary Heart Disease And Bypass Surgery In Urban Blacks. Tables, notes. Levi (Jr.) Watkins and others. *National Medical Association Journal*. 75: 381-383 (Apr 83)

Correspondence Schools And Courses

Correspondence Courses. James P. Duffy. *Essence*. 14: 30 (May 83)

Cosby, Bill (about)

Bill Cosby Plays Santa Claus To Needy Children. Illustrated. *Jet*. 65: 54-55 (26 Dec 83)

Bill Cosby, Sammy Davis: First Time To Headline Club Date Together. Illustrated. Aldore D. Collier. *Jet*. 63: 58-62 (7 Mar 83)

Bill Cosby Tells Why He Is Tough On His Children. Illustrated. *Jet*. 64: 60-63 (30 May 83)

Comedian Bill Cosby Is Honored At Annual PUSH Grande Reception. Illustrated. *Jet*. 64: 12-14 (23 May 83)

Cosmetics Industry—Texas—Dallas

How This Sister Turned A Winning Bid Into A Gold Mine! Illustrated. Lloyd Gite. *Essence*. 14: 31 (Jul 83)

Cost Of Medical Care

See Medical Care, Cost Of

Coughtry, Jay

The Notorious Triangle, Rhode Island And The African Slave Trade, 1700-1807. Book review. John E. Fleming. *Journal of Negro History*. 68: 113-114 (Winter 83)

Council On Interracial Books For Children

CIBC Responds To Charges. Editorial. *Interracial Books for Children*. 14: No. 1: 3+ (83)

Counseling

Minority Identity Development And Preference For Counselor Race. Notes, tables. George Morten and Donald R. Atkinson. *Journal of Negro Education*. 52: 156-161 (Spring 83)

Cousins, Dorothy (about)

Essence Women: Dorothy Cousins. Illustrated. Margo Walker Williams. *Essence*. 13: 25 (Feb 83)

Cowell, Daniel D.

Aging Research, Black Americans, And The National Institute On Aging.. *National Medical Association Journal*. 75: 99+ (Jan 83)

Cowings, Patricia (about)

Space Science: The African-American Contribution. Illustrated. Curtis M. Graves and Ivan Van Sertima. *Journal of African Civilizations*. 05: 238-257 (Apr-Nov 83)

Cox, Clinton

Ten Ways To Upgrade Your Home. Illustrated. *Black Enterprise*. 13: 72+ (Apr 83)

Cox, Oliver Cromwell (1901-1974) (about)

Oliver C. Cox: A Biographical Sketch Of His Life And Work. Notes. Herbert M. Hunter. *Phylon*. 44: 249-261 (Dec 83)

Cox, Taylor (Jr.)

Blacks And Higher Education: Where Do We Stand And What Difference Does It Make Anyway? Notes , tables. *Negro Educational Review*. 34: 4-11 (Jan 83)

Craft, Juanita Jewel (about)

Juanita Jewel Craft: Just Look At Her "Kids".
Illustrated. Ann L. Reagins. *Crisis*. 90: 36-37
(Jun-Jul 83)

Craig, Dennis R.

Teaching Standard English To Nonstandard
Speakers: Some Methodological Issues. Notes.
Journal of Negro Education. 52: 65-74 (Winter 83)

Credit Cards

Cash Or Charge? Illustrated. Frank Emerson. *Black
Enterprise*. 14: 97-98 + (Dec 83)

Creighton, H. Campbell

Ethnocultural Processes And National Problems In
The Modern World. Book review. Alonzo T.
Stephens. *Journal of Negro History*. 68: 128-129
(Winter 83)

Crime And Criminals

Can Black Mayors Stop Crime? Illustrated. Walter
Leavy. *Ebony*. 39: 116 + (Dec 83)

The Malady Of Violent Crime. Illustrated. Earl G.
   Graves. *Black Enterprise*. 13: 11 (Apr 83)

   See Also Prisoners
      Victims Of Crimes

Crime Prevention

Closing Down On Crime. Illustrated. R. G.
Collazo. *Black Enterprise*. 13: 39-41 + (Apr 83)

Report From Houston. . . Community Involvement
Is Key To Future Success. Illustrated. Lee P.
Brown. *Crisis*. 90: 38-39 (Feb 83)

Criss, Ola B.

A Piller Of Fire To Follow: American Indian
Dramas, 1808-1859. Book review. *Phylon*. 44:
90-91 (Mar 83)

Criticism

   See Also Aesthetics
      Drama—History And Criticism
      Fiction—History And Criticism
      Poetry—History And Criticism

Crockett, George W. (Jr.)

American Policy In Southern Africa. Illustrated.
Negro History Bulletin. 46: 104-105 (Oct-Dec 83)

An Open Letter On The Middle East..
Freedomways. 23: No. 3: 176-178 (83)

Reagan Foreign Policy: War On The Doorstep?
Illustrated. *Crisis*. 90: 48-49 (Dec 83)

Cromartie, E. W. (II) (about)

Two Blacks Win Seats On S. Carolina City
Council. First facts, Illustrated. *Jet*. 64: 4 (25 Apr
83)

Crosswaith, Frank R. (about)

Frank R. Crosswaith And Labor Unionization In
Harlem, 1939 - 1945. Notes. John C. Walter.
Afro-Americans in New York Life and History. 07:
47-58 (Jul 83)

Cruelty To Children

   See Also Child Abuse

Cuban Music

   See Music, Cuban

Cudjoe, Selwyn R.

Grenada.. *Freedomways*. 23: No. 4: 270-277 (83)

Cuffay, William (1788-1870) (about)

William Cuffay: London's Black Chartist. Notes.
Norbert J. Gossman. *Phylon*. 44: 56-65 (Mar 83)

Cullen, Countee (1903-1946)

A Brown Girl Dead. Poem. *Ebony*. 38: 154 (Oct
83)

For A Lady I Know. Poem. *Ebony*. 38: 154 (Oct
83)

From The Dark Tower. Poem. *Ebony*. 38: 154 (Oct
83)

Heritage (For Harold Jackman). Poem. *Ebony*. 38:
154 (Oct 83)

Incident (For Eric Walrond). Poem. *Ebony*. 38: 155
(Oct 83)

Simon The Cyrenian Speaks. Poem. *Ebony*. 38: 155
(Oct 83)

Yet Do I Marvel. Poem. *Ebony*. 38: 152 (Oct 83)

Youth Sings A Song Of Rosebuds (To Roberta).
Poem. *Ebony*. 38: 155 (Oct 83)

Cults

Body Buried For Six Years Unearthed, Skull
Removed; Suspect Cult Ritualists. Illustrated.
Clarence Waldron. *Jet*. 64: 28-31 (11 Jul 83)

Cults—Trinidad And Tobago

African Cults And Christian Churches In Trinidad:
The Spiritual Baptist Case. Notes. Stephen D.
Glazier. *Journal of Religious Thought*. 39: 17-25
(Fall-Winter 83)

Cultural Relations

The Ideological Significance Of Afrocentricity In
Intercultural Communication. Notes, bibliography.
Molefi Kete Asante. *Journal of Black Studies*. 14:
3-19 (Sep 83)

Culture

Development Of Culture By Black Artisans. Notes.
Sharon F. Patton. *Negro History Bulletin*. 46: 43-45
(Apr-Jun 83)

The Foundations Of Black Culture. W. H.
McClendon. *Black Scholar*. 14: 18-20 (Summer 83)

Needed: A Culture Of Development, Rather Than
Mere Survival. Illustrated. Haki R. Madhubuti.
Black Collegian. 13: 126 + (Feb-Mar 83)

The Survival Of A Cultural Legacy. Adolphus
Ealey. *Negro History Bulletin*. 46: 90 (Oct-Dec 83)

Culture And Language

   See Language And Culture

Cummings, Alban and others

Children Of The Caribbean: A Study Of Diversity..
Journal of Black Studies. 13: 489-495 (Jun 83)

Cummings, Terry (about)

Terry Cummings: Basketball's Million-Dollar Minister. Illustrated. Marilyn Marshall. *Ebony.* 38: 42-44 (Feb 83)

Cunningham, Mirna and Chrisman, Robert

The Black Scholar Interviews: Mirna Cunningham. Interview. *Black Scholar.* 14: 17-27 (Mar-Apr 83)

Cureau, Harold G.

The Visual Arts In Black Colleges: From Benign Neglect To Progress. Notes. *Negro Educational Review.* 34: 27-36 (Jan 83)

Current, Gloster B. (about)

Gloster B. Current Recalled From Retirement To Be Deputy Director. Illustrated. *Crisis.* 90: 5 (Oct 83)

National Association Of Negro Musicians, Inc., Salutes R. Nathaniel Dett's 100th Birthday. Illustrated. *Crisis.* 90: 18-20 (Feb 83)

Curry, Leonard P.

The Free Black In Urban America: 1800-1850. Book review. Janice Sumler-Lewis. *Black Law Journal.* 08: 162-163 (Spring 83)

The Free Black In Urban America, 1800-1850. Book review, Notes. James O. Horton. *Afro-Americans in New York Life and History.* 07: 63-70 (Jan 83)

Custody Of Children

Fla. Interracial Couple Loses Custody Battle. Illustrated. D. Michael Cheers. *Jet.* 64: 36-38 (28 Mar 83)

Joint Custody: Sharing The Love. Illustrated. Joan Hopewell. *Essence.* 14: 122+ (May 83)

Dalgish, Gerard M.

A Dictionary Of Africanisms: Contributions Of Sub-Saharan Africa To The English Language. Book review. David F. Dorsey. *Phylon.* 44: 88-90 (Mar 83)

A Dictionary of Africanisms: Contributions Of Sub-Saharan Africa To The English Language. Book review. Baruch Elimelech. *CAAS Newsletter.* 07: 13+ (May 83)

Dallas, Texas

Dallas: A "New Frontier" For Blacks. Illustrated. Frank (III) White. *Ebony.* 38: 52-54+ (Jan 83)

See Also Bombings—Texas—Dallas
Cosmetics Industry—Texas—Dallas

Dancers

Dancing In The Dark: The Life And Times Or Margot Webb In AfrAmerican Vaudeville Of The Swing Era. Illustrated, notes. Brenda Dixon-Stowell. *Black American Literature Forum.* 17: 3-7 (Spring 83)

Whatever Happened To The Nicholas Brothers? Illustrated. Aldore Collier. *Ebony.* 38: 103-104+ (May 83)

Daniel, Jack L.

Black Children.. *Interracial Books for Children.* 14: No. 7: 8 (83)

Daniel, Johnnie

Regional And Industry Differences In The Employment Of Minority Managers. Notes, tables. *The Urban League Review.* 07: 74-90 (Summer 83)

Daniels, Belinda S.

Black Athletes In The United States: A Bibliography Of Books, Articles, Autobiographies, And Biographies On Black Professional Athletes In The United States, 1800-1981. Book review. Harry Edwards. *Crisis.* 90: 30-31 (May 83)

Daramola, J. O. (joint author)

See Ajagbe, H. A.

Darden, Christine (about)

Space Science: The African-American Contribution. Illustrated. Curtis M. Graves and Ivan Van Sertima. *Journal of African Civilizations.* 05: 238-257 (Apr-Nov 83)

Darden, Joe T.

Racial Differences In Unemployment: A Spatial Perspective. Tables, Notes. *Review of Black Political Economy.* 12: 93-105 (Spring 83)

Darwish, Mahmoud

Identity Card. Poem. *Freedomways.* 23: No. 2: 112-113 (83)

Dash, J. Michael

Literature And Ideology In Haiti, 1915-1961. Book review. Andrew Salkey. *Research in African Literatures.* 14: 564-566 (Winter 83)

Data Processing

See Electronic Data Processing

Daughters And Fathers

See Fathers And Daughters

Davenport, Doris

The Mojo Hands Call/I Must Go. Book review. *Black American Literature Forum.* 17: 177-179 (Winter 83)

Narratives: Poems In The Tradition Of Black Women. Book review. *Black American Literature Forum.* 17: 177-179 (Winter 83)

Waves & License. Book review. *Black American Literature Forum.* 17: 177-179 (Winter 83)

Davidson, Arthur T.

Human Histocompatibility Antigens And Organ Transplantation. Notes. *National Medical Association Journal.* 75: 526-527+ (May 83)

The Role Of The Historic Black Colleges In The Training Of Black Professionals. Notes. *National Medical Association Journal.* 75: 1019-1022 (Oct 83)

Sexual Exploitation Of Children: A Call To Action. Editorial, Notes. *National Medical Association Journal.* 75: 925-927 (Oct 83)

Davidson, Arthur T. and Coleman, Arthur H.

Legal Options In Securing Hospital Appointments. Notes. *National Medical Association Journal.* 75: 318-320 (Mar 83)

Death—Psychological Aspects

A Healthful Approach To Death And Dying. Editorial, Notes. Abbasi J. Akhtar. *National Medical Association Journal.* 75: 350 (Apr 83)

Debtor And Creditor

On The Money: When A Collector Gets On Your Case. . . . Aurelia Toyer Miller and Ruth Dolores Manuel. *Essence.* 14: 21 (May 83)

Decision-Making

Black Decision Makers: An Exploratory Study In Role Perception And Role Performances. Tables, notes. Odell Uzzell. *Journal of Black Studies.* 14: 83-98 (Sep 83)

Dee, Merri (about)

Where There's A Will. . . This Woman Should Not Be Alive: The Miracle Of Merri Dee. Illustrated. Roger Witherspoon. *Essence.* 13: 72-74+ (Apr 83)

Dee, Ruby (about)

Lights! Camera! Action! Illustrated. S. Lee Hilliard and Nelson George. *Black Enterprise.* 14: 48-50+ (Dec 83)

What's Right About Black Men? Illustrated. *Ebony.* 38: 86+ (Aug 83)

DeGange, Stephen

America-From Hitler To MX. Motion picture review. *Freedomways.* 23: No. 01: 37-41 (83)

DeLain, Martha A. and Blount, Carolyne S.

Family Life Education: Strengthening Family Life Through Counseling. Interview, Illustrated. *about. . . time.* 11: 10-13+ (Sep 83)

DeLerma, Dominique-Rene

Bibliography Of Black Music Volume 3: Geographical Studies. Book review. Doris Evans McGinty. *The Black Perspective in Music.* 11: 79-82 (Spring 83)

Black Music In America: A Bibliography. Book review. *Negro History Bulletin.* 46: 85-86 (Jul-Sep 83)

Canto Nero. Book review. *The Black Perspective in Music.* 11: 78-79 (Spring 83)

A Concordance Of Black-Music Entries In Five Encyclopedias: Baker's, Ewen, Grove's, MGG, And Rich.. *The Black Perspective in Music.* 11: 190-209 (Fall 83)

Delinquency, Juvenile

See Juvenile Delinquency—Africa

Demby, William (about)

The Achievement Of William Demby. Notes. Jay R. Berry. *CLA Journal.* 26: 434-451 (Jun 83)

Democratic Party

Democratic Presidential Hopefuls. Bebe Moore Campbell. *Black Enterprise.* 14: 35 (Oct 83)

Demonstrations

See Protests, Demonstrations, Etc.

Denga, Daniel I.

The Effect Of Mobile Group Counseling On Nomadic Fulani's Attitudes Toward Formal Education. Notes, tables. *Journal of Negro Education.* 52: 170-175 (Spring 83)

Dennis, Lloyd

March On Washington '83. Illustrated. *Black Collegian.* 14: 35-37 (Nov-Dec 83)

Denniston, Dorothy L.

Faulkner's Image Of Blacks In Go Down, Moses. Notes. *Phylon.* 44: 33-43 (Mar 83)

Dent, David J.

Boycotting For Jobs. Illustrated. *Black Enterprise.* 13: 28 (Mar 83)

Champagne Celebration. Illustrated. *Black Enterprise.* 14: 116-118 (Dec 83)

Plagued By AIDS Scare. Tables. *Black Enterprise.* 14: 24 (Dec 83)

A Surge In Infant Deaths. Tables. *Black Enterprise.* 14: 22 (Oct 83)

UNCF Schools In Crisis.. *Black Enterprise.* 13: 20 (May 83)

Dent, Tom

The Antioch-Suite Jazz. Book review. *Freedomways.* 23: No. 01: 42-49 (83)

Exits And Entrances. Book review. *Freedomways.* 23: No. 01: 42-49 (83)

For Robeson (From New Orleans). Poem. *Freedomways.* 23: No. 4: 243 (83)

Season Of Hunger/Cry Of Rain. Book review. *Freedomways.* 23: No. 01: 42-49 (83)

Dental Care

A Clinic On Wheels. Illustrated. Britt Robson. *Black Enterprise.* 13: 18 (Jul 83)

Dentists

A Clinic On Wheels. Illustrated. Britt Robson. *Black Enterprise.* 13: 18 (Jul 83)

Denver, Colorado

See Also Executions And Executioners—Colorado—Denver

Department Of Defense

See United States. Department Of Defense

Department Of Education

See United States. Department of Education

Department Of Housing And Urban Development

See United States. Department Of Housing And Urban Development

Department of Justice

See United States. Department Of Justice

DePaur, Leonard (about)

Leonard De Paur And The WPA Theatre. Glenda E. Gill. *Freedomways.* 23: No. 4: 240-242 (83)

Depo-Provera

Is This Drug Dangerous? Joan Hopewell. *Essence*. 14: 42 (Jul 83)

DeRamus, Betty

How You Can Get What You Want.. *Essence*. 13: 67+ (Jan 83)

DeRamus, Betty and Gourse, Leslie

Remembering Dinah, Queen Of The Blues. Illustrated. *Essence*. 14: 76-78+ (May 83)

Derrick, W. Edwin

Shades Of Brown: New Perspectives On School Desegregation. Book review. *Journal of Negro Education*. 52: 177-178 (Spring 83)

Derricks, Cleavant (about)

The Dream Guys Of 'Dreamgirls'. Illustrated. *Ebony*. 38: 74-76+ (Apr 83)

Derricotte, Toi

Natural Birth: Poems. Book review. Joe Weixlmann. *Black American Literature Forum*. 17: 180-182 (Winter 83)

The Anesthesia Is Taking Effect. Poem. *Black American Literature Forum*. 17: 155 (Winter 83)

Beau Monde. Poem. *Black American Literature Forum*. 17: 155 (Winter 83)

The House Is The Enemy. Poem. *Black American Literature Forum*. 17: 155 (Winter 83)

The Night She Dreamed She Was Mad. Poem. *Black American Literature Forum*. 17: 155 (Winter 83)

The Sculpture At Night. Poem. *Black American Literature Forum*. 17: 155 (Winter 83)

Desegregation In Education

See School Integration

Detroit

See Also Banks And
Banking—Michigan—Detroit
Private Schools—Michigan—Detroit

Detroit—Economic Conditions

Hunger In Detroit. Illustrated. Lloyd Gite. *Black Enterprise*. 13: 19 (Apr 83)

Joblessness In Detroit Is "Devastating". Illustrated. Kevin Moss. *Crisis*. 90: 14 (Apr 83)

New Detroit, Inc.. Illustrated. Kevin Moss. *Crisis*. 90: 24-25 (Apr 83)

Dett, R. Nathaniel (1882-1943)

National Association Of Negro Musicians, Inc., Salutes R. Nathaniel Dett's 100th Birthday. Illustrated. Gloster B. Current. *Crisis*. 90: 18-20 (Feb 83)

DeVeaux, Alexis

Black South Africa: One Day Soon. Illustrated. *Essence*. 14: 80-81+ (Jul 83)

Blood Ties. Illustrated. *Essence*. 13: 62-64+ (Jan 83)

Sister Love. Illustrated. *Essence*. 14: 82-84+ (Oct 83)

Developing Countries

See Underdeveloped Areas

Development, Economic

See Economic Development

DeVore, Ophelia (about)

Essence Women: Ophelia DeVore. Illustrated. Ruth Dolores Manuel. *Essence*. 14: 50 (Aug 83)

Dickens, Floyd

The Black Manager: Making It In The Corporate World. Book review. Elza Terera Dinwiddie. *Black Enterprise*. 13: 30 (Jun 83)

Dickens, Jacqueline

The Black Manager: Making It In The Corporate World. Book review. Elza Terera Dinwiddie. *Black Enterprise*. 13: 30 (Jun 83)

Dickerson, Morgan W. F.

Problems Of Black High-Risk Elderly. Notes, tables. *Journal of Black Studies*. 14: 251-260 (Dec 83)

Diet

Sis Diets. . . Brother Does Too! Illustrated. Nancy Arnott. *Essence*. 14: 128 (Dec 83)

See Also Reducing Diets
Vegetarianism

Dieting

See Reducing

Dillard, Peggy (about)

Peggy Dillard: A Model Life Of Health And Beauty. Illustrated. Stephanie Stokes Oliver. *Essence*. 13: 100-101 (Jan 83)

Dingle, Derek T.

Black GOP Warns Reagan.. *Black Enterprise*. 14: 20 (Nov 83)

Bohana Bets On Insurance. Illustrated. *Black Enterprise*. 14: 24+ (Nov 83)

Breaking Bottlenecks.. *Black Enterprise*. 14: 19 (Oct 83)

Shagari Faces Economic Woes. Illustrated. *Black Enterprise*. 14: 26 (Dec 83)

Supplying Demand. Illustrated. *Black Enterprise*. 14: 26 (Oct 83)

Dinwiddie, Elza

The Black Student's Guide To Colleges. Book review. *Black Enterprise*. 13: 23 (Feb 83)

Dinwiddie, Elza Teresa

All About Success For The Black Woman. Book review. *Black Enterprise*. 13: 31 (Jun 83)

Black Life In Corporate America: Swimming In The Mainstream. Book review. *Black Enterprise*. 13: 27+ (Jun 83)

The Black Manager: Making It In The Corporate World. Book review. *Black Enterprise*. 13: 30 (Jun 83)

The Black Woman's Career Guide. Book review. *Black Enterprise*. 13: 30-31 (Jun 83)

Raising The Bottom Line: Business Leadership In A Changing Society. Book review. *Black Enterprise*. 13: 30 (Jun 83)

Diplomatic And Consular Service

Why Aren't There More Blacks In Foreign Service? Illustrated. D. Michael Cheers. *Ebony*. 38: 89-90+ (May 83)

Diplomats

Racism Toward Black African Diplomats During The Kennedy Administration. Notes. Calvin B. Holder. *Journal of Black Studies*. 14: 31-48 (Sep 83)

Directors, Television

See Television Producers And Directors

Directors, Theatrical

See Theatrical Producers And Directors

Disarmament

Social, Psychological And Ethical Aspects Of The Arms Race, War And Disarmament.. *Black Scholar*. 14: 56-58 (Nov-Dec 83)

See Also Peace

Disarmament And Atomic Weapons

See Atomic Weapons And Disarmament

Discrimination

Interconnections. James S. Tinney. *Interracial Books for Children*. 14: No. 3: 4-6+ (83)

There Is No Hierarchy Of Oppressions. Aundre Lorde. *Interracial Books for Children*. 14: No. 3: 9 (83)

Discrimination In Education—Law And Legislation

No Tax Breaks For Racism. Illustrated. Dennis Williams. *Black Enterprise*. 14: 17 (Sep 83)

Supreme Court Rules: Coleman Wins Case To Deny Biased School Tax Exemptions. Illustrated. *Jet*. 64: 21-22 (13 Jun 83)

Discrimination In Employment

Blacks In Labor Markets: A Historical Assessment. Notes. Denys Vaughn-Cooke. *The Urban League Review*. 07: 8-18 (Summer 83)

The Challenge For Black Students: Confronting New Forms Of Discrimination. Illustrated. Clarence Thomas. *Black Collegian*. 13: 44-46+ (Feb-Mar 83)

A Critical Analysis Of Judicial Opinions In Professional Employment Discrimination Cases. Notes. Jane Howard-Martin. *Howard Law Journal*. 26: No. 2: 723-757 (83)

The Critical Choice: Facing The Contradictions Of Life In America. Editorial. *Black Collegian*. 13: 14 (Apr-May 83)

Fair Representation In Employment: A Historical Look. Notes. Afife Sayin. *The Urban League Review*. 07: 19-32 (Summer 83)

Occupational Cancer In The Black Population: The Health Effects Of Job Discrimination. Notes. David Michaels. *National Medical Association Journal*. 75: 1014-1018 (Oct 83)

Orthodox And Systemic Explanations For Unemployment And Racial Inequality: Implications For Policy. Notes. David H. Swinton. *Review of Black Political Economy*. 12: 9-25 (Spring 83)

Regional And Industry Differences In The Employment Of Minority Managers. Notes, tables. Johnnie Daniel. *The Urban League Review*. 07: 74-90 (Summer 83)

So You Want To Be In The Movies? Illustrated. Curtis E. Rodgers. *Crisis*. 90: 6-10 (Jan 83)

Wage Secrecy At IBM. Steve Askin. *Black Enterprise*. 13: 24 (Apr 83)

See Also Affirmative Action Programs

Discrimination In Housing—Law And Legislation

Fair Housing Bills Proposed. Bebe Moore Campbell. *Black Enterprise*. 14: 31 (Nov 83)

Diseases, Occupational

See Occupational Diseases

Dissertations, Academic

Dissertations.. *Research in African Literatures*. 14: 196-199 (Summer 83)

Distler, Jed

Jazz Masters/Art Tatum. Book review. James Remel Burden. *The Black Perspective in Music*. 11: 86-88 (Spring 83)

Distribution (Economic Theory)

Biological Differences, Social Inequality, And Distributive Goods: An Exploratory Argument. Notes. A. J. Williams-Myers. *Journal of Black Studies*. 13: 399-416 (Jun 83)

Diverticulitis

Meckel's Diverticulum: The False-Negative Examination. Illustrated, notes. L. Keith Madison and Ruc Manh Tran. *National Medical Association Journal*. 75: 519-522 (May 83)

Divorce

Divorce: How Black Women Cope With Their Broken Marriages. Illustrated. Lynn Norment. *Ebony*. 39: 59-60+ (Nov 83)

Divorced Fathers

Who's Supporting The Kids? Why Men Leave Their Children: One Man's Story. Paul W. Price. *Essence*. 14: 74+ (Jul 83)

Dixon, Calvin

The Bronchial Challenge Test: A New Direction In Asthmatic Management. Tables, notes. *National Medical Association Journal*. 75: 199-204 (Feb 83)

Dixon, Melvin

Change Of Territory. Book review. Adam David Miller. *Black American Literature Forum*. 17: 179-180 (Winter 83)

Dixon-Stowell, Brenda

Dancing In The Dark: The Life And Times Or Margot Webb In AfrAmerican Vaudeville Of The Swing Era. Illustrated, notes. *Black American Literature Forum*. 17: 3-7 (Spring 83)

Doctors

　See Physicians

Dodson, Owen (about)

Remembering Owen Dodson. Aaron Kramer. *Freedomways*. 23: No. 4: 258-269 (83)

Black Theatre: Present Condition. Book review. *Black American Literature Forum*. 17: 94-95 (Summer 83)

Dogons (African People)

African Observers Of The Universe: The Sirius Question. Illustrated, notes, tables. Hunter Havelin (III) Adams. *Journal of African Civilizations*. 05: 27-46 (Apr-Nov 83)

New Light On The Dogon And Sirius. Notes. Hunter Havelin (III) Adams. *Journal of African Civilizations*. 05: 47-49 (Apr-Nov 83)

Dole, Elizabeth and Rouselle, William

The Black College Initiative: A Conversation With Elizabeth Dole. Interview, Illustrated. *Black Collegian*. 14: 44-46 (Nov-Dec 83)

Dole, Robert

"A Holiday for All The People". Illustrated. *Crisis*. 90: 17-18 (Nov 83)

Domestic Animals—Kenya—History

African Cattle Bones Stir Scientific Debate. Bayard Webster. *Journal of African Civilizations*. 05: 65-66 (Apr-Nov 83)

Dominica—Description And Travel

Dominica: A Lush And Inviting Wilderness. Illustrated. Emile Milne. *Black Enterprise*. 13: 68+ (May 83)

Dominican Republic—History—1844-1930

Frederick Douglass And American Diplomacy In The Caribbean. Notes, bibliography. Merline Pitre. *Journal of Black Studies*. 13: 457-475 (Jun 83)

Donaldson, Jeff

John A. Kendrick: A Salute. Illustrated. *Black Collegian*. 13: 130-131 (Feb-Mar 83)

Donegan, Dorothy (about)

Dorothy Donegan: Bouncy As Ever At Age 61. Illustrated. Clarence Waldron. *Ebony*. 39: 87-88+ (Dec 83)

Dongala, Emmanuel

Un Fusil Dans La Main, Un Poème Dans La Poche. Book review. Thelma Ravell-Pinto. *Journal of Black Studies*. 13: 369-371 (Mar 83)

Dooley, Charlie A. (about)

First Black Elected As Mayor Of Northwoods, Mo. First facts. *Jet*. 64: 4 (25 Apr 83)

Dorsey, David F.

A Dictionary Of Africanisms: Contributions Of Sub-Saharan Africa To The English Language. Book review. *Phylon*. 44: 88-90 (Mar 83)

Dosumu-Johnson, T. O.

Reflections Of An African Nationalist. Book review. Sulayman S. Nyang. *Phylon*. 44: 164-168 (Jun 83)

Douglas, Kordice (about)

Keeping It In The Family. Illustrated. Lloyd Gite. *Essence*. 14: 36 (Dec 83)

Douglas, Pamela

Teaching Your Kids The ABC's Of Dollars And Cents. Illustrated. *Black Enterprise*. 13: 205-206+ (Jun 83)

Teaching Your Kids The Financial Facts Of Life. Illustrated. *Black Enterprise*. 14: 106-108+ (Oct 83)

Douglas, Ronalda (about)

New Faces In Hollywood. Illustrated. *Ebony*. 38: 62-64+ (Apr 83)

Douglass, Frederick (1817-1895) (about)

Frederick Douglass: Agitator For Liberty, Justice, Equality And Afro-American Uplift. Illustrated. Frederick Douglass (Jr.) Jefferson. *about. . . time*. 11: 8-11+ (Feb 83)

Frederick Douglass And American Diplomacy In The Caribbean. Notes, bibliography. Merline Pitre. *Journal of Black Studies*. 13: 457-475 (Jun 83)

Frederick Douglass And Woman Suffrage. Notes. S. Jay Walker. *Black Scholar*. 14: 18-25 (Sep-Oct 83)

Vision And Revision In The Autobiographies Of Frederick Douglass. Notes. Thomas De Pieto. *CLA Journal*. 26: 384-396 (Jun 83)

Dozier, Carol (joint author)

　See Taylor, Henry

Drake, James A.

Popular Culture And American Life: Selected Topics In The Study Of American Popular Culture. Book review. Doris Evans McGinty. *The Black Perspective in Music*. 11: 212-214 (Fall 83)

Drama

A Look At The Contemporary Black Theatre Movement. Notes. A. Peter Bailey. *Black American Literature Forum*. 17: 19-21 (Spring 83)

See Also Nigerian Drama
Theater

Drama—History And Criticism

Comic Irony In Vanbrugh's The Relapse: Worthy's Repentance. Notes. James S. Malek. *CLA Journal*. 26: 353-361 (Mar 83)

Conflicting Impulses In The Plays Of Ntozake Shange. Illustrated, notes. Sandra L. Richards. *Black American Literature Forum*. 17: 73-78 (Summer 83)

The Dramatic Structure Of Dutchman. Illustrated, notes. Andrzej Ceynowa. *Black American Literature Forum.* 17: 15-18 (Spring 83)

Journey Toward Light: Athol Fugard's Tsotsi . Notes. Robert M. Post. *CLA Journal.* 26: 415-421 (Jun 83)

The Sighted Eyes And Feeling Heart Of Lorraine Hansberry. Notes. Margaret B. Wilkerson. *Black American Literature Forum.* 17: 8-13 (Spring 83)

Drama—Indexes

An Index Of Proper Nouns For "The Place Of The Negro In The Evolution Of The American THeatre, 1767 To 1940," A Dissertation By Fannin Saffore Belcher, Jr. (Yale University, 1945). Neil Conboy and James V. Hatch. *Black American Literature Forum.* 17: 38-47 (Spring 83)

Draper, Charla L.

Casserole Cuisine. Illustrated. *Ebony.* 38: 100-102+ (Oct 83)

Chocolate Temptations. Illustrated. *Ebony.* 38: 109-110+ (Sep 83)

Designing Your Space For You. Illustrated. *Ebony.* 38: 131-133 (May 83)

Fish Stories. Illustrated. *Ebony.* 38: 100-102+ (Apr 83)

His Turn To Cook. Illustrated. *Ebony.* 38: 119-120+ (Aug 83)

The Holiday Feast. Illustrated. *Ebony.* 39: 100-102+ (Dec 83)

Holiday Gifts From The Kitchen. Illustrated. *Ebony.* 39: 113-114+ (Nov 83)

Simply Salads. Illustrated. *Ebony.* 38: 114-116+ (Jun 83)

Summer Cookin'. Illustrated. *Ebony.* 38: 92-94+ (Jul 83)

Vegetable Variety. Illustrated. *Ebony.* 38: 118-120+ (May 83)

Dreams

Making Sense Of Your Dreams. Illustrated. Ruthe Stein. *Ebony.* 38: 51+ (Oct 83)

Drinkard, Mildred Elizabeth Nero

Miracles Of Ministry. Poem. *Journal of Religious Thought.* 40: 72 (Spring-Summer 83)

Drug Abuse

See Also Narcotic Habit

Drug Addicts

See Narcotic Addicts

Drugs And Youth

Is Your Child Hooked On Drugs? Illustrated. *Ebony.* 39: 75-76+ (Nov 83)

Drugs—Side Effects

Is This Drug Dangerous? Joan Hopewell. *Essence.* 14: 42 (Jul 83)

Drum

The Social Evolution Of The Afro-Cuban Drum. Illustrated, notes. Roberto Nodal. *The Black Perspective in Music.* 11: 157-177 (Fall 83)

Drumwright, Frank E. (Jr.)

Paul's Apocalyptic In The Key Of Beker: A Student Response. Notes. *Journal of Religious Thought.* 40: 16-17 (Spring-Summer 83)

DuBois, William Edward Burghardt (1868-1963) (about)

On Reconsidering Park, Johnson, DuBois, Frazier And Reid: Reply To Benjamin Bowser's "The Contribution Of Blacks To Sociological Knowledge.". Notes. Jerry G. Watts. *Phylon.* 44: 273-291 (Dec 83)

Private Consequences Of A Public Controversy. . . Grandmother, Grandfather, W.E.B. Du Bois And Booker T. Washington. Illustrated. Adele Logan Alexander. *Crisis.* 90: 8-11 (Feb 83)

W. E. B. DuBois And The Concepts Of Race And Class. Notes. Dan S. Green and Earl Smith. *Phylon.* 44: 262-272 (Dec 83)

W. E. B. DuBois And The First Scientific Study Of Afro-America. Notes, tables. Werner J. Lange. *Phylon.* 44: 135-146 (Jun 83)

DuBois, William Edward Burghardt (1868-1963) —Criticism And Interpretation

Psychic Duality Of Afro-Americans In The Novels Of W. E. B. DuBois. Notes. James B. Stewart. *Phylon.* 44: 93-107 (Jun 83)

Ducker, Dan

"Pow!" "Snap!" "Pouf!": The Modes Of Communication In Who's Afraid Of Virgina Woolf? Notes. *CLA Journal.* 26: 465-477 (Jun 83)

Duckett, Joy

Essence Women: Cheryl Glass. Illustrated. *Essence.* 13: 29 (Mar 83)

Essence Women: Dorothy Pitman Hughes. Illustrated. *Essence.* 13: 22 (Feb 83)

Money Management: There Is A Better Way. Illustrated. *Essence.* 14: 74-75+ (Jun 83)

NMBC Is A-OK.. *Black Enterprise.* 13: 38 (Jun 83)

Dudley, Willie

Due Process Safeguarding The Right To An Impartial Jury: The Adequacy Of Post-Trial Hearings Smith Vs Phillips. Notes. *Black Law Journal.* 08: 338-347 (Fall 83)

Due Process Of Law—United States

Due Process Safeguarding The Right To An Impartial Jury: The Adequacy Of Post-Trial Hearings Smith Vs Phillips. Notes. Willie Dudley. *Black Law Journal.* 08: 338-347 (Fall 83)

Leis V. Flynt - Yet Another Perspective. Notes. Carlton Bailey. *Black Law Journal.* 08: 95-126 (Spring 83)

Duffy, James P.

Correspondence Courses.. *Essence*. 14: 30 (May 83)

Dukes, Bethel

In Memoriam: Doris Mossie Thomas.. *Journal of Negro History*. 68: 144-145 (Winter 83)

Dummett, Clifton O.

Prevention Began Early: Charles Edwin Bentley, DDS 1859-1926.. *National Medical Association Journal*. 75: 1235-1236 (Dec 83)

Dunbar, Paul Laurence (1872-1906) (about)

Paul Laurence Dunbar: Master Player In A Fixed Game. Notes. Ralph Story. *CLA Journal*. 27: 30-55 (Sep 83)

Dunbar, Sybil

After Farewell. Poem. *Essence*. 14: 89 (Oct 83)

Duncan, Titus D. and McCord, Dolores

Thyroid Carcinoma: Criteria In Selection Of Patients For Total And Subtotal Thyroidectomy. Notes. *National Medical Association Journal*. 75: 401-404 (Apr 83)

Dupree, Adolph

Andrew Langston: Mighty Like A River. Illustrated. *about. . . time*. 11: 14-21 (Apr 83)

Caribbean Sea Circle: A Brass Ring For 40,000 Years. Illustrated. *about. . . time*. 11: 13-21 + (Dec 83)

Prescription For Success. Illustrated. *about. . . time*. 11: 14-16 (Aug 83)

The Quality Of Leadership: Gary A. Scott (July 11, 1945-March 29, 1968). Illustrated. *about. . . time*. 11: 22-26 (Nov 83)

Running For Political Office. Illustrated. *about. . . time*. 11: 8-19 (Oct 83)

Through A Magnifying Glass: An Examination Of Family Relations. Illustrated. *about. . . time*. 11: 14-20 + (Sep 83)
Gibson, Kenneth A.
Jacob, John E.

Dupree, David (joint author)

See Shields, Portia H.

Durham, Dianne (about)

Dianne Durham: Going For The Gold In '84 Olympics. Illustrated. D. Michael Cheers. *Ebony*. 38: 52-54 + (Sep 83)

Gary's Dianne Durham Is Top U.S. Female Gymnast. Illustrated. D. Michael Cheers. *Jet*. 64: 46-50 (27 Jun 83)

Dursy, Rose (about)

New Faces In Hollywood. Illustrated. *Ebony*. 38: 62-64 + (Apr 83)

Duval County, Florida

See Also School Integration—Duval County, Florida

Dvorkiu, Elizabeth

Becoming A Lawyer: A Humanistic Perspective On Legal Education And Professionalism. Book review. Elana Yancey. *Black Law Journal*. 08: 164-166 (Spring 83)

Dwight, Margaret L.

The Belle Of Ashby Street: Helen Douglas Mankin And Georgia Politics. Book review. *Journal of Negro History*. 68: 102-104 (Winter 83)

Dworkin, Ronald (about)

Controversial Propositions Of Law And The Positivist Embarrassment: The Hart/Dworkin Debate Reconsidered. Notes. Simeon Charles Randolph McIntosh. *Howard Law Journal*. 26: No. 2: 699-722 (83)

Dye, William E. (about)

Columbia, Mo., Gets First Black Police Chief. Illustrated, first facts. *Jet*. 63: 57 (10 Jan 83)

E.E.O.C.

See United States—Equal Employment Opportunity Commission

Ealey, Adolphus

The Survival Of A Cultural Legacy.. *Negro History Bulletin*. 46: 90 (Oct-Dec 83)

Eanes, Marcie

Essence Women: Barbara J. Mahone. Illustrated. *Essence*. 14: 56 (Dec 83)

Have A Happy Halloween.. *Essence*. 14: 136 (Oct 83)

Earles, Lucius C. (III)

Message From The Class Of 1963.. *National Medical Association Journal*. 75: 1125-1129 (Dec 83)

President's Inaugural Address: Priorities.. *National Medical Association Journal*. 75: 1139-1143 (Dec 83)

Ebony Jr! (Periodical)

Ebony Jr! Celebrates Its Tenth Anniversary With Special May Issue. First facts, Illustrated. *Jet*. 64: 14 + (9 May 83)

Economic Development

Alternative Economic Strategies For Blacks. Illustrated. Fred H. Rasheed. *Crisis*. 90: 8-9 (Oct 83)

Black Survival In America. Illustrated. Glenn C. Loury. *Black Enterprise*. 13: 33 (May 83)

Outlook For Black Economic Development. Illustrated. Frederick V. Boyd. *Black Enterprise*. 13: 247-248 + (Jun 83)

Technology As A Means Of Promoting Black Development. Charles E. Tate. *The Urban League Review*. 08: 9-13 (Winter 83)

The Value Of Black Dollars.. *Crisis*. 90: 9 (Oct 83)

Economic Policy, Foreign

See International Economic Relations

Economics

See Also Supply And Demand
Urban Economics

Economics—Study And Teaching

The Political Economy Of Black Americans:
Perspectives On Curriculum Development. Lloyd L.
Hogan. *Review of Black Political Economy*. 12:
145-161 (Winter 83)

Education

Can Computers Close The Educational Equity Gap?
Notes. James P. Johnson. *The Urban League
Review*. 08: 21-25 (Winter 83)

An Interview With The Secretary Of Education:
Terrell Bell. Interview, Illustrated. Terrel Bell and
Hughes Jones. *Black Collegian*. 13: 51-53
(Apr-May 83)

Persistent And Emergent Legal Issues In Education:
1983 Yearbook. Editorial. Faustine C.
Jones-Wilson. *Journal of Negro Education*. 52:
187-188 (Summer 83)

The State Of Education For Black Americans.
Beverly P. Cole. *Crisis*. 90: 42-45 (May 83)

See Also Illiteracy

Education—Africa

African Traditional Education: A Method Of
Disseminating Cultural Values. Notes. Felix
Boateng. *Journal of Black Studies*. 13: 321-336
(Mar 83)

Education And State

Schooling And Democracy. Editorial. Faustine C.
Jones-Wilson. *Journal of Negro Education*. 52:
91-93 (Spring 83)

Education—Appalachian Region, Southern

Blacks In Appalachian America: Reflections On
Biracial Education And Unionism. Notes. William
H. Turner. *Phylon*. 44: 198-208 (Sep 83)

Education, Bilingual

A Survey OF Bidialectal Language Arts Programs
In The United States. Notes, tables. Orlando L.
Taylor and others. *Journal of Negro Education*. 52:
35-45 (Winter 83)

Education, Higher

Blacks And Higher Education: Where Do We Stand
And What Difference Does It Make Anyway? Notes
, tables. Taylor (Jr.) Cox. *Negro Educational
Review*. 34: 4-11 (Jan 83)

Higher Education For Minorities: The Challenge Of
The 1980s. Notes. Bernard W. Harleston. *Journal
of Negro Education*. 52: 94-101 (Spring 83)

See Also Universities And Colleges

Education, Higher—Tennessee—History

The Effect Of Higher Education On Black
Tennesseeans After The Civil War. Notes. Cynthia
Griggs Flemming. *Phylon*. 44: 209-216 (Sep 83)

Education—Integration

See School Integration

Education, Intercultural

See Intercultural Education

Education of Children

A Better Chance. Illustrated. Lynn Norment.
Ebony. 38: 46+ (Jun 83)

Childcare Shapes The Future: Racism, Related
Problems, Research And Strategies. Illustrated.
Interracial Books for Children. 14: No. 7: 6+ (83)

Children Of The Caribbean: A Study Of Diversity.
Alban Cummings and others. *Journal of Black
Studies*. 13: 489-495 (Jun 83)

Gain The Competitive Edge. Illustrated. Dennis A.
Williams. *Black Enterprise*. 14: 34-38+ (Sep 83)

Education—Philosophy

The Educational Panacea Of The Black Man: Black
Americans Faith In America Education, 1954-1983.
Notes. Clarence (Jr.) White. *Negro Educational
Review*. 34: 61-73 (Apr 83)

Education—Puerto Rico—History

U.S. Influence On Puerto Rican Schools: A
Tragi-Comedy.. *Interracial Books for Children*. 14:
No. 1: 28-29 (83)

Education—Segregation

See Segregation In Education

Education—Standards

An Educational Dilemma. James M. Blount.
about. . . time. 11: 4 (May 83)

A Nation At Risk: A Black Perspective On
American Education: An Interview With Norman
Francis. Interview, Illustrated. Norman Francis and
William Rouselle. *Black Collegian*. 14: 69-72
(Nov-Dec 83)

Educational Discrimination

See Discrimination In Education

Educational Equalization

Minority Tokenism In American Law Schools.
Notes, tables. Portia T. Hamlar. *Howard Law
Journal*. 26: No. 2: 443-599 (83)

Real Education Equity: A One-System Approach.
Editorial. Chalmers (Jr.) Archer. *Journal of Negro
Education*. 52: 375-377 (Fall 83)

Educational Fund Raising

UNCF Starts D.C. Drive For $9.9 Million, R.J.
Reynolds Makes Gift Of $1 Million. Illustrated.
Jet. 64: 14-16 (11 Jul 83)

Educational Games

The Significance Of Black American Children's
Singing Games In An Educational Setting. Notes.
Linda F. Wharton-Boyd. *Journal of Negro
Education*. 52: 46-56 (Winter 83)

Educational Television

See Television In Education

Educational Tests And Measurements

Florida Test Causes Furor. Valerie J. Hill. *Black
Enterprise*. 13: 17 (Jul 83)

Educators

Dr. Kenneth B. Clark: Fighter For Educational Opportunity. Interview, Illustrated. James M. Blount. *about. . . time.* 11: 14-15+ (May 83)

In Memoriam: Nick Aaron Ford (1904-1982). Therman B. O'Daniel. *Black American Literature Forum.* 17: 99 (Fall 83)

In Memoriam: Rayford W. Logan. Illustrated. Michael R. Winston. *Negro History Bulletin.* 46: 68 (Jul-Sep 83)

The Legacy Of George E. Kent. Notes. James W. Coleman and Joanne Veal Gabbin. *Black American Literature Forum.* 17: 143-147 (Winter 83)

A Man For All Sessions. Illustrated. Don Armstrong. *Crisis.* 90: 32 (Apr 83)

Mary Hatwood Futrell: Top Teacher. Illustrated. Steve Askin. *Black Enterprise.* 14: 124-126+ (Oct 83)

Noted Educator Says. . . "Blacks Must Never Give Up Pursuit Of Equality". Illustrated. *Crisis.* 90: 38-39 (Oct 83)

Remembering Owen Dodson. Aaron Kramer. *Freedomways.* 23: No. 4: 258-269 (83)

Superwomen Of Public Education. Illustrated. *Ebony.* 38: 88+ (Jun 83)

Teachers Union Boss. Illustrated. *Ebony.* 38: 140+ (Oct 83)

A Tribute To Vivian Wilson Henderson. Barbara A. P. Jones. *Review of Black Political Economy.* 12: 5-7 (Spring 83)

Edwards, Audrey

Black Women In Corporate America: Managing The Game. Illustrated. *Essence.* 13: 70-72+ (Mar 83)

Money Is The Root Of All Evil. . . And Other Bad Ideas That Keep Us Poor.. *Essence.* 14: 72-73 (Jun 83)
Miles, Patrice

Edwards, Harry

The Struggle That Must Be. Book review. Manning Carlyle Peterson. *Journal of Black Studies.* 14: 99-102 (Sep 83)

Athletic Performance In Exchange For An Education - A Contract Unfulfilled. Illustrated. *Crisis.* 90: 10-14 (May 83)

Black Athletes In The United States: A Bibliography Of Books, Articles, Autobiographies, And Biographies On Black Professional Athletes In The United States, 1800-1981. Book review. *Crisis.* 90: 30-31 (May 83)

Relections On Olympic Sportpolitics: History And Prospects, 1968-1984. Illustrated. *Crisis.* 90: 20-24 (May 83)

Egypt

See Also Aeronautics—Egypt—History
Agriculture—Egypt—Origin

Egypt—Description And Travel

Life On The Nile: One Woman's Travels Through Egypt-Land Of The Pharaohs. Illustrated. Kathleen Wyer Lane. *Essence.* 14: 38+ (Jul 83)

Egypt—Kings And Rulers

African King In Confederate Capital. Illustrated, bibliography. V. Spottswood Simon. *Negro History Bulletin.* 46: 9-10 (Jan-Mar 83)

Egyptian Medicine

See Medicine, Egyptian

Ekpo, Michael (joint author)

See Famuyiwa, Oluwole O.

El Beheiry, Kawsar Abdel Salam

L'Influence De La Littérature Française Sur Le Roman Arabe. Book review. Evelyne Accad. *Research in African Literatures.* 14: 203-207 (Summer 83)

Election

See Also Women—Suffrage

Elections

1982 Election Returns. Illustrated. Emile Milne. *Black Enterprise.* 13: 13 (Jan 83)

The 1984 Elections: A Checklist For Black Voters. Norman Hill. *about. . . time.* 11: 36 (Nov 83)

See Also Campaign Funds
Presidents—United States—Election
Voters, Registration Of
Voting

Elections—California—Campaign Funds

Bradley Got Major Backing In Calif. Governor's Race. Illustrated. *Jet.* 64: 8 (21 Mar 83)

Elections—Chicago—Campaign Funds

Unity Banquet Draws 5,500: Washington Supporters Told Beware Of 'False Security'. Illustrated. *Jet.* 64: 6-8 (18 Apr 83)

Elections—Illinois—Chicago

Race And The 1983 Chicago Election. Illustrated. Edward (III) Thompson. *Crisis.* 90: 14-15 (Oct 83)

Elections—Mississippi

Alleged Irregularities: Blacks Turn Out In Record Numbers For Miss. Primary Vote. Illustrated. D. Michael Cheers. *Jet.* 64: 12-14 (22 Aug 83)

Elections—Ohio

The Election Of An Ohio Congressman. Notes. Philip A. (Jr.) Grant. *Negro History Bulletin.* 46: 60-62 (Apr-Jun 83)

Electronic Data Processing—Vocational Guidance

Ready Or Not, Here Comes The Computer Future. Rosemary L. Bray. *Essence.* 14: 99-100+ (Oct 83)

Elegbeleye, O. O. (joint author)

See Bandele, E. O.

Elethea, Abba

The Antioch-Suite Jazz. Book review. Tom Dent. *Freedomways.* 23: No. 01: 42-49 (83)

Elhelu, Mohamed A. and others

Growth Of Trichinella Spiralis Larvae In Rats Receiving Folic-Acid-Deficient Diet. Tables, notes. *National Medical Association Journal*. 75: 501-502 (May 83)

The Role Of Macrophages In Immunology.. *National Medical Association Journal*. 75: 314-317 (Mar 83)

Elimelech, Baruch

A Dictionary of Africanisms: Contributions Of Sub-Saharan Africa To The English Language. Book review. *CAAS Newsletter*. 07: 13+ (May 83)

Ellison, Mary

Black Perceptions And Red Images: Indian And Black Literary Links. Notes. *Phylon*. 44: 44-55 (Mar 83)

Ellison, Ralph—Criticism And Interpretation

Imagery Of Imprisonment In Ralph Ellison's Invisible Man. Notes. Per Winther. *Black American Literature Forum*. 17: 115-119 (Fall 83)

Emergency Rooms

See Hospitals—Emergency Service

Emerson, Frank

Cash Or Charge? Illustrated. *Black Enterprise*. 14: 97-98+ (Dec 83)

The Write Stuff.. *Black Enterprise*. 14: 73-74+ (Nov 83)

Emigration And Immigration—Africa

Africans In Search Of Work: Migration And Diaspora. Notes, tables. Lenneal J. Henderson. *The Urban League Review*. 07: 58-73 (Summer 83)

Emigration And Immigration—United States

From Other Shores. Illustrated. Udayan Gupta. *Black Enterprise*. 13: 51-54 (Mar 83)

Emihovich, Catherine A.

The Color Of Misbehaving: Two Case Studies Of Deviant Boys. Notes. *Journal of Black Studies*. 13: 259-273 (Mar 83)

Eminent Domain

Harris Neck: Georgia Blacks Fight To Regain Ancestral Land. Illustrated. Thad Martin. *Ebony*. 38: 36-38+ (Jul 83)

Emotions

See Also Anger
Bashfulness
Jealousy
Love

Emoungu, Paul-Albert

Black-White Contact In Schools: Its Social And Academic Effects. Book review. *Journal of Negro Education*. 52: 182-184 (Spring 83)

Employee Seniority

See Seniority, Employee

Employees, Relocation Of

Moving On! Illustrated. Britt Robson. *Black Enterprise*. 14: 99-100+ (Oct 83)

Employment Agencies

Knocking On The Right Doors: How To Use Employment Agencies To Your Advantage. Robert Half. *Essence*. 14: 26 (Jul 83)

Employment And Foreign Trade

See Foreign Trade And Employment

Employment And Marriage

See Marriage And Employment

Employment Discrimination

See Discrimination In Employment

Employment (Economic Theory)

Deindustrialization And Unemployment In America. Tables, Notes. Barry Bluestone. *Review of Black Political Economy*. 12: 27-42 (Spring 83)

Orthodox And Systemic Explanations For Unemployment And Racial Inequality: Implications For Policy. Notes. David H. Swinton. *Review of Black Political Economy*. 12: 9-25 (Spring 83)

Employment Forecasting

Employment Outlook 1983. Illustrated, tables. Edmund Newton. *Black Enterprise*. 13: 43-45 (Feb 83)

Employment Interviewing

Preparing For The On-Campus Interview. Thelma Upperman Cook. *Black Collegian*. 14: 86+ (Nov-Dec 83)

Super Interviewing Tips From A Corporate Recruiter. Illustrated. Bethany L. Spotts. *Black Collegian*. 14: 92+ (Nov-Dec 83)

Tips For Preparing For An Interview. Chris Bardwell. *Black Collegian*. 13: 85 (Feb-Mar 83)

Employment Of Women

See Women—Employment

Employment Of Youth

See Youth—Employment

Employment, Summer

See Summer Employment

Engineering—Scholarships, Fellowships, Etc.

Financial Aid For Engineering Students. Illustrated. Ammatullah Saburah Khaliq. *Black Collegian*. 13: 134-136+ (Dec-Jan 83)

Engineering Schools

Black Engineering Schools. Illustrated. William Rouselle and James Borders. *Black Collegian*. 13: 96+ (Dec-Jan 83)

Engineering Students

NACME Works For Engineering Students. Illustrated. Lloyd M. Cooke. *Black Collegian*. 13: 38+ (Dec-Jan 83)

Summer Job Opportunities For Engineering Students. Illustrated. Kuumba Na Kazi. *Black Collegian*. 13: 85-88 (Dec-Jan 83)

Ten Steps To Success: How To Succeed In Engineering School. Benson E. Penick. *Black Collegian*. 13: 70+ (Dec-Jan 83)

Engineering—Vocational Guidance

Engineering Options. Illustrated. Martin Booker. *Black Collegian*. 13: 32-34+ (Dec-Jan 83)

Laser Technology: An Engineering Area Of The Future. Illustrated. Claire Gavin. *Black Collegian*. 13: 62+ (Dec-Jan 83)

Professional Engineering Opportunities.. *Black Collegian*. 13: 110-114+ (Dec-Jan 83)

Engineers

Lincoln Hawkins: A Black Engineering Pioneer. Illustrated. Kim Pearson. *Black Collegian*. 13: 48-50+ (Dec-Jan 83)

On Being An Engineer: Making The Transition From School To Career. Pamela G. Johnson. *Black Collegian*. 13: 56+ (Dec-Jan 83)

Pioneering Black Bell Labs Engineer Still At Work At 71. Illustrated. Kim E. Pearson. *Crisis*. 90: 40-41 (Apr 83)

English Language—Study And Teaching

A Perspective On Teaching Black Dialect Speaking Students To Write Standard English. Notes. Judith P. Nembhard. *Journal of Negro Education*. 52: 75-82 (Winter 83)

Teaching Standard English To Nonstandard Speakers: Some Methodological Issues. Notes. Dennis R. Craig. *Journal of Negro Education*. 52: 65-74 (Winter 83)

Engram, Eleanor

Science, Myth, Reality: The Black Family In One-Half Century Of Research. Book review. Dorothy Linder. *Phylon*. 44: 87-88 (Mar 83)

Entertainers

Bill Cosby, Sammy Davis: First Time To Headline Club Date Together. Illustrated. Aldore D. Collier. *Jet*. 63: 58-62 (7 Mar 83)

Bricktop. Excerpt. *Ebony*. 39: 59-60+ (Dec 83)

Gladys Knight And Billy Dee Williams: Stars Of 'EbonysJet Celebrity Showcase'. Illustrated. *Jet*. 64: 54-56 (1 Aug 83)

Lola Falana: On Tour With Sexy Show And Witty Thoughts. Illustrated. Robert E. Johnson. *Jet*. 64: 58-61 (18 Jul 83)

Redd Foxx And Smokey Robinson Reveal Sides They Have Kept Private. Illustrated. *Jet*. 64: 56-58 (8 Aug 83)

See Also Circus Performers
Comedians
Dancers
Musicians
Singers

Entertainers—Religious Life

Born-Again Stars. Illustrated. Aldore Collier. *Ebony*. 39: 51-52+ (Dec 83)

Entertaining

Champagne Celebration. Illustrated. David J. Dent. *Black Enterprise*. 14: 116-118 (Dec 83)

Making Your Party Special.. *Essence*. 14: 109-110+ (Dec 83)

A Super Holiday Party. Illustrated. *Black Enterprise*. 14: 111-112+ (Dec 83)

Entrepreneur

Entrepreneurship: A Viable Alternative. Illustrated. Philip A. Loyd. *about. . . time*. 11: 14-16+ (Mar 83)

The New Black Entrepreneurs. Illustrated. Pamela Noel. *Ebony*. 38: 160+ (Aug 83)

Epic Poetry, African

Introduction [To volume 14 Number 3, 1983]. Notes. Dan Ben-Amos. *Research in African Literatures*. 14: 277-282 (Fall 83)

Epic Poetry, African—History And Criticism

A Few Reflections On Narrative Structures Of Epic Texts: A Case Example Of Bambara And Fulani Epics. Notes. Christiane Seydou. *Research in African Literatures*. 14: 312-331 (Fall 83)

Epic Poetry, Gambian—History And Criticism

Stability And Change In The Performances Of Ohafia Igbo Singers Of tales. Tables, bibliography, notes. Chukwuma Azuonye. *Research in African Literatures*. 14: 332-380 (Fall 83)

Epic Poetry, Tanzanian

The Nanga Bards Of Tanzania: Are They Epic Artists? Illustrated, tables, notes. M. Mulukozi. *Research in African Literatures*. 14: 283-311 (Fall 83)

Epps, Anna Cherrie (joint author)

See Pisano, Joseph C.

Epps, Anne Cherrie (joint author)

See Pisano, Joseph C.

Equal Educational Opportunity

See Educational Equalization

Equal Employment Opportunity

See Affirmative Action Programs
Discrimination In Employment

Equal Employment Opportunity Commission

See United States—Equal Employment Opportunity Commission

Equality

Black/White Equality: The Socioeconomic Conditions Of Blacks In America, Part II. Notes. Sidney M. Willhelm. *Journal of Black Studies*. 14: 151-184 (Dec 83)

Equality Before The Law

Should Color Blindness And Representativeness Be A Part Of American Justice. Notes. Damon J. Keith. *Howard Law Journal*. 26: No. 1: 1-7 (83)

Equality Before The Law—United States

Equal Protection Fourteenth Amendment - State Requirement Of Citizenship To Be Peace Officer Sugarman Exception Cabell Vs Chavez-Salido. Notes. Ronald Low. *Black Law Journal*. 08: 322-337 (Fall 83)

Plyer V. Doe - Education And Illegal Alien Children. Notes. Ruth Jones. *Black Law Journal.* 08: 132-137 (Spring 83)

Equiano, Olaudah (about)

Retrospective Glance: The Interesting Narrative Of The Life Of Olaudah Equiano Reconsidered. Notes. Wilfred D. Samuels. *Negro History Bulletin.* 46: 99-100 (Oct-Dec 83)

Erskine, Noel Leo

Decolonizing Theology: A Caribbean Perspective. Book review. John B. Eubanks. *Journal of Religious Thought.* 39: 70-71 (Fall-Winter 83)

Erythrocytes

Effect Of Storage On Insulin Receptor Binding In Human Erythrocytes. Tables, notes. Kanwal K. Gambhir and others. *National Medical Association Journal.* 75: 503-507 (May 83)

Esophagus—Tumors

A Nonclassifiable Anaplastic Tumor Of The Esophagus. Illustrated, notes. Lloyd G. (Jr.) Phillips and others. *National Medical Association Journal.* 75: 205-207 (Feb 83)

Ethics And Law

See Law And Ethics

Ethics Of Wealth

See Wealth, Ethics Of

Ethiopian Refugees

See Refugees, Ethiopian

Ethnocentrism

The Ideological Significance Of Afrocentricity In Intercultural Communication. Notes, bibliography. Molefi Kete Asante. *Journal of Black Studies.* 14: 3-19 (Sep 83)

Ethnology—Study And Teaching

W. E. B. DuBois And The First Scientific Study Of Afro-America. Notes, tables. Werner J. Lange. *Phylon.* 44: 135-146 (Jun 83)

Eubanks, John B.

Decolonizing Theology: A Caribbean Perspective. Book review. *Journal of Religious Thought.* 39: 70-71 (Fall-Winter 83)

The Relational Self Ethics And Therapy From A Black Church Perspective. Book review. *Journal of Religious Thought.* 40: 73-74 (Spring-Summer 83)

Europe—Defenses

European Security And Disarmament.. *Black Scholar.* 14: 46-48 (Nov-Dec 83)

Evans, Arthur S.

Role Relations Of Black Sociologists With The Black Community: Perceptions Of Sociologists. Tables, notes. *Journal of Black Studies.* 13: 477-487 (Jun 83)

Evans, Ruppert L.

The Implications Of Labor Market Orientation Programs For Black Teenage Job Entry: A Response To Nelms And Pentecoste. Notes. *Negro Educational Review.* 34: 79-82 (Apr 83)

Eve, Anita

Constitutional Law- A 40-Year Sentence of Imprisonment Within The Limits Of A Statute Does Not Amount To Cruel And Unusual Punishment. Notes. *Howard Law Journal.* 26: No. 1: 305-325 (83)

Everette, Cheryl

The "Dream" Revisited. Illustrated. *Essence.* 14: 50 (Aug 83)

Evers, Myrlie

Myrlie Evers' Painful Odyssey. Illustrated. Chester A. (Sr.) Higgins. *Crisis.* 90: 34-36 (May 83)

Evidence (Law)—United States

Confessions-Evidence Obtained Pursuant To An Illegal Arrest Is Inadmissible At Trial Taylor Vs Alabama. Notes. Debra D. Palmer. *Black Law Journal.* 08: 348-360 (Fall 83)

Ex-convicts

Preacher Wages 30-Year Fight To Clear Name Of Rape Charge Against Him. Illustrated. D. Michael Cheers. *Jet.* 63: 14-16 (7 Mar 83)

Two Innocents Who Suffered On Death Row. Illustrated. Raymond Lang. *Ebony.* 38: 29-30+ (Sep 83)

Exceptional Children

See Also Gifted Children

Exceptional Children—Diagnosis

Improving The Assessment Of Black Students. Notes. LaDelle Olion and Marion Gillis-Olion. *Negro Educational Review.* 34: 52-60 (Apr 83)

Exceptional Children—Education

Affective Attributes Of Special Education And Regular Class Preprofessionals. Notes. Wilfred A. Johnson and Brenda A. Caple. *Negro Educational Review.* 34: 73-78 (Apr 83)

Executions And Executioners—Colorado —Denver

The End Of An Era: Denver's Last Legal Public Execution, July 27, 1886. Notes. William M. King. *Journal of Negro History.* 68: 37-53 (Winter 83)

Executives

Alexander Dies At 51. Connie Green. *Black Enterprise.* 14: 22 (Aug 83)

Black Managers In Corporate America: A Good Fit? Notes, tables. Regina Nixon. *The Urban League Review.* 07: 44-57 (Summer 83)

Party Politics! Liz Moore. *Essence.* 14: 32 (Dec 83)

Regional And Industry Differences In The Employment Of Minority Managers. Notes, tables. Johnnie Daniel. *The Urban League Review.* 07: 74-90 (Summer 83)

Strategy Sessions For Corporate Success. Illustrated. Jan Alexander. *Black Enterprise.* 14: 61-62+ (Aug 83)

Struggling In The Mainstream: An Excerpt From Black Life In Corporate America. Excerpt, Illustrated. George Davis and Glegg Watson. *Black Collegian*. 14: 58-64 (Nov-Dec 83)

See Also Women Executives

Exercise

Body Strategy. Illustrated. *Ebony*. 38: 108-110+ (Jan 83)

Sweat Without Tears. Illustrated. Evalyn Kaufman. *Black Enterprise*. 14: 74+ (Sep 83)

Existentialism In Literature

Facing The Abyss: The Floating Opera And End Of The Road. Notes. Ben Satterfield. *CLA Journal*. 26: 341-352 (Mar 83)

Expectation (Psychology)

Great Expectations. Illustrated. Judy Simmons. *Essence*. 13: 64+ (Feb 83)

Explorers

Matt Henson: Black Explorer Is Part Of Controversy In Flim 'Race To The Pole'. Illustrated. Thad Martin. *Ebony*. 39: 80-82+ (Nov 83)

F.B.I.

See United States—Federal Bureau Of Investigation

Fabre, Geneviève

Le Thèâtre Noir Aux États-Unis. Book review. Andrzej Ceynowa. *Black American Literature Forum*. 17: 95-96 (Summer 83)

Fabre, Geneviève

The Free Southern Theatre, 1963-1979. Notes. *Black American Literature Forum*. 17: 55-59 (Summer 83)

Fadahunsi, Patrick Kola

Gastric Cancer In An Urban Hospital: A 25-Year Review. Notes. *National Medical Association Journal*. 75: 623-625 (Jun 83)

Fader, Shirley Sloan

How To Get Paid What You're Worth. Illustrated. *Essence*. 14: 81+ (Jun 83)

Faduma, Orishatukeh (1857?-1946) (about)

Orishatukeh Faduma: A Man Of Two Worlds. Notes. Rina L. Okonkwo. *Journal of Negro History*. 68: 24-36 (Winter 83)

Faggins, Barbara

Teddy Pendergrass Cheered At First Public Appearance Since Paralyzing Accident. Illustrated. *Jet*. 63: 62-64 (28 Feb 83)

Fair Housing Act Of 1968

Havens Realty Corp. V. Coleman: Standing To Sue Under The Fair Housing Act. Notes. Terry L. White. *Black Law Journal*. 08: 127-131 (Spring 83)

Faith

How To Believe If The Worst Should Come. Samuel D. Proctor. *Journal of Religious Thought*. 40: 34-44 (Spring-Summer 83)

You've Got To Believe. Editorial. Susan L. Taylor. *Essence*. 14: 67 (Dec 83)

Falana, Lola (about)

Lola Falana: On Tour With Sexy Show And Witty Thoughts. Illustrated. Robert E. Johnson. *Jet*. 64: 58-61 (18 Jul 83)

Falconer-Blake, Martha

Unemployment Is Not Leisure.. *Crisis*. 90: 41 (Jan 83)

Family

African Patterns In The Afro-American Family. Illustrated, notes. Herbert J. Foster. *Journal of Black Studies*. 14: 201-232 (Dec 83)

Black Families In White Suburbs Retain Positive Image - Study Shows.. *Crisis*. 90: 39 (Dec 83)

An Evaluation Of Black Family Life. Editorial. Carolyne S. Blount. *about. . . time*. 11: 4 (Sep 83)

Improving The Quality Of Family Life. Frances M. Mazique. *National Medical Association Journal*. 75: 123 (Feb 83)

Leaves From Our Family Tree. Illustrated. Jessica Harris. *Black Enterprise*. 14: 77-79 (Aug 83)

Test Your Family Values. Illustrated. Carolyne S. Blount. *about. . . time*. 11: 8-9 (Sep 83)

Through A Magnifying Glass: An Examination Of Family Relations. Illustrated. Adolph Dupree. *about. . . time*. 11: 14-20+ (Sep 83)

See Also Brothers And Sisters
Fathers
Marriage
Mothers
Parent And Child
Parenthood
Quintuplets
Single-Parent Family
Twins

Family In Literature

The Motif Of The Ancestor In The Conservationist . Notes. Michael Thorpe. *Research in African Literatures*. 14: 184-192 (Summer 83)

Family Life Education

Family Life Education: Strengthening Family Life Through Counseling. Interview, Illustrated. Martha A. DeLain and Carolyne S. Blount. *about. . . time*. 11: 10-13+ (Sep 83)

Famuyiwa, Oluwole O. and Ekpo, Michael

The Othello Syndrome. Notes. *National Medical Association Journal*. 75: 207-209 (Feb 83)

Farm Ownership

Agriculture Secretary Says Special Task Force To Study Decline In Black Farms. Illustrated. *Jet*. 64: 6-7 (9 May 83)

The Decline Of Black Farming In America: A Call To Alert. Notes. Kenneth A. Glenn. *Black Law Journal*. 08: 292-305 (Fall 83)

Farrakhan, Louis

Minister Louis Farrakhan's Stirring Address. Illustrated. *Black Collegian*. 14: 36-37 (Nov-Dec 83)

Farrell, Walter C. (Jr.) and others

Genocide Fears In A Rural Black Community: An Empirical Examination. Notes, tables. *Journal of Black Studies*. 14: 49-67 (Sep 83)

Farris, Vera King (about)

New Jersey Gets First Black Woman President At Stockton State College. Illustrated, first facts. *Jet*. 64: 23 (20 Jun 83)

Fashion

Action Wear For Active People. Illustrated. Eunice W. Johnson. *Ebony*. 38: 108-110+ (Jun 83)

Career Connections. Illustrated. *Essence*. 14: 76-81 (Aug 83)

Closing The Gap With Look Alikes. Illustrated. Eunice W. Johnson. *Ebony*. 38: 126-128+ (Apr 83)

The Drama Of Italian Couture. Illustrated. Eunice W. Johnson. *Ebony*. 39: 120-122+ (Nov 83)

The Ebony Man: Selecting A Suit For All Seasons. Illustrated. *Ebony*. 38: 114 (Oct 83)

Everybody's Perfect. Illustrated. *Essence*. 14: 62-63+ (Aug 83)

Expression Of Grand Elegance. Illustrated. Eunice W. Johnson. *Ebony*. 38: 116-118 (Sep 83)

Fashion's Best From Europe. Illustrated. Eunice W. Johnson. *Ebony*. 39: 108-110+ (Dec 83)

Getting Suited For The Work Force. Illustrated. *Essence*. 14: 78-85 (Nov 83)

It's Leather Weather! Illustrated. *Essence*. 14: 66-74 (Sep 83)

Italian Ready-To-Wear: A Vintage Year. Illustrated. Eunice W. Johnson. *Ebony*. 38: 100-102 (Jul 83)

Men's Fall Fashions. Illustrated. Alfred (Jr.) Fornay. *Ebony*. 38: 124-126+ (Oct 83)

A New Direction: Summer Couture From Paris 1983. Illustrated. Eunice W. Johnson. *Ebony*. 38: 136-138+ (May 83)

Performance In Black And White. Illustrated. Eunice W. Johnson. *Ebony*. 38: 96-98+ (Feb 83)

The Resort Look Cool And Casual. Illustrated. *Ebony*. 38: 68+ (Apr 83)

Rhapsody In Black. Illustrated. *Essence*. 14: 80-92 (Dec 83)

Sunsational Beachwear. Illustrated. Eunice W. Johnson. *Ebony*. 38: 70-72+ (Jan 83)

Urban Casuals And Classics. Illustrated. *Ebony*. 38: 148-150 (Aug 83)

5'4" And Under: Fashions For The Petite Figure. Illustrated. Eunice W. Johnson. *Ebony*. 38: 110-112 (Oct 83)

See Also Men's Clothing

Fasion Models

See Models, Fashion

Fasting

See Also Starvation

Fathers

A Father For All Seasons. Illustrated. Frank (III) White. *Ebony*. 38: 112-114+ (Aug 83)

I Had To Make Many Adjustments Trying To Build A Relationship With A Woman Who Was A Mother. Illustrated. Peter Harris. *Essence*. 14: 31 (Oct 83)

See Also Divorced Fathers

Fathers And Daughters

Fathers And Daughters. Mari P. Saunders. *Essence*. 14: 85-86+ (Aug 83)

Fathers And Daughters: The Men Behind Their Success. Illustrated. Pamela Noel. *Ebony*. 39: 124+ (Dec 83)

Shari And Harry. Illustrated. Michele Wallace. *Essence*. 14: 82-83 (Aug 83)

Fathers And Sons

"This Culture Fosters The View That Men Are Supposed To Leave Children, Not Assume Responsibility For Them". Illustrated. Wesley Brown. *Essence*. 14: 22 (Jun 83)

Faulkner, William (1897-1962)—Criticism And Interpretation

Dilsey: Faulkner's Black Mammy In The Sound And The Fury. Notes. Sandra D. Milloy. *Negro History Bulletin*. 46: 70-71 (Jul-Sep 83)

Faulkner's Image Of Blacks In Go Down, Moses. Notes. Dorothy L. Denniston. *Phylon*. 44: 33-43 (Mar 83)

Fauset, Jessie (1882-1961) (about)

Jessie Fauset Of The Crisis: Novelist, Feminist, Centenarian. Illustrated. Joseph J. Feeney. *Crisis*. 90: 20+ (Jun-Jul 83)

Fax, Elton C.

Reflections On A Journey To Southern India.. *Freedomways*. 23: No. 01: 14-16 (83)

Federal Aid To Minority Business Enterprises

8(A) Graduates: Unwilling Victims Of Success? Illustrated. Bebe Campbell Moore. *Black Enterprise*. 13: 49-50 (Jun 83)

Federal Aid To The Theater

Leonard De Paur And The WPA Theatre. Glenda E. Gill. *Freedomways*. 23: No. 4: 240-242 (83)

Federal Bureau Of Investigation

See United States—Federal Bureau Of Investigation

Federal Government

Federalism, "Civil Rights" And Black Progress. Notes. Ronald W. Walters. *Black Law Journal*. 08: 220-234 (Fall 83)

Nationalism, Federalism And Political Consensus. Notes. Linda S. Greene. *Black Law Journal*. 08: 399-407 (Winter 83)

The New Federalism And The Unfinished Civil Rights Agenda. Notes. Marguerite Ross Barnett. *Black Law Journal*. 08: 375-386 (Winter 83)

Federal Theatre Project

Leonard De Paur And The WPA Theatre. Glenda E. Gill. *Freedomways*. 23: No. 4: 240-242 (83)

Federalism

See Federal Government

Feeney, Joseph J.

Jessie Fauset Of The Crisis: Novelist, Feminist, Centenarian. Illustrated. *Crisis*. 90: 20+ (Jun-Jul 83)

Felder, Cain H.

New Testament Apocalyptic. Book review. *Journal of Religious Thought*. 39: 72-73 (Fall-Winter 83)

Partiality And God's Law: An Exegesis Of James 2:1-13. Notes. *Journal of Religious Thought*. 39: 51-69 (Fall-Winter 83)

Paul's Reinterpretation Of Jewish Apocalypticism: A Faculty Response To J. Christian Beker. Notes. *Journal of Religious Thought*. 40: 18-22 (Spring-Summer 83)

Felix, Catherine

Black Woman. Poem. *Black American Literature Forum*. 17: 170-171 (Winter 83)

Fellowships

See Scholarships

Felton, Reginald

The Advantages Of Working For The Federal Government.. *Black Collegian*. 13: 72+ (Apr-May 83)

Feminism

Black Feminism In Indiana, 1893-1933. Notes. Erlene Stetson. *Phylon*. 44: 292-298 (Dec 83)

Black Women, White Women: Separate Paths To Liberation. Notes. Elizabeth F. Hood. *Black Scholar*. 14: 26-37 (Sep-Oct 83)

Racism And Anti-Feminism.Chisholm Shirley. *Black Scholar*. 14: 2-7 (Sep-Oct 83)

See Also Women's Rights

Ferdinand, Val

See Salaam, Kalamu Ya

Ferguson, Linda Taylor (about)

Profiles: Linda Taylor Ferguson. Portrait. Sandra K. Mitchell. *Black Law Journal*. 08: 144-146 (Spring 83)

Foreword [To Vol. 8 No.1]. Notes. *Black Law Journal*. 08: 4-6 (Spring 83)

Fergusson, Isaac

Rita Marley: Showstopper. Illustrated. *Essence*. 14: 51 (Jul 83)

See George, Nelson

Ferman, Irving

The Brandeis/Frankfurter Connection. Book review, Notes. *Howard Law Journal*. 26: No. 1: 345-358 (83)

Fernandez, Elizabeth

Virna Canson: Fighting Fire With Fire. Illustrated. *Crisis*. 90: 26+ (Jun-Jul 83)

Ferris, William

Folk Music And Modern Sound. Book review. Doris Evans McGinty. *The Black Perspective in Music*. 11: 212-214 (Fall 83)

Ferry, Henry Justin

Gifts Of Power: The Writings Or Rebecca Jackson. Book review. *Journal of Religious Thought*. 39: 71-72 (Fall-Winter 83)

Festivals

See Also Music Festivals

Fiction

See Also Nigerian Fiction

Fiction—History And Criticism

The Achievement Of William Demby. Notes. Jay R. Berry. *CLA Journal*. 26: 434-451 (Jun 83)

Authorial Displacement In Herman Melville's "The Piazza". Notes. Michael Clark. *CLA Journal*. 27: 69-80 (Sep 83)

Beyond Mimetic Exhaustion: The Reflex And Bone Structure Experiment. Notes. Larry D. Bradfield. *Black American Literature Forum*. 17: 120-123 (Fall 83)

Imagery Of Imprisonment In Ralph Ellison's Invisible Man. Notes. Per Winther. *Black American Literature Forum*. 17: 115-119 (Fall 83)

Loomings Of An Awakened Consciousness: Mardi, A Reinterpretation. Notes. Khalil Husni. *CLA Journal*. 27: 56-68 (Sep 83)

Repeated Images In Part One Of Cane. Notes. Herbert W. Rice. *Black American Literature Forum*. 17: 100-105 (Fall 83)

Fiction—Technique

Miltons's Choices: Styron's Use Of Robert Frost's Poetry In Lie Down In Darkness. Notes. Judith Ruderman. *CLA Journal*. 27: 141-151 (Dec 83)

Fiction—Themes, Motives

Roots And The Heroic Search For Identity. Notes. Helen Chavis Othow. *CLA Journal*. 26: 311-324 (Mar 83)

Fiction, West Indian—Themes, Motives

Complacency And Community: Psychocultural Patterns In The West Indian Novel. Notes. Melvin B. Rahming. *CLA Journal*. 26: 288-302 (Mar 83)

Field, Phyllis F.

The Politics Of Race In New York: The Struggle For Black Suffrage In The Civil War. Book review. Charles T. Haley. *Journal of Negro History*. 68: 125-126 (Winter 83)

Fields Kim (about)

Showstopper: Kim Fields. Illustrated. Craig Reid. *Essence.* 14: 47 (Aug 83)

Fields, Mike

Betting It All Together. Book review. Paula S. White. *Essence.* 14: 48 (Nov 83)

Fiji—Description And Travel

A South Pacific Island Paradise. Illustrated. Christina Jackson. *about. . . time.* 11: 22-23 (Dec 83)

Finance, Personal

All About Credit.. *Essence.* 14: 78-79 + (Jun 83)

Bankruptcy: Is It The Answer To Your Money Problems? Phil W. Petrie. *Essence.* 14: 24 + (Jun 83)

The Bonanza In Tax-free Bonds. Illustrated. Udayan Gupta. *Black Enterprise.* 14: 31 (Aug 83)

Choosing A Financial Planner. Udayan Gupta. *Black Enterprise.* 14: 41 (Dec 83)

Countdown To Tax Time. Flora Johnson. *Black Enterprise.* 14: 67-68 + (Nov 83)

Grocery-Shopping Make-Over. Illustrated. Sally Sherwin. *Essence.* 13: 98 (Jan 83)

A Home Of Your Own-Buy Or Rent? Illustrated. Udayan Gupta. *Black Enterprise.* 13: 26 (Jul 83)

How To Get That Bank Loan. Renee Michael. *Black Enterprise.* 14: 43-44 + (Sep 83)

Initial Public Stock Offerings The Start Of Something Big. Illustrated. Udayan Gupta. *Black Enterprise.* 13: 61 (Jun 83)

Keep Your Health Insurance Package Up To Date. Illustrated. Udayan Gupta. *Black Enterprise.* 13: 31 (May 83)

Maneuvering Through The Mortgage Maze. Hershel Lee Johnson. *Black Enterprise.* 14: 80-82 + (Dec 83)

Money Is The Root Of All Evil. . . And Other Bad Ideas That Keep Us Poor. Audrey Edwards. *Essence.* 14: 72-73 (Jun 83)

Money Management: There Is A Better Way. Illustrated. Joy Duckett. *Essence.* 14: 74-75 + (Jun 83)

Money Power! Editorial. Susan L. Taylor. *Essence.* 14: 71 (Jun 83)

Mutual Funds Make Good Investments In A Rising Market. Illustrated. Udayan Gupta. *Black Enterprise.* 13: 35 (Feb 83)

Mutual Funds With Social Conscience. Udayan Gupta. *Black Enterprise.* 14: 35 (Nov 83)

On The Money: When A Collector Gets On Your Case. . . . Aurelia Toyer Miller and Ruth Dolores Manuel. *Essence.* 14: 21 (May 83)

Sharing Two Incomes: How To Make It Work. Aurelia Toyer Miller. *Essence.* 13: 38 + (Mar 83)

Shopping The Financial Supermarkets. Tables. Udayan Gupta. *Black Enterprise.* 14: 59-60 + (Oct 83)

Should You Buy Your Own Phone? Stephanie Stokes Oliver and Vanessa J. Gallman. *Essence.* 13: 124 (Mar 83)

Stock Market Outlook. Illustrated. Udayan Gupta. *Black Enterprise.* 14: 69-70 + (Oct 83)

Surviving A Tax Audit. Illustrated. Udayan Gupta. *Black Enterprise.* 14: 29 (Sep 83)

Taking A Second Mortgage Or Refinancing Your Home For Extra Cash. Illustrated. Udayan Gupta. *Black Enterprise.* 13: 31 (Apr 83)

Teaching Your Kids The Financial Facts Of Life. Illustrated. Pamela Douglas. *Black Enterprise.* 14: 106-108 + (Oct 83)

Turning Tykes On To Dow Jones. Udayan Gupta. *Black Enterprise.* 14: 112 (Oct 83)

See Also Investments

Finch, Charles S.

The African Background Of Medical Science. Illustrated, notes. *Journal of African Civilizations.* 05: 140-156 (Apr-Nov 83)

Finch, Minnie

Shadow & Substance: Afro-American Experience In Contemporary Children's Fiction. Book review. *Journal of Negro Education.* 52: 184-185 (Spring 83)

Fine, Jerome L. (joint author)

See Botwin, Carol

First Facts

Air Force Graduates First Black Woman Pilot. By Women Air Pilots and Theresa ClaiborneUnited States. Air Force—Officers. *Ebony.* 38: 46 + (Jan 83)

Air Guard Appoints First Black General. By Russell C. DavisUnited States—Air National Guard. *Jet.* 63: 53 (24 Jan 83)

Author Alice Walker Wins Pulitzer Prize For Novel. By Alice WalkerPulitzer Prizes. *Jet.* 64: 9 (9 May 83)

Baptist Church Appoints First Black Woman Pastor. By Women Clergy. *Jet.* 64: 25 (13 Jun 83)

Black College Leaders Tackle Issues At First PUSH/EXCEL Conference. By Arthur E. Thomas and Inc. Push For Excellence. *Jet.* 63: 40-41 (24 Jan 83)

Black Woman Judge Is Named To Missouri Court. By Evelyn Marie BakerWomen Judges. *Jet.* 64: 30 (2 May 83)

Chicago Mayor Names City's First Black Police Supt. By Fred RicePolice Chiefs. *Jet.* 65: 8 (12 Sep 83)

Columbia, Mo., Gets First Black Police Chief. By Police Chiefs—Missouri and William E. Dye. *Jet.* 63: 57 (10 Jan 83)

Ebony Jr! Celebrates Its Tenth Anniversary With Special May Issue. By Ebony Jr! (Periodical)Childrens Periodicals. *Jet.* 64: 14 + (9 May 83)

First Black Appointed To Virginia Supreme Court. By John Charles ThomasJudges—Virginia. *Jet.* 64: 30 (2 May 83)

First Black Elected As Mayor Of Northwoods, Mo. By Charlie A. DooleyMayors—Missouri—Northwoods. *Jet.* 64: 4 (25 Apr 83)

First Black Elected To Iowa State Senate. By Thomas (Jr.) MannLegislators—Iowa. *Jet.* 63: 6 (10 Jan 83)

First Black Installed As Mayor Of Harvey, Ill. By David JohnsonMayors—Illinois—Harvey. *Jet.* 64: 8 (23 May 83)

Food Stamp Administrator Named Aide To Head Of Department Of Agriculture. By Samuel J. CorneliusUnited States—Officials And Employees. *Jet.* 63: 4 (7 Feb 83)

Guy Bluford: Black Astronaut Makes First Space Mission. By Guion BlufordAstronauts. Reviewed by Clarence Waldron. *Jet.* 64: 20-22 + (5 Sep 83)

Harold Washington Wins Hot Race To Become First Black Mayor Of Chicago. By Harold WashingtonMayors—Illinois—ChicagoChicago—Mayors. *Jet.* 64: 4-6 + (2 May 83)

New Jersey Gets First Black Woman President At Stockton State College. By Vera King FarrisWomen College Presidents. *Jet.* 64: 23 (20 Jun 83)

Two Blacks Win Seats On S. Carolina City Council. By E. W. (II) Cromartie and Luther (III) BattisteCity Councilmen—South Carolina—Columbia City. *Jet.* 64: 4 (25 Apr 83)

Veteran New York Cop Is Named City's First Black Commissioner Of Police. By Benjamin WardPolice Chiefs—New York (State)—New York (City). *Jet.* 65: 12 (28 Nov 83)

Women Cadets Make Coast Guard History. By United States. Coast Guard AcademyWomen College Students. Reviewed by Marilyn Marshall. *Ebony.* 38: 138 + (Apr 83)

Fish As Food

See Also Cookery (Fish)

Fisher, Bob

The Illustrated Encyclopedia Of Black Music. Book review. Doris Evans McGinty. *The Black Perspective in Music.* 11: 212-214 (Fall 83)

Fisher, Miles Mark (about)

Miles Mark Fisher: Minister, Historian And Cultural Philosopher. Illustrated, notes. Lenwood G. Davis. *Negro History Bulletin.* 46: 19-21 (Jan-Mar 83)

Fisher, Paul A. and Neas, Ralph G.

Civil Rights Challenges For The 1980's. Illustrated. *about. . . time.* 11: 10-13 + (May 83)

Fitzgerald, Ella (about)

Jazz Great Ella Fitzgerald Performs In-Flight Concert. Illustrated. Clarence Waldron. *Jet.* 63: 62 + (31 Jan 83)

Flannigan, Arthur

Studies In 20th Century Literature. Book review. *Research in African Literatures.* 14: 121-123 (Spring 83)

Fleissner, Robert F.

New Light On Tennyson's Blackness. Notes. *CLA Journal.* 26: 334-340 (Mar 83)

Fleming, John E.

The Notorious Triangle, Rhode Island And The African Slave Trade, 1700-1807. Book review. *Journal of Negro History.* 68: 113-114 (Winter 83)

Flemming, Cynthia Griggs

The Effect Of Higher Education On Black Tennesseeans After The Civil War. Notes. *Phylon.* 44: 209-216 (Sep 83)

Fletcher, Winona L.

A Slender Thread Of Hope: The Kennedy Center Black Theatre Project. Notes. *Black American Literature Forum.* 17: 65-68 (Summer 83)

Florida

See Also Judges—Florida
Murder—Florida

Florida A&M University—Curricula

The Florida A And M University Preservice And Inservice Multicultural Education Model. Notes, tables. Walter A. Mercer. *Negro Educational Review.* 34: 37-44 (Jan 83)

Flowers, William K.

Ritodrine Use In Placenta Previa. Notes. *National Medical Association Journal.* 75: 427-428 (Apr 83)

Floyd, Samuel

An Oral History: The Great Lakes Experience. Illustrated, notes. *The Black Perspective in Music.* 11: 41-61 (Spring 83)

Flute-Players

Bobbi Humphrey Toots Her Own Flute. Illustrated. Bonnie Allen. *Essence.* 13: 66-68 (Mar 83)

Foley-Davis, Lelia (about)

Her Honor, The Mayor. Illustrated. Julie Chenault. *Essence.* 14: 14 + (Jul 83)

Folk Literature

Black Perceptions And Red Images: Indian And Black Literary Links. Notes. Mary Ellison. *Phylon.* 44: 44-55 (Mar 83)

Folk-Lore

See Also Oral Tradition

Folk-lore In Literature

Folklore And The Creative Artist: Lydia Cabrera And Zora Neale Hurston. Notes. Miriam DeCosta Willis. *CLA Journal.* 27: 81-90 (Sep 83)

Folkloric Aspects Of Wright's "The Man Who Killed A Shadow". Notes. Eugene E. Miller. *CLA Journal.* 27: 210-223 (Dec 83)

Folk Medicine

Root Doctors As Providers Of Primary Care. Notes. Van J. (Jr.) Stitt. *National Medical Association Journal*. 75: 719-721 (Jul 83)

Football

The USFL: A Whole New Ball Game. Illustrated. *Ebony*. 38: 33-34+ (Jun 83)

Football Coaches

Eddie Robinson: Grambling's Living Legend. Illustrated. Walter Leavy. *Ebony*. 38: 60-62+ (Jan 83)

Grambling Grabs Title, Coach Robinson Becomes Third All-Time Winner. Illustrated. *Jet*. 65: 44-45 (19 Dec 83)

Football Players

Darryl Stingley: Happy To Be Alive. Illustrated. Darryl Stingley. *Ebony*. 38: 68+ (Oct 83)

Football's Controversial Multimillion Dollar Man. Illustrated. Norman O. Unger. *Jet*. 64: 46-48+ (4 Apr 83)

Marcus Allen: Raider Running Back May Be The Best Ever In The NFL. Illustrated. *Ebony*. 39: 143-144+ (Nov 83)

Rozier Gets Early Xmas, 10th Straight Black To Win Coveted Heisman Trophy. Illustrated. *Jet*. 65: 48 (26 Dec 83)

Running For The Money. Illustrated. Roger Witherspoon. *Black Enterprise*. 13: 18 (May 83)

Ford Foundation

Aid For Poor Kids. Michael Beaubien. *Black Enterprise*. 13: 20 (Apr 83)

Essence Man: Franklin Thomas. Illustrated. Eric Copage. *Essence*. 14: 40 (Nov 83)

Ford, Harold E. (about)

Federal Budget: Harold E. Ford (D. Tenn.). Illustrated. Bebe Moore Campbell. *Black Enterprise*. 14: 54 (Oct 83)

Ford, Nick Aaron (1904-1982) (about)

In Memoriam: Nick Aaron Ford (1904-1982). Therman B. O'Daniel. *Black American Literature Forum*. 17: 99 (Fall 83)

Foreign Service

See Diplomatic And Consular Service

Foreign Trade And Employment

Auto Trade Policy: What It Means For African-Americans. Notes. Emory West. *The Urban League Review*. 07: 100-112 (Summer 83)

Foreman, George (about)

Ex-Champ George Foreman Donates Title Belt, Robe To Job Corps, LBJ Library. Illustrated. *Jet*. 65: 30-31 (21 Nov 83)

Fornay, Alfred

Fragrance: The Perfect Holiday Gift. Illustrated. *Ebony*. 39: 126-128+ (Nov 83)

Fornay, Alfred (Jr.)

The Best Of Fall. Illustrated. *Ebony*. 38: 146-148+ (Sep 83)

A Grooming Guide For Black Men. Illustrated. *Ebony*. 38: 140-142+ (Aug 83)

Men's Fall Fashions. Illustrated. *Ebony*. 38: 124-126+ (Oct 83)

Speaking of Lips: Luscious, Voluptuous Lips. . . Are In. Illustrated. *Ebony*. 38: 94-96+ (Jan 83)

Spring Radiance. Illustrated. *Ebony*. 38: 146-148+ (Apr 83)

Foster-Davis, Frankie (joint author)

See Reid, Herbert O. (Sr.)

Foster, Herbert J.

African Patterns In The Afro-American Family. Illustrated, notes. *Journal of Black Studies*. 14: 201-232 (Dec 83)

Fournier, Collette (joint author)

See Wilson, Robin

Fourth World

See Underdeveloped Areas

Foxx, Redd (about)

Redd Foxx And Smokey Robinson Reveal Sides They Have Kept Private. Illustrated. *Jet*. 64: 56-58 (8 Aug 83)

France—Colonies

Brown France Vs. Black Africa: The Tide Turned In 1932. Notes. Martin Steins. *Research in African Literatures*. 14: 474-497 (Winter 83)

Frances, Hector

The War Of Terror Against Nicaragua. Illustrated. *Black Scholar*. 14: 2-16 (Mar-Apr 83)

Franchises (Retail Trade)

Voulez-Vous Un Big Mac? Illustrated. Wendell Gault. *Black Enterprise*. 14: 39 (Dec 83)

Francis, Cleveland (about)

Juggling Careers In Medicine And Music. Illustrated. Frank (III) White. *Ebony*. 38: 156-158 (Oct 83)

Francis, Norman and Rouselle, William

A Nation At Risk: A Black Perspective On American Education: An Interview With Norman Francis. Interview, Illustrated. *Black Collegian*. 14: 69-72 (Nov-Dec 83)

Franklin, Vincent P.

White Supremacy: A Comparative Study In American And South African History. Book review. *Phylon*. 44: 160-163 (Jun 83)

Franklin, Yvette and Rouselle, William

How Placement Copes When Recruiters Don't Come. Illustrated. *Black Collegian*. 13: 20+ (Apr-May 83)

Job Outlook '83 Gloomy With A Ray Of Hope. Illustrated. *Black Collegian*. 13: 112+ (Feb-Mar 83)

Outlook For Liberal Arts Majors. Illustrated. *Black Collegian*. 13: 20-22 (Dec-Jan 83)

Fraser, C. Gerald

A Great Artist Passes. Illustrated. *Black Enterprise*. 14: 22 (Aug 83)

Fraser, Walter J. (Jr.)

From The Old South To The New: Essays On The Transitional South. Book review. H. Leon (Sr.) Prather. *Journal of Negro History*. 68: 120-122 (Winter 83)

Frazier, E. Franklin (about)

On Reconsidering Park, Johnson, DuBois, Frazier And Reid: Reply To Benjamin Bowser's "The Contribution Of Blacks To Sociological Knowledge.". Notes. Jerry G. Watts. *Phylon*. 44: 273-291 (Dec 83)

Frederickson, George

White Supremacy: A Comparative Study In American And South African History. Book review. Vincent P. Franklin. *Phylon*. 44: 160-163 (Jun 83)

Fredland, Richard A.

Integration And Disintegration In East Africa. Book review. Frank M. Chiteji. *Review of Black Political Economy*. 12: 243-245 (Winter 83)

Free Southern Theatre

The Free Southern Theatre, 1963-1979. Notes. Genevieve Fabre. *Black American Literature Forum*. 17: 55-59 (Summer 83)

Freydberg, Elizabeth Hadley

The Concealed Dependence Upon White Culture In Baraka's 1969 Aesthetic. Notes. *Black American Literature Forum*. 17: 27-29 (Spring 83)

Fried, Eunice

The Art Of Savoring Wine. Illustrated. *Black Enterprise*. 14: 104 (Nov 83)

Beaujolais Wine Of Spring. Illustrated. *Black Enterprise*. 13: 78 (Apr 83)

Bordeaux: A Grand Red. Illustrated. *Black Enterprise*. 13: 112 (Feb 83)

A Rose Is A Rose Is A Rose. Illustrated. *Black Enterprise*. 14: 82 (Aug 83)

Rum: Choice Of The Islands. Illustrated. *Black Enterprise*. 13: 76+ (May 83)

Spicy Foods, Racy Wines. Illustrated. *Black Enterprise*. 14: 70+ (Sep 83)

Spirited Summer Drinks. Illustrated. *Black Enterprise*. 13: 66 (Jul 83)

Touring Napa Valley Wine Country. Illustrated. *Black Enterprise*. 13: 264 (Jun 83)

The Warming Glow Of Cognac. Illustrated. *Black Enterprise*. 13: 60 (Jan 83)

What You'd Like To Know About Scotch. Illustrated. *Black Enterprise*. 14: 140 (Oct 83)

Wines Of The Veneto. Illustrated. *Black Enterprise*. 13: 84 (Mar 83)

Friedland, Elaine A.

The South African Freedom Movement: Factors Influencing Its Ideological Development, 1912-1980s. Notes. *Journal of Black Studies*. 13: 337-354 (Mar 83)

Friendship

Can Women And Men Be Friends? Illustrated. Rosemary L. Bray. *Essence*. 14: 71-72+ (Jul 83)

Fugard, Athol—Criticism And Interpretation

Journey Toward Light: Athol Fugard's Tsotsi . Notes. Robert M. Post. *CLA Journal*. 26: 415-421 (Jun 83)

Fulahs—Education

The Effect Of Mobile Group Counseling On Nomadic Fulani's Attitudes Toward Formal Education. Notes, tables. Daniel I. Denga. *Journal of Negro Education*. 52: 170-175 (Spring 83)

Full Employment Policies—United States

The Employment Challenge: A Job For Every Worker. Illustrated. Bernard E. Anderson. *Black Enterprise*. 13: 24 (Jan 83)

Fuller, Charles (about)

The Descent Of Charlie Fuller Into Pulitzerland And The Need For African-American Institutions. Amiri Baraka. *Black American Literature Forum*. 17: 51-54 (Summer 83)

Furman, Roger (about)

The Magic Of Technical Theatre. Illustrated. A. Peter Bailey. *Black Collegian*. 14: 75+ (Sep-Oct 83)

Futrell, Jon

The Illustrated Encyclopedia Of Black Music. Book review. Doris Evans McGinty. *The Black Perspective in Music*. 11: 212-214 (Fall 83)

Futrell, Mary (about)

Teachers Union Boss. Illustrated. *Ebony*. 38: 140+ (Oct 83)

Futrell, Mary Hatwood (about)

Essense Women: Mary Hatwood Futrell. Illustrated. Celeste Bullock. *Essence*. 14: 38 (Nov 83)

Mary Hatwood Futrell: Top Teacher. Illustrated. Steve Askin. *Black Enterprise*. 14: 124-126+ (Oct 83)

Gérard, Albert S.

African Language Literatures: An Introduction To The Literary History Of Sub-Saharan Africa. Book review. Vladimír Klíma. *Research in African Literatures*. 14: 200-202 (Summer 83)

Gabbin, Joanne Veal (joint author)

See Coleman, James W.

Gaines-Carter, Patrice

Going To College On Uncle Sam. Illustrated. *Black Enterprise*. 13: 79-80+ (Feb 83)

Keeping Your Child Afloat. Illustrated. *Black Enterprise*. 13: 272+ (Jun 83)

The Price Of Integration. Illustrated. *Essence*. 14: 150 (Jul 83)

Gaines, Ernest

A Gathering Of Old Men [Excerpt]. Novel. *Black Scholar*. 14: 42-49 (Summer 83)

Galimore, Ron (about)

Introducing: Ron Galimore. Illustrated. *Ebony*. 38: 42+ (Jan 83)

Gallman, Vanessa

Are Discount Long-Distance Services All They're Wired Up To Be? Illustrated. *Essence*. 14: 120 (May 83)

Gallman, Vanessa J.

What To Say When Someone Tells You, 'It Pays To Be A Black Woman'.. *Essence*. 13: 89-90 (Mar 83)

Working Temp: Temporary Jobs Now Offer Full-Time Benefits And Other Options. Illustrated. *Essence*. 14: 36 (Jun 83)
Oliver, Stephanie Stokes

Gambhir, Kanwal K. and others

Effect Of Storage On Insulin Receptor Binding In Human Erythrocytes. Tables, notes. *National Medical Association Journal*. 75: 503-507 (May 83)

Gambian Epic Poetry

See Epic Poetry, Gambian

Gambling—New Jersey—Atlantic City

Will The Gamble Pay Off? Illustrated. Nelson George. *Black Enterprise*. 13: 58-60+ (Mar 83)

Games

A "Kontrast" In Card Games. Illustrated. Lloyd Gite. *Black Enterprise*. 14: 32 (Dec 83)

Playing With Black History. Illustrated. *Black Enterprise*. 14: 32 (Dec 83)

See Also Educational Games

García-Barrio, Constance

Grant Master In A Flash.. *Essence*. 14: 16 (Aug 83)

Real Life 101: What You've Learned In Life May Be Worth College Credits.. *Essence*. 14: 36 (Jul 83)

Garcia-Barrio, Constance

Preparing Your Child For A Hospital Stay.. *Essence*. 14: 136 (Oct 83)

Speak Easy: Making Presentations Without Falling Apart.. *Essence*. 13: 34+ (Apr 83)

Gardner, Edward G. (about)

Give The Man A Hand. Illustrated. Ruth Dolores Manuel. *Essence*. 14: 54 (Jul 83)

Gardner, Kevin (joint author)

See Watkins, Levi (Jr.)

Garland, Brock

"Selecting A Mate And Having Children Means Commitment And An End To Self-Indulgence". Illustrated. *Essence*. 14: 27 (Dec 83)

Garland Enterprises

Garland Lands Nigeria Deal. Illustrated. Jill Nelson. *Black Enterprise*. 13: 25 (Feb 83)

Garner, Thurmon

Cooperative Communication Strategies: Observations In A Black Community. Notes, bibliography. *Journal of Black Studies*. 14: 233-250 (Dec 83)

Garnet, Henry Highland (1815-1882) (about)

Henry Highland Garnet Revisited Via His Diplomatic Correspondence: The Correction Of Misconceptions And Errors. Notes. Hanes (Jr.) Walton and others. *Journal of Negro History*. 68: 80-92 (Winter 83)

Garrison, George R.

Historical Traditions In Civil Dissent And Their Corresponding Conceptions Of Law. Notes. *Black Law Journal*. 08: 198-219 (Fall 83)

Garrison, Zina (about)

Essence Women: Zina Garrison. Illustrated. Elizabeth Wheeler. *Essence*. 13: 30 (Mar 83)

Garrow, David J.

The FBI And Martin Luther King, Jr. Book review. Gerald C. Horne. *Freedomways*. 23: No. 4: 290-294 (83)

Garth-Taylor, Mikki and White, Paula S.

Put Your Best Self Forward. Illustrated. *Essence*. 13: 69+ (Jan 83)

Garvey, Marcus M. (1887-1940) (about)

Henrietta Vinton Davis And The Garvey Movement. Notes. William Seraile. *Afro-Americans in New York Life and History*. 07: 7-24 (Jul 83)

Gates, Henry-Louis (Jr.)

The Art Of Slave Narrative: Original Essays In Criticism And Theory. Book review. *Black American Literature Forum*. 17: 131-134 (Fall 83)

The Terrible Twos. Book review. *Black Enterprise*. 13: 16 (Apr 83)

Gatlin, June (about)

Psychic June Gatlin Looks 1984. Patrice Miles. *Essence*. 14: 79+ (Dec 83)

The Song. Poem. *Essence*. 13: 17 (Jan 83)

Gault, Wendell

Voulez-Vous Un Big Mac? Illustrated. *Black Enterprise*. 14: 39 (Dec 83)

Gavin, Claire

Laser Technology: An Engineering Area Of The Future. Illustrated. *Black Collegian*. 13: 62+ (Dec-Jan 83)

Gay, Geneva

Perspectives In Multicultural Education. Book review. *Journal of Negro Education*. 52: 461-463 (Fall 83)

Gaye, Marvin (about)

Marvin Gaye: Talks About His Troubled Life. Illustrated. Robert E. Johnson. *Jet.* 64: 56-60 (15 Aug 83)

What's Going On With Marvin Gaye? Illustrated. David Ritz. *Essence.* 13: 58-60+ (Jan 83)

Gayle, Misani

Carnival In Trinidad And Tobago. Illustrated. *Black Enterprise.* 13: 78 (Mar 83)

Genealogists

Essence Women: Sandi Brewster-Walker. Illustrated. Sid Cassese. *Essence.* 13: 22+ (Apr 83)

Genet, Jean—Criticism And Interpretation

Les Négres: A Look At Genet's Excursion Into Black Consciousnes. Notes. Keith Q. Warner. *CLA Journal.* 26: 397-414 (Jun 83)

Genocide—Psychological Aspects—Research

Genocide Fears In A Rural Black Community: An Empirical Examination. Notes, tables. Walter C. (Jr.) Farrell and others. *Journal of Black Studies.* 14: 49-67 (Sep 83)

Gentemann, Karen M. and Whitehead, Tony L.

The Cultural Broker Concept In Bicultural Education. Notes. *Journal of Negro Education.* 52: 118-129 (Spring 83)

Gentleman, Kirstie

African-American Contributions To Information Technology. Illustrated. *Journal of African Civilizations.* 05: 273-292 (Apr-Nov 83)

George, Herman (Jr.)

Black Violence: Political Impact Of The 1960s Riots. Book review. *Afro-Americans in New York Life and History.* 07: 72-73 (Jul 83)

George, Michael

Traveling Music.. *Black Enterprise.* 14: 86+ (Nov 83)

George, Nelson

Caring For Records And Tapes. Illustrated. *Essence.* 14: 54 (Jun 83)

My 'Dream Girl' Is Beautiful, Smart, Ambitious, But Can I Deal With Her In Real Life? Illustrated. *Essence.* 14: 14 (Aug 83)

The New Bidding Game In Sports. Illustrated. *Black Enterprise.* 13: 28-32 (Jan 83)

Riffs For A Summer Day. Illustrated. *Black Enterprise.* 13: 68 (Jul 83)

Will The Gamble Pay Off? Illustrated. *Black Enterprise.* 13: 58-60+ (Mar 83)
Hilliard, S. Lee

George, Nelson and Fergusson, Isaac

Jamming In Jamaica. Illustrated. *Black Enterprise.* 13: 59-60+ (May 83)

Georges-Abeyie, Daniel E.

The Social Ecology Of Bomb Threats: Dallas, Texas. Notes, tables. *Journal of Black Studies.* 13: 305-320 (Mar 83)

Georgia

See Also Capital Punishment—Georgia Legislators—Georgia

Gerardi, Robert J. (joint author)

See Benedict, Gary C.

Gerber, David A.

Ethnic Relations In America. Book review. Notes. *Afro-Americans in New York Life and History.* 07: 75-76 (Jul 83)

Ghana

See Also Teachers Of Handicapped Children, Training Of—Ghana

Gibbs, James

Critical Perspectives On Wole Soyinka. Book review. T. V. Prakash. *Research in African Literatures.* 14: 102-107 (Spring 83)

Ake, The Years Of Childhood. Book review. *Research in African Literatures.* 14: 98-102 (Spring 83)

Tear The Painted Masks; Join The Poison Stains: A Preliminary Study Of Wole Soyinka's Writings For The Nigerian Press. Notes. *Research in African Literatures.* 14: 3-44 (Spring 83)

Gibbs, Marla (about)

Marla Gibbs. Illustrated. Craig W. Reid. *Essence.* 13: 15 (Mar 83)

Gibbs, Tyson (joint author)

See McLean, Archie H.

Gibson, Kenneth A. and Dupree, Adolph

Kenneth Allen Gibson: Mayor Of Newark, New Jersey. Interview, Illustrated. *about. . . time.* 11: 10-13+ (Jul 83)

Gifted Children

Gifted Children: How To Recognize Them And Help Them Reach Their Potential. Illustrated. *Ebony.* 38: 123-124+ (Sep 83)

Gifted Children—Education

When Your Child Is Young, Gifted And Black. Illustrated. Dennis Williams. *Black Enterprise.* 14: 68-69 (Sep 83)

Giles, Llewellyn Ivory

Songs From My Father's Pockets. Book review. Adam David Miller. *Black American Literature Forum.* 17: 179-180 (Winter 83)

Gill, Chris

The Illustrated Encyclopedia Of Black Music. Book review. Doris Evans McGinty. *The Black Perspective in Music.* 11: 212-214 (Fall 83)

Gill, Glenda E.

Leonard De Paur And The WPA Theatre.. *Freedomways.* 23: No. 4: 240-242 (83)

Gillam, Isaac (IV) (about)

Space Science: The African-American Contribution. Illustrated. Curtis M. Graves and Ivan Van Sertima. *Journal of African Civilizations.* 05: 238-257 (Apr-Nov 83)

Gilliam, Angela M.

An Afro-American Perspective On The Middle
East. Bibliography. *Freedomways*. 23: No. 2: 81-89
(83)

See Patterson, Tiffany R.

Gillis-Olion, Marion (joint author)

See Olion, LaDelle

Giovanni, Nikki

Communication. Poem. *Ebony*. 38: 48 (Feb 83)

I Wrote A Good Omelet. Poem. *Essence*. 14: 88
(Oct 83)

Girls

See Also Youth

Gite, Lloyd

Charles Allen's Declaration Of Independence.
Illustrated, tables. *Black Enterprise*. 13: 113-114 +
(Jun 83)

A Dallas Paralegal Builds Her Own Lucrative
Business. Illustrated. *Essence*. 14: 22 (May 83)

Essence Man: Joe Madison. Illustrated. *Essence*.
14: 38 (Nov 83)

Essence Women: Elta L. Hambrick. Illustrated.
Essence. 14: 54 (Jul 83)

Giving That Winning Presentation. Illustrated.
Black Enterprise. 14: 49-50 + (Sep 83)

How This Sister Turned A Winning Bid Into A
Gold Mine! Illustrated. *Essence*. 14: 31 (Jul 83)

How To Buy A House With A Friend.. *Black
Enterprise*. 13: 57-58 (Jul 83)

Hunger In Detroit. Illustrated. *Black Enterprise*. 13:
19 (Apr 83)

Keeping It In The Family. Illustrated. *Essence*. 14:
36 (Dec 83)

A "Kontrast" In Card Games. Illustrated. *Black
Enterprise*. 14: 32 (Dec 83)

Making That Move: Relocating For A Better Job..
Essence. 13: 32 + (Jan 83)

No Prospects For Work. Illustrated. *Black
Enterprise*. 14: 17 (Aug 83)

Taking Care Of Business. Illustrated. *Essence*. 13:
28 (Jan 83)

Two Women In Houston Turn Their Dreams Of
Owning A Bookstore Into A Successful Reality.
Illustrated. *Essence*. 13: 32 + (Mar 83)

Up, Up And Away. Illustrated. *Essence*. 14: 44
(Oct 83)

Gite, Lloyd and Perry, Jean

Diet Right! Losing Weight Soulfully. Illustrated.
Essence. 14: 117-118 (Aug 83)

Glass, Cheryl (about)

Essence Women: Cheryl Glass. Illustrated. Joy
Duckett. *Essence*. 13: 29 (Mar 83)

Glaucoma

Laser Therapy Of Glaucoma. Tables, illustrated,
notes. Kevin C. Greenidge. *National Medical
Association Journal*. 75: 373-377 (Apr 83)

Glazier, Stephen D.

African Cults And Christian Churches In Trinidad:
The Spiritual Baptist Case. Notes. *Journal of
Religious Thought*. 39: 17-25 (Fall-Winter 83)

Glenn, John (joint author)

See Mondale, Walter F.

Glenn, Kenneth A.

The Decline Of Black Farming In America: A Call
To Alert. Notes. *Black Law Journal*. 08: 292-305
(Fall 83)

Glock, Charles Y.

The Anatomy Of Racial Attitudes. Book review.
Keith A. Winsell. *Phylon*. 44: 246-248 (Sep 83)

Glover, John D. (about)

The FBI's Top-Ranking Black. Illustrated. *Ebony*.
38: 108 + (Apr 83)

God (African Religion)

Concepts Of God In Africa. Notes. William A.
Brown. *Journal of Religious Thought*. 39: 5-16
(Fall-Winter 83)

Godfathers

See Sponsors

Gold, Richard H.

Mammography, Thremography And Ultrasound In
Breast Cancer Detection. Book review. Cornelius
W. Merrick. *National Medical Association Journal*.
75: 1023 (Oct 83)

Golden, Marita

My Father, My Mother, Myself. Illustrated.
Essence. 14: 72-74 + (May 83)

Golden, Martia

Migrations Of The Heart. Book review. Gerald D.
Kendrick. *CLA Journal*. 26: 362-363 (Mar 83)

Goldstein, Michael

How Ronald Reagan, Henry Hyde, And William
French Smith Became Voting Rights Heroes:
Political Actors And The Press Fool The Public..
CAAS Newsletter. 07: 1 + (May 83)

Golf

Golfing With Calvin Peete. Illustrated. John Putnam
Ross. *Black Enterprise*. 13: 70 (Jul 83)

Gonsalves, Sandra Virginia

Women, Race And Class. Book review. *Journal of
Negro History*. 68: 109-110 (Winter 83)

Goode, Wilson (about)

Black Power At The Polls. Illustrated. Frank
McRae. *Black Enterprise*. 13: 17 (May 83)

Gordimer, Nadine—Criticism And Interpretation

The Motif Of The Ancestor In The Conservationist
. Notes. Michael Thorpe. *Research in African
Literatures*. 14: 184-192 (Summer 83)

Gordon, Beverly M.

Reflections On Desegregation: Columbus, Ohio - A Case In Point. Notes. *Negro Educational Review.* 34: 12-19 (Jan 83)

Gordon, Jacob U.

Minority Aging: Sociological And Social Psychological Issues. Book review. *Journal of Negro History.* 68: 110-111 (Winter 83)

Gordon, Walter

Strict Legal Liability, Upper Class Criminality, And The Model Penal Code. Notes. *Howard Law Journal.* 26: No. 2: 781-797 (83)

Gordon, Walter L. (III)

Corporate Crime. Book review, Notes. *Black Law Journal.* 08: 152-159 (Spring 83)

Gorman, G. E.

Books In Print South Africa 1980/Suid Afrikaanse Boeke Tans In Druk. Book review. *Research in African Literatures.* 14: 266-268 (Summer 83)

Gospel Music

Charles Albert Tindley: Progenitor Of Black-American Gospel Music. Illustrated, tables, notes. Horace Clarence Boyer. *The Black Perspective in Music.* 11: 103-132 (Fall 83)

Gospel Goes To The Holy Land. Illustrated. Charles Sanders and Vandell Cobb. *Ebony.* 39: 36-38+ (Dec 83)

Gossett, Louis (Jr.) (about)

Gossett Wins An Oscar; Urges Hollywood To Use More Blacks In Movies. Illustrated. *Jet.* 64: 60 (2 May 83)

Louis Gossett, Natalie Cole Tell Of Changes In Their Lives. Illustrated. *Jet.* 64: 60-63 (23 May 83)

Gossman, Norbert J.

William Cuffay: London's Black Chartist. Notes. *Phylon.* 44: 56-65 (Mar 83)

Gourse, Leslie

Essense Women: Carrie Alston. Illustrated. *Essence.* 13: 22 (Apr 83)

See DeRamus, Betty

Government Contracts

See Public Contracts

Government Employees

See Civil Service

Government, Resistance To

Historical Traditions In Civil Dissent And Their Corresponding Conceptions Of Law. Notes. George R. Garrison. *Black Law Journal.* 08: 198-219 (Fall 83)

Graduate Work

See Universities And Colleges—Graduate Work

Graham, Maryemma

The Color Purple. Book review. *Freedomways.* 23: No. 4: 278-280 (83)

Grant, Philip A. (Jr.)

The Election Of An Ohio Congressman. Notes. *Negro History Bulletin.* 46: 60-62 (Apr-Jun 83)

Graphics, Computer

See Computer Graphics

Graves, Curtis M. and Van Sertima, Ivan

Space Science: The African-American Contribution. Illustrated. *Journal of African Civilizations.* 05: 238-257 (Apr-Nov 83)

Graves, Earl G.

Blacks Exhibit Clout At The Ballot Box. Illustrated. *Black Enterprise.* 13: 11 (Feb 83)

Carrying On The Struggle. Illustrated. *Black Enterprise.* 14: 9 (Aug 83)

The Malady Of Violent Crime. Illustrated. *Black Enterprise.* 13: 11 (Apr 83)

Our Organizations Can Be Vehicles For Change. Illustrated. *Black Enterprise.* 14: 11 (Dec 83)

Scandal In The Sports Business. Illustrated. *Black Enterprise.* 13: 7 (Jan 83)

Gray, Stephen

Modern South African Stories. Book review. Linda Susan Beard. *Research in African Literatures.* 14: 219-222 (Summer 83)

Perspectives On South African Fiction. Book review. *Research in African Literatures.* 14: 216-218 (Summer 83)

Great Britain

See Also Political Parties—Great Britain Racism—Great Britain

Great Zimbabwe

Great Zimbabwe: An Ancient African City-State. Illustrated. Molefi Asante and Kariamu Asante. *Journal of African Civilizations.* 05: 84-91 (Apr-Nov 83)

Greek Letter Societies

Fraternities And Sororities: A Dramatic Comeback On Campus. Illustrated. *Ebony.* 39: 93-94+ (Dec 83)

New Wave Networkers. Pat King. *Black Enterprise.* 14: 89-90+ (Dec 83)

Green, Connie

Alexander Dies At 51.. *Black Enterprise.* 14: 22 (Aug 83)

Black Enterprise Readers Rate The Consumer And Professional Services.. *Black Enterprise.* 14: 73-74 (Aug 83)

Green, Dan S. and Smith, Earl

W. E. B. DuBois And The Concepts Of Race And Class. Notes. *Phylon.* 44: 262-272 (Dec 83)

Green, Janice

NBA To Boost Voting Ranks.. *Black Enterprise.* 14: 24 (Dec 83)

Green, Jeffrey P.

In Dahomey In London In 1903.. *The Black Perspective in Music.* 11: 22-40 (Spring 83)

Green, Robert L. (about)

Dr. Robert Green Named New President of UDC.. *Jet.* 64: 30 (15 Aug 83)

Greenberg, Jack

Civil Rights Enforcement Activity Of The Department Of Justice. Notes. *Black Law Journal.* 08: 60-67 (Spring 83)

Greenblatt, Susan L.

Community Politics And Educational Change: Ten School Systems Under Court Order. Book review. George L. Mims. *Journal of Black Studies.* 13: 375-376 (Mar 83)

Greene, Carroll (Jr.)

A State Recalls Its Heritage: A Museum For Maryland. Illustrated. *Crisis.* 90: 12+ (Feb 83)

Greene, Janice L.

Bargaining: For What You're Worth. Illustrated. *Black Enterprise.* 13: 47-49 (May 83)

Tracking Down A Technical School.. *Black Enterprise.* 13: 71-72 (Feb 83)

What Goes Up. . . . Illustrated. *Black Enterprise.* 13: 64-65 (Jul 83)

Greene, Linda S.

Nationalism, Federalism And Political Consensus. Notes. *Black Law Journal.* 08: 399-407 (Winter 83)

Greenfield, Eloise

Honey, I Love. Book review. Nieda Spigner. *Freedomways.* 23: No. 01: 55-56 (83)

Greenidge, Kevin C.

Laser Therapy Of Glaucoma. Tables, illustrated, notes. *National Medical Association Journal.* 75: 373-377 (Apr 83)

Gregg, Elaine

Riding In Style. Illustrated. *Black Enterprise.* 14: 91-92 (Nov 83)

Gregg, Sandra

Keeping A Winning Smile. Illustrated. *Black Enterprise.* 13: 82 (Mar 83)

Gregg, Sandra R.

The Black Enterprise Guide To Good Health. Illustrated. *Black Enterprise.* 13: 39-43 (May 83)

Hypertension: What You Know Can Save Your Life. Illustrated. *Black Enterprise.* 13: 114 (Feb 83)

Gregory, Carole E.

Black Women Writers At Work. Book review. *Freedomways.* 23: No. 4: 287-289 (83)

Confirmation: An Anthology Of African American Women. Book review. *Freedomways.* 23: No. 4: 287-289 (83)

A Little Computer Literacy Goes A Long Way.. *Black Collegian.* 14: 77-78+ (Nov-Dec 83)

Gregory, Frederick D. (about)

Space Science: The African-American Contribution. Illustrated. Curtis M. Graves and Ivan Van Sertima. *Journal of African Civilizations.* 05: 238-257 (Apr-Nov 83)

Grenada

See Also Women—Grenada

Grenada—Invasion, 1983

Grenada & Black America: Two Views. Illustrated. Norman Hill. about. . . time. 11: 8-9 (Dec 83)

Grenada: The Events, The Future. Michael Frank Wright. *Black Scholar.* 14: 21-25 (Nov-Dec 83)

Invitation To Invade Black Nation Called 'Gunboat Diplomacy'. Illustrated. Simeon Booker. *Jet.* 65: 8-9+ (14 Nov 83)

Reagan Foreign Policy: War On The Doorstep? Illustrated. George W. (Jr.) Crockett. *Crisis.* 90: 48-49 (Dec 83)

Grenada—Politics And Government

Grenada. Selwyn R. Cudjoe. *Freedomways.* 23: No. 4: 270-277 (83)

Griffin, Judith Berry (about)

A Better Chance. Illustrated. Lynn Norment. *Ebony.* 38: 46+ (Jun 83)

Griffiths, Gareth

Writers In Exile: The Creative Use Of Home In Modern Literature. Book review. *Research in African Literatures.* 14: 222-225 (Summer 83)

Grigulevich, I. R.

Ethnocultural Processes And National Problems In The Modern World. Book review. Alonzo T. Stephens. *Journal of Negro History.* 68: 128-129 (Winter 83)

Grimes, Elwyn M. and others

Urinary Estrogen And Serum Gonadotropin Profiles In Women Ingesting Oral Contraceptive Steroid Formulations With Variable Estrogen Content. Tables, notes. *National Medical Association Journal.* 75: 575-580 (Jun 83)

Grooming For Men

A Grooming Guide For Black Men. Illustrated. Alfred (Jr.) Fornay. *Ebony.* 38: 140-142+ (Aug 83)

Gruening, Martha

Two Suffrage Movements [September, 1912]. Tables. *Crisis.* 90: 6-8 (Jun-Jul 83)

Guillaume, Robert (about)

Robert Guillaume: Behind The Scenes With TV's 'Benson'. Illustrated. Aldore Collier. *Ebony.* 39: 133-134+ (Nov 83)

Gullah Dialect

Contemporary Gullah Speech: Some Persistent Linguistic Features. Notes. Patricia Jones-Jackson. *Journal of Black Studies.* 13: 289-303 (Mar 83)

Gupta, Udayan

The Bonanza In Tax-free Bonds. Illustrated. *Black Enterprise*. 14: 31 (Aug 83)

Choosing A Financial Planner.. *Black Enterprise*. 14: 41 (Dec 83)

From Other Shores. Illustrated. *Black Enterprise*. 13: 51-54 (Mar 83)

A Home Of Your Own-Buy Or Rent? Illustrated. *Black Enterprise*. 13: 26 (Jul 83)

House Work. Illustrated. *Black Enterprise*. 13: 59-60+ (Apr 83)

Individual Retirement Accounts: Everyman's Tax Shelter. Tables. *Black Enterprise*. 13: 22 (Jan 83)

Initial Public Stock Offerings The Start Of Something Big. Illustrated. *Black Enterprise*. 13: 61 (Jun 83)

Joint Ventures: A Marriage Of Convenience.. *Black Enterprise*. 13: 191-192+ (Jun 83)

Keep Your Health Insurance Package Up To Date. Illustrated. *Black Enterprise*. 13: 31 (May 83)

Mutual Funds Make Good Investments In A Rising Market. Illustrated. *Black Enterprise*. 13: 35 (Feb 83)

Mutual Funds With Social Conscience.. *Black Enterprise*. 14: 35 (Nov 83)

Shopping The Financial Supermarkets. Tables. *Black Enterprise*. 14: 59-60+ (Oct 83)

Stock Market Outlook. Illustrated. *Black Enterprise*. 14: 69-70+ (Oct 83)

Surviving A Tax Audit. Illustrated. *Black Enterprise*. 14: 29 (Sep 83)

Taking A Second Mortgage Or Refinancing Your Home For Extra Cash. Illustrated. *Black Enterprise*. 13: 31 (Apr 83)

Turning Tykes On To Dow Jones.. *Black Enterprise*. 14: 112 (Oct 83)

Gurr, Andrew

Writers In Exile: The Creative Use Of Home In Modern Literature. Book review. Gareth Griffiths. *Research in African Literatures*. 14: 222-225 (Summer 83)

Guy-Sheftall, Beverly

Ain't I A Woman: Black Woman And Feminism. Book review. *Phylon*. 44: 84-85 (Mar 83)

Gymnasts

Dianne Durham: Going For The Gold In '84 Olympics. Illustrated. D. Michael Cheers. *Ebony*. 38: 52-54+ (Sep 83)

Gary's Dianne Durham Is Top U.S. Female Gymnast. Illustrated. D. Michael Cheers. *Jet*. 64: 46-50 (27 Jun 83)

Introducing: Ron Galimore. Illustrated. *Ebony*. 38: 42+ (Jan 83)

H. Councill Trenholm Memorial Program

H. Councill Trenholm Memorial Program. Illustrated. *Negro History Bulletin*. 46: 15-18 (Jan-Mar 83)

Hacker, Benjamin T. (about)

Admiral Hacker Takes Command. Illustrated. *Ebony*. 38: 74+ (Feb 83)

Hackett, Obra V.

The Dilemma Of Access: Minorities In Two Year Colleges. Book review. *Journal of Negro History*. 68: 130-131 (Winter 83)

Hackley, Lloyd V.

We Need To Educate Our Athletes! Illustrated. *Black Collegian*. 13: 35-37 (Apr-May 83)

Haddy, Theresa B. and Castro, Oswaldo L.

Sickled Hypochromic Red Blood Cells. Illustrated, notes. *National Medical Association Journal*. 75: 423+ (Apr 83)

Hahn, H. George

The Orchard And The Street: The Political Mirror Of The Tragic In Julius Caesar And Coriolanus. Notes. *CLA Journal*. 27: 169-186 (Dec 83)

Hair—Dyeing And Bleaching

Your Hair: Color It Rich! Illustrated. *Essence*. 14: 96-97 (May 83)

Haircutting

The Great Cut. Illustrated. *Essence*. 13: 48 (Mar 83)

Hairdressing

The Best Of Fall. Illustrated. Alfred (Jr.) Fornay. *Ebony*. 38: 146-148+ (Sep 83)

Crown Jewels: Beauty Assets That Shimmer! Illustrated. *Essence*. 14: 98-101 (Jun 83)

Hairstyles 1983. Illustrated. *Ebony*. 38: 100-102+ (Jan 83)

The History And Significance Of Hair Braiding. Illustrated. Tulani L. C. Jordan. *Black Collegian*. 13: 64-66 (Apr-May 83)

Short Takes. Illustrated. *Essence*. 14: 110-113 (Oct 83)

Hairston, Andrea

If You Just Change The Key, It's Still The Same Old Song.. *Black American Literature Forum*. 17: 36-37 (Spring 83)

Hairston, Loyle

The Women Of Brewster Place. Book review. *Freedomways*. 23: No. 4: 282-285 (83)

Haiti

See Also Americans In Haiti—History

Haitian Refugees

See Refugees, Haitian

Haitians In The United States

Plagued By AIDS Scare. Tables. David J. Dent. *Black Enterprise*. 14: 24 (Dec 83)

Haley, Alex

Alex Haley Remembers Malcolm X. Illustrated. *Essence*. 14: 52-54+ (Nov 83)

Haley, Alex—Criticism And Interpretation

The Plastic Arts Motif In Roots. Notes. Carol P. Marsh. *CLA Journal*. 26: 325-333 (Mar 83)

Roots And The Heroic Search For Identity. Notes. Helen Chavis Othow. *CLA Journal*. 26: 311-324 (Mar 83)

Haley, Charles

The Klan In Their Midst: The Ku Klux Klan In Upstate New York Communities. Notes. *Afro-Americans in New York Life and History*. 07: 41-53 (Jan 83)

Haley, Charles T.

The Politics Of Race In New York: The Struggle For Black Suffrage In The Civil War. Book review. *Journal of Negro History*. 68: 125-126 (Winter 83)

Half, Robert

Knocking On The Right Doors: How To Use Employment Agencies To Your Advantage.. *Essence*. 14: 26 (Jul 83)

Hall, Jaki (about)

Essence Women: Jaki Hall. Illustrated. Sandra Harley. *Essence*. 14: 54 (Jun 83)

Hall, Jean

The Transforming Image: A Study Of Shelley's Major Poetry. Book review. Elizabeth J. Higgins. *CLA Journal*. 27: 228-230 (Dec 83)

Hall, Julie E.

Exclusion Zoning - City Of Memphis V. Greene. Notes. *Black Law Journal*. 08: 138-143 (Spring 83)

Profiles: LaDoris Hazzard Cordell. Portrait. *Black Law Journal*. 08: 150-151 (Spring 83)

Hall, Katie (about)

New Faces On Capitol Hill. Illustrated. *Ebony*. 38: 36-38 + (Feb 83)

Hall, Macy (Jr.) (joint author)

See Walker, Mark

Halloween

Have A Happy Halloween. Marcie Eanes. *Essence*. 14: 136 (Oct 83)

Hambrick, Elta L. (about)

Essence Women: Elta L. Hambrick. Illustrated. Lloyd Gite. *Essence*. 14: 54 (Jul 83)

Hamilton Bobb

Moments. Poem. *Essence*. 13: 16 (Apr 83)

Hamilton, Stephanie Renfrow

Music. Illustrated. *Essence*. 13: 18 (Feb 83)

Take Note!. *Essence*. 14: 49 (Oct 83)

Hamilton, Thomas (about)

Education To What End? An Englishman Comments On The Plight Of Blacks In The "Free" States, 1830. Notes. Ivan D. Steen. *Afro-Americans in New York Life and History*. 07: 55-57 (Jan 83)

Men And Manners In America (1833). Notes. *Afro-Americans in New York Life and History*. 07: 58-60 (Jan 83)

Hamilton, Virginia

Sweet Whispers Brother Rush. Book review. Geraldine Wilson. *Interracial Books for Children*. 14: No. 1: 32 (83)

Hamlar, Portia T.

Minority Tokenism In American Law Schools. Notes, tables. *Howard Law Journal*. 26: No. 2: 443-599 (83)

Hammond, Allen S. (IV)

Now You See It, Now You Don't: Federal Policy And Minority Ownership In The Video Industry. Notes. *The Urban League Review*. 08: 26-39 (Winter 83)

Handicapped

See Also Mentally Ill—Home Care

Handicapped Children

Adopted Dwarf, 10, Has Happy Childhood With A Dwarf Father And An Average-Sized Mother. Illustrated. Clarence Waldron and James Mitchell. *Jet*. 65: 20-24 (12 Sep 83)

Handicapped Youth

Who's Handicapped? Not Sharpshooter Norris McAdoo. Illustrated. *Ebony*. 38: 96 + (Jun 83)

Handicrafts

The Work Of Four Creative Expressions In Crocheting, Drawing, Sewing And Furniture. Illustrated. *about. . . time*. 11: 18-20 (May 83)

Handler, Diana S. and others

Health Career Preview: A Summer Internship For Minority Students In A Teaching Hospital. Tables, notes. *National Medical Association Journal*. 75: 1007-1009 + (Oct 83)

Handy, D. Antoinette

American Women In Jazz: 1900 To The Present. Book review. *The Black Perspective in Music*. 11: 83-85 (Spring 83)

Mother Of The Blues: A Study Of Ma Rainey. Book review. *The Black Perspective in Music*. 11: 83-85 (Spring 83)

Hankerson, Henry E.

Teacher/Student Work Manual: A Model Evaluating Traditional U.S. History Textbooks. Book review. *Journal of Negro Education*. 52: 89-90 (Winter 83)

Hansberry, Lorraine (1930-1965)—Criticism And Interpretation

The Sighted Eyes And Feeling Heart Of Lorraine Hansberry. Notes. Margaret B. Wilkerson. *Black American Literature Forum*. 17: 8-13 (Spring 83)

Harlan, Louis R.

Booker T. Washington: The Wizard Of Tuskegee, 1901-1915. Book review. Adele Logan Alexander. *Crisis*. 90: 32 (Dec 83)

Harlem

See New York (City)—Harlem

Harlem Third World Trade Institute

Trade Pact For Guinea. Jill Nelson. *Black Enterprise*. 13: 40 (Jun 83)

Harleston, Bernard W.

Higher Education For Minorities: The Challenge Of The 1980s. Notes. *Journal of Negro Education*. 52: 94-101 (Spring 83)

Harley, Sandra

Essence Women: Jaki Hall. Illustrated. *Essence*. 14: 54 (Jun 83)

Harney, Ben (about)

The Dream Guys Of 'Dreamgirls'. Illustrated. *Ebony*. 38: 74-76+ (Apr 83)

Harney, James

Video Terminals And Your Health.. *Essence*. 14: 50 (Oct 83)

Harper, Robert Berkley

Accountability Of Law Enforcement Officers In The Use Of Deadly Force. Notes. *Howard Law Journal*. 26: No. 1: 119-151 (83)

Harper, Shari Belafonte

See Belafonte-Harper, Shari

Harris, Carl G. (Jr.)

Lift Every Voice And Sing: A Collection Of Afro-American Spirituals And Other Songs. Book review. *The Black Perspective in Music*. 11: 82-83 (Spring 83)

Harris, Donald J.

Economic Growth, Structural Change And The Relative Income Status Of Blacks In The U.S. Economy, 1947-78. Tables, Notes. *Review of Black Political Economy*. 12: 75-92 (Spring 83)

Harris, Frank (III)

Black Teenage Unemployment.. *Crisis*. 90: 38-39 (Jan 83)

Harris, Ian M.

Criteria For Evaluating School Desegregation In Milwaukee. Notes, tables. *Journal of Negro Education*. 52: 423-435 (Fall 83)

Harris, Jessica

Afternoon Tea: An Island Tradition.. *Black Enterprise*. 13: 72+ (May 83)

Antiquing In The Caribbean. Illustrated. *Black Enterprise*. 13: 78-79 (May 83)

Leaves From Our Family Tree. Illustrated. *Black Enterprise*. 14: 77-79 (Aug 83)

Harris, Jessica B.

Your Chair, My Couch: Sharing Furniture And Space With Someone You Love. Illustrated. *Black Enterprise*. 13: 106+ (Feb 83)

Harris, Joan

Touring Kenya's Fabulous Coast. Illustrated. *Black Enterprise*. 13: 80 (Apr 83)

Harris, Neck, Georgia

Harris Neck: Georgia Blacks Fight To Regain Ancestral Land. Illustrated. Thad Martin. *Ebony*. 38: 36-38+ (Jul 83)

Harris, Peter

I Had To Make Many Adjustments Trying To Build A Relationship With A Woman Who Was A Mother. Illustrated. *Essence*. 14: 31 (Oct 83)

Harris, Robert L. (Jr.)

From Slavery To Achievement: Keep On A Goin'. Illustrated. *Black Collegian*. 13: 142-147 (Feb-Mar 83)

Harris, Ron

The House That Willie Built. Illustrated, tables. *Black Enterprise*. 13: 90-92+ (Jun 83)

Harris, Wilson

Kaiso! The Trinidad Calypso. Book review. *Research in African Literatures*. 14: 417-421 (Fall 83)

Harrison, Dorothy D.

Relaxation Therapy: Adjunctive Therapy For The Physician. Tables, notes. *National Medical Association Journal*. 75: 193-198 (Feb 83)

Harrow, Kenneth

A Sufi Interpretation Of Le Regard Du Roi . Notes. *Research in African Literatures*. 14: 135-164 (Summer 83)

Hart, Armando

Opening Speech In The Meeting Of Intellectuals For The Sovereignty Of The Peoples Of Our America.. *Black Scholar*. 14: 2-12 (Summer 83)

Hart, H. L. A. (about)

Controversial Propositions Of Law And The Positivist Embarrassment: The Hart/Dworkin Debate Reconsidered. Notes. Simeon Charles Randolph McIntosh. *Howard Law Journal*. 26: No. 2: 699-722 (83)

Hart, Mary L.

Folk Music And Modern Sound. Book review. Doris Evans McGinty. *The Black Perspective in Music*. 11: 212-214 (Fall 83)

Harvery, William (about)

The President Is A Colonel. Illustrated. Kendall Wilson. *Black Collegian*. 13: 46 (Apr-May 83)

Harvey, Joan

America-From Hitler To MX. Motion picture review. Stephen DeGange. *Freedomways*. 23: No. 01: 37-41 (83)

Harvin, Cassandra Byers

Our Nig, Or Sketches From The Life Of A Free Black In A Two-Story House, North. Book review. *Essence*. 13: 20 (Feb 83)

Hatch, James V. (joint author)

See Conboy, Neil

Hawaii—Description And Travel

Maui: A Hawaiian Adventure. Roger Witherspoon. *Black Enterprise*. 14: 153 (Oct 83)

Hawkins, Augustus F. (about)

U.S. Rep. Hawkins Honored For 50 Years In Politics. Illustrated. *Jet*. 64: 12-13 (27 Jun 83)

Hawkins, Lincoln (about)

Lincoln Hawkins: A Black Engineering Pioneer. Illustrated. Kim Pearson. *Black Collegian*. 13: 48-50+ (Dec-Jan 83)

Hawkins, W. Lincoln (about)

Pioneering Black Bell Labs Engineer Still At Work At 71. Illustrated. Kim E. Pearson. *Crisis*. 90: 40-41 (Apr 83)

Hawley, Willis D.

Effective School Desegregation: Equity, Quality, And Feasibility. Book review. Muriel Moore. *Journal of Black Studies*. 13: 371-375 (Mar 83)

Hayden, Robert C.

Black Americans In The Field Of Science And Invention. Illustrated. *Journal of African Civilizations*. 05: 215-228 (Apr-Nov 83)

Hayes, Charles (about)

Washington's Successor. Steve Askin. *Black Enterprise*. 14: 19 (Nov 83)

Hayes, Dennis F. (joint author)

See Sweezer, William P. (Jr.)

Hazelton, Lynette

A Salary With Fringe On Top.. *Essence*. 14: 26 (May 83)

Uncovering Fronts. Illustrated. *Black Enterprise*. 14: 24 (Nov 83)

Health

The Black Enterprise Guide To Good Health. Illustrated. Sandra R. Gregg. *Black Enterprise*. 13: 39-43 (May 83)

Destination: Getting Fit, Getting Free. Illustrated. *Essence*. 13: 89-101 (Apr 83)

How To Cope With Ten Of The Most Worrisome Health Problems. Illustrated. *Ebony*. 38: 52+ (Feb 83)

Wellness: The Happy Art Of Living Well. Roberto G. Collazo. *Essence*. 13: 49+ (Jan 83)

Health Insurance

See Insurance, Health

Health, Mental

See Mental Health

Health, Public

See Public Health

Heart—Diseases

The Black Enterprise Guide To Good Health. Illustrated. Sandra R. Gregg. *Black Enterprise*. 13: 39-43 (May 83)

Idiopathic Hypertrophic Subaortic Stenosis And Acute Myocardial Infarction: An Uncommon Association. Tables, illustrated. Michael Bachik and others. *National Medical Association Journal*. 75: 305-309 (Mar 83)

Heffernan, Virgie S.

Sullivan Inaugurated As First President Of Morehouse School Of Medicine. Illustrated. *National Medical Association Journal*. 75: 826+ (Aug 83)

Helmreich, William H.

The Things They Say Behind Your Back: Stereotypes And The Myths Behind Them. Book review. Keith A. Winsell. *Phylon*. 44: 246-248 (Sep 83)

Helms, Jesse (about)

King's Son Answers Helm's Communist Slur Of His Dad.. *Jet*. 65: 22-23 (24 Oct 83)

Hemphill, Essex

The Black Community Cannot Afford To Indulge In Excluding Black Homosexuals Or In Condemning Us!. *Essence*. 14: 15 (Nov 83)

Henderson, Kaye (about)

Up, Up And Away. Illustrated. Lloyd Gite. *Essence*. 14: 44 (Oct 83)

Henderson, Lenneal J.

Africans In Search Of Work: Migration And Diaspora. Notes, tables. *The Urban League Review*. 07: 58-73 (Summer 83)

Henderson, Lenneal J. and Murphy, Charles

Perils Of Black Postal Workers In A Technological Age: Some Strategies For Survival. Tables, notes. *The Urban League Review*. 07: 33-43 (Summer 83)

Henderson, Rickey (about)

Baseball's Greatest 'Thief'. Illustrated. Walter Leavy. *Ebony*. 38: 135-136+ (Jun 83)

Henderson, Vivian Wilson (about)

A Tribute To Vivian Wilson Henderson. Barbara A. P. Jones. *Review of Black Political Economy*. 12: 5-7 (Spring 83)

Hendricks, Leo E. and others

The NIMH Diagnostic Interview Schedule: A Test Of Its Validity In A Population Of Black Adults. Tables, notes. *National Medical Association Journal*. 75: 667-671 (Jul

Hendryx, Nona (about)

Nona! Illustrated. Michele Wallace. *Essence*. 14: 78-79 (Jul 83)

Henley, David

The International Hearing On The Israeli Invasion Of Lebanon.. *Freedomways*. 23: No. 2: 99-111 (83)

Henry, Diane

Creative Home. Illustrated. *Essence*. 14: 105-106+ (Sep 83)

Henry, Nancy (about)

Her Honor, The Mayor. Illustrated. Julie Chenault. *Essence*. 14: 14+ (Jul 83)

Hensley, Dennis E. and Johnson, Wista

How To Overcome Shyness.. *Essence*. 14: 71+ (Aug 83)

Henson, Josiah

See Also Postage Stamps—Topics—Henson, Josiah

Henson, K. T.

America's Public Schools In Transition: Future Trends And Issues. Book review. Wilfred A. Johnson. *Journal of Negro Education*. 52: 459-461 (Fall 83)

Henson, Matthew (about)

Matt Henson: Black Explorer Is Part Of Controversy In Flim 'Race To The Pole'. Illustrated. Thad Martin. *Ebony*. 39: 80-82+ (Nov 83)

Henson, Reggie

Rallies (For Michael). Poem. *Black American Literature Forum*. 17: 175 (Winter 83)

Young Being. Poem. *Black American Literature Forum*. 17: 175 (Winter 83)

Hequet, Marc

Everything For The Office, Inc. Illustrated. *Black Enterprise*. 14: 95-96 (Dec 83)

Herber, Avril (about)

Conversations: Some People, Some Place, Some Time-South Africa. Book review. *Research in African Literatures*. 14: 252-253 (Summer 83)

Heritage Foundation

CIBC Responds To Charges. Editorial. *Interracial Books for Children*. 14: No. 1: 3+ (83)

Hernandez-Cruz, Juan

The Black Presence In Puerto Rico.. *Interracial Books for Children*. 14: No. 1: 23-24 (83)

Hernandez, Enrique and Rosenshein, Neil B.

Salpingo-Oophorectomy In Women With Previous Hysterectomy. Illustrated. *National Medical Association Journal*. 75: 106-107 (Jan 83)

Hernandez, Pa-Mela (about)

Breakthrough Under The Big Top. Illustrated. *Ebony*. 39: 69-70+ (Dec 83)

Hershman, James H. (Jr.)

Public School Bonds And Virginia's Massive Resistance. Notes, tables. *Journal of Negro Education*. 52: 398-409 (Fall 83)

Heuman, Gad J.

Between Black And White: Race, Politics, And The Free Colored In Jamaica. Book review. Glenn O. Phillips. *Afro-Americans in New York Life and History*. 07: 73-74 (Jul 83)

Higgens, Elizabeth J.

Faulkner: The House Divided. Book review. *CLA Journal*. 27: 97-101 (Sep 83)

Higgins, Chester A. (Sr.)

The Color Purple. Book review, Illustrated. *Crisis*. 90: 49 (Jun-Jul 83)

Forsaking All Others. Book review. *Crisis*. 90: 36 (Apr 83)

Hit Hard. Book review. *Crisis*. 90: 44-47 (Nov 83)

Many U.S. Cities Need A Visit From Conyers Committee. Illustrated. *Crisis*. 90: 23-24 (Nov 83)

Myrlie Evers' Painful Odyssey. Illustrated. *Crisis*. 90: 34-36 (May 83)

A Salute To Detroit. . . Dynamic Detroit NAACP Branch Sets Most Lavish Life Membership Table In The U.S.. Illustrated. *Crisis*. 90: 8-11 (Apr 83)

"We Are Going To Enforce The Law.". Illustrated. *Crisis*. 90: 50-52+ (Feb 83)

Higgins, Elizabeth J.

The Transforming Image: A Study Of Shelley's Major Poetry. Book review. *CLA Journal*. 27: 228-230 (Dec 83)

High School Students

Salute To Black Scholars: Bringing Scholarships And Students Together. Illustrated. Elizabeth Knight. *about. . . time*. 11: 12-13 (Jun 83)

Higher Education

See Education, Higher

Hill, Anthony D.

Rituals At The New Lafayette Theatre. Notes. *Black American Literature Forum*. 17: 31-35 (Spring 83)

Hill, Norman

Grenada & Black America: Two Views. Illustrated. *about. . . time*. 11: 8-9 (Dec 83)

The Threat To American Steel Independence.. *about. . . time*. 11: 11 (Aug 83)

The 1984 Elections: A Checklist For Black Voters.. *Crisis*. 90: 31-32 (Nov 83)

The 1984 Elections: A Checklist For Black Voters.. *about. . . time*. 11: 36 (Nov 83)

Hill, Valerie J.

Florida Test Causes Furor.. *Black Enterprise*. 13: 17 (Jul 83)

No Checks; Cash Only.. *Black Enterprise*. 13: 22 (Apr 83)

Hillard, Asa G. (III)

IQ And The Courts: Larry P. Vs. Wilson Riles And PASE Vs Hann. Notes. *Journal of Black Psychology*. 10: 1-18 (Aug 83)

Hilliard, Alphonso W. (joint author)

See Morrow, LaVert

Hilliard, Asa G. (III)

Psychological Factors Associated With Language In
The Education Of The African-American Child.
Notes. *Journal of Negro Education.* 52: 24-34
(Winter 83)

Hilliard, Asa (III)

In Memoriam: Robert A. Thornton.. *Journal of
Negro History.* 68: 142-143 (Winter 83)

Hilliard, Robert L. M.

The Black Female Physician: A Double Jeopardy..
National Medical Association Journal. 75: 253-254
(Mar 83)

Health Care For Black Americans: A Priority..
Crisis. 90: 24 (Oct 83)

Increasing NMA Membership: A Challenge To
Minority Physicians.. *National Medical Association
Journal.* 75: 341-344 (Apr 83)

A Matter Of Concern.. *National Medical
Association Journal.* 75: 931-932 (Oct 83)

The Medical Colleges Alumni Dinner: A Major
Event At NMA Conventions. Editorial. *National
Medical Association Journal.* 75: 1045-1046 (Nov
83)

President's Farewell Address ''So Short The
Season''.. *National Medical Association Journal.*
75: 1049-1050 (Nov 83)

The President's Inaugural Address: Insuring Quality
Health Care. Illustrated. *National Medical
Association Journal.* 75: 81-83 (Jan 83)

Providing Sound And Effective Health Care
Delivery For All Americans. Editorial. *National
Medical Association Journal.* 75: 1135-1138 (Dec
83)

Will There Be A Physician Glut OR An
Exaggeration Of The Present Maldistribution Of
Physicians? Another View. Illustrated. *National
Medical Association Journal.* 75: 855-859 (Sep 83)

Hilliard, S. Lee

The Business Of Getting Elected. Illustrated. *Black
Enterprise.* 14: 57-58 + (Nov 83)

See Hooks, Benjamin L.

Hilliard, S. Lee and George, Nelson

Lights! Camera! Action! Illustrated. *Black
Enterprise.* 14: 48-50 + (Dec 83)

Himmelstein, Jack

Becoming A Lawyer: A Humanistic Perspective On
Legal Education And Professionalism. Book
review. Elana Yancey. *Black Law Journal.* 08:
164-166 (Spring 83)

Hinds, Patricia M.

Bringing Home African Textiles. Illustrated.
Essence. 14: 112-113 (Jul 83)

Hines, Geraldine S. (joint author)

See Washington, Harold R.

Historians

Chronicles Of Black Courage (Part III): Father Of
Black History Changed Vision Of Black America.
Illustrated. Lerone (Jr.) Bennett. *Ebony.* 38:
31-32 + (Feb 83)

Historical Museums—Maryland

A State Recalls Its Heritage: A Museum For
Maryland. Illustrated. Carroll (Jr.) Greene. *Crisis.*
90: 12 + (Feb 83)

History—Bibliography

Important Black History Books: Some Fundamental
Readings. Maulana Karenga. *Black Collegian.* 13:
142 + (Dec-Jan 83)

History—Study And Teaching

Black Historical Scholarship And The Black
Historian. Notes. *Negro History Bulletin.* 46: 38-40
(Apr-Jun 83)

Hobson, Patricia (about)

Beer Brewery Boss. Illustrated. Pamela Noel.
Ebony. 38: 40 + (Jun 83)

Hobson, Robert W. (II) (joint author)

See Lazaro, Eric J.

Hocutt, Thomas R. (about)

Hocutt: Genesis Of Brown. Notes. Gilbert Ware.
Journal of Negro Education. 52: 227-233 (Summer
83)

Hoffman, Lyla

Circle Of Fire. Book review. *Interracial Books for
Children.* 14: No. 5: 25 (83)

Hogan, Lloyd L.

The Political Economy Of Black Americans:
Perspectives On Curriculum Development.. *Review
of Black Political Economy.* 12: 145-161 (Winter
83)

Holder, Calvin B.

Racism Toward Black African Diplomats During
The Kennedy Administration. Notes. *Journal of
Black Studies.* 14: 31-48 (Sep 83)

Holidays

Celebrating Kwanza: One Family's Story.
Illustrated. Beverley Seawright Taliaferro. *Essence.*
14: 103 + (Dec 83)

King Holiday Bill Passes; He Becomes 2nd
American Honored By A National Day. Illustrated.
Jet. 65: 4-6 (7 Nov 83)

President Reagan Praises King, Signs Holiday Bill.
Illustrated. Simeon Booker. *Jet.* 65: 4-7 (21
Nov 83)

See Also Christmas
Kwanza

Holloway, William J.

School Desegregation In The United States,
1973-1982: An Annotated Bibliography.. *Negro
Educational Review.* 34: 115-138 (Jul-Oct 83)

Home Ownership

Black Women And Homeownership: The Financial Challenge Of The '80s. Tables, notes. Shirley Better. *Black Scholar*. 14: 38-45 (Sep-Oct 83)

Creative Home. Illustrated. Diane Henry. *Essence*. 14: 105-106+ (Sep 83)

A Home Of Your Own-Buy Or Rent? Illustrated. Udayan Gupta. *Black Enterprise*. 13: 26 (Jul 83)

Sources Of Variability In Rates Of Black Home Ownership In 1900. Notes, tables. Steven Mintz. *Phylon*. 44: 312-331 (Dec 83)

Homosexuality

The Black Community Cannot Afford To Indulge In Excluding Black Homosexuals Or In Condemning Us! Essex Hemphill. *Essence*. 14: 15 (Nov 83)

Homophobia: Why Bring It Up? Barbara Smith. *Interracial Books for Children*. 14: No. 3: 7-8 (83)

See Also Lesbianism

Honeywood, Stephanie

Varnette Honeywood: Art That Hits Home. Illustrated. *Essence*. 14: 97+ (Aug 83)

Honeywood, Varnette (about)

Varnette Honeywood: Art That Hits Home. Illustrated. Stephanie Honeywood. *Essence*. 14: 97+ (Aug 83)

Hood, Elizabeth F.

Black Women, White Women: Separate Paths To Liberation. Notes. *Black Scholar*. 14: 26-37 (Sep-Oct 83)

Hooks, Bell

Ain't I A Woman: Black Woman And Feminism. Book review. Beverly Guy-Sheftall. *Phylon*. 44: 84-85 (Mar 83)

Ain't I A Woman: Black Woman And Feminism. Book review. Maria K. Mootry Ikerionwu. *Phylon*. 44: 85-86 (Mar 83)

Ain't I A Woman: Black Women And Feminism. Book review. Barbara Smith. *Black Scholar*. 14: 38-45 (Jan-Feb 83)

Ain't I A Woman: Black Women And Feminism. Book review. Dorothy Randall-Tsuruta. *Black Scholar*. 14: 46-52 (Jan-Feb 83)

Hooks, Benjamin L. and Hilliard, S. Lee

Demanding A Fair Share. Interview, Illustrated. *Black Enterprise*. 14: 40-42 (Aug 83)

". . . Plus Three, For A Stronger NAACP!".. *Crisis*. 90: 4 (Apr 83)

"Fair Share Approach Is Fourfold".. *Crisis*. 90: 4 (Oct 83)

Fair Share Points The Way. . . "We Are Laying A Foundation To Change The Face Of America".. *Crisis*. 90: 10-11 (Oct 83)

"God Will Not Do For Us What We Can Do For Ourselves. . . ".. *Crisis*. 90: 4 (Nov 83)

Hollywood's Racism Affects Our Black African Brothers, Too.. *Crisis*. 90: 5 (Jan 83)

An Interview With Benjamin L. Hooks. . . Demanding A Fair Share. Interview, Illustrated. *Crisis*. 90: 6-7 (Oct 83)

"Much More Will Be Done. . . ".. *Crisis*. 90: 4 (Aug-Sep 83)

Profile Of Black America - A Grim Picture.. *Crisis*. 90: 4 (Dec 83)

"Struggle On!". Illustrated. *Crisis*. 90: 22-24 (Aug-Sep 83)

Twentieth Anniversary Mobilization Jobs, Peace, And Freedom. Illustrated. *Crisis*. 90: 22-23 (Oct 83)

Why Black History Month? Illustrated. *Crisis*. 90: 4 (Feb 83)

Hooks, William H.

Circle Of Fire. Book review. Lyla Hoffman. *Interracial Books for Children*. 14: No. 5: 25 (83)

Hope, Julius C. (about)

The Importance Of Politics And Prayer. Illustrated. Don Armstrong. *Crisis*. 90: 30 (Apr 83)

Hopewell, Joan

How To Choose A Summer Camp.. *Essence*. 13: 124+ (Apr 83)

Is This Drug Dangerous?. *Essence*. 14: 42 (Jul 83)

Joint Custody: Sharing The Love. Illustrated. *Essence*. 14: 122+ (May 83)

Horne, Gerald

A Case Of Black And White: Northern Volunteers And The Southern Freedom Summers, 1964-65. Book review. *Journal of Negro History*. 68: 107-109 (Winter 83)

Horne, Gerald C.

Black Life In Corporate America: Swimming In The Mainstream. Book review. *Freedomways*. 23: No. 01: 51-54 (83)

The FBI And Martin Luther King, Jr. Book review. *Freedomways*. 23: No. 4: 290-294 (83)

Let The Trumpet Sound: The Life Of Martin Luther King, Jr.. Book review. *Freedomways*. 23: No. 4: 290-294 (83)

Live And Off-Color: News Biz. Book review. *Freedomways*. 23: No. 01: 51-54 (83)

Horne, Lena (about)

Lena Horne Finds Roots In Atlanta During Visit. Illustrated. Harmon Perry. *Jet*. 64: 28-30 (18 Jul 83)

Spingarn Medal Presentation To. . . Lena Horne-A Living Legend. Vernon E. (Jr.) Jordan. *Crisis*. 90: 36 (Aug-Sep 83)

Spingarn Medalist's Acceptance Recalls. . . A Measure Of What Has Gone Before. Illustrated. *Crisis*. 90: 38-40 (Aug-Sep 83)

Horton, James O.

The Free Black In Urban America, 1800-1850. Book review, Notes. *Afro-Americans in New York Life and History*. 07: 63-70 (Jan 83)

Horton, Linda

Pilgrim's Progress. Illustrated, tables. *Black Enterprise*. 13: 145-146+ (Jun 83)

See King, Charles H. (Jr.)

Hospital Administrators

The Life Blood Of America's Hospitals. Illustrated. Roger Witherspoon. *Black Enterprise*. 13: 49-50+ (Jul 83)

Hospitals

See Also Psychiatric Hospitals—Emergency Services

Hospitals—Emergency Service

Emergency Service Nursing Staff: A Survey Of Knowledge, Attitudes, And Concerns. Tables, notes. F. M. Baker and Barbara Moynihan. *National Medical Association Journal*. 75: 417-421 (Apr 83)

Hospitals—Illinois—Chicago

The New Provident Medical Center.. *National Medical Association Journal*. 75: 727 (Jul 83)

Provident Medical Center: Fulfillment Of A Need. Editorial. Calvin C. Sampson. *National Medical Association Journal*. 75: 665-666 (Jul 83)

Hostutler, John D. and Blount, Carolyne S.

The Industrial Management Council. Interview, Illustrated. *about. . . time*. 11: 12-13+ (Aug 83)

Hot Air Balloons

What Goes Up. . . . Illustrated. Janice L. Greene. *Black Enterprise*. 13: 64-65 (Jul 83)

House Buying

How To Buy A House With A Friend. Lloyd Gite. *Black Enterprise*. 13: 57-58 (Jul 83)

House Construction

Avoid Home Improvement Fraud. Illustrated. *Black Enterprise*. 13: 76 (Apr 83)

Housing

See Also Discrimination In Housing

Housing, Cooperative

Co-op Living In The Suburbs. Illustrated. *Ebony*. 38: 116-118 (Oct 83)

Houston, Texas

See Also Police Chiefs—Texas—Houston

Hovet, Grace Ann and Loansberry, Barbara

Flying As Symbol And Legend In Toni Morrison's The Bluest Eye, Sula, And Song Of Solomon. Notes. *CLA Journal*. 27: 119-140 (Dec 83)

Howard-Martin, Jane

A Critical Analysis Of Judicial Opinions In Professional Employment Discrimination Cases. Notes. *Howard Law Journal*. 26: No. 2: 723-757 (83)

Howard University. Divinity School—Annual Convocation, 1982

Photo Essay: The Sixty-Sixth Annual Convocation, November 3-4, 1982. Illustrated. *Journal of Religious Thought*. 40: 45-61 (Spring-Summer 83)

Howard, Victor B.

Black Liberation In Kentucky: Emancipation And Freedom. Book review. Thomas J. Davis. *Negro History Bulletin*. 46: 85 (Jul-Sep 83)

Howe, Gary L. and others

Munchausen's Syndrome Or Chronic Factitious Illness: A Review And Case Presentation. Tables, notes. *National Medical Association Journal*. 75: 175-181 (Feb 83)

Hudson, Gossie Harold

Black Americans vs. Citizenship: The Dred Scott Decision.. *Negro History Bulletin*. 46: 26-28 (Jan-Mar 83)

Huff, Claudia (joint author)

See Witherspoon, Roger

Hughes, Dorothy Pitman (about)

Essence Women: Dorothy Pitman Hughes. Illustrated. Joy Duckett. *Essence*. 13: 22 (Feb 83)

Hull, Everson

Money Growth And The Employment Aspirations Of Black Americans. Tables, Notes. *Review of Black Political Economy*. 12: 64-74 (Spring 83)

Hull, Gloria T.

But Some Of Us Are Brave. Book review. Hortense D. Lloyd. *Negro Educational Review*. 34: 45-46 (Jan 83)

Human Relations

See Interpersonal Relations

Humez, Jean McMahon

Gifts Of Power: The Writings Or Rebecca Jackson. Book review. Henry Justin Ferry. *Journal of Religious Thought*. 39: 71-72 (Fall-Winter 83)

Humphrey, Bobbi (about)

Bobbi Humphrey Toots Her Own Flute. Illustrated. Bonnie Allen. *Essence*. 13: 66-68 (Mar 83)

Humphrey, Patricia A. (joint author)

See Lee, Clarence

Hundertmark, Connie Von

New Year's Peas & Rice—Why?. *Essence*. 14: 51 (Dec 83)

Hunger

Hunger In Detroit. Illustrated. Lloyd Gite. *Black Enterprise*. 13: 19 (Apr 83)

Hunt, Dennis

Dionne Warwick: Speaks Out For Strong Black Women. Illustrated. *Ebony*. 38: 95-96+ (May 83)

Hunter, Herbert M.

Oliver C. Cox: A Biographical Sketch Of His Life And Work. Notes. *Phylon*. 44: 249-261 (Dec 83)

Hurd, Myles

Shakespeare's Paulina: Characterization And Craftsmanship In the Winter's Tale. Notes. *CLA Journal*. 26: 303-310 (Mar 83)

Hurston, Zora Neale (1903-1960)—Criticism And Interpretation

Folklore And The Creative Artist: Lydia Cabrera And Zora Neale Hurston. Notes. Miriam DeCosta Willis. *CLA Journal*. 27: 81-90 (Sep 83)

"Tuh de Horizon And Back": The Female Quest In Their Eyes Were Watching God. Notes. Missy Dehn Kubitschek. *Black American Literature Forum*. 17: 109-115 (Fall 83)

Husni, Khalil

Loomings Of An Awakened Consciousness: Mardi, A Reinterpretation. Notes. *CLA Journal*. 27: 56-68 (Sep 83)

Hutchings, Geoffrey

Perspectives On South African Fiction. Book review. Stephen Gray. *Research in African Literatures*. 14: 216-218 (Summer 83)

Hyde-Rowan, M. Deborah (about)

Neurosurgery: Two Black Women Surgeons Are Pioneers In Highly Specialized Medical Field. Illustrated. Marilyn Marshall. *Ebony*. 38: 72-74 + (Sep 83)

Hyman, Lateifa Ramona L.

Seasons Of Hunger/Cry Of Rain. Book review. *Black American Literature Forum*. 17: 182 (Winter 83)

Hypertension

Hypertension: Controlling It May Save Your Life. Linda Villarosa. *Essence*. 14: 30 + (Sep 83)

Hypertension: What You Know Can Save Your Life. Illustrated. Sandra R. Gregg. *Black Enterprise*. 13: 114 (Feb 83)

The Nurse Practitioner's Role In Complex Patient Management: Hypertension. Tables, notes. Michael J. Reichgott and others. *National Medical Association Journal*. 75: 1197-1204 (Dec 83)

Precursors Of Hypertension: A Review. Notes. John Thomas and others. *National Medical Association Journal*. 75: 359-369 (Apr 83)

Simultaneous Treatment Of Hypertension And Opiate Withdrawal Using An α_2-Adrenergic Agonist. Carl C. Bell. *National Medical Association Journal*. 75: 89-93 (Jan 83)

Hypothermia

Baby, It's Cold Outside: 10 Ways To Take The B-r-r-r Out Of Winter. Illustrated. Frances E. Ruffin. *Black Enterprise*. 13: 57-58 (Jan 83)

Hypothyroidism

Hypothyroidism Causing Macrocytic Anemia Unresponsive To B_{12} And Folate. Notes. Edward G. Sims. *National Medical Association Journal*. 75: 429-431 (Apr 83)

I.B.M.

See International Business Machines

Iacocca, Lee

Rebuilding America: Strong Spirits And Common Sense. Illustrated. *Black Collegian*. 14: 90 + (Sep-Oct 83)

Igoe, Lynn Moody

A Checklist Of Afro-American Art Exhibits In The State Of New York, 1913 - 1983.. *Afro-Americans in New York Life and History*. 07: 59-70 (Jul 83)

Ikerionwu, Maria K. Mootry

Ain't I A Woman: Black Woman And Feminism. Book review. *Phylon*. 44: 85-86 (Mar 83)

The Heart Of A Woman. Book review. *Phylon*. 44: 86-87 (Mar 83)

Iko, Benny O.

Radiological Management Of Obstructive Jaundice. Tables, illustrated, notes. *National Medical Association Journal*. 75: 51-56 (Jan 83)

Ikonné, Chidi

From DuBois To Van Vechten: The Early New Negro Literature, 1903-1926. Book review. Houston A. (Jr.) Baker. *Research in African Literatures*. 14: 554-560 (Winter 83)

Illinois

See Also Legislators—United States—Illinois

Illiteracy

Battling Illiteracy Among Prisoners. Latique Adrian Jamel. *Crisis*. 90: 40-41 + (Nov 83)

Imagination In Literature

Wordsworth's Secular Imagination And "Spots On Time". Notes. Allen Chavkin. *CLA Journal*. 26: 452-464 (Jun 83)

Iman (about)

Iman! Illustrated. Michele Wallace. *Essence*. 14: 64-65 + (Sep 83)

Imes, Elmer Samuel (about)

Blackspace. Illustrated, notes. James G. Spady. *Journal of African Civilizations*. 05: 258-265 (Apr-Nov 83)

Imlay, John P. (Jr.)

The Information Revolution: A Declaration For Survival.. *The Urban League Review*. 08: 82-87 (Winter 83)

Immunology

The Role Of Macrophages In Immunology. Mohamed A. Elhelu. *National Medical Association Journal*. 75: 314-317 (Mar 83)

Incest

Recognizing The Incestuous Family. Tables, notes. Mark S. Johnson. *National Medical Association Journal*. 75: 757-761 (Aug 83)

Income

See Also Wages

Income Tax—Rates And Tables

A Flat-Rate Tax Will Hurt The Middle Class.
Alfred E. (Jr.) Osborne. *Black Enterprise*. 14: 31
(Sep 83)

Income—United States

An Assessment Of Minority Income Differences
And Governmental Policies. Notes. Raphael
Thelwell. *Black Law Journal*. 08: 387-398 (Winter
83)

Economic Growth, Structural Change And The
Relative Income Status Of Blacks In The U.S.
Economy, 1947-78. Tables, Notes. Donald J.
Harris. *Review of Black Political Economy*. 12:
75-92 (Spring 83)

Economics, Politics, And Blacks. Notes. Glenn C.
Loury. *Review of Black Political Economy*. 12:
43-54 (Spring 83)

Sources Of Income For Blacks Vs. Whites. Tables.
Andrew F. Brimmer. *Black Enterprise*. 14: 33 (Aug
83)

India—Description And Travel

Settings Sights For India. Illustrated. Mira Nair.
Essence. 14: 22+ (Sep 83)

India—Economic Conditions

Reflections On A Journey To Southern India. Elton
C. Fax. *Freedomways*. 23: No. 01: 14-16 (83)

Indiana Association Of Colored Women's Clubs

Black Feminism In Indiana, 1893-1933. Notes.
Erlene Stetson. *Phylon*. 44: 292-298 (Dec 83)

Indianapolis

Indianapolis: Blacks Seek A Greater Role In The
City's Growth And Development. Illustrated.
Marilyn Marshall. *Ebony*. 38: 64+ (Jun 83)

Indians Of Central America

See Also Mosquito Indians

Indians Of North America

A Black Chief's Inspiring Saga. Illustrated. William
Loren Katz. *Crisis*. 90: 38-39 (Apr 83)

Individual Retirement Accounts

Individual Retirement Accounts: Everyman's Tax
Shelter. Tables. Udayan Gupta. *Black Enterprise*.
13: 22 (Jan 83)

Industry And State

Blacks And The Industrial Policy Debate.
Illustrated. Ernest J. (III) Wilson. *about. . . time*.
11: 8-10 (Aug 83)

Rebuilding America: Strong Spirits And Common
Sense. Illustrated. Lee Iacocca. *Black Collegian*.
14: 90+ (Sep-Oct 83)

Industry—Social Aspects

A New Role For Corporations: Linking Technology
To Socioeconomic Development. William C.
Norris. *The Urban League Review*. 08: 88-94
(Winter 83)

Infants—Mortality

A Surge In Infant Deaths. Tables. David J. Dent.
Black Enterprise. 14: 22 (Oct 83)

Inflation (Finance)

Eliminate Both Unemployment And Inflation.
Illustrated. W. Arthur Lewis. *Crisis*. 90: 40 (Jan
83)

Ingram, Robert (about)

Man Of God And Gun. Illustrated. Raymond Lang.
Ebony. 38: 102-104 (Sep 83)

Insanity

See Also Schizophrenia

Insurance Companies

The Benefits Of Innovation: Insurance Overview.
Tables. *Black Enterprise*. 13: 137-138 (Jun 83)

Insurance Companies—Directories

Insurance. Tables. *Black Enterprise*. 13: 142-143
(Jun 83)

Insurance Companies—Georgia—Augusta

Pilgrim's Progress. Illustrated, tables. Linda
Horton. *Black Enterprise*. 13: 145-146+ (Jun 83)

Insurance, Health

Keep Your Health Insurance Package Up To Date.
Illustrated. Udayan Gupta. *Black Enterprise*. 13: 31
(May 83)

Insurance, Life

Life Insurance: What's Right For You. Mimi Brien.
Essence. 13: 52+ (Apr 83)

Insurance, Social

See Social Security

Integration In Education

See School Integration

Integration In Higher Education

See College Integration

Intelligence Levels

Biological Differences, Social Inequality, And
Distributive Goods: An Exploratory Argument.
Notes. A. J. Williams-Myers. *Journal of Black
Studies*. 13: 399-416 (Jun 83)

Intelligence Levels—Trinidad

Racial Stratification, Sex, And Mental Ability: A
Comparison Of Five Groups In Trinidad. Tables,
notes. Lennard M. Shangi. *Journal of Black
Studies*. 14: 69-82 (Sep 83)

Intelligence Tests

IQ And The Courts: Larry P. Vs. Wilson Riles And
PASE Vs Hann. Notes. Asa G. (III) Hillard.
Journal of Black Psychology. 10: 1-18 (Aug 83)

Intercultural Education

The Cultural Broker Concept In Bicultural
Education. Notes. Karen M. Gentemann and Tony
L. Whitehead. *Journal of Negro Education*. 52:
118-129 (Spring 83)

The Florida A And M University Preservice And
Inservice Multicultural Education Model. Notes,
tables. Walter A. Mercer. *Negro Educational
Review*. 34: 37-44 (Jan 83)

Fostering Constructive Intergroup Contact In Desegregated Schools: Suggestions For Future Research. Notes. William B. Lacy and others. *Journal of Negro Education.* 52: 130-141 (Spring 83)

See Also Race Awareness

Interior Decoration

Bringing Home African Textiles. Illustrated. Patricia M. Hinds. *Essence.* 14: 112-113 (Jul 83)

A Closet Case. Illustrated. Dolly Calhoun and Tony Moses. *Essence.* 13: 127-128 (Mar 83)

Decorating With Your Fashion Favorites. Illustrated. Dolly Calhoun and Tony Moses. *Essence.* 14: 119 (May 83)

Designing Your Space For You. Illustrated. Charla L. Draper. *Ebony.* 38: 131-133 (May 83)

Hang It All: The Art Of Exhibiting Paintings, Posters, Photos And Prints. Illustrated. Evalyn Kaufman. *Black Enterprise.* 14: 134 (Oct 83)

Making Old Stuff New (For Under $100). Illustrated. Dolly Calhoun and Tony Moses. *Essence.* 14: 117 (Jun 83)

New Ways To Dress Up Windows. Illustrated. Dolly Calhoun and Tony Moses. *Essence.* 14: 111 (Aug 83)

Stow It: Get More Room From Less Space. Illustrated. Nanine Alexander. *Black Enterprise.* 13: 70-71 (Apr 83)

Ten Ways To Upgrade Your Home. Illustrated. Clinton Cox. *Black Enterprise.* 13: 72+ (Apr 83)

Internal Migration

See Migration, Internal

International Business Enterprises—Social Aspects

The Impact Of Multinational Corporations On Power Relations In South Africa. Notes. Timothy Bates. *Review of Black Political Economy.* 12: 133-143 (Winter 83)

International Business Machines

Wage Secrecy At IBM. Steve Askin. *Black Enterprise.* 13: 24 (Apr 83)

International Communication

See Communication, International

International Conference On Central America And The Caribbean Basin

Conference At MLK Center Focuses On Turmoil In Latin America, Caribbean. Illustrated. *Jet.* 63: 12-13 (24 Jan 83)

International Economic Relations

Development, The Arms Race And Disarmament International Economic Cooperation.. *Black Scholar.* 14: 55-56 (Nov-Dec 83)

Interns

Internship Programs. Sandra Roberts. *Black Enterprise.* 14: 63-64+ (Sep 83)

Internships Offer Valuable Work Experience. Illustrated. Carson (Jr.) Carr. *Black Collegian.* 13: 118+ (Feb-Mar 83)

Interpersonal Communication

Talking To Someone You Love. Illustrated. Patrice Miles. *Essence.* 13: 70-72+ (Feb 83)

Interpersonal Relations

Any Man Won't Do! Carol Botwin and Jerome L. Fine. *Essence.* 13: 74-75+ (Feb 83)

Great Expectations. Illustrated. Judy Simmons. *Essence.* 13: 64+ (Feb 83)

Human Relations: Closing The Gap Between Rights And Opportunity. Illustrated. Willie O. Davis. *about. . . time.* 11: 16-17+ (May 83)

Interracial Marriage

The Black Male-White Female: An Update. Illustrated. Alvin F. Poussaint. *Ebony.* 38: 124+ (Aug 83)

Black Men And White Women 13 Years Later. Illustrated. Orde Coombs. *Essence.* 14: 80-82+ (May 83)

Black Women And White Men. Patrice Miles and Audrey Edwards. *Essence.* 14: 94-95+ (Oct 83)

Interviewing

See Also Employment Interviewing

Intestines—Diseases

Pneumatosis Coli: A Case Presentation And Review Of The Literature. Illustrated, notes. Joyce Moore Stovall. *National Medical Association Journal.* 75: 626-629 (Jun 83)

Retroperitoneal Abscess. Tables, illustrated, notes. Soji F. Oluwole and others. *National Medical Association Journal.* 75: 693-700 (Jul 83)

Intracranial Aneurysms

Cerebral Aneurysm: Report Of Two Cases And Clinical Update. Notes. LaVert Morrow and Alphonso W. Hilliard. *National Medical Association Journal.* 75: 263-266 (Mar 83)

Intravenous Catherization

A Technique For Safe Internal Jugular Vein Catheterization. Illustrated. Michael G. Sarr. *National Medical Association Journal.* 75: 105-106 (Jan 83)

Inventors

Black Americans In The Field Of Science And Invention. Illustrated. Robert C. Hayden. *Journal of African Civilizations.* 05: 215-228 (Apr-Nov 83)

Lewis Latimer-Bringer Of The Light. Illustrated, notes. John Henrik Clarke. *Journal of African Civilizations.* 05: 229-237 (Apr-Nov 83)

See Also Engineers

Investments

Blacks In The Stock Market. Andrew F. Brimmer. *Black Enterprise.* 14: 41-42 (Oct 83)

The Bonanza In Tax-free Bonds. Illustrated. Udayan Gupta. *Black Enterprise.* 14: 31 (Aug 83)

Initial Public Stock Offerings The Start Of Something Big. Illustrated. Udayan Gupta. *Black Enterprise*. 13: 61 (Jun 83)

Mutual Funds Make Good Investments In A Rising Market. Illustrated. Udayan Gupta. *Black Enterprise*. 13: 35 (Feb 83)

Mutual Funds With Social Conscience. Udayan Gupta. *Black Enterprise*. 14: 35 (Nov 83)

Stock Market Outlook. Illustrated. Udayan Gupta. *Black Enterprise*. 14: 69-70+ (Oct 83)

See Also Speculation

Iowa

See Also Legislators—Iowa

Iraquis In The United States

Blacks And Iraqis Collide In Detroit. Abdeen Jabara and Ndel J. Saleh. *Freedomways*. 23: No. 3: 179-185 (83)

Irony In Literature

Comic Irony In Vanbrugh's The Relapse: Worthy's Repentance. Notes. James S. Malek. *CLA Journal*. 26: 353-361 (Mar 83)

Irvine, Russell W.

The Impact Of The Desegregation Process On The Education Of Black Students: Key Variables. Notes , tables. *Journal of Negro Education*. 52: 410-422 (Fall 83)

Ischinger, Barbara

Literatur Und Geschichte In Afrika: Darstellung Der Vorkolonialen Und Kultur Afrikas In Der English-Und Frazosischsprachig. en Fiktionalen Afrikanischen Literatur. Book review. *Research in African Literatures*. 14: 545-549 (Winter 83)

Islam And Capitalism

Prayers And Profits. Illustrated. Curtis G. Bunn. *Black Enterprise*. 14: 28 (Dec 83)

Islam And Literature

A Sufi Interpretation Of Le Regard Du Roi . Notes. Kenneth Harrow. *Research in African Literatures*. 14: 135-164 (Summer 83)

Israel

See Also Prisoners Of War—Israel

Israel—Foreign Relations—Lebanon

Israel's Plan For Lebanon. Notes. Claudia A. Sampson. *Freedomways*. 23: No. 2: 114-117 (83)

Israel—Foreign Relations—United States

America In The Wrong. Gus Savage. *Freedomways*. 23: No. 3: 171-175 (83)

An Open Letter On The Middle East. George W. (Jr.) Crockett. *Freedomways*. 23: No. 3: 176-178 (83)

Israel—Politics And Government

Liberation Theology And The Middle East Conflict. Wyatt Tee Walker. *Freedomways*. 23: No. 3: 147-152 (83)

Jabara, Abdeen and Saleh, Ndel J.

Blacks And Iraqis Collide In Detroit.. *Freedomways*. 23: No. 3: 179-185 (83)

Jackson, Anna Mitchell

A Theoretical Model For The Practice Of Psychotherapy With Black Populations. Tables, notes. *Journal of Black Psychology*. 10: 19-27 (Aug 83)

Jackson, Charles (Sr.)

Black Woman. Poem. *about. . . time*. 11: 24 (May 83)

Jackson, Christina

A South Pacific Island Paradise. Illustrated. *about. . . time*. 11: 22-23 (Dec 83)

Jackson, Irene V.

Lift Every Voice And Sing: A Collection Of Afro-American Spirituals And Other Songs. Book review. Carl G. (Jr.) Harris. *The Black Perspective in Music*. 11: 82-83 (Spring 83)

Jackson, Isaiah (about)

Isaiah Jackson - A Leader In The Classic Sense. Illustrated. Sarah D. Kash. *Crisis*. 90: 36-38 (Dec 83)

Jackson, Janet (about)

Todd Bridges And Janet Jackson: The Problems Of Teen-Age Stars. Illustrated. Aldore Collier. *Ebony*. 38: 58-59+ (Feb 83)

Jackson, Jesse L.

Back From Europe Jesse Leaves PUSH: To Run For President? Illustrated. *Jet*. 65: 8-9 (3 Oct 83)

Jackson, Jesse L. (about)

Jackson Steals Show At Democratic Fundraisers. Illustrated. *Jet*. 65: 6-8 (26 Dec 83)

Jesse Jackson Begins Run For U.S. President. Illustrated. *Jet*. 65: 14-16 (21 Nov 83)

Jesse Jackson Goes South With Crusade To Register Voters. Illustrated. Charles Sanders. *Jet*. 64: 6-8+ (13 Jun 83)

Jesse Jackson's Push For Power. Illustrated. Frank Dexter Brown. *Black Enterprise*. 14: 44-46+ (Nov 83)

Jesse Jackson Tells Why He Wants To Be President. Illustrated. *Jet*. 65: 4-6 (14 Nov 83)

Ministers As Apocalyptic Advocates For The Poor.. *Journal of Religious Thought*. 40: 23-28 (Spring-Summer 83)

Jackson, Jesse L. and Cassese, Sid

Jesse Jackson: The Leader Of PUSH Urges Boycotts For Dollar Power. Interview, Illustrated. *Essence*. 14: 14+ (Jun 83)

Jackson, Michael (about)

Diana and Michael: They Are Undisputed King And Queen Of Entertainment. Illustrated. Charles L. Sanders. *Ebony*. 39: 29-30+ (Nov 83)

Jackson-Opoku, Sandra

Avoid Foreign Faux Pas. Illustrated. *Black Enterprise*. 13: 241-245 (Jun 83)

How To Make Traveling For Business A Breeze.. *Essence*. 13: 42 + (Mar 83)

Pick The Right Telephone Service For Your Personal Needs. Illustrated, tables. *Black Enterprise*. 14: 56-58 (Aug 83)

A Tale Of Three Islands. Illustrated. *Essence*. 13: 41-42 + (Apr 83)

Three Isles Of Diversity. Illustrated. *Essence*. 14: 38 + (Oct 83)

Well, After All What Is There To Say? Poem. *Essence*. 14: 89 (Oct 83)

Winter-Proofing Your Boots.. *Essence*. 14: 40 (Nov 83)

Jackson, Reggie (about)

Reggie Jackson Admits Second Love Is For His 50 Cars. Illustrated. Norman O. Unger. *Jet*. 63: 46-49 (17 Jan 83)

Jackson, Trent (about)

What Happens When. . . The Active Career In Sports Is Over? Illustrated. Willis Anderson. *about. . . time*. 11: 14-19 (Jan 83)

Jackson, W. Sherman

"The Civil Rights Movement And The Black Church: A Conservative Or Militant Force". Notes. *Negro History Bulletin*. 46: 41-42 (Apr-Jun 83)

Jacob, John E.

Black Americans In Reagan's America. Notes. *Black Law Journal*. 08: 417-426 (Winter 83)

Jacob, John E. and Dupree, Adolph

John E. Jacob: President, National Urban League. Interview, Illustrated. *about. . . time*. 11: 10-15 + (Nov 83)

Jacob, John E. and McNatt, Robert

Lobbying: The Power Brokers. Interview, Illustrated. *Black Enterprise*. 14: 44-45 + (Aug 83)

Jacobs, Bruce

Black Theatre In Rochester-A Coming Of Age. Illustrated. *about. . . time*. 11: 20-23 (Jun 83)

Jacobs, Rosevelt

Psychological Aspects Of Chronic Pain. Notes. *National Medical Association Journal*. 75: 387-391 (Apr 83)

Jacobs, Sylvia M.

Black Americans And The Missionary Movement In Africa. Book review. L. B. J. Machobane. *Journal of Negro History*. 68: 118-119 (Winter 83)

An Empire For The Masses: The French Popular Image Of Africa, 1870-1900. Book review. *Journal of Negro History*. 68: 116-117 (Winter 83)

Jacobson, Cardell K.

Black Support For Affirmative Action Programs. Notes, tables. *Phylon*. 44: 299-311 (Dec 83)

Jamaica

Sharing Natural Rhythms Of Growth. Illustrated. Robin Wilson and Collette Fournier. *about. . . time*. 11: 10-12 (Dec 83)

Jamaican Cookery

See Cookery, Jamaican

Jamel, Latique Adrian

Battling Illiteracy Among Prisoners.. *Crisis*. 90: 40-41 + (Nov 83)

James, C. L.

Black And Beautiful Dolls. Illustrated. *Essence*. 14: 106 + (Nov 83)

James, Curtia

Avoiding After-College Panic.. *Essence*. 14: 20 + (Aug 83)

A Bajan Buffet. Illustrated. *Essence*. 13: 104-105 (Apr 83)

A Black-Native American Harvest. Illustrated. *Essence*. 14: 87-88 (Nov 83)

Essence Women: Barbara Banks. Illustrated. *Essence*. 13: 20 + (Jan 83)

How To Make Your Barbecue Sizzlin' Good. Illustrated. *Essence*. 14: 95 + (Jul 83)

The Joy Of Chicken. Illustrated. *Essence*. 14: 93-94 + (Sep 83)

Star-Studded Dishes. Illustrated. *Essence*. 13: 95 + (Feb 83)

Stir-Fry! Illustrated. *Essence*. 13: 89 + (Jan 83) Newborn, Venezuela

James, Joanette Pete

I Taught My Children To Manage Money. Illustrated. *Essence*. 14: 136 + (Jun 83)

James, Rick (about)

Rick James Talks About Life With Fast Women And Hot Cars. Illustrated. Aldore D. Collier. *Jet*. 65: 58-61 (26 Sep 83)

Jansen, Karl Heinz

Literatur Und Geschichte In Afrika: Darstellung Der Vorkolonialen Und Kultur Afrikas In Der English-Und Frazosischsprachig. en Fiktionalen Afrikanischen Literatur. Book review. Barbara Ischinger. *Research in African Literatures*. 14: 545-549 (Winter 83)

Japanese-Americans—Evacuation And Relocation, 1942-1945

The Press, Japanese Americans, And The Concentration Camps. Notes. Gary Y. Okihiro and Julie Sly. *Phylon*. 44: 66-83 (Mar 83)

Jaundice, Obstructive

Radiological Management Of Obstructive Jaundice. Tables, illustrated, notes. Benny O. Iko. *National Medical Association Journal*. 75: 51-56 (Jan 83)

Jaws—Tumors

Fibro-Osseous Lesions Of The Jaw: A Review Of 133 Cases From Nigeria. Illustrated, notes. H. A. Ajagbe and J. O. Daramola. *National Medical Association Journal*. 75: 593-598 (Jun 83)

Jazz Music

Will Jazz Survive? Thoughts On The State Of The Great American Art. Playthell Benjamin. *Freedomways*. 23: No. 4: 212-225 (83)

Jazz Musicians

Bobbi Humphrey Toots Her Own Flute. Illustrated. Bonnie Allen. *Essence*. 13: 66-68 (Mar 83)

Dorothy Donegan: Bouncy As Ever At Age 61. Illustrated. Clarence Waldron. *Ebony*. 39: 87-88 + (Dec 83)

The "Louisana Troupes" In Europe. Illustrated. Rainer E. Lotz. *The Black Perspective in Music*. 11: 133-142 (Fall 83)

Patrice Rushen. Illustrated. Gerrie E. Summers. *Essence*. 13: 15 (Feb 83)

Wynton Marsalis: Jazz Musician Of The Year. Illustrated. Kalamu Ya Salaam. *Black Collegian*. 14: 54-56 (Nov-Dec 83)

Jealousy

The Othello Syndrome. Notes. Oluwole O. Famuyiwa and Michael Ekpo. *National Medical Association Journal*. 75: 207-209 (Feb 83)

Jeffers, Lance and Laryea, Doris L.

A Black Poet's Vision: An Interview With Lance Jeffers. Interview. *CLA Journal*. 26: 422-433 (Jun 83)

Youngblood. Book review. *Black Scholar*. 14: 49-50 (Sep-Oct 83)

Jefferson, Frederick Douglass (Jr.)

Frederick Douglass: Agitator For Liberty, Justice, Equality And Afro-American Uplift. Illustrated. *about. . . time*. 11: 8-11 + (Feb 83)

Jemie, Onwuchekwa

Towards The Decolonization Of African Literature. Book review. Gerald Moore. *Research in African Literatures*. 14: 549-553 (Winter 83)

Jenkins, Melvin E.

In Memoriam Frederic C. Bartter, MD 1914-1983.. *National Medical Association Journal*. 75: 1111 (Nov 83)

Jeter, Michael A.

Criminal Law-The Right To An Impartial Trial Is Protected By An Opportunity To Prove That Juror Bias Or Prosecutorial Misconduct Affected The Outcome of The Trial: Smith V. Phillips. Notes. *Howard Law Journal*. 26: No. 2: 799-817 (83)

United States Vs Ross: Final Obliteration Of Fourth Amendment Protection From Warrantless Searches Of Cars And Their Contents. Notes. *Black Law Journal*. 08: 306-321 (Fall 83)

Jewish-Arab Relations

The Road To Jerusalem: Beirut September. Illustrated. Ellen Siegel. *Freedomways*. 23: No. 2: 90-98 (83)

Job Satisfaction

From Praises To Raises. Sherry Chastain. *Essence*. 14: 32 (Jun 83)

Making The Right Moves. Patricia Stinson. *Black Enterprise*. 14: 55-56 + (Sep 83)

Job Vacancies

Job Outlook '83 Gloomy With A Ray Of Hope. Illustrated. Yvette Franklin and William Rouselle. *Black Collegian*. 13: 112 + (Feb-Mar 83)

1983 Job Index.. *Black Collegian*. 13: 88 + (Feb-Mar 83)

Jockeys

Riding High At Seventeen. Illustrated. Marilyn Marshall. *Ebony*. 38: 60-61 + (May 83)

Johnson, Arthur L. (about)

A Man For All Sessions. Illustrated. Don Armstrong. *Crisis*. 90: 32 (Apr 83)

Johnson, Brent (joint author)

See Campbell, Norm

Johnson, Charles (about)

On Reconsidering Park, Johnson, DuBois, Frazier And Reid: Reply To Benjamin Bowser's "The Contribution Of Blacks To Sociological Knowledge.". Notes. Jerry G. Watts. *Phylon*. 44: 273-291 (Dec 83)

Johnson, David (about)

First Black Installed As Mayor Of Harvey, Ill. First facts. *Jet*. 64: 8 (23 May 83)

Johnson, Dwight L. (joint author)

See Mathey, William C. (Jr.)

Johnson, Edwin T.

Nosocomial Infection: Update. Tables, notes. *National Medical Association Journal*. 75: 147-154 (Feb 83)

Johnson, Eunice W.

Action Wear For Active People. Illustrated. *Ebony*. 38: 108-110 + (Jun 83)

Closing The Gap With Look Alikes. Illustrated. *Ebony*. 38: 126-128 + (Apr 83)

The Drama Of Italian Couture. Illustrated. *Ebony*. 39: 120-122 + (Nov 83)

Expression Of Grand Elegance. Illustrated. *Ebony*. 38: 116-118 (Sep 83)

Fashion's Best From Europe. Illustrated. *Ebony*. 39: 108-110 + (Dec 83)

Italian Ready-To-Wear: A Vintage Year. Illustrated. *Ebony*. 38: 100-102 (Jul 83)

A New Direction: Summer Couture From Paris 1983. Illustrated. *Ebony*. 38: 136-138 + (May 83)

Performance In Black And White. Illustrated. *Ebony*. 38: 96-98 + (Feb 83)

Sunsational Beachwear. Illustrated. *Ebony*. 38: 70-72+ (Jan 83)

5'4" And Under: Fashions For The Petite Figure. Illustrated. *Ebony*. 38: 110-112 (Oct 83)

Johnson, Flora

Countdown To Tax Time.. *Black Enterprise*. 14: 67-68+ (Nov 83)

Johnson, Guy

The Warrior. Poem. *Essence*. 14: 122 (Aug 83)

Johnson, Herschel

Cab Calloway: After 50 Years In Show Business The Hi-De-Ho Man Is Still Going Strong. Illustrated. *Ebony*. 38: 66-67+ (Feb 83)

To Mareta. Poem. *Ebony*. 38: 50 (Feb 83)

Johnson, Hershel Lee

Maneuvering Through The Mortgage Maze.. *Black Enterprise*. 14: 80-82+ (Dec 83)

Johnson, James P.

Can Computers Close The Educational Equity Gap? Notes. *The Urban League Review*. 08: 21-25 (Winter 83)

Johnson, James Weldon (1871-1938)

Beauty That Is Never Old. Poem. *Ebony*. 38: 48 (Feb 83)

Johnson, Janice (joint author)

　See Penn, William H. (Sr.)

Johnson, John H. (about)

Publisher John H. Johnson Wins Praise As New Owner Of Station WLOU. Illustrated. *Jet*. 63: 10-15 (10 Jan 83)

Publisher Johnson Among 10 Enshrined In Chicago Business Hall Of Fame. Illustrated. *Jet*. 65: 6-8 (31 Oct 83)

Johnson, Leandrew L. (about)

Test Your Family Values. Illustrated. Carolyne S. Blount. *about. . . time*. 11: 8-9 (Sep 83)

Johnson, Mark S.

Recognizing The Incestuous Family. Tables, notes. *National Medical Association Journal*. 75: 757-761 (Aug 83)

Johnson, Pamela G.

On Being An Engineer: Making The Transition From School To Career.. *Black Collegian*. 13: 56+ (Dec-Jan 83)

Johnson, Patrice

A Primer For Small Landlords: How To Reduce Hassles And Raise Profits. Illustrated. *Black Enterprise*. 13: 233-234+ (Jun 83)

Johnson Publishing Company

Johnson Publishing Company Sues Revlon, Inc; Charges Infringement Of Trademarks. Illustrated. *Jet*. 65: 14-15 (7 Nov 83)

Johnson, Robert E. and Sutton, Isaac

George Benson: Move To Hawaii Helps Him Survive Crises. Illustrated. *Jet*. 63: 58-62+ (21 Feb 83)

Gladys Knight Talks About Her Family And Career. Illustrated. *Jet*. 64: 54-57 (18 Apr 83)

Harold Washington: Makes Bold Bid To Become Chicago's First Black Mayor. Illustrated. *Jet*. 64: 12-16+ (21 Mar 83)

Harry Belafonte: Daughter Pays Father's Day Tribute To Her Famous Father. Illustrated. *Jet*. 64: 58-61 (20 Jun 83)

Lola Falana: On Tour With Sexy Show And Witty Thoughts. Illustrated. *Jet*. 64: 58-61 (18 Jul 83)

Marvin Gaye: Talks About His Troubled Life. Illustrated. *Jet*. 64: 56-60 (15 Aug 83)

Washington Upsets Foes To Win Democratic Bid In Chicago Mayoral Race. Illustrated. *Jet*. 63: 6-7+ (14 Mar 83)

Johnson, Ronald

Supply-Side Economics: The Rise To Prominence. Notes. *Review of Black Political Economy*. 12: 189-202 (Winter 83)

Johnson, Suzan D. (about)

Essence Women: Suzan D. Johnson. Illustrated. Mai Brown. *Essence*. 14: 42 (Sep 83)

Johnson, Wilfred A. and Caple, Brenda A.

Affective Attributes Of Special Education And Regular Class Preprofessionals. Notes. *Negro Educational Review*. 34: 73-78 (Apr 83)

America's Public Schools In Transition: Future Trends And Issues. Book review. *Journal of Negro Education*. 52: 459-461 (Fall 83)

Johnson, Willard R.

The Ancient Akan Script: A Review Of Sankofa, By Niangoran-Bouah. Illustrated. *Journal of African Civilizations*. 05: 197-207 (Apr-Nov 83)

Johnson, Wista

Diet Right. Illustrated. *Essence*. 13: 107 (Jan 83)

Easing Cramps, Naturally. Tables. *Essence*. 14: 42 (Sep 83)

How To Tame The Stress In Your Life.. *Essence*. 13: 82-83 (Apr 83)

A Man's Body Pleasure Points.. *Essence*. 14: 62-64+ (Nov 83)

Should Children Believe In Santa Claus?. *Essence*. 14: 124+ (Dec 83) Hensley, Dennis E.

Jones, Barbara A. P.

A Tribute To Vivian Wilson Henderson.. *Review of Black Political Economy*. 12: 5-7 (Spring 83)

Jones, Hughes (joint author)

　See Bell, Terrel

Jones, J. E. M.

I Smile Just A Little. Poem. *about. . . time*. 11: 22 (Sep 83)

Jones-Jackson, Patricia

Alive: African Traditions On The Sea Islands. Illustrated. *Negro History Bulletin.* 46: 95-96 + (Oct-Dec 83)

The Audience In Gullah And Igbo: A Comparison Of Oral Traditions. Notes. *CLA Journal.* 27: 197-209 (Dec 83)

Contemporary Gullah Speech: Some Persistent Linguistic Features. Notes. *Journal of Black Studies.* 13: 289-303 (Mar 83)

Jones, James Nathan

In Retrospect: Alfred Jack Thomas: Performer, Composer, Educator. Notes. *The Black Perspective in Music.* 11: 62-75 (Spring 83)

Jones, Ken

Stars To Shine At The Apollo. Illustrated. *Black Enterprise.* 14: 18 (Sep 83)

Jones, Lawrence N.

Urban Black Churches: Conservators Of Value And Sustainers Of Community. Notes. *Journal of Religious Thought.* 39: 41-50 (Fall-Winter 83)

Jones, Marcus E.

Female Immigrants To The United States: Caribbean, Latin American, And African Experience. Book review. *Phylon.* 44: 245-246 (Sep 83)

Jones-Miller, Alice and Ray, Elaine C.

The Essence Working Woman's Guide: Take Charge! Illustrated. *Essence.* 13: 75-82 (Mar 83)

Frost Came Too Early This Year. Poem. *Essence.* 13: 22 (Mar 83)

Jones, Monica C.

Planning A Successful Career: Taking It One Step At A Time. Illustrated. *Black Collegian.* 14: 78-80 (Sep-Oct 83)

Jones, Oliver (Jr.)

The Black Muslim Movement And The American Constitutional System. Tables, notes. *Journal of Black Studies.* 13: 417-437 (Jun 83)

Jones, Rhett S.

Social-Scientific Perspectives On The Afro-American Arts.. *Black American Literature Forum.* 17: 130-131 (Fall 83)

Jones, Ruth

Plyer V. Doe - Education And Illegal Alien Children. Notes. *Black Law Journal.* 08: 132-137 (Spring 83)

Jones, Thomas David

The International Law Of Maritime Blockade-A Measure Of Naval Economic Interdiction. Notes. *Howard Law Journal.* 26: No. 2: 759-779 (83)

Jones-Wilson, Faustine C.

Persistent And Emergent Legal Issues In Education: 1983 Yearbook. Editorial. *Journal of Negro Education.* 52: 187-188 (Summer 83)

Schooling And Democracy. Editorial. *Journal of Negro Education.* 52: 91-93 (Spring 83)

Jordan, June

Black Folks And Foreign Policy. Illustrated. *Essence.* 14: 162 (Jun 83)

DeLiza Spend The Day In The City. Poem. *Freedomways.* 23: No. 4: 234-235 (83)

Grace. Poem. *Essence.* 14: 124 (Aug 83)

Greensboro: North Carolina: Poem. *Freedomways.* 23: No. 4: 235 (83)

With Fire. Book review. *Freedomways.* 23: No. 01: 50 (83)

Jordan, Norman

Maya-2. Poem. *Essence.* 14: 20 (Sep 83)

Jordan, Tulani L. C.

The History And Significance Of Hair Braiding. Illustrated. *Black Collegian.* 13: 64-66 (Apr-May 83)

Jordan, Vernon E. (Jr.)

Spingarn Medal Presentation To. . . Lena Horne-A Living Legend.. *Crisis.* 90: 36 (Aug-Sep 83)

Jordon, Boji

Reflections On The Sharpville-Langa Massacres Of 1960. Illustrated. *Crisis.* 90: 44-45 (Apr 83)

Jordon, Harold W. (joint author)

See Howe, Gary L.

Joseph, Gloria I.

Zami - A New Spelling Of My Name. Book review. *Black Scholar.* 14: 48-49 (Sep-Oct 83)

Josey, E. J. (about)

Librarians Group Elects E.J. Josey To Top Post. Illustrated. *Jet.* 64: 23 (22 Aug 83)

Journal Of Black Psychology

An Empirical And Theoretical Review Of Articles In The Journal Of Black Psychology: 1974-1980. Tables, notes. Robert E. Steele and Sherry E. Davis. *Journal of Black Psychology.* 10: 29-42 (Aug 83)

Journalism—Objectivity

The Press, Japanese Americans, And The Concentration Camps. Notes. Gary Y. Okihiro and Julie Sly. *Phylon.* 44: 66-83 (Mar 83)

Journalists

Ed Bradley At Ease. Illustrated. Michele Wallace. *Essence.* 14: 66-67 (Nov 83)

Joseph Robert Love, 1839-1914: West Indian Extraordinary. Notes. Joy Lumsden. *Afro-Americans in New York Life and History.* 07: 25-39 (Jan 83)

See Also Women Journalists

Judges

Justice At The Top. Illustrated. *Ebony.* 38: 160-162 (Apr 83)

See Also Women Judges

Judges—Florida

Fla. Gov. Appoints Black To State Supreme Court.. *Jet.* 63: 4 (17 Jan 83)

Judges—Virginia

First Black Appointed To Virginia Supreme Court. First facts. *Jet.* 64: 30 (2 May 83)

Jury

Criminal Law-The Right To An Impartial Trial Is Protected By An Opportunity To Prove That Juror Bias Or Prosecutorial Misconduct Affected The Outcome of The Trial: Smith V. Phillips. Notes. Michael A. Jeter. *Howard Law Journal.* 26: No. 2: 799-817 (83)

Justice, Administration Of

Reagan Civil Rights: The First Twenty Months. Notes. *Black Law Journal.* 08: 68-94 (Spring 83)

Justice, Administration Of—United States

Without Justice. NotesLeadership Conference On Civil Rights. *Black Law Journal.* 08: 24-59 (Spring 83)

Juvenile Delinquency—Africa

The Onyenualagu (Godparent) In Traditional And Modern African Communities: Implications For Juvenile Delinquency. Notes. J. A. Sofola. *Journal of Black Studies.* 14: 21-30 (Sep 83)

Kabnick, Earl M. (joint author)

See Sobo, Steven

Kahle, Jane B.

Double Dilemma: Minorities And Women In Science Education. Book review. Julia V. Clark. *Journal of Negro Education.* 52: 85-87 (Winter 83)

Kai, Barbara

Collecting Pre-Columbian Art. Illustrated. *Black Enterprise.* 13: 108+ (Feb 83)

Kairys, David

The Politics Of Law: A Progressive Critique. Book review. Meredith L. Caliman. *Black Law Journal.* 08: 462-463 (Winter 83)

Kaposi's Sarcoma

A Descriptive Study Of Kaposi's Sarcoma In South Florida. Tables, notes. C. G. Torres and T. E. Aldrich. *National Medical Association Journal.* 75: 422-423 (Apr 83)

Karenga, Maulana

Important Black History Books: Some Fundamental Readings.. *Black Collegian.* 13: 142+ (Dec-Jan 83)

Karenga, Mulana

Introduction To Black Studies. Book review. Kuumba Na Kazi. *Black Collegian.* 13: 139 (Dec-Jan 83)

Karrer, Wolfgang

The Afro-American Novel Since 1960. Book review. Joe Weixlmann. *Black American Literature Forum.* 17: 134-136 (Fall 83)

Kash, Sarah D.

Isaiah Jackson - A Leader In The Classic Sense. Illustrated. *Crisis.* 90: 36-38 (Dec 83)

Kashif (about)

Kashif: A Musical Inventor For The '80s. Illustrated. Kalamu Ya Salaam. *Black Collegian.* 14: 118+ (Sep-Oct 83)

Kasim, Ahmed A. (joint author)

See Elhelu, Mohamed A.

Katz, Vera J. (joint author)

See Boston, Taquiena

Katz, William Loren

A Black Chief's Inspiring Saga. Illustrated. *Crisis.* 90: 38-39 (Apr 83)

Zionism In The Age Of The Dictators: A Reappraisal. Book review. *Freedomways.* 23: No. 3: 199-202 (83)

Kaufman, Evalyn

Good Health Guide For Travelers. Illustrated. *Black Enterprise.* 13: 80 (Mar 83)

Hang It All: The Art Of Exhibiting Paintings, Posters, Photos And Prints. Illustrated. *Black Enterprise.* 14: 134 (Oct 83)

Sweat Without Tears. Illustrated. *Black Enterprise.* 14: 74+ (Sep 83)

Tips On Renting A Vacation Home.. *Black Enterprise.* 13: 236 (Jun 83)

Kazi-Ferrouillet, Kuumba

The New Miss America: Beauty, Brains And Blackness. Illustrated. *Black Collegian.* 14: 48-49+ (Nov-Dec 83)

Kazi, Kuumba Na

Introduction To Black Studies. Book review. *Black Collegian.* 13: 139 (Dec-Jan 83)

Sassafrass, Cypress And Indigo. Book review. *Black Collegian.* 13: 132+ (Feb-Mar 83)

Summer Job Opportunities For Engineering Students. Illustrated. *Black Collegian.* 13: 85-88 (Dec-Jan 83)

Zami: A Spelling Of My Name. Book review, Illustrated. *Black Collegian.* 13: 68 (Apr-May 83)

Keith, Bea

Winning At Office Politics. Illustrated. *Essence.* 14: 79-80+ (Sep 83)

Keith, Damon J.

Should Color Blindness And Representativeness Be A Part Of American Justice. Notes. *Howard Law Journal.* 26: No. 1: 1-7 (83)

Keith, Stephen N.

Prospective Payment For Hospital Costs Using Diagnosis-Related Groups: Will Cost Inflation Be Reduced? Notes. *National Medical Association Journal.* 75: 609+ (Jun 83)

Kelley, Ernece B.

The Color Purple: A Moral Tale. Book review. *CLA Journal*. 27: 91-96 (Sep 83)

Kemp, Jack

Martin, Luther King Day Commemorates American Ideals. Illustrated. *about. . . time*. 11: 33 (Nov 83)

Kemp, James (about)

Labor Leader James Kemp Named National President Of NAACP At New York Meet. Illustrated. *Jet*. 63: 6 (21 Feb 83)

Kendrick, Gerald D.

Migrations Of The Heart. Book review. *CLA Journal*. 26: 362-363 (Mar 83)

Kendrick, John A. (about)

John A. Kendrick: A Salute. Illustrated. Jeff Donaldson. *Black Collegian*. 13: 130-131 (Feb-Mar 83)

Kennedy, Jayne (about)

Jayne Kennedy: Portrait Of A Woman Who Lost Her Husband And Found Herself. Illustrated. Laura B. Randolph. *Ebony*. 38: 107-108 + (Jul 83)

Jayne Kennedy: Portrait Of A Woman Who Lost Her Husband And Found Herself. Illustrated. Laura B. Randolph. *Ebony*. 38: 107-108 + (Jul 83)

Kennedy, John F. (1917-1963) (about)

Racism Toward Black African Diplomats During The Kennedy Administration. Notes. Calvin B. Holder. *Journal of Black Studies*. 14: 31-48 (Sep 83)

Kennedy, Stetson

Bid For Murder Tape Gets Cold Shoulder. Illustrated. *Crisis*. 90: 48-49 (Nov 83)

Kennington, Donald

The Literature Of Jazz: A Critical Guide. Book review. George L. Starks. *The Black Perspective in Music*. 11: 215-218 (Fall 83)

Kent, George E. (about)

The Legacy Of George E. Kent. Notes. James W. Coleman and Joanne Veal Gabbin. *Black American Literature Forum*. 17: 143-147 (Winter 83)

Kent, Rosanne

How To Speak Effectively: Tips For Coeds. Illustrated. *Black Collegian*. 13: 30 + (Apr-May 83)

Kentucky

See Also Republican Party. Kentucky

Kenya

See Also Astronomy—Kenya
Domestic Animals—Kenya—History

Kenya—Description And Travel

Touring Kenya's Fabulous Coast. Illustrated. Joan Harris. *Black Enterprise*. 13: 80 (Apr 83)

Kern-Foxworth, Marilyn

A Basic Guide To Resumes. Tables. *Black Collegian*. 14: 84-88 (Sep-Oct 83)

How To Get Into Grad School And Survive. Illustrated. *Black Collegian*. 14: 110 + (Nov-Dec 83)

Kerr, Catherine

Camping. Illustrated. *Black Enterprise*. 13: 260-262 (Jun 83)

Khaliq, Ammatullah Saburah

Financial Aid For Engineering Students. Illustrated. *Black Collegian*. 13: 134-136 + (Dec-Jan 83)

Kidneys—Diseases

Renal Angiomyolipoma With Retroperitoneal Adenopathy. Illustrated. Kiran Chawla and others. *National Medical Association Journal*. 75: 431-434 (Apr 83)

Kilgore, James C.

Another Ecclesiastical Morning. Poem. *Black American Literature Forum*. 17: 172 (Winter 83)

Like The Drunk. Poem. *Black American Literature Forum*. 17: 173 (Winter 83)

Page 3. Poem. *Black American Literature Forum*. 17: 173 (Winter 83)

Time Is More Than Money. Poem. *Black American Literature Forum*. 17: 173 (Winter 83)

Killam, G. D.

An Introduction To The Writings Of Ngugi. Book review. Govind Narain Sharma. *Research in African Literatures*. 14: 238-242 (Summer 83)

European And African Stereotypes In Twentieth-Century Fiction. Book review. *Research in African Literatures*. 14: 225-228 (Summer 83)

Killens, John Oliver

Youngblood. Book review. Lance Jeffers. *Black Scholar*. 14: 49-50 (Sep-Oct 83)

Youngblood. Book review. Elizabeth Nunez-Harrell. *Crisis*. 90: 42-43 (Oct 83)

Great Black Russian: Chapter Five - Part 5. Novel, Illustrated. *Crisis*. 90: 44-49 (Oct 83)

Praisesong For The Widow. Book review. *Crisis*. 90: 49-50 (Aug-Sep 83)

Run Like Hell And Holler Fire! (Part I). Novel. *Freedomways*. 23: No. 4: 244-256 (83)

Kinamore, Angela

Essence Women! Lenora T. Cartright. Illustrated. *Essence*. 14: 40 (Sep 83)

Fitness Fun And Healthful Habits For Kids. Illustrated. *Essence*. 13: 108 + (Jan 83)

Kindle, Valerie (about)

A Dallas Paralegal Builds Her Own Lucrative Business. Illustrated. Lloyd Gite. *Essence*. 14: 22 (May 83)

King, Bernice (about)

Whatever Happened To Bernice King? Illustrated. *Ebony*. 38: 160 + (Oct 83)

King, Charles H. (Jr.) and Horton, Linda

A Conversation With Dr. Charles H. King Jr. Interview, Illustrated. *Essence*. 14: 15 + (Dec 83)

King, Coretta Scott (about)

Coretta Scott King's Dedication To 'Dream' Rekindles Rights Drive. Illustrated. *Jet*. 65: 4-8 + (19 Sep 83)

King, D. E.

The Preacher For These Days.. *Journal of Religious Thought*. 40: 29-33 (Spring-Summer 83)

King, Evelyn (about)

Evelyn King. Frederick D. Murphy. *Essence*. 13: 13 (Apr 83)

King, Martin Luther (Jr.) (1929-1968) (about)

Comic Richard Pryor Puts All Jokes Aside To Give King Tribute. Illustrated. *Jet*. 63: 7-9 (31 Jan 83)

The Keepers Of The King Dream 15 Years Later. Illustrated. *Ebony*. 38: 31-32 + (Apr 83)

King's Son Answers Helm's Communist Slur Of His Dad.. *Jet*. 65: 22-23 (24 Oct 83)

A Living Memorial To The Drum Major For Justice. Illustrated. Walter Leavy. *Ebony*. 38: 120 + (Feb 83)

A Message To Black College Students. Illustrated. Stevie Wonder. *Black Collegian*. 13: 24-25 (Dec-Jan 83)

**King, Martin Luther (Jr.) (1929-1968)
—Anniversaries, Etc.**

The "Dream" Revisited. Illustrated. Cheryl Everette. *Essence*. 14: 50 (Aug 83)

"A Holiday for All The People". Illustrated. Robert Dole. *Crisis*. 90: 17-18 (Nov 83)

King Holiday Bill Passes; He Becomes 2nd American Honored By A National Day. Illustrated. *Jet*. 65: 4-6 (7 Nov 83)

Martin, Luther King Day Commemorates American Ideals. Illustrated. Jack Kemp. *about. . . time*. 11: 33 (Nov 83)

President Reagan Praises King, Signs Holiday Bill. Illustrated. Simeon Booker. *Jet*. 65: 4-7 (21 Nov 83)

King, Pat

New Wave Networkers.. *Black Enterprise*. 14: 89-90 + (Dec 83)

King, William M.

The End Of An Era: Denver's Last Legal Public Execution, July 27, 1886. Notes. *Journal of Negro History*. 68: 37-53 (Winter 83)

King, Woodie (Jr.)

Black Theatre: Present Condition. Book review. Owen Dodson. *Black American Literature Forum*. 17: 94-95 (Summer 83)

The Politics Of Black Arts.. *Black American Literature Forum*. 17: 30 (Spring 83)

Kirp, David L.

Just Schools: The Ideal Of Racial Equality In American Education. Book review. Peter Sola. *Journal of Negro Education*. 52: 457-459 (Fall 83)

Klíma, Vladimír

African Language Literatures: An Introduction To The Literary History Of Sub-Saharan Africa. Book review. *Research in African Literatures*. 14: 200-202 (Summer 83)

Klinkowitz, Jerome

God Made Alaska For The Indians: Selected Essays. Book review. *Black American Literature Forum*. 17: 137-139 (Fall 83)

Knappert, Jan

Namibia: Land And Peoples, Myths And Fables. Book review. Megan Biesele. *Research in African Literatures*. 14: 405-407 (Fall 83)

Knight, Elizabeth

Salute To Black Scholars: Bringing Scholarships And Students Together. Illustrated. *about. . . time*. 11: 12-13 (Jun 83)

Students On Civil Rights Progress: It's An Era Of Challenge For Them. Illustrated. *about. . . time*. 11: 16-18 (Nov 83)

Knight, Gladys (about)

Gladys Knight And Billy Dee Williams: Stars Of 'EbonysJet Celebrity Showcase'. Illustrated. *Jet*. 64: 54-56 (1 Aug 83)

Gladys Knight Talks About Her Family And Career. Illustrated. Robert E. Johnson. *Jet*. 64: 54-57 (18 Apr 83)

Knight, Kathleen (about)

Up, Up And Away. Illustrated. Lloyd Gite. *Essence*. 14: 44 (Oct 83)

Knights Of Labor

The 1886 Convention Of The Knights Of Labor. Notes. Claudia Miner. *Phylon*. 44: 147-159 (Jun 83)

Knipp, Margaret M.

Baba Of Karo: A Woman Of The Muslim Hausa. Book review. *Research in African Literatures*. 14: 407-409 (Fall 83)

Knipp, Thomas R.

African Writing Today. Book review. *Research in African Literatures*. 14: 116-119 (Spring 83)

Knox, W. J. (Jr.) (joint author)

See Cooper, W.

Koblenz, Jay

Archives For Auto Buffs. Illustrated. *Black Enterprise*. 14: 87-88 (Nov 83)

Family Trucking. Illustrated. *Black Enterprise*. 14: 87 (Aug 83)

Kom, Ambroise

Le Harlem De Chester Himes. Book review. Edward F. Taylor. *CLA Journal*. 27: 224-225 (Dec 83)

Kontrast (Game)

A "Kontrast" In Card Games. Illustrated. Lloyd Gite. *Black Enterprise*. 14: 32 (Dec 83)

Kornegay, Sharron

Pauline Strayhorne Is Major Federal's Prime Asset. Illustrated, tables. *Black Enterprise*. 13: 129-130 + (Jun 83)

Kosciuszko Tadeusz (about)

Tadeusz Kosciuszko And The Black Connection. E. P. Kulawiec. *Negro History Bulletin*. 46: 46 (Apr-Jun 83)

Kozlov, S. Ya

Ethnocultural Processes And National Problems In The Modern World. Book review. Alonzo T. Stephens. *Journal of Negro History*. 68: 128-129 (Winter 83)

Kramer, Aaron

Remembering Owen Dodson.. *Freedomways*. 23: No. 4: 258-269 (83)

Krampah, D. E. K.

Helping With Literature. Book review. Chikwenye Okonjo Ogunyemi. *Research in African Literatures*. 14: 254-255 (Summer 83)

Kratz, Corinne

Socio-Political Aspects Of The Palaver In Some African Countries. Book review. *Research in African Literatures*. 14: 409-412 (Fall 83)

Kreps, Karen

Diet Right: You Can Keep It Off!. *Essence*. 13: 131 (Apr 83)

Ku Klux Klan

Anti-Klan Network Seeks To End Racist Violence. Illustrated. *Jet*. 63: 43 (24 Jan 83)

Inside The Klan. Illustrated. Jerry Thompson. *Ebony*. 38: 100-102 + (Jun 83)

Ku Klux Klan In New York (State)

The Klan In Their Midst: The Ku Klux Klan In Upstate New York Communities. Notes. Charles Haley. *Afro-Americans in New York Life and History*. 07: 41-53 (Jan 83)

Kubitschek, Missy Dehn

"Tuh de Horizon And Back": The Female Quest In Their Eyes Were Watching God. Notes. *Black American Literature Forum*. 17: 109-115 (Fall 83)

Kulawiec, E. P.

Tadeusz Kosciuszko And The Black Connection.. *Negro History Bulletin*. 46: 46 (Apr-Jun 83)

Kumar, Ashir

Cephalosporins: Recent Developments. Notes. *National Medical Association Journal*. 75: 218-223 (Feb 83)

Kuzma, Kay

You Can Raise Well-Disciplined Kids. Illustrated. *Essence*. 13: 132 (Mar 83)

Kwanza

Celebrating Kwanza: One Family's Story. Illustrated. Beverley Seawright Taliaferro. *Essence*. 14: 103 + (Dec 83)

Celebrities See Christmas As Something Special Too At Kwanza Celebration. Illustrated. *Jet*. 65: 56-58 (26 Dec 83)

The New Soul Christmas. Illustrated. Frank (III) White. *Ebony*. 39: 29-30 + (Dec 83)

Kweli, Kujaatele

The Information Age: Promise Or Nightmare? Editorial. *The Urban League Review*. 08: 5-8 (Winter 83)

Kweli, Kujaatele and Randolph, Marc L.

Satellite Teleconferencing: A New Tool For Community And Economic Development. Illustrated , notes. *The Urban League Review*. 08: 40-54 (Winter 83)

Labor And Laboring Classes

Blacks In Labor Markets: A Historical Assessment. Notes. Denys Vaughn-Cooke. *The Urban League Review*. 07: 8-18 (Summer 83)

See Also Alien Labor
Middle Classes
Unemployed

Labor, Complicated

The Active Management Of Prolonged Labor. Illustrated, notes. Charles H. Wright. *National Medical Association Journal*. 75: 223-226 (Feb 83)

Labor Laws And Legislation

Good Intentions Gone Wrong: 8(A)(3) Supreme Court And Circuit Round-Up/With A Look At Wright Line. Notes. Madelyn C. Squire. *Howard Law Journal*. 26: No. 1: 9-52 (83)

Labor Laws And Legislation—United States

Fair Representation In Employment: A Historical Look. Notes. Afife Sayin. *The Urban League Review*. 07: 19-32 (Summer 83)

Labor Mobility—Africa

Africans In Search Of Work: Migration And Diaspora. Notes, tables. Lenneal J. Henderson. *The Urban League Review*. 07: 58-73 (Summer 83)

Labor Supply

Addressing Unemployment Problems: A Jobs Bill Is Needed From The Federal Government. Illustrated. William Clay and Lillian Roberts. *about. . . time*. 11: 12-13 (Jan 83)

Bombs Or Bread: Black Unemployment And The Pentagon Budget. Tables. Marion Anderson. *Black Scholar*. 14: 2-11 (Jan-Feb 83)

Deindustrialization And Unemployment In America. Tables, Notes. Barry Bluestone. *Review of Black Political Economy*. 12: 27-42 (Spring 83)

Eliminate Both Unemployment And Inflation. Illustrated. W. Arthur Lewis. *Crisis*. 90: 40 (Jan 83)

Money Growth And The Employment Aspirations Of Black Americans. Tables, Notes. Everson Hull. *Review of Black Political Economy*. 12: 64-74 (Spring 83)

Orthodox And Systemic Explanations For Unemployment And Racial Inequality: Implications For Policy. Notes. David H. Swinton. *Review of Black Political Economy*. 12: 9-25 (Spring 83)

Racial Differences In Unemployment: A Spatial Perspective. Tables, Notes. Joe T. Darden. *Review of Black Political Economy*. 12: 93-105 (Spring 83)

The Unemployment Dilemma. Editorial. Carolyne S. Blount. *about. . . time*. 11: 4+ (Mar 83)

Labor Supply—History

Yesterday (1929) In The Crisis. . . Exploitation Or Cooperation? Tables. William C. Matney. *Crisis*. 90: 20-22 (Dec 83)

Labor-Unions

See Trade-Unions

Lacob, Miriam

South Africa's Black Middle Class. Illustrated. *Black Enterprise*. 13: 49-50+ (Apr 83)

Lacy, William B. and others

Fostering Constructive Intergroup Contact In Desegregated Schools: Suggestions For Future Research. Notes. *Journal of Negro Education*. 52: 130-141 (Spring 83)

Laforse, Martin

Popular Culture And American Life: Selected Topics In The Study Of American Popular Culture. Book review. Doris Evans McGinty. *The Black Perspective in Music*. 11: 212-214 (Fall 83)

Lake, Edwin B.

A Voice Of The People. Illustrated. *Black Enterprise*. 13: 42 (Jun 83)

Lake, Marvin Leon

The President That Time Forgot.. *Negro History Bulletin*. 46: 51-52 (Apr-Jun 83)

Land Use

See Eminent Domain

Landlord And Tenant

A Primer For Small Landlords: How To Reduce Hassles And Raise Profits. Illustrated. Patrice Johnson. *Black Enterprise*. 13: 233-234+ (Jun 83)

Tips On Renting A Vacation Home. Evalyn Kaufman. *Black Enterprise*. 13: 236 (Jun 83)

Landrum, Larry N.

American Popular Culture: A Guide To Information Sources. Book review. Doris Evans McGinty. *The Black Perspective in Music*. 11: 212-214 (Fall 83)

Lane Isaac (about)

From Slavery To Achievement: Keep On A Goin'. Illustrated. Robert L. (Jr.) Harris. *Black Collegian*. 13: 142-147 (Feb-Mar 83)

Lane, Kathleen Wyer

Life On The Nile: One Woman's Travels Through Egypt-Land Of The Pharaohs. Illustrated. *Essence*. 14: 38+ (Jul 83)

Lang, Raymond

Man Of God And Gun. Illustrated. *Ebony*. 38: 102-104 (Sep 83)

Two Innocents Who Suffered On Death Row. Illustrated. *Ebony*. 38: 29-30+ (Sep 83)

Lange, Gerri

Bay Area: California Dreamin'. Illustrated. *Essence*. 14: 38+ (May 83)

Lange, Werner J.

W. E. B. DuBois And The First Scientific Study Of Afro-America. Notes, tables. *Phylon*. 44: 135-146 (Jun 83)

Langston, Andrew (about)

Andrew Langston: Mighty Like A River. Illustrated. Adolph Dupree. *about. . . time*. 11: 14-21 (Apr 83)

Language And Culture

If You Just Change The Key, It's Still The Same Old Song. Andrea Hairston. *Black American Literature Forum*. 17: 36-37 (Spring 83)

Language And Liberation. Notes. Geneva Smitherman. *Journal of Negro Education*. 52: 15-23 (Winter 83)

Language And Education

Functional Language, Socialization, And Academic Achievement. Notes. Richard L. Wright. *Journal of Negro Education*. 52: 3-14 (Winter 83)

Psychological Factors Associated With Language In The Education Of The African-American Child. Notes. ASA G. (III) Hilliard. *Journal of Negro Education*. 52: 24-34 (Winter 83)

Language And Languages—Study And Teaching

The College Language Association And The Profession Of Languages And Literature. Notes. Eleanor Q. Tignor. *CLA Journal*. 26: 367-383 (Jun 83)

Language Arts—Africa

Education In Indigenous Languages: The West African Model Of Language Education. Notes. Ayo Bamgbose. *Journal of Negro Education*. 52: 57-64 (Winter 83)

Lapchick, Richard and Williams, Franklin H.

We Say "No" To Apartheid Sport. Illustrated. *Crisis*. 90: 42-45 (Jan 83)

Larsen, David C.

Will Power: Don't Leave Life Without It.. *Essence*. 14: 35+ (Oct 83)

Laryea, Doris L. (joint author)

See Jeffers, Lance

Lassiter, Wright (Jr.) (about)

Dr Wright Lassitar Jr. New Bishop College Prexy. Illustrated. *Jet*. 64: 24 (8 Aug 83)

Latimer, Lewis (1848-1928) (about)

Lewis Latimer-Bringer Of The Light. Illustrated, notes. John Henrik Clarke. *Journal of African Civilizations*. 05: 229-237 (Apr-Nov 83)

Latin America—Foreign Relations—United States

Opening Speech In The Meeting Of Intellectuals For The Sovereignty Of The Peoples Of Our America. Armando Hart. *Black Scholar*. 14: 2-12 (Summer 83)

Laubich, Arnold

Art Tatum: A Guide To His Recorded Music. Book review. James Remel Burden. *The Black Perspective in Music*. 11: 86-88 (Spring 83)

Launius, Roger D.

Walter Hines Page And The World's Work, 1900-1913. Book review. *Journal of Negro History*. 68: 104-105 (Winter 83)

Law And Ethics

Controversial Propositions Of Law And The Positivist Embarrassment: The Hart/Dworkin Debate Reconsidered. Notes. Simeon Charles Randolph McIntosh. *Howard Law Journal*. 26: No. 2: 699-722 (83)

Law, Labor

See Labor Laws And Legislation

Law, Medical

See Medical Laws And Legislation

Law Schools

Minority Tokenism In American Law Schools. Notes, tables. Portia T. Hamlar. *Howard Law Journal*. 26: No. 2: 443-599 (83)

Peoples' College Of Law.. *Black Law Journal*. 08: 456-458 (Winter 83)

Law Schools—Curricula

A Plan For The Special Preparation Of Attorneys In Effective Writing Skills. Notes. Elizabeth Walker Stone. *Journal of Negro Education*. 52: 314-331 (Summer 83)

Lawrence, D. Baloti

Body Alive: Quick Relief For Back Pain. Illustrated. *Essence*. 14: 129 (May 83)

Lawrence, Leonard E.

Stress And The Black Medical Family. Illustrated. *National Medical Association Journal*. 75: 749-753 (Aug 83)

Lawrence, Loeta S.

Women In Caribbean Literature: The African Presence. Notes. *Phylon*. 44: 1-10 (Mar 83)

Lawson, Edward (about)

A Case Of Anonymity. Illustrated. Jill Nelson. *Black Enterprise*. 13: 26 (Mar 83)

Lawson, Ellen N. and Merrill, Marlene

The Antebellum "Talented Thousandth": Black College Students At Oberlin Before The Civil War. Notes, tables. *Journal of Negro Education*. 52: 142-155 (Spring 83)

Lawyers

Foreword [To Vol. 8 No.1]. Notes. Linda Taylor Ferguson. *Black Law Journal*. 08: 4-6 (Spring 83)

Louis Rothschild Mehlinger: The First One Hundred Years. Notes. J. Clay (Jr.) Smith. *Howard Law Journal*. 26: No. 2: 359-441 (83)

The Role Of Primary And Secondary Teachers In The Motivation Of Black Youth To Become Lawyers. Notes. J. Clay (Jr.) Smith. *Journal of Negro Education*. 52: 302-313 (Summer 83)

See Also Attorney And Client
Bar Associations
Judges
Women Lawyers

Laye, Camara—Criticism And Interpretation

A Sufi Interpretation Of Le Regard Du Roi . Notes. Kenneth Harrow. *Research in African Literatures*. 14: 135-164 (Summer 83)

Lazaro, Eric J. and others

A Critical Analysis Of Clerkship Grading Procedures. Tables, notes. *National Medical Association Journal*. 75: 1083-1086 (Nov 83)

Leadership

Breakthroughs. Illustrated. *Ebony*. 38: 176-178 + (Aug 83)

If We Are Not For Ourselves. Illustrated. Les Payne. *Essence*. 13: 130 (Feb 83)

The Pan African Movement, 1900-1945: A Study In Leadership Conflicts Among The Disciples Of Pan Africanism. Notes. Alexandre Mboukou. *Journal of Black Studies*. 13: 275-287 (Mar 83)

The Quality Of Leadership: Gary A. Scott (July 11, 1945-March 29, 1968). Illustrated. Adolph Dupree. *about. . . time*. 11: 22-26 (Nov 83)

A Theory Of Liberation Leadership. Notes. Charles V. Willie. *Journal of Negro History*. 68: 1-7 (Winter 83)

The 100 Most Influential Black Americans. Illustrated. *Ebony*. 38: 109-110 + (May 83)

50 Young Leaders Of The Future. Illustrated. *Ebony*. 38: 65-66 + (Sep 83)

Leadership Conference On Civil Rights

Without Justice. Notes. *Black Law Journal*. 08: 24-59 (Spring 83)

Leanness

Everything To Gain, Nothing To Lose. Illustrated. *Ebony*. 38: 44 + (Jul 83)

Leavy, Walter

Aaron Pryor: His Own Boss Inside And Outside The Ring. Illustrated. *Ebony*. 38: 35-36 + (May 83)

Baseball's Greatest 'Thief'. Illustrated. *Ebony*. 38: 135-136 + (Jun 83)

Can Black Mayors Stop Crime? Illustrated. *Ebony*. 39: 116 + (Dec 83)

Eddie Murphy: An Incredible Leap To Superstardom. Illustrated. *Ebony*. 38: 35-36 + (Oct 83)

Eddie Murphy: Will Movie Hit Create Problems For Controversial Comic? Illustrated. *Ebony*. 38: 88 + (Apr 83)

Eddie Robinson: Grambling's Living Legend.
Illustrated. *Ebony*. 38: 60-62 + (Jan 83)

Is The Black Male An Endangered Species?
Illustrated. *Ebony*. 38: 41-42 + (Aug 83)

A Living Memorial To The Drum Major For
Justice. Illustrated. *Ebony*. 38: 120 + (Feb 83)

Lt. Col. Guion S. Bluford Jr. Takes. . . A Historic
Step Into Space. Illustrated. *Ebony*. 39: 162-164 +
(Nov 83)

The Runningest, Jumpingest Athlete In The World.
Illustrated. *Ebony*. 38: 139-140 + (Sep 83)

Lebanon

See Also Massacres—Lebanon

Lebanon—Foreign Relations—Israel

Israel's Plan For Lebanon. Notes. Claudia A.
Sampson. *Freedomways*. 23: No. 2: 114-117 (83)

Lebanon—Israeli Invasion, 1982

The International Hearing On The Israeli Invasion
Of Lebanon. David Henley. *Freedomways*. 23: No.
2: 99-111 (83)

Lederman, Michael M. and others

Measurement Of Glycosylated Hemoglobins In
Black Diabetic Patients: A Note Of Caution.
Illustrated, notes. *National Medical Association
Journal*. 75: 353-355 (Apr 83)

Lee, Clarence and others

Interaction Of Nutrition And Infection: Effect Of
Zinc Deficiency On Immunoglobulin Levels In
Trypanosoma Musculi Infection. Tables, notes.
National Medical Association Journal. 75: 677-682
(Jul 83)

Lee, Clarence M. and Best, Yvette

Immunobiology Of Trichinosis. Notes. *National
Medical Association Journal*. 75: 565-570 (Jun 83)

Lee, Don L.

See Madhubuti, Haki R.

Lee, Elliott D. (joint author)

See Campbell, Bebe Moore

Lee, Mildred K. (joint author)

See Cummings, Alban

Lee, Susan

Mastectomy: Some Hopeful Facts You Should
Know. Illustrated. *Essence*. 13: 53-54 (Feb 83)

Leeman, Clive

The Writing Of Peter Abrahams. Book review.
Research in African Literatures. 14: 245-248
(Summer 83)

Legal Aid—California—Los Angeles

South Central Legal Services Program. Elaine
Mallette. *Black Law Journal*. 08: 147-149 (Spring
83)

Legal Positivism

Controversial Propositions Of Law And The
Positivist Embarrassment: The Hart/Dworkin Debate
Reconsidered. Notes. Simeon Charles Randolph
McIntosh. *Howard Law Journal*. 26: No. 2:
699-722 (83)

Legislators—Georgia

The Private Side Of Julian Bond. Illustrated.
Stephanie Stokes Oliver. *Essence*. 14: 103-104 +
(Nov 83)

Legislators—Iowa

First Black Elected To Iowa State Senate.
Illustrated, first facts. *Jet*. 63: 6 (10 Jan 83)

Legislators—New York (State)

Essence Women: Gloria Davis. Illustrated. Ruth
Manuel. *Essence*. 14: 56 (Jul 83)

Legislators—United States

New Faces On Capitol Hill. Illustrated. *Ebony*. 38:
36-38 + (Feb 83)

Legislators—United States—California

U.S. Rep. Hawkins Honored For 50 Years In
Politics. Illustrated. *Jet*. 64: 12-13 (27 Jun 83)

Legislators—United States—Illinois

Washington's Successor. Steve Askin. *Black
Enterprise*. 14: 19 (Nov 83)

Legislators—United States—New York

Federal Budget: Charles B. Rangel (D. N. Y.).
Illustrated. Bebe Moore Campbell. *Black
Enterprise*. 14: 56 (Oct 83)

Legislators—United States—Ohio

The Election Of An Ohio Congressman. Notes.
Philip A. (Jr.) Grant. *Negro History Bulletin*. 46:
60-62 (Apr-Jun 83)

Legislators—United States—Tennessee

Federal Budget: Harold E. Ford (D. Tenn.).
Illustrated. Bebe Moore Campbell. *Black
Enterprise*. 14: 54 (Oct 83)

Leiner, Jacqueline

Imaginaire, Langage-Identité Culturelle, Négritude.
Book review. Martin Steins. *Research in African
Literatures*. 14: 553-554 (Winter 83)

LeNoire, Rosetta (about)

Rosetta LeNoire: The Lady And Her Theatre.
Notes. Linda Kerr Norflett. *Black American
Literature Forum*. 17: 69-72 (Summer 83)

Leonard, Jeanette J. (joint author)

See Tollett, Kenneth S.

Leonard, Sugar Ray (about)

Sugar Ray Leonard Replaces Boxing With Family,
TV Show And New $2 Million Home. Illustrated.
Norman O. Unger. *Jet*. 65: 20-23 (14 Nov 83)

Lesbianism

Sister Love. Illustrated. Alexis DeVeaux. *Essence*.
14: 82-84 + (Oct 83)

Lesnick, Howard

Becoming A Lawyer: A Humanistic Perspective On Legal Education And Professionalism. Book review. Elana Yancey. *Black Law Journal*. 08: 164-166 (Spring 83)

Lewis, Carl (about)

The Runningest, Jumpingest Athlete In The World. Illustrated. Walter Leavy. *Ebony*. 38: 139-140 + (Sep 83)

Lewis, Emmanuel (about)

Emmanuel Lewis: Star Of TV Commercials To Debut In TV Series. Illustrated. Trudy S. Moore. *Jet*. 64: 60-64 (22 Aug 83)

Lewis, W. Arthur

Eliminate Both Unemployment And Inflation. Illustrated. *Crisis*. 90: 40 (Jan 83)

Liberation Theology

Liberation Theology And The Middle East Conflict. Wyatt Tee Walker. *Freedomways*. 23: No. 3: 147-152 (83)

Liberia

See Also Music—Liberia

Liberia—History—1847-1944

European Imperialism In Liberia: The Scramble And Partition - 1882-1914. Notes. Monday B. Akpan. *Negro History Bulletin*. 46: 93-94 (Oct-Dec 83)

Liberty Of The Press

See Also Censorship

Librarians

Librarians Group Elects E.J. Josey To Top Post. Illustrated. *Jet*. 64: 23 (22 Aug 83)

Liburd-Jordan, Sondra

Fueling His Way To The Top. Illustrated. *Black Enterprise*. 13: 169-170 + (Jun 83)

Lieb, Sandra R.

Mother Of The Blues: A Study Of Ma Rainey. Book review. D. Antoinette Handy. *The Black Perspective in Music*. 11: 83-85 (Spring 83)

Liebman, Lance

Ethnic Relations In America. Book review, Notes. David A. Gerber. *Afro-Americans in New York Life and History*. 07: 75-76 (Jul 83)

Life Insurance

See Insurance, Life

Lightfoot, Orlando B.

Preventive Issues And The Black Elderly: A Biopsychosocial Perspective. Notes, tables. *National Medical Association Journal*. 75: 957-963 (Oct 83)

Lim, Sook K. and others

Virilizing Lipid Cell Tumor Of The Ovary: Light And Electron Microscopic Studies. Tables, illustrated, notes. *National Medical Association Journal*. 75: 722-726 (Jul 83)

Lincoln Independent Party

Black Political Insurgency In Louisville, Kentucky: The Lincoln Independent Party Of 1921. Notes. George C. Wright. *Journal of Negro History*. 68: 8-23 (Winter 83)

Linder, Dorothy

Science, Myth, Reality: The Black Family In One-Half Century Of Research. Book review. *Phylon*. 44: 87-88 (Mar 83)

Lipids

Comparative Study Of The Lipid Composition Of Particular Pathogenic And Nonpathogenic Species Of Mycobacterium. Tables, illustrated. Arvind K. N. Nandedkar. *National Medical Association Journal*. 75: 69-74 (Jan 83)

Lippert, Anne

C.D.S.H., Centre De Documentation Des Sciences Humaines, Algeria.. *Research in African Literatures*. 14: 193-195 (Summer 83)

Literary Research

C.D.S.H., Centre De Documentation Des Sciences Humaines, Algeria. Anne Lippert. *Research in African Literatures*. 14: 193-195 (Summer 83)

Literature

See Also Autobiography
Cameroonian Literature (English)
Caribbean Literature
Characters And Characteristics In Literature
Children's Literature
Fiction
Folk Literature
Imagination In Literature
Nigerian Literature
Poetry
Race Awareness In Literature
Women In Literature

Literature And Folk-Lore

See Also Folk-Lore In Literature

Literature And Islam

See Islam And Literature

Literature And Society

Social-Scientific Perspectives On The Afro-American Arts. Rhett S. Jones. *Black American Literature Forum*. 17: 130-131 (Fall 83)

Literature, South African

See South African Literature

Little, Malcolm

See Malcolm X (1925-1965)

Little Rock, Arkansas

See Also School Integration—Little Rock, Arkansas

Lloyd, Ed (about)

Everything For The Office, Inc. Illustrated. Marc Hequet. *Black Enterprise*. 14: 95-96 (Dec 83)

Lloyd, Hortense D.

But Some Of Us Are Brave. Book review. *Negro Educational Review*. 34: 45-46 (Jan 83)

Lloyd, R. Grann

The Constitution And The Black American.. *Negro Educational Review*. 34: 2-3 (Jan 83)

The Major Problems And Concerns Of Black Students In The Duval County Public Schools. Tables, notes. *Negro Educational Review*. 34: 92-114 (Jul-Oct 83)

Three-Fifths Of A Professor, Too?. *Negro Educational Review*. 34: 50-51 (Apr 83)

Loansberry, Barbara (joint author)

See Hovet, Grace Ann

Lobbyists

Lobbying: The Power Brokers. Interview, Illustrated. John E. Jacob and Robert McNatt. *Black Enterprise*. 14: 44-45+ (Aug 83)

Locus Standi

Havens Realty Corp. V. Coleman: Standing To Sue Under The Fair Housing Act. Notes. Terry L. White. *Black Law Journal*. 08: 127-131 (Spring 83)

Logan, Adella Hunt

Colored Women As Voters (September, 1912).. *Crisis*. 90: 11 (Feb 83)

Logan, Adella Hunt (1863-1915) (about)

Private Consequences Of A Public Controversy. . . Grandmother, Grandfather, W.E.B. Du Bois And Booker T. Washington. Illustrated. Adele Logan Alexander. *Crisis*. 90: 8-11 (Feb 83)

Logan, Hal J.

Harnessing The Information Explosion. Illustrated. *Black Enterprise*. 13: 223-224+ (Jun 83)

Logan, Harold J.

Maxima's 8a Dilemma. Illustrated. *Black Enterprise*. 13: 42-45 (Jan 83)

Logan, Rayford W.

Dictionary Of American Negro Biography. Book review. *Crisis*. 90: 58 (Feb 83)

Dictionary Of American Negro Biography. Book review. Eunice Shaed Newton. *Journal of Negro Education*. 52: 454-455 (Fall 83)

Logan, Rayford W. (1897-1982) (about)

In Memoriam: Rayford W. Logan. Illustrated. Michael R. Winston. *Negro History Bulletin*. 46: 68 (Jul-Sep 83)

Logan, Warren (about)

Private Consequences Of A Public Controversy. . . Grandmother, Grandfather, W.E.B. Du Bois And Booker T. Washington. Illustrated. Adele Logan Alexander. *Crisis*. 90: 8-11 (Feb 83)

Long, Samuel

Psychopolitical Orientations Of White And Black Youth: A Test Of Five Models. Tables, notes. *Journal of Black Studies*. 13: 439-456 (Jun 83)

Lorde, Audre

Zami - A New Spelling Of My Name. Book review. Gloria I. Joseph. *Black Scholar*. 14: 48-49 (Sep-Oct 83)

Zami: A New Spelling Of My Name. Book review. Carole Bovoso. *Essence*. 13: 20 (Mar 83)

Zami: A Spelling Of My Name. Book review, Illustrated. Kuumba Na Kazi. *Black Collegian*. 13: 68 (Apr-May 83)

Black Women's Anger. Illustrated. *Essence*. 14: 90-92+ (Oct 83)

The Seventh Sense. Poem. *Essence*. 14: 17 (Dec 83)

Lorde, Audre

There Is No Hierarchy Of Oppressions.. *Interracial Books for Children*. 14: No. 3: 9 (83)

Los Angeles

See Also Legal Aid—California—Los Angeles

Lotan, Yael

Middle East Crossroads.. *Freedomways*. 23: No. 3: 165-170 (83)

Lotz, Rainer E.

The "Louisana Troupes" In Europe. Illustrated. *The Black Perspective in Music*. 11: 133-142 (Fall 83)

Lou, Mary Ann (joint author)

See Popoola, Dapo

Louis, Joe (1914-1981) (about)

Joe Louis-Model For The Physician. Illustrated. *Crisis*. 90: 22-23 (Apr 83)

Louisville, Kentucky

See Also Radio Stations—Kentucky—Louisville

Louisville, Kentucky—Politics And Government —History

Black Political Insurgency In Louisville, Kentucky: The Lincoln Independent Party Of 1921. Notes. George C. Wright. *Journal of Negro History*. 68: 8-23 (Winter 83)

Loury, Glenn C.

Black Survival In America. Illustrated. *Black Enterprise*. 13: 33 (May 83)

Economics, Politics, And Blacks. Notes. *Review of Black Political Economy*. 12: 43-54 (Spring 83)

Love

Making Love Work. Editorial. Susan L. Taylor. *Essence*. 13: 59 (Feb 83)

Love, Joseph Robert (1839-1914) (about)

Joseph Robert Love, 1839-1914: West Indian Extraordinary. Notes. Joy Lumsden. *Afro-Americans in New York Life and History*. 07: 25-39 (Jan 83)

Low, Ronald

Equal Protection Fourteenth Amendment - State Requirement Of Citizenship To Be Peace Officer Sugarman Exception Cabell Vs Chavez-Salido. Notes. *Black Law Journal*. 08: 322-337 (Fall 83)

Low, W. Augustus

Encyclopedia Of Black America. Book review.
Doris Evans McGinty. *The Black Perspective in
Music.* 11: 79-82 (Spring 83)

Loyalty-Security Program, 1947-

Louis Rothschild Mehlinger: The First One Hundred
Years. Notes. J. Clay (Jr.) Smith. *Howard Law
Journal.* 26: No. 2: 359-441 (83)

Loyd, Philip A.

Entrepreneurship: A Viable Alternative. Illustrated.
about. . . time. 11: 14-16+ (Mar 83)

Make Your Own Breaks. Illustrated. *about. . . time.*
11: 13 (Apr 83)

Luciano, Felipe

Puerto Rico's Cerromar Beach. Illustrated. *Black
Enterprise.* 13: 67 (May 83)

Lumpkin, Beatrice

Senefer And Hatshepsut. Book review. Claudia
Zaslavsky. *Freedomways.* 23: No. 4: 294-296 (83)

Africa In The Mainstream Of Mathematics History.
Notes. *Journal of African Civilizations.* 05: 100-109
(Apr-Nov 83)

The Pyramids: Ancient Showcase Of African
Science And Technology. Illustrated, notes, tables.
Journal of African Civilizations. 05: 67-83
(Apr-Nov 83)

Lumpkin, Margaret (joint author)

See Britton, Gwyneth

Lumpkins, Lola and Oestreich, Alan E.

Rickets As An Unexpected X-Ray Finding.
Illustrated, notes. *National Medical Association
Journal.* 75: 255-258 (Mar 83)

Lumsden, Joy

Joseph Robert Love, 1839-1914: West Indian
Extraordinary. Notes. *Afro-Americans in New York
Life and History.* 07: 25-39 (Jan 83)

Lungs—Cancer

Lung Cancer Incidence Among Nonwhites In Erie
County, New York. Notes, tables. John E. Vena.
National Medical Association Journal. 75:
1229-1231 (Dec 83)

Lungs—Dust Diseases

See Also Asbestosis

Lyles, Barbara D.

In The Eye Of The Beholder: Contemporary Issues
In Stereotyping. Book review. *Journal of Negro
Education.* 52: 83-85 (Winter 83)

Lynch, B. M. and Robbins, L. H.

Namoratunga: The First Archaeoastronomical
Evidence In Sub-Saharan Africa. Illustrated, tables,
notes. *Journal of African Civilizations.* 05: 51-56
(Apr-Nov 83)

M & M Products Company, Inc.

Prescription FOr Success. Illustrated. Adolph
Dupree. *about. . . time.* 11: 14-16 (Aug 83)

Machado de Assis, Joaquim Maria (1839-1908)
(about)

An Artist's Identity Versus The Social Role Of The
Writer: The Case For Joaquim Maria Machado De
Assis. Notes. Maria Luisa Nunes. *CLA Journal.* 27:
187-196 (Dec 83)

Machobane, L. B. J.

Black Americans And The Missionary Movement In
Africa. Book review. *Journal of Negro History.* 68:
118-119 (Winter 83)

Mack, Ally Faye

Political Process And The Development Of Black
Insurgency 1930-1970. Book review. *Journal of
Negro History.* 68: 127-128 (Winter 83)

Mack, Eva (about)

Her Honor, The Mayor. Illustrated. Julie Chenault.
Essence. 14: 14+ (Jul 83)

Maclennan, Don

Perspectives On South African Fiction. Book
review. Stephen Gray. *Research in African
Literatures.* 14: 216-218 (Summer 83)

Macrophages

The Role Of Macrophages In Immunology.
Mohamed A. Elhelu. *National Medical Association
Journal.* 75: 314-317 (Mar 83)

Madgett, Naomi Long

Exits And Entrances. Book review. Tom Dent.
Freedomways. 23: No. 01: 42-49 (83)

Madhubuti, Haki R.

Needed: A Culture Of Development, Rather Than
Mere Survival. Illustrated. *Black Collegian.* 13:
126+ (Feb-Mar 83)

Madison, Joe (about)

Essence Man: Joe Madison. Illustrated. Lloyd Gite.
Essence. 14: 38 (Nov 83)

Madison, Joseph E.

The Coming Of Age Of Black Political Power.
Tables. *Crisis.* 90: 30 (Aug-Sep 83)

Madison, L. Keith and Tran, Ruc Manh

Meckel's Diverticulum: The False-Negative
Examination. Illustrated, notes. *National Medical
Association Journal.* 75: 519-522 (May 83)

Madubuike, Ihechukwu

Towards The Decolonization Of African Literature.
Book review. Gerald Moore. *Research in African
Literatures.* 14: 549-553 (Winter 83)

Magazines

See Periodicals

Mahone, Barbara J. (about)

Essence Women: Barbara J. Mahone. Illustrated.
Marcie Eanes. *Essence.* 14: 56 (Dec 83)

Major, Clarence—Criticism And Interpretation

Beyond Mimetic Exhaustion: The Reflex And Bone
Structure Experiment. Notes. Larry D. Bradfield.
Black American Literature Forum. 17: 120-123
(Fall 83)

Major, Reggie

South Africa And Its Firm Foundations.. *Black Scholar*. 14: 12-20 (Jan-Feb 83)

Makouta-M'Boukou, Jean-Pierre

Introduction À L' Étude Du Roman Nœgro-Africain De Langue Française: Problemes Culturels Et Littèraires. Book review. Jonathan Ngaté. *Research in African Literatures*. 14: 207-209 (Summer 83)

Malcolm X (1925-1965) (about)

Alex Haley Remembers Malcolm X. Illustrated. Alex Haley. *Essence*. 14: 52-54 + (Nov 83)

The Evolution Of The Attitude Of Malcolm X Toward Whites. Notes. Raymond Rodgers and Jimmie N. Rogers. *Phylon*. 44: 108-115 (Jun 83)

Malek, James S.

Comic Irony In Vanbrugh's The Relapse: Worthy's Repentance. Notes. *CLA Journal*. 26: 353-361 (Mar 83)

Mallette, Elaine

South Central Legal Services Program.. *Black Law Journal*. 08: 147-149 (Spring 83)

Malloy, Stewart C.

Traditional African Watercraft: A New Look. Illustrated, tables, notes. *Journal of African Civilizations*. 05: 163-176 (Apr-Nov 83)

Malveaux, Julianne

Last-Minute Tax Saving.. *Essence*. 14: 28-29 (Dec 83)

Mamonsono, L. P.

Bio-Bibliographie Des Ecrivains Congolais: Belles Lettres - Littérature. Book review. Daniel Whitman. *Research in African Literatures*. 14: 215-216 (Summer 83)

Man

See Also Women

Managers

See Executives

Mande Writing

See Writing, Mande

Mandela, Nelson (about)

Mandela: Man Of The Resistance. Illustrated. *Crisis*. 90: 42-43 (Feb 83)

Mann, Joseph B. (Jr.) (about)

The Life Blood Of America's Hospitals. Illustrated. Roger Witherspoon. *Black Enterprise*. 13: 49-50 + (Jul 83)

Mann, Thomas (Jr.) (about)

First Black Elected To Iowa State Senate. Illustrated, first facts. *Jet*. 63: 6 (10 Jan 83)

Manning, Marable

Jobs, Peace, Freedom: A Political Assessment Of The August 27 March On Washington. Notes. *Black Scholar*. 14: 2-20 (Nov-Dec 83)

Manuel, Ron C.

Minority Aging: Sociological And Social Psychological Issues. Book review. Jacob U. Gordon. *Journal of Negro History*. 68: 110-111 (Winter 83)

Manuel, Ruth

Essence Women: Gloria Davis. Illustrated. *Essence*. 14: 56 (Jul 83)

Manuel, Ruth Dolores

An Actor Trades Pounds For Jobs! Illustrated. *Essence*. 14: 116 (Nov 83)

Do You Need A Beeper?. *Essence*. 14: 35 (Nov 83)

Essence Women: Ophelia DeVore. Illustrated. *Essence*. 14: 50 (Aug 83)

Give The Man A Hand. Illustrated. *Essence*. 14: 54 (Jul 83)

Showstopper: Darnell Williams. Illustrated. *Essence*. 14: 35 (Nov 83)

Untitled. Poem. *Essence*. 13: 16 (Apr 83) Miller, Aurelia Toyer

Marasmus—Nigeria

Growth Of Nigerian Children With Marasmus After Hospital Treatment. Tables. Theodore C. Okeahialam. *National Medical Association Journal*. 75: 75-80 (Jan 83)

Marichal, Juan (about)

Marichal, Robinson In Hall 9 Black Players Fall Short. Illustrated. *Jet*. 63: 53 (31 Jan 83)

Markwalder, Don

A Response To Timothy Bates' Comment. Notes. *Review of Black Political Economy*. 12: 241-242 (Winter 83)

Marley, Rita (about)

Rita Marley: Showstopper. Illustrated. Isaac Fergusson. *Essence*. 14: 51 (Jul 83)

Marquard, Jean

A Century Of South African Short Stories. Book review. Linda Susan Beard. *Research in African Literatures*. 14: 219-222 (Summer 83)

Marriage

First Marriage After 40. Illustrated. Lynn Norment. *Ebony*. 38: 28-30 + (Jan 83)

Why Some Women Prefer Older Men. Illustrated. Lynn Norment. *Ebony*. 38: 132 + (Apr 83)

See Also Divorce
Family
Sex In Marriage

Marriage, Interracial

See Interracial Marriage

Married People

'American Dream' Couples. Illustrated. *Ebony*. 38: 73-74 + (Jul 83)

Your Chair, My Couch: Sharing Furniture And Space With Someone You Love. Illustrated. Jessica B. Harris. *Black Enterprise*. 13: 106 + (Feb 83)

Married People—Employment

Sharing Two Incomes: How To Make It Work. Aurelia Toyer Miller. *Essence*. 13: 38+ (Mar 83)

  See Also Wives—Employment

Marsalis, Wynton (about)

Wynton Marsalis: Jazz Musician Of The Year. Illustrated. Kalamu Ya Salaam. *Black Collegian*. 14: 54-56 (Nov-Dec 83)

Marsh, Carol P.

The Plastic Arts Motif In Roots. Notes. *CLA Journal*. 26: 325-333 (Mar 83)

Shakespeare's Sonnets. Book review. *CLA Journal*. 26: 478-479 (Jun 83)

Marsh, Iders

Marketing: Social Conscience. Illustrated. *Black Enterprise*. 13: 39-41 (Jan 83)

Marsh-Joiner, Trena T.

I Am. Poem. *Essence*. 14: 142 (Nov 83)

Marshall, Marilyn

Are Black Women Taking Black Men's Jobs? Illustrated. *Ebony*. 38: 60+ (Aug 83)

Indianapolis: Blacks Seek A Greater Role In The City's Growth And Development. Illustrated. *Ebony*. 38: 64+ (Jun 83)

Neurosurgery: Two Black Women Surgeons Are Pioneers In Highly Specialized Medical Field. Illustrated. *Ebony*. 38: 72-74+ (Sep 83)

Riding High At Seventeen. Illustrated. *Ebony*. 38: 60-61+ (May 83)

Terry Cummings: Basketball's Million-Dollar Minister. Illustrated. *Ebony*. 38: 42-44 (Feb 83)

Woman At The Helm Of Philadelphia Presbytery. Illustrated. *Ebony*. 38: 51-52+ (Jul 83)

Women Cadets Make Coast Guard History. Illustrated, first facts. *Ebony*. 38: 138+ (Apr 83)

Marshall, Paule

Praisesong For The Widow. Book review. John Oliver Killens. *Crisis*. 90: 49-50 (Aug-Sep 83)

Praisesong For The Widow. Book review. Carole Bovoso. *Essence*. 13: 19 (Apr 83)

Martin, Damon

State Prisoners' Rights To Medical Treatment: Merely Elusive Or Wholly Illusory? Notes. *Black Law Journal*. 08: 427-455 (Winter 83)

Martin Luther King Jr. Center For Nonviolent Social Change

A Living Memorial To The Drum Major For Justice. Illustrated. Walter Leavy. *Ebony*. 38: 120+ (Feb 83)

Martin, Marlene Hodge

The Color Crutch. Illustrated. *Essence*. 14: 140 (Aug 83)

Martin, Thad

The Bahamas: A Decade Of Independence. Illustrated. *Ebony*. 38: 117-118+ (Apr 83)

Bracing For Hard Times. Illustrated. *Ebony*. 38: 78+ (Aug 83)

Can Black Public Colleges Be Saved? Illustrated. *Ebony*. 38: 130+ (Feb 83)

Harris Neck: Georgia Blacks Fight To Regain Ancestral Land. Illustrated. *Ebony*. 38: 36-38+ (Jul 83)

Matt Henson: Black Explorer Is Part Of Controversy In Flim 'Race To The Pole'. Illustrated. *Ebony*. 39: 80-82+ (Nov 83)

Private Back Colleges: Struggle Against The Odds. Illustrated. *Ebony*. 38: 84+ (Oct 83)

Martinez, Cervando (Jr.)

Physician And Health Professional Manpower. Illustrated, notes. *National Medical Association Journal*. 75: 545-546 (Jun 83)

Maryland

  See Also Historical Museums—Maryland

Masilela, Johnny

Let's Write A Novel. Book review. *Research in African Literatures*. 14: 253-254 (Summer 83)

Mason, E. J. (joint author)

  See Lacy, William B.

Mason, Ernest

Black Art And The Configurations Of Experience: The Philosophy Of The Black Aesthetic. Notes. *CLA Journal*. 27: 1-17 (Sep 83)

Mass Communication

  See Communication

Mass Media

  See Also Newspapers
    Women In The Mass Media Industry

Mass Media—Africa

The Voice Of One Crying In The Wilderness: Constructing The African Mass Communication Pyramid. Notes, tables. Mamadi Chinyelu. *Black Law Journal*. 08: 285-291 (Fall 83)

Mass Media—Political Aspects

The Role Of Mass Media In U. S. Imperialism. Robert Chrisman. *Black Scholar*. 14: 13-17 (Summer 83)

Mass Media—Social Aspects

The Activist Black Press. Frank Dexter Brown. *Black Enterprise*. 13: 38 (Jun 83)

Mass Media—United States

The Voice Of One Crying In The Wilderness: Constructing The African Mass Communication Pyramid. Notes, tables. Mamadi Chinyelu. *Black Law Journal*. 08: 285-291 (Fall 83)

Mass Media—Vocational Guidance

Make Your Own Breaks. Illustrated. Philip A. Loyd. *about. . . time*. 11: 13 (Apr 83)

Massacres—Lebanon

The Road To Jerusalem: Beirut September.
Illustrated. Ellen Siegel. *Freedomways*. 23: No. 2:
90-98 (83)

Massacres—South Africa

Reflections On The Sharpville-Langa Massacres Of
1960. Illustrated. Boji Jordon. *Crisis*. 90: 44-45
(Apr 83)

Mastectomy

Mastectomy: Some Hopeful Facts You Should
Know. Illustrated. Susan Lee. *Essence*. 13: 53-54
(Feb 83)

Mathematics, Ancient

Africa In The Mainstream Of Mathematics History.
Notes. Beatrice Lumpkin. *Journal of African
Civilizations*. 05: 100-109 (Apr-Nov 83)

Mathematics—Vocational Guidance

You Can Count On Mathematics! Harriet Jackson
Scarupa. *Essence*. 13: 30 (Feb 83)

Matney, William C.

Yesterday (1929) In The Crisis. . . Exploitation Or
Cooperation? Tables. *Crisis*. 90: 20-22 (Dec 83)

Matney, William C. (Jr.) and Johnson, Dwight L.

America's Black Population: 1970 To 1982 - A
Statistical View. Tables. *Crisis*. 90: 10-18 (Dec 83)

Black Economic Plight - A Look Into The Past
Forecasts Challenge To The Present. Illustrated.
Crisis. 90: 6-7 (Dec 83)

Maxima Corporation

Maxima's 8a Dilemma. Illustrated. Harold J.
Logan. *Black Enterprise*. 13: 42-45 (Jan 83)

Maynard, Robert (about)

Maynard Buys Tribune. Illustrated. Rose Ragsdale.
Black Enterprise. 13: 18 (Jul 83)

Maynard, Robert C. (about)

Give The Man A Hand. Illustrated. Elaine C. Ray.
Essence. 14: 50 (Aug 83)

Mayors—Illinois—Chicago

Harold Washington Wins Hot Race To Become
First Black Mayor Of Chicago. Illustrated, first
facts. *Jet*. 64: 4-6+ (2 May 83)

Mayor Harold Washington: Changing Of The Guard
In Chicago. Illustrated. Lynn Norment. *Ebony*. 38:
27-30+ (Jul 83)

Mayors—Illinois—Harvey

First Black Installed As Mayor Of Harvey, Ill. First
facts. *Jet*. 64: 8 (23 May 83)

Mayors—Missouri—Northwoods

First Black Elected As Mayor Of Northwoods, Mo.
First facts. *Jet*. 64: 4 (25 Apr 83)

Mayors—New Jersey—Newark

Kenneth Allen Gibson: Mayor Of Newark, New
Jersey. Interview, Illustrated. Kenneth A. Gibson
and Adolph Dupree. *about. . . time*. 11: 10-13+
(Jul 83)

Mayors—United States

Can Black Mayors Stop Crime? Illustrated. Walter
Leavy. *Ebony*. 39: 116+ (Dec 83)

Her Honor, The Mayor. Illustrated. Julie Chenault.
Essence. 14: 14+ (Jul 83)

Taking Over City Hall. Illustrated, tables. Edmund
Newton. *Black Enterprise*. 13: 155-160 (Jun 83)

Mazique, Frances M.

Improving The Quality Of Family Life.. *National
Medical Association Journal*. 75: 123 (Feb 83)

Mboukou, Alexandre

The Pan African Movement, 1900-1945: A Study In
Leadership Conflicts Among The Disciples Of Pan
Africanism. Notes. *Journal of Black Studies*. 13:
275-287 (Mar 83)

McAdam, Doug

Political Process And The Development Of Black
Insurgency 1930-1970. Book review. Ally Faye
Mack. *Journal of Negro History*. 68: 127-128
(Winter 83)

McAdoo, Norris

Who's Handicapped? Not Sharpshooter Norris
McAdoo. Illustrated. *Ebony*. 38: 96+ (Jun 83)

McCabe, Jewell Jackson

Black Women-Meeting Today's Challenges.
Illustrated. *Crisis*. 90: 10-12 (Jun-Jul 83)

McCarroll, Thomas

Back To The Drawing Board. Illustrated. *Black
Enterprise*. 13: 75-76+ (Feb 83)

McClendon, W. H.

The Foundations Of Black Culture.. *Black Scholar*.
14: 18-20 (Summer 83)

McClure, John A.

Kipling And Conrad: The Colonial Fiction. Book
review. Martin Tucker. *Research in African
Literatures*. 14: 228-232 (Summer 83)

McCluskey, John A. (Jr.)

Graduate School: CIC Fellowships.. *Black
Collegian*. 14: 124-127 (Nov-Dec 83)

McCoo, Marilyn (about)

Marilyn McCoo: How She Keeps Fit. Illustrated.
Ebony. 38: 80-82+ (Feb 83)

McCord, Dolores (joint author)

   See Duncan, Titus D.

McCoy, Jonathan Mark

What Has The NAACP Done For Me? Poem.
Crisis. 90: 46 (May 83)

McDougall, Gay J.

Palestinian Prisoners: Are They Prisoners Of War?
Notes. *Freedomways*. 23: No. 2: 126-139 (83)

McDougall, Harold

Love (For Diane). Poem. *Essence*. 14: 108 (Nov
83)

McDowell, Melody M.

Rumbling In Chicago. Illustrated. *Black Enterprise*. 14: 19 (Nov 83)

McGinty, Doris Evans

American Popular Culture: A Guide To Information Sources. Book review. *The Black Perspective in Music*. 11: 212-214 (Fall 83)

Bibliography Of Black Music Volume 3: Geographical Studies. Book review. *The Black Perspective in Music*. 11: 79-82 (Spring 83)

Biographical Dictionary Of Afro-American And African Musicians. Book review. *The Black Perspective in Music*. 11: 79-82 (Spring 83)

Encyclopedia Of Black America. Book review. *The Black Perspective in Music*. 11: 79-82 (Spring 83)

Folk Music And Modern Sound. Book review. *The Black Perspective in Music*. 11: 212-214 (Fall 83)

The Illustrated Encyclopedia Of Black Music. Book review. *The Black Perspective in Music*. 11: 212-214 (Fall 83)

Popular Culture And American Life: Selected Topics In The Study Of American Popular Culture. Book review. *The Black Perspective in Music*. 11: 212-214 (Fall 83)

Who's Who In Rock. Book review. *The Black Perspective in Music*. 11: 212-214 (Fall 83)

McGougan, Mike

The Navy's Black Professionals: In Fields From Nuclear Propulsion To Computerized Electronics. Illustrated. *about. . . time*. 11: 18-20 (Feb 83)

McGuire, Phillip

War And Race: The Black Officer In The American Military, 1915-1941. Book review. *Journal of Negro History*. 68: 114-116 (Winter 83)

McIntosh, Simeon Charles Randolph

Controversial Propositions Of Law And The Positivist Embarrassment: The Hart/Dworkin Debate Reconsidered. Notes. *Howard Law Journal*. 26: No. 2: 699-722 (83)

McLean, Archie H. and others

An Enrichment Program For South Carolina High School Students Interested In Future Biomedical Science Professions. Notes. *National Medical Association Journal*. 75: 603-605 (Jun 83)

McMillan, Terry

Don't Beg To Be Loved.. *Essence*. 14: 172 (Oct 83)

McNair, Marcia

Get Somewhere In Travel.. *Essence*. 13: 29 (Apr 83)

Star Teacher: Training Kids For TV Ads. Illustrated. *Essence*. 14: 18 + (Sep 83)

Where To Find: Black Books By Mail.. *Essence*. 14: 54 (Jul 83)

Working On Your Diet. Illustrated. *Essence*. 13: 135 (Mar 83)
Scarupa, Harriet Jackson

McNamara, Robert S.

The Road Ahead. . . South Africa Faces Bloody Future. Illustrated. *Crisis*. 90: 46-49 (Apr 83)

McNatt, Robert

Debate Grows Over Rule 48.. *Black Enterprise*. 13: 18 (May 83)

Risky Business Of Broadway. Illustrated. *Black Enterprise*. 14: 69-70 + (Dec 83)

South Africans speak Out In America.. *Black Enterprise*. 13: 54 (Apr 83)
Jacob, John E.

McQuater, Gregory V. (joint author)

See Banks, W. Curtis

McRae, Frank

Black Power At The Polls. Illustrated. *Black Enterprise*. 13: 17 (May 83)

Medical Care

See Also Child Health Services

Medical Care, Cost Of

Prospective Payment For Hospital Costs Using Diagnosis-Related Groups: Will Cost Inflation Be Reduced? Notes. Stephen N. Keith. *National Medical Association Journal*. 75: 609 + (Jun 83)

Medical Care For The Aged

See Aged—Medical Care

Medical Care—Nicaragua

The Black Scholar Interviews: Mirna Cunningham. Interview. Mirna Cunningham and Robert Chrisman. *Black Scholar*. 14: 17-27 (Mar-Apr 83)

Medical Care—Tanzania

Radiotherapy In Tanzania. Illustrated, tables. George A. Alexander. *National Medical Association Journal*. 75: 289-295 (Mar 83)

Medical Care—United States

Health Care For Black Americans: A Priority. Robert L. M. Hilliard. *Crisis*. 90: 24 (Oct 83)

The President's Inaugural Address: Insuring Quality Health Care. Illustrated. Robert L. M. Hilliard. *National Medical Association Journal*. 75: 81-83 (Jan 83)

President's Inaugural Address: Priorities. Lucius C. (III) Earles. *National Medical Association Journal*. 75: 1139-1143 (Dec 83)

Providing Sound And Effective Health Care Delivery For All Americans. Editorial. Robert L. M. Hilliard. *National Medical Association Journal*. 75: 1135-1138 (Dec 83)

Medical Colleges—Admission

The Impact Of MCAT Intervention Efforts on Medical Student Acceptance Rates. Tables, notes. Joseph C. Pisano and Anna Cherrie Epps. *National Medical Association Journal*. 75: 773-777 (Aug 83)

Medical Colleges—Georgia—Atlanta

The Morehouse School Of Medicine: A State Of Mind, Of Mission, And Of Commitment. Louis W. Sullivan. *National Medical Association Journal*. 75: 837-839 (Aug 83)

Medical Education

Medical Education - The Basis For Tomorrow's Medical Care. Illustrated. James H. Sammons. *National Medical Association Journal*. 75: 663-664 (Jul 83)

New Government Proposals: The Effect On Minority Medical Education. Velma Gibson Watts. *National Medical Association Journal*. 75: 247-249 (Mar 83)

Medical Folk-Lore

See Folk Medicine

Medical Laws And Legislation

Legal Options In Securing Hospital Appointments. Notes. Arthur T. Davidson and Arthur H. Coleman. *National Medical Association Journal*. 75: 318-320 (Mar 83)

Medical Personnel

The Impact Of A Medical-School-Based Summer Program On The Acceptance Of Minority Undergraduate Students Into Health Professional Schools. Tables. Joseph C. Pisano and Anne Cherrie Epps. *National Medical Association Journal*. 75: 17-23 (Jan 83)

Physician And Health Professional Manpower. Illustrated, notes. Cervando (Jr.) Martinez. *National Medical Association Journal*. 75: 545-546 (Jun 83)

See Also Physicians

Medical Students

Am I My Brother's Keeper? Editorial. Cheryl Lynn Walker. *National Medical Association Journal*. 75: 867-868 (Sep 83)

Strengthening Our Ties. Illustrated. Alexis A. Thompson. *National Medical Association Journal*. 75: 459-460 (May 83)

Medicare

Medicare Switches To Prospective Payment Plan. Illustrated. Bebe Moore Campbell. *Black Enterprise*. 14: 37 (Dec 83)

Medicine, Ancient

The African Background Of Medical Science. Illustrated, notes. Charles S. Finch. *Journal of African Civilizations*. 05: 140-156 (Apr-Nov 83)

Medicine And Psychology

See Also Sick—Psychology

Medicine, Clinical—Hospital Reports

Computerization Of Procedural Requests And Reports Of Clinical Laboratory Data: A Case Study. Tables. T. A. (III) Nowlin and G. Y. Webster. *National Medical Association Journal*. 75: 409-414 (Apr 83)

Medicine, Egyptian

Black Contributions To The Early History Of Western Medicine. Illustrated. Frederick Newsome. *Journal of African Civilizations*. 05: 127-139 (Apr-Nov 83)

Medicine—Practice

Hispanic Cultural Influences On Medical Practice. Notes. Pedro A. Poma. *National Medical Association Journal*. 75: 941-946 (Oct 83)

Medicine, Psychosomatic

Relaxation Therapy: Adjunctive Therapy For The Physician. Tables, notes. Dorothy D. Harrison. *National Medical Association Journal*. 75: 193-198 (Feb 83)

Medicine—Study And Teaching

A Critical Analysis Of Clerkship Grading Procedures. Tables, notes. Eric J. Lazaro and others . *National Medical Association Journal*. 75: 1083-1086 (Nov 83)

Medicine—Vocational Guidance

An Enrichment Program For South Carolina High School Students Interested In Future Biomedical Science Professions. Notes. Archie H. McLean and others. *National Medical Association Journal*. 75: 603-605 (Jun 83)

Meharry Medical College

Meharry Med School Gets New Dental School Dean. Illustrated. *Jet*. 63: 39 (24 Jan 83)

Satcher Inaugurated Meharry's Eighth President. Illustrated. *National Medical Association Journal*. 75: 210+ (Feb 83)

Mehlinger, Louis Rothschild (about)

Louis Rothschild Mehlinger: The First One Hundred Years. Notes. J. Clay (Jr.) Smith. *Howard Law Journal*. 26: No. 2: 359-441 (83)

Melhem, D. H.

Dudley Randall: A Humanist View. Illustrated, notes. *Black American Literature Forum*. 17: 157-167 (Winter 83)

Melton, Nellie G. (about)

Her Honor, The Mayor. Illustrated. Julie Chenault. *Essence*. 14: 14+ (Jul 83)

Melville, Herman (1819-1891)—Criticism And Interpretation

Authorial Displacement In Herman Melville's "The Piazza". Notes. Michael Clark. *CLA Journal*. 27: 69-80 (Sep 83)

Loomings Of An Awakened Consciousness: Mardi, A Reinterpretation. Notes. Khalil Husni. *CLA Journal*. 27: 56-68 (Sep 83)

Men

Is It True What They Say About Southern Men? Illustrated. Lynn Norment. *Ebony*. 38: 104+ (Feb 83)

Is The Black Male An Endangered Species? Illustrated. Walter Leavy. *Ebony*. 38: 41-42+ (Aug 83)

Michael, Renee

How To Get That Bank Loan.. *Black Enterprise*.
14: 43-44+ (Sep 83)

Michaels, David

Occupational Cancer In The Black Population: The
Health Effects Of Job Discrimination. Notes.
National Medical Association Journal. 75:
1014-1018 (Oct 83)

Michaels, Marsha (about)

Star Teacher: Training Kids For TV Ads.
Illustrated. Marcia McNair. *Essence*. 14: 18+ (Sep
83)

Middle Classes—Attitudes

"A Woman's Place": The Attitudes Of
Middle-Class Black Men. Notes, tables. Noel A.
Cazenaye. *Phylon*. 44: 12-32 (Mar 83)

Middle Classes—South Africa

South Africa's Black Middle Class. Illustrated.
Miriam Lacob. *Black Enterprise*. 13: 49-50+ (Apr
83)

South Africans speak Out In America. Robert
McNatt. *Black Enterprise*. 13: 54 (Apr 83)

Middle Classes—United States

'American Dream' Couples. Illustrated. *Ebony*. 38:
73-74+ (Jul 83)

Migone, Paolo (joint author)

See Caracci, Giovanni

Migration Internal—Africa

Africans In Search Of Work: Migration And
Diaspora. Notes, tables. Lenneal J. Henderson. *The
Urban League Review*. 07: 58-73 (Summer 83)

Mikell, Carla A.

Make The Rest Of Your Life The Best Of Your
Life.. *Essence*. 14: 67-68 (May 83)

Milbury-Steen, Sarah L.

European And African Stereotypes In
Twentieth-Century Fiction. Book review. G. D.
Killam. *Research in African Literatures*. 14:
225-228 (Summer 83)

Miles, Patrice and Edwards, Audrey

Black Women And White Men.. *Essence*. 14:
94-95+ (Oct 83)

Psychic June Gatlin Looks 1984.. *Essence*. 14:
79+ (Dec 83)

Talking To Someone You Love. Illustrated.
Essence. 13: 70-72+ (Feb 83)

Miller, Adam David

Change Of Territory. Book review. *Black American
Literature Forum*. 17: 179-180 (Winter 83)

Songs From My Father's Pockets. Book review.
Black American Literature Forum. 17: 179-180
(Winter 83)

Miller, Arthur G.

In The Eye Of The Beholder: Contemporary Issues
In Stereotyping. Book review. Barbara D. Lyles.
Journal of Negro Education. 52: 83-85 (Winter 83)

Miller, Aurelia Toyer and Manuel, Ruth Dolores

On The Money: When A Collector Gets On Your
Case..... *Essence*. 14: 21 (May 83)

Sharing Two Incomes: How To Make It Work..
Essence. 13: 38+ (Mar 83)

Miller, Carroll L.

Role Model Blacks: Known But Little Known.
Book review. Samuel L. Banks. *Journal of Negro
Education*. 52: 87-89 (Winter 83)

Miller, Cheryl (about)

'Playing' Your Way Through College. Illustrated.
Knolly Moses. *Essence*. 14: 52 (Aug 83)

Miller, E. Ethelbert

Season Of Hunger/Cry Of Rain. Book review. Tom
Dent. *Freedomways*. 23: No. 01: 42-49 (83)

Seasons Of Hunger/Cry Of Rain. Book review.
Lateifa Ramona L. Hyman. *Black American
Literature Forum*. 17: 182 (Winter 83)

Miller, Eugene E.

Folkloric Aspects Of Wright's "The Man Who
Killed A Shadow". Notes. *CLA Journal*. 27:
210-223 (Dec 83)

Miller, Joseph M. and others

Isoenzymes Of Lactate Dehydrogenase In Amnionic
Fluid In Early Pregnancy. Tables, notes. *National
Medical Association Journal*. 75: 687-689 (Jul 83)

Miller, M. Sammye

The National Endowment For The Humanities: A
Selected Bibliography For Two Years Of Funded
Projects On The Black Experience 1977-1978.
Notes. *Journal of Negro History*. 68: 59-79 (Winter
83)

Miller, Russell L. and others

Studies Of The Kallikrein-Kinin System In Patients
With Sickle Cell Anemia. Tables, notes. *National
Medical Association Journal*. 75: 551-556 (Jun 83)

Millionaires

Learning To Live With $5 Million. Illustrated.
Trudy S. Moore. *Ebony*. 38: 52+ (Apr 83)

Turning Points In The Lives of Self-Made
Millionaires. Illustrated. *Ebony*. 38: 53-54+ (May
83)

$5 Million Lottery Winner Has $50,000 Wedding
To Remember. Illustrated. Trudy S. Moore and
Moneta (Jr.) Sleet. *Jet*. 64: 14-16+ (18 Jul 83)

$5 Million Man To Take Bride. Illustrated. Trudy
S. Moore. *Jet*. 63: 20-27 (31 Jan 83)

Milloy, Sandra D.

Dilsey: Faulkner's Black Mammy In The Sound
And The Fury. Notes. *Negro History Bulletin*. 46:
70-71 (Jul-Sep 83)

Milne, Emile

Dominica: A Lush And Inviting Wilderness.
Illustrated. *Black Enterprise*. 13: 68+ (May 83)

1982 Election Returns. Illustrated. *Black
Enterprise*. 13: 13 (Jan 83)

Milwaukee, Wisconsin

See Also School Integration—Milwaukee,
Wisconsin

Mims, A. Grace Lee

Spirituals. Record review. Josephine Wright. *The
Black Perspective in Music*. 11: 93-95 (Spring 83)

Mims, George L.

Community Politics And Educational Change: Ten
School Systems Under Court Order. Book review.
Journal of Black Studies. 13: 375-376 (Mar 83)

Minear, Paul S.

New Testament Apocalyptic. Book review. Cain H.
Felder. *Journal of Religious Thought*. 39: 72-73
(Fall-Winter 83)

Miner, Claudia

The 1886 Convention Of The Knights Of Labor.
Notes. *Phylon*. 44: 147-159 (Jun 83)

Ministers Of The Gospel

See Clergy

Minority Business Enterprises

Are The Promises Being Kept? Illustrated. Isaiah J.
Poole. *Black Enterprise*. 14: 117-118+ (Oct 83)

Uncovering Fronts. Illustrated. Lynette Hazelton.
Black Enterprise. 14: 24 (Nov 83)

Minority Business Enterprises—Finance

See Also Federal Aid To Minority Business
Enterprises

Minority Business Enterprises—New York (State)—Rochester

Implementing The MBE Program. Ruth Scott.
about. . . time. 11: 1 (Sep 83)

Mintz, Steven

Sources Of Variability In Rates Of Black Home
Ownership In 1900. Notes, tables. *Phylon*. 44:
312-331 (Dec 83)

Minyono-Nkodo, M. F.

Le Vieux Nègre Et La Médaille De Ferdinand
Oyono. Book review. Simon P. X. Battestini.
Research in African Literatures. 14: 237-238
(Summer 83)

Miss America Pageant

The New Miss America: Beauty, Brains And
Blackness. Illustrated. Kuumba Kazi-Ferrouillet.
Black Collegian. 14: 48-49+ (Nov-Dec 83)

Missionaries—Angola

Héli Chatelain: Pioneer Of A National Language
And Literature For Angola. Notes. Gerald Moser.
Research in African Literatures. 14: 516-537
(Winter 83)

Missionaries, Women

Essence Women: Eleanor Workman. Illustrated.
Kitty Oliver. *Essence*. 14: 54 (Dec 83)

Mississippi

See Also Elections—Mississippi
Theater—Mississippi

Mississippi Minority Supplier Development Council

Supplying Demand. Illustrated. Derek T. Dingle.
Black Enterprise. 14: 26 (Oct 83)

Mitchell, James (joint author)

See Moore, Trudy S.
Waldron, Clarence

Mitchell-Kernan, Claudia and Tucker, M. Belinda

Familial Support Among Mildly Mentally Retarded
Afro-Americans.. *CAAS Newsletter*. 07: 6-7+
(May 83)

Mitchell, Leona (about)

Leona Mitchell: An All-American Opera Star.
Illustrated. Aldore Collier. *Ebony*. 38: 37-38+ (Sep
83)

Mitchell, Louis D. (joint author)

See Bush, Ann Marie

Mitchell, Sandra K.

Profiles: Linda Taylor Ferguson. Portrait. *Black
Law Journal*. 08: 144-146 (Spring 83)

Mobility

See Labor Mobility
Occupational Mobility

Mobley, Callie (about)

Her Honor, The Mayor. Illustrated. Julie Chenault.
Essence. 14: 14+ (Jul 83)

Mobley, Leroy

The Bottomless Pit. Book review. *Crisis*. 90: 50
(Aug-Sep 83)

Models, Fashion

Billie Blair: Model Close-Up. Illustrated. *Essence*.
14: 74 (Oct 83)

Essence Women: Ophelia DeVore. Illustrated. Ruth
Dolores Manuel. *Essence*. 14: 50 (Aug 83)

Iman! Illustrated. Michele Wallace. *Essence*. 14:
64-65+ (Sep 83)

Peggy Dillard: A Model Life Of Health And
Beauty. Illustrated. Stephanie Stokes Oliver.
Essence. 13: 100-101 (Jan 83)

Wanakee. Illustrated. Paula S. White. *Essence*. 14:
62 (Dec 83)

Moffett, Maxine Anderson

'Loving Myself Came Hard'. Illustrated. *Essence*.
13: 116 (Feb 83)

Mondale, Walter F. and others

Excerpts From. . . What Presidential Candidates
Told NAACP Convention Delegates.. *Crisis*. 90:
32-35 (Aug-Sep 83)

Money Supply—United States

Money Growth And The Employment Aspirations
Of Black Americans. Tables, Notes. Everson Hull.
Review of Black Political Economy. 12: 64-74
(Spring 83)

Morgan, Gordon D.

Saints, Slaves And Blacks: The Changing Place Of Black People Within Mormonism. Book review. *Journal of Negro History*. 68: 111-112 (Winter 83)

Morris, Byron

Honey, I Love. Book review. Nieda Spigner. *Freedomways*. 23: No. 01: 55-56 (83)

Morris, Madeline L.

Undocumented Workers: In Search Of A Profile. Notes. *The Urban League Review*. 07: 91-99 (Summer 83)

Morrison, Toni—Criticism And Interpretation

Flying As Symbol And Legend In Toni Morrison's The Bluest Eye, Sula, And Song Of Solomon. Notes. Grace Ann Hovet and Barbara Loansberry. *CLA Journal*. 27: 119-140 (Dec 83)

Morrow, LaVert and Hilliard, Alphonso W.

Cerebral Aneurysm: Report Of Two Cases And Clinical Update. Notes. *National Medical Association Journal*. 75: 263-266 (Mar 83)

Morten, George and Atkinson, Donald R.

Minority Identity Development And Preference For Counselor Race. Notes, tables. *Journal of Negro Education*. 52: 156-161 (Spring 83)

Mortgage Loans

Taking A Second Mortgage Or Refinancing Your Home For Extra Cash. Illustrated. Udayan Gupta. *Black Enterprise*. 13: 31 (Apr 83)

Mortgages

Maneuvering Through The Mortgage Maze. Hershel Lee Johnson. *Black Enterprise*. 14: 80-82 + (Dec 83)

Mortimer, Delores M.

Female Immigrants To The United States: Caribbean, Latin American, And African Experience. Book review. Marcus E. Jones. *Phylon*. 44: 245-246 (Sep 83)

Moser, Gerald

Héli Chatelain: Pioneer Of A National Language And Literature For Angola. Notes. *Research in African Literatures*. 14: 516-537 (Winter 83)

Moses, Knolly

In The Chips! Illustrated. *Essence*. 14: 30 (Aug 83)

'Playing' Your Way Through College. Illustrated. *Essence*. 14: 52 (Aug 83)

Moses, Tony (joint author)

See Calhoun, Dolly

Mosquito Indians

The Black Scholar Interviews: Mirna Cunningham. Interview. Mirna Cunningham and Robert Chrisman. *Black Scholar*. 14: 17-27 (Mar-Apr 83)

Moss, Kevin

Arthur McDuffee's Ghost Still Haunts. . . Racial Injustice In Miami. Illustrated. *Crisis*. 90: 48-49 (Jan 83)

Joblessness In Detroit Is "Devastating". Illustrated. *Crisis*. 90: 14 (Apr 83)

New Detroit, Inc.. Illustrated. *Crisis*. 90: 24-25 (Apr 83)

Moss, Thylias

Rush Hour. Poem. *Essence*. 14: 134 (Dec 83)

Mothers

Coping With First-Baby Blues. Irene Pickhardt. *Essence*. 13: 112 (Feb 83)

An Open Letter To Mommie. Illustrated. Madeline Sulaiman. *about. . . time*. 11: 22-23 (May 83)

Super Mom, Super Kids. Illustrated. Pamela Noel. *Ebony*. 38: 44 + (Oct 83)

See Also Adolescent Mothers

Mothers And Sons

His Mama! Diane Weathers. *Essence*. 14: 57 + (Nov 83)

Motion Picture Reviews

America-From Hitler To MX. By Joan Harvey. Reviewed by Stephen DeGange. *Freedomways*. 23: No. 01: 37-41 (83)

Motivation (Psychology)

Delayed Gratification In Black: A Critical Review. Notes, tables. W. Curtis Banks and others. *Journal of Black Psychology*. 09: 43 56 (Feb 83)

Moton, Robert Russa (about)

Chronicles Of Black Courage (Part IV). Illustrated. Lerone (Jr.) Bennett. *Ebony*. 38: 131-134 (Sep 83)

Motor-Trucks

Family Trucking. Illustrated. Jay Koblenz. *Black Enterprise*. 14: 87 (Aug 83)

Moving-Picture Industry

Black Films In Search Of A Home. Notes. Clyde Taylor. *Freedomways*. 23: No. 4: 226-233 (83)

So You Want To Be In The Movies? Illustrated. Curtis E. Rodgers. *Crisis*. 90: 6-10 (Jan 83)

Moving-Pictures

Where To Find. . . Black Films For Rental Or Purchase. Kathe Sandler. *Essence*. 14: 50 (May 83)

See Also Characters And Characteristics In Moving-Pictures

Moving-Pictures—Awards

See Also Academy Awards (Moving-Pictures)

Moving-Pictures For Children

AV Materials On Puerto Rican Themes: What Are The Messages. Anaida Colon-Muniz. *Interracial Books for Children*. 14: No. 1: 25-27 (83)

Moving-Pictures—Plots, Themes, Etc.

'D.C. Cab' Rolls With Mr T And High-Speed Cast. Illustrated. *Jet*. 65: 54-56 + (19 Dec 83)

Eddie Murphy: Hot Comic Sizzles In '48 Hrs.' Film. Illustrated. Clarence Waldron. *Jet*. 63: 28-31 (14 Feb 83)

Richard, Pryor, Jackie Gleason Team For Laughs And Lesson In 'The Toy'. Illustrated. Trudy S. Moore. *Jet*. 63: 60-62 (10 Jan 83)

Moynihan, Barbara (joint author)

See Baker, F. M.

Mphahlele, Es'kia

Let's Write A Novel. Book review. Johnny Masilela. *Research in African Literatures*. 14: 253-254 (Summer 83)

Mr. T. (about)

'D.C. Cab' Rolls With Mr T And High-Speed Cast. Illustrated. *Jet*. 65: 54-56+ (19 Dec 83)

Mr. T Among Stars In Hottest New TV Show. Illustrated. *Jet*. 64: 54-56 (28 Mar 83)

Muigai, Waithira (joint author)

See Brown, Frank

Muir, Kenneth

Shakespeare's Sonnets. Book review. Carol P. Marsh. *CLA Journal*. 26: 478-479 (Jun 83)

Mullen, Andrea Kirsten

A Browser's Guide To Black-American Museums. Illustrated. *Black Enterprise*. 13: 266+ (Jun 83)

Mullen, Edward J.

The Life And Poems Of A Cuban Slave: Juan Francisco Manzano, 1797-1854. Book review. Ian I. Smart. *Research in African Literatures*. 14: 414-417 (Fall 83)

Mulukozi, M.

The Nanga Bards Of Tanzania: Are They Epic Artists? Illustrated, tables, notes. *Research in African Literatures*. 14: 283-311 (Fall 83)

Murder—Florida

Bid For Murder Tape Gets Cold Shoulder. Illustrated. Stetson Kennedy. *Crisis*. 90: 48-49 (Nov 83)

Murphy, Bruce Allen

The Brandeis/Frankfurter Connection. Book review, Notes. Irving Ferman. *Howard Law Journal*. 26: No. 1: 345-358 (83)

Murphy, Charles (joint author)

See Henderson, Lenneal J.

Murphy, Eddie (about)

Eddie Murphy: An Incredible Leap To Superstardom. Illustrated. Walter Leavy. *Ebony*. 38: 35-36+ (Oct 83)

Eddie Murphy: Black Humor With An Edge. Illustrated. Bonnie Allen. *Essence*. 13: 12 (Jan 83)

Eddie Murphy: Hot Comic Sizzles In '48 Hrs.' Film. Illustrated. Clarence Waldron. *Jet*. 63: 28-31 (14 Feb 83)

Eddie Murphy: Will Movie Hit Create Problems For Controversial Comic? Illustrated. Walter Leavy. *Ebony*. 38: 88+ (Apr 83)

Murphy, Frederick D.

Evelyn King.. *Essence*. 13: 13 (Apr 83)

Murphy, Larry

I Wouldn't Take Nothin For My Journey: Two Centuries Of An Afro American Minister's Family. Book review. *National Medical Association Journal*. 75: 1232-1234 (Dec 83)

Murray, Barbara (about)

Essence Women: Barbara Murray. Illustrated. Ken Smikle. *Essence*. 14: 56 (Jun 83)

Museums

A Browser's Guide To Black-American Museums. Illustrated. Andrea Kirsten Mullen. *Black Enterprise*. 13: 266+ (Jun 83)

See Also Historical Museums—Maryland

Music

See Also Concerts
Jazz Music
Operas

Music And Morals

Music. Illustrated. Stephanie Renfrow Hamilton. *Essence*. 13: 18 (Feb 83)

Music Conductors

See Conductors (Music)

Music, Cuban

The Social Evolution Of The Afro-Cuban Drum. Illustrated, notes. Roberto Nodal. *The Black Perspective in Music*. 11: 157-177 (Fall 83)

Music Festivals

Riffs For A Summer Day. Illustrated. Nelson George. *Black Enterprise*. 13: 68 (Jul 83)

Music, Gospel

See Gospel Music

Music—Indexes

A Concordance Of Black-Music Entries In Five Encyclopedias: Baker's, Ewen, Grove's, MGG, And Rich. Dominique-Rene DeLerma. *The Black Perspective in Music*. 11: 190-209 (Fall 83)

Music—Liberia

The Conceptual Nature Of Music Among The Vai Of Liberia. Illustrated, notes. Lester P. Monts. *The Black Perspective in Music*. 11: 143-156 (Fall 83)

Music, Popular (Songs, Etc.)—Jamaica

See Also Reggae Music

Musical Groups

The 'Jackson Five' Of England. Illustrated. *Ebony*. 38: 126-128+ (Jul 83)

Pieces Of A Dream: A Young College Trio Puts It Together. Illustrated. Kalamu Ya Salaam. *Black Collegian*. 13: 122-124 (Feb-Mar 83)

Musical Review, Comedy, Etc.

In Dahomey In London In 1903. Jeffrey P. Green. *The Black Perspective in Music*. 11: 22-40 (Spring 83)

Musical Revues, Comedy, Etc.

'Dreamgirls' A Smash Hit In Hollywood. Illustrated. *Jet*. 64: 28-31 (27 Jun 83)

Musical Youth (Musical Group)

The 'Jackson Five' Of England. Illustrated. *Ebony.* 38: 126-128 + (Jul 83)

Musicians

Barry White & Glodean White: How He Divides His Love Between His Wife And His Music. Illustrated. *Jet.* 65: 58-59 (24 Oct 83)

George Benson: Move To Hawaii Helps Him Survive Crises. Illustrated. Robert E. Johnson and Isaac Sutton. *Jet.* 63: 58-62 + (21 Feb 83)

In Retrospect: Alfred Jack Thomas: Performer, Composer, Educator. Notes. James Nathan Jones. *The Black Perspective in Music.* 11: 62-75 (Spring 83)

National Association Of Negro Musicians, Inc., Salutes R. Nathaniel Dett's 100th Birthday. Illustrated. Gloster B. Current. *Crisis.* 90: 18-20 (Feb 83)

See Also Bandsmen
Composers
Flute-Players
Jazz Musicians
Pianists
Singers

Mycobacteria

Comparative Study Of The Lipid Composition Of Particular Pathogenic And Nonpathogenic Species Of Mycobacterium. Tables, illustrated. Arvind K. N. Nandedkar. *National Medical Association Journal.* 75: 69-74 (Jan 83)

Myers, Hector F. and others

Life Stress, Health, And Blood Pressure In Black College Students. Notes, tables. *Journal of Black Psychology.* 09: 1-25 (Feb 83)

N.A.A.C.P.

See National Association For The Advancement Of Colored People

N.A.S.A.

See United States—National Aeronautics And Space Administration

N.C.A.A.

See National Collegiate Athletic Association

N.E.A.

See National Education Association

N.M.A.

See National Medical Association

N'Namdi, Carmen (about)

Essence Women: Carmen N'Namdi. Illustrated. Bethany L. Spotts. *Essence.* 13: 22 + (Feb 83)

N.O.W.

See National Organizaiton For Women

N.U.L.

See National Urban League

NAACP Image Awards, 1983

15th Annual Image Awards: An Historic Event. Illustrated. Joan Webb. *Crisis.* 90: 22-27 (Jan 83)

Nails (Anatomy)

How To Have A Perfect Ten! Illustrated. *Essence.* 13: 106-107 (Mar 83)

Nair, Mira

Settings Sights For India. Illustrated. *Essence.* 14: 22 + (Sep 83)

Namibia—Foreign Relations—South Africa

No Progress On Namibia. Illustrated. Jeanne M. Woods. *Black Enterprise.* 14: 22 (Nov 83)

Namibia—Politics And Government

Namibian Independence Stands On Its Own; South Africa's Murderous Raid Deplored. Charles E. Cobb. *Crisis.* 90: 34 (Jan 83)

UN Debate On Namibia. Illustrated. Jeanne M. Woods. *Black Enterprise.* 14: 18 (Aug 83)

Nandedkar, Arvind K. N.

Comparative Study Of The Lipid Composition Of Particular Pathogenic And Nonpathogenic Species Of Mycobacterium. Tables, illustrated. *National Medical Association Journal.* 75: 69-74 (Jan 83)

Narcotic Addicts—Rehabilitation

Where There's A Will: Antonia's Incredible Triumph. Illustrated. Roger Witherspoon and Claudia Huff. *Essence.* 14: 69-70 + (Dec 83)

Narcotic Habit

See Also Cocaine Habit

Narcotic Habit—Treatment

Simultaneous Treatment Of Hypertension And Opiate Withdrawal Using An α_2-Adrenergic Agonist. Carl C. Bell. *National Medical Association Journal.* 75: 89-93 (Jan 83)

National Action Council For Minorities In Engineering

NACME Works For Engineering Students. Illustrated. Lloyd M. Cooke. *Black Collegian.* 13: 38 + (Dec-Jan 83)

National Aeronautics And Space Administration

See United States—National Aeronautics And Space Administration

National Anti-Klan Network

Anti-Klan Network Seeks To End Racist Violence. Illustrated. *Jet.* 63: 43 (24 Jan 83)

National Association For The Advancement Of Colored People

Baptist Convention Of America Pledges $100,000 To NAACP. Illustrated. *Crisis.* 90: 16-17 (Oct 83)

Carrying On The Struggle. Illustrated. Earl G. Graves. *Black Enterprise.* 14: 9 (Aug 83)

Demanding A Fair Share. Interview, Illustrated. Benjamin L. Hooks and S. Lee Hilliard. *Black Enterprise.* 14: 40-42 (Aug 83)

". . . Plus Three, For A Stronger NAACP!". Benjamin L. Hooks. *Crisis.* 90: 4 (Apr 83)

The Era Of Diminished Expectations. Alfreda Y. Buckner. *Crisis.* 90: 33 (Apr 83)

Gloster B. Current Recalled From Retirement To Be Deputy Director. Illustrated. *Crisis*. 90: 5 (Oct 83)

Labor Leader James Kemp Named National President Of NAACP At New York Meet. Illustrated. *Jet*. 63: 6 (21 Feb 83)

"Much More Will Be Done. . . ". Benjamin L. Hooks. *Crisis*. 90: 4 (Aug-Sep 83)

NAACP Membership- Your Fight For Freedom Insurance. Illustrated. Althea T. L. Simmons. *Crisis*. 90: 20-21 (Apr 83)

NAACP's Spingarn Medal To Lena Horne Climaxes 75th Annual Convention. Illustrated. *Jet*. 64: 12-14 (1 Aug 83)

NAACP Victory In Name Case. Illustrated. *Ebony*. 38: 140+ (Jun 83)

A New Special Project. . . NAACP Regional Membership Coordinators. Illustrated. William H. (Sr.) Penn and Janice Johnson. *Crisis*. 90: 18-19 (Apr 83)

Stand Up! Be Counted In '83! Join The NAACP!. . . The 74th NAACP Annual Convention. Illustrated. William H. (Sr.) Penn. *Crisis*. 90: 6-13 (Aug-Sep 83)

National Association For The Advancement Of Colored People—Detroit

A Salute To Detroit. . . Dynamic Detroit NAACP Branch Sets Most Lavish Life Membership Table In The U.S.. Illustrated. Chester A. (Sr.) Higgins. *Crisis*. 90: 8-11 (Apr 83)

National Association Of Black Social Workers

Collective Goods And Black Interest Groups. Notes , tables. Dianne M. Pinderhughes. *Review of Black Political Economy*. 12: 219-236 (Winter 83)

National Association Of Negro Musicians, Inc.

National Association Of Negro Musicians, Inc., Salutes R. Nathaniel Dett's 100th Birthday. Illustrated. Gloster B. Current. *Crisis*. 90: 18-20 Feb 83)

National Baptist Convention Of America

Baptist Convention Of America Pledges $100,000 To NAACP. Illustrated. *Crisis*. 90: 16-17 (Oct 83)

National Bar Association

Attorneys Aim For Greater Black Voter Participation In '80s. Illustrated. *Jet*. 64: 17-18 (9 May 83)

NBA To Boost Voting Ranks. Janice Green. *Black Enterprise*. 14: 24 (Dec 83)

National Black Nurses' Association

The National Black Nurses' Association. Illustrated. E. Lorraine Baugh and Beryl Elyese Shorter. *Black Collegian*. 13: 62 (Apr-May 83)

National Black United Front

Make The Past Serve The Present: Strategies For Black Liberation. Notes. Oba Simba T'Shaka. *Black Scholar*. 14: 21-37 (Jan-Feb 83)

National Center For Neighborhood Enterprise

Neighborhoods Reach For The Stars. Illustrated, notes. Pamela A. Taylor. *The Urban League Review*. 08: 77-81 (Winter 83)

National Collegiate Athletic Association

Debate Grows Over Rule 48. Robert McNatt. *Black Enterprise*. 13: 18 (May 83)

National Conference Of Black Lawyers

Foreword [To Vol. 8 No.1]. Notes. Linda Taylor Ferguson. *Black Law Journal*. 08: 4-6 (Spring 83)

National Conference On Black Business Enterprises, 1982

Joint Ventures And Mergers: Keys To Black Business Development. Illustrated. Bebe Moore Campbell. *Black Enterprise*. 13: 19 (Jan 83)

National Council For Black Studies, Inc.

National Council For Black Studies, Inc. Holds Seventh Annual Conference In Berkeley, California. Illustrated. *Black Scholar*. 14: 56-57 (Summer 83)

National Education Association

Mary Hatwood Futrell: Top Teacher. Illustrated. Steve Askin. *Black Enterprise*. 14: 124-126+ (Oct 83)

National Foundation On The Arts And The Humanities

See United States—National Foundation On The Arts And The Humanities

National Institute On Aging

See United States—National Institute On Aging

National Medical Association

Collective Goods And Black Interest Groups. Notes , tables. Dianne M. Pinderhughes. *Review of Black Political Economy*. 12: 219-236 (Winter 83)

Dawson Receives NMA's 1982 Distinguished Service Award.. *National Medical Association Journal*. 75: 321 (Mar 83)

Increasing NMA Membership: A Challenge To Minority Physicians. Robert L. M. Hilliard. *National Medical Association Journal*. 75: 341-344 (Apr 83)

A Matter Of Concern. Robert L. M. Hilliard. *National Medical Association Journal*. 75: 931-932 (Oct 83)

The Medical Colleges Alumni Dinner: A Major Event At NMA Conventions. Editorial. Robert L. M. Hilliard. *National Medical Association Journal*. 75: 1045-1046 (Nov 83)

NMA Dedicates New Headquarters In Washington. Illustrated. Pamela Noel. *Ebony*. 38: 85-86+ (Jul 83)

National Minority Business Council, Inc.

NMBC Is A-OK. Joy Duckett. *Black Enterprise*. 13: 38 (Jun 83)

National Opera Ebony

National Opera Ebony Is Alive And Doing Well. Helen R. Williams. *Crisis*. 90: 25 (Apr 83)

National Organization For Women

Joint Ventures And Mergers: Keys To Black Business Development. Illustrated. Bebe Moore Campbell. *Black Enterprise.* 13: 19 (Jan 83)

National Socialism

Is Israel On The Road To Nazism? Israel Shahak. *Freedomways.* 23: No. 3: 153-164 (83)

National Urban League

Carrying On The Struggle. Illustrated. Earl G. Graves. *Black Enterprise.* 14: 9 (Aug 83)

John E. Jacob: President, National Urban League. Interview, Illustrated. John E. Jacob and Adolph Dupree. *about. . . time.* 11: 10-15 + (Nov 83)

Lobbying: The Power Brokers. Interview, Illustrated. John E. Jacob and Robert McNatt. *Black Enterprise.* 14: 44-45 + (Aug 83)

Navy

See United States. Navy

Naylor Gloria

The Women Of Brewster Place. Book review. Loyle Hairston. *Freedomways.* 23: No. 4: 282-285 (83)

Nazism

See National Socialism

Neas, Ralph G. (joint author)

See Fisher, Paul A.

Necrosis—Bacteriology

Necrotizing Fasciitis: The Howard University Hospital Experience. Tables, illustrated, notes. Mark Walker and Macy (Jr.) Hall. *National Medical Association Journal.* 75: 159-163 (Feb 83)

Negro History Bulletin

The "Bulletin" In The Eighties: The Legacy And The Challenge. Illustrated. *Negro History Bulletin.* 46: 69 (Jul-Sep 83)

Origin; First Quarter Of A Century. Illustrated. *Negro History Bulletin.* 46: 74-77 (Jul-Sep 83)

Negro Labor Committee

Frank R. Crosswaith And Labor Unionization In Harlem, 1939 - 1945. Notes. John C. Walter. *Afro-Americans in New York Life and History.* 07: 47-58 (Jul 83)

Neisser, Eric

Affirmative Action In Hiring Court Staff: The Ninth Circuit's Experience. Notes, tables. *Howard Law Journal.* 26: No. 1: 53-89 (83)

Nelson, Jill

A Case Of Anonymity. Illustrated. *Black Enterprise.* 13: 26 (Mar 83)

Cruel And Unusual Punishment.. *Black Enterprise.* 13: 53 + (May 83)

The Fortune That Madame Built. Illustrated. *Essence.* 14: 84-86 + (Jun 83)

Garland Lands Nigeria Deal. Illustrated. *Black Enterprise.* 13: 25 (Feb 83)

NY Paper In Trouble. Illustrated. *Black Enterprise.* 13: 20 (May 83)

Politics And Education. Illustrated. *Black Enterprise.* 13: 17 (Jul 83)

Trade Pact For Guinea.. *Black Enterprise.* 13: 40 (Jun 83)

Nembhard, Judith P.

A Perspective On Teaching Black Dialect Speaking Students To Write Standard English. Notes. *Journal of Negro Education.* 52: 75-82 (Winter 83)

Nerurkar, S. G. (joint author)

See Gambhir, Kanwal K.

Neser, William B. (joint author)

See Thomas, John

Networking

New Wave Networkers. Pat King. *Black Enterprise.* 14: 89-90 + (Dec 83)

Neubauer, Carol E.

Displacement And Autobiographical Style In Maya Angelou's The Heart Of A Woman. Notes. *Black American Literature Forum.* 17: 123-129 (Fall 83)

Neurasthenia

Are You Headed For A Nervous Breakdown? Illustrated. *Ebony.* 38: 92 + (Oct 83)

New Detroit, Inc.

New Detroit, Inc.. Illustrated. Kevin Moss. *Crisis.* 90: 24-25 (Apr 83)

New Heritage Repertory Theatre

The Magic Of Technical Theatre. Illustrated. A. Peter Bailey. *Black Collegian.* 14: 75 + (Sep-Oct 83)

New Lafayette Theatre

Rituals At The New Lafayette Theatre. Notes. Anthony D. Hill. *Black American Literature Forum.* 17: 31-35 (Spring 83)

New Orleans

See Also Police—Complaints Against—New Orleans

New Orleans—Description

New Orleans: Rich In Tradition. Illustrated. Phil W. Petrie. *Essence.* 14: 46 + (Dec 83)

New Orleans. Louisiana World's Exposition, 1984

Black History On Display. Illustrated. Lovell Beaulieu. *Black Enterprise.* 14: 28 (Oct 83)

New York (City)

See Also Police Chiefs—New York (State)—New York (City) Theater—New York (State)—New York (City) Theaters—New York (State)—New York (City) Trade-Unions—New York (State)—New York (City)—History

New York (City)—Harlem

Can Harlem Be Saved? Illustrated. A. Peter Bailey *Ebony.* 38: 80-82 + (Jan 83)

New York (City)—Public Schools—History

The New York African Free School, 1827-1836: Conflict Over Community Control Of Black Education. Notes. John L. Rury. *Phylon*. 44: 187-197 (Sep 83)

New York (State)

See Also Ku Klux Klan In New York (State)
  Legislators—New York (State)
  Legislators—United States—New York (State)

New York (State)—History

The Klan In Their Midst: The Ku Klux Klan In Upstate New York Communities. Notes. Charles Haley. *Afro-Americans in New York Life and History*. 07: 41-53 (Jan 83)

Men And Manners In America (1833). Notes. Thomas Hamilton. *Afro-Americans in New York Life and History*. 07: 58-60 (Jan 83)

New York (State)—Politics And Government

Running For Political Office. Illustrated. Adolph Dupree. *about. . . time*. 11: 8-19 (Oct 83)

Newark, New Jersey—Mayors

Kenneth Allen Gibson: Mayor Of Newark, New Jersey. Interview, Illustrated. Kenneth A. Gibson and Adolph Dupree. *about. . . time*. 11: 10-13+ (Jul 83)

Newborn, Venezuela

Fix Food Fast.. *Essence*. 14: 106+ (May 83)

No Time To Cook? These Quick And Tasty Recipes Will Make Every Meal This Month A Joy.. *Essence*. 13: 113-114+ (Mar 83)

Newborn, Venezuela and James, Curtia

Good And Cheap. Illustrated. *Essence*. 14: 103-105+ (Jun 83)

News Agencies—Africa

African News Agency Opens. Jennifer Beaumont. *Black Enterprise*. 14: 18 (Aug 83)

Newsom, Lionel and Rouselle, William

The Struggle To Save A Black School: An Interview With Central State President Newsom. Interview, Illustrated. *Black Collegian*. 13: 38+ (Apr-May 83)

Newsome, Frederick

Black Contributions To The Early History Of Western Medicine. Illustrated. *Journal of African Civilizations*. 05: 127-139 (Apr-Nov 83)

Newspaper Publishing—California—Oakland

Maynard Buys Tribune. Illustrated. Rose Ragsdale. *Black Enterprise*. 13: 18 (Jul 83)

Newspapers

America's Ten Oldest Black Newspapers. Illustrated, notes. J. William Snorgrass. *Negro History Bulletin*. 46: 11-14 (Jan-Mar 83)

NY Paper In Trouble. Illustrated. Jill Nelson. *Black Enterprise*. 13: 20 (May 83)

See Also Periodicals

Newton, Edmund

Employment Outlook 1983. Illustrated, tables. *Black Enterprise*. 13: 43-45 (Feb 83)

An Eye For An Eye.. *Black Enterprise*. 13: 52+ (May 83)

Glamour Careers Without A Sheepskin. Illustrated. *Black Enterprise*. 13: 66-68+ (Feb 83)

Planning For Your Retirement. Illustrated. *Black Enterprise*. 14: 89-92+ (Oct 83)

Taking Over City Hall. Illustrated, tables. *Black Enterprise*. 13: 155-160 (Jun 83)

Newton, Eunice Shaed

Dictionary Of American Negro Biography. Book review. *Journal of Negro Education*. 52: 454-455 (Fall 83)

Newton, Patricia A.

An Evaluation Of The Cost Effectiveness Of Day Hospitalization For Black Male Schizophrenics. Tables. *National Medical Association Journal*. 75: 273-285 (Mar 83)

Ngaté, Jonathan

Introduction À L' Étude Du Roman Nœgro-Africain De Langue Française: Problemes Culturels Et Littèraires. Book review. *Research in African Literatures*. 14: 207-209 (Summer 83)

Nicaragua

See Also Medical Care—Nicaragua
  Revolutions—Nicaragua

Nicaragua—Economic Policy

Nicaragua: Economic Planning For The Future. Tables, illustrated. *Black Scholar*. 14: 28-47 (Mar-Apr 83)

Nicaragua—Foreign Relations—United States

The War Of Terror Against Nicaragua. Illustrated. Hector Frances. *Black Scholar*. 14: 2-16 (Mar-Apr 83)

Nicaragua—Politics And Government

Nicaragua: The Path To Peace. Editorial. Robert Chrisman. *Black Scholar*. 14: 1 (Mar-Apr 83)

Nicholas Brothers

Whatever Happened To The Nicholas Brothers? Illustrated. Aldore Collier. *Ebony*. 38: 103-104+ (May 83)

Nichols, Charles H.

Arna Bontemps-Langston Hughes: Letters 1925-1967. Book review. Maria K. Mootry-Ikerionwu. *CLA Journal*. 27: 226-228 (Dec 83)

Nicole, Lydia (about)

New Faces In Hollywood. Illustrated. *Ebony*. 38: 62-64+ (Apr 83)

Nieto, Sonia

Children's Literature On Puerto Rican Themes- Part I: The Messages Of Fiction. Illustrated. *Interracial Books for Children*. 14: No. 1: 6-9 (83)

Children's Literature On Puerto Rican Themes- Part
II: Non-fiction. Illustrated. *Interracial Books for
Children*. 14: No. 1: 10-12+ (83)

Nigeria

See Also Marasmus—Nigeria
Oral Tradition—Nigeria
Petroleum Industry And Trade—Nigeria
Teachers Of Handicapped Children, Training
Of—Nigeria

Nigeria—Economic Conditions

Shagari Faces Economic Woes. Illustrated. Derek
T. Dingle. *Black Enterprise*. 14: 26 (Dec 83)

Nigerian Drama—History And Criticism

Metaphor As Basis Of Form In Soyinka's Drama.
Notes. 'Ropo Sekoni. *Research in African
Literatures*. 14: 45-57 (Spring 83)

A Nigerian Version Of A Greek Classic: Soyinka's
Transformation Of The Bacchae. Notes. Norma
Bishop. *Research in African Literatures*. 14: 68-80
(Spring 83)

Nigerian Fiction—History And Criticism

"Leaders And Left-Overs": A Reading Of
Soyinka's: Death And The King's Horseman.
Notes. Mark Ralph-Bowman. *Research in African
Literatures*. 14: 81-97 (Spring 83)

Nigerian Literature—History And Criticism

No Longer At Ease: Chinua Achebe's "Heart Of
Whiteness". Notes. Philip Rogers. *Research in
African Literatures*. 14: 165-183 (Summer 83)

Nigerian Poetry—History And Criticism

The Voice And Viewpoint Of The Poet In Wole
Soyinka's "Four Archetypes". Notes. Tanure
Ojaide. *Research in African Literatures*. 14: 58-67
(Spring 83)

Niven, Alastair

A Critical View On Elechi Amadi's. Book review.
Robert M. Wren. *Research in African Literatures*.
14: 110-111 (Spring 83)

Nivens, Beatryce

The Black Woman's Career Guide. Book review.
Elza Teresa Dinwiddie. *Black Enterprise*. 13: 30-31
(Jun 83)

The Black Woman's Career Guide. Book review.
Carole Bovoso. *Essence*. 13: 20 (Mar 83)

Hot Careers In The Eighties.. *Essence*. 14: 32 (Aug
83)

Nixon, Regina

Black Managers In Corporate America: A Good
Fit? Notes, tables. *The Urban League Review*. 07:
44-57 (Summer 83)

Nodal, Roberto

The Social Evolution Of The Afro-Cuban Drum.
Illustrated, notes. *The Black Perspective in Music*.
11: 157-177 (Fall 83)

Noel, Pamela

Beer Brewery Boss. Illustrated. *Ebony*. 38: 40+
(Jun 83)

Cheap Chic. Illustrated. *Ebony*. 38: 58-59+ (Sep
83)

A Family Affair At West Point. Illustrated. *Ebony*.
39: 45-46+ (Nov 83)

Fasting: The Myths And The Facts. Illustrated.
Ebony. 38: 36+ (Jan 83)

Fathers And Daughters: The Men Behind Their
Success. Illustrated. *Ebony*. 39: 124+ (Dec 83)

The New Black Entrepreneurs. Illustrated. *Ebony*.
38: 160+ (Aug 83)

NMA Dedicates New Headquarters In Washington.
Illustrated. *Ebony*. 38: 85-86+ (Jul 83)

Super Mom, Super Kids. Illustrated. *Ebony*. 38:
44+ (Oct 83)

Noguchi, Jean (joint author)

See Van Pham, Cao

Non-Wage Payments

A Salary With Fringe On Top. Lynette Hazelton.
Essence. 14: 26 (May 83)

Norflett, Linda Kerr

Rosetta LeNoire: The Lady And Her Theatre.
Notes. *Black American Literature Forum*. 17: 69-72
(Summer 83)

Norfolk (Virginia) State University

The President That Time Forgot. Marvin Leon
Lake. *Negro History Bulletin*. 46: 51-52 (Apr-Jun
83)

Norman, Beverly J.

Weeding Out Black Scholars. Illustrated. *Black
Enterprise*. 13: 97-98+ (Feb 83)

Norman, Fran

All That Glitters May Not Be Gold! Short story.
about. . . time. 11: 35 (Nov 83)

Dads Only: Better Husbands, Fathers And Men.
Illustrated. *about. . . time*. 11: 20-21 (Jul 83)

One Of These Days. Short story. *about. . . time*.
11: 21 (Sep 83)

Unrecognized Musicians. Short story, Illustrated.
about. . . time. 11: 12-13 (Feb 83)

Norment, Lynn

Are Black Refugees Getting A Dirty Deal?
Illustrated. *Ebony*. 38: 132-134+ (Oct 83)

A Better Chance. Illustrated. *Ebony*. 38: 46+ (Jun
83)

Divorce: How Black Women Cope With Their
Broken Marriages. Illustrated. *Ebony*. 39: 59-60+
(Nov 83)

A Family Affair: Patricia Shaw Succeeds Father As
President Of Universal Life. Illustrated. *Ebony*. 38:
75-76+ (May 83)

Farewell To Ragtime's Apostle Of Happiness.
Illustrated. *Ebony*. 38: 27-28+ (May 83)

First Marriage After 40. Illustrated. *Ebony*. 38:
28-30+ (Jan 83)

Here She Is. . . Miss America. Illustrated. *Ebony*.
39: 132-134+ (Dec 83)

Is It True What They Say About Southern Men? Illustrated. *Ebony*. 38: 104+ (Feb 83)

Mayor Harold Washington: Changing Of The Guard In Chicago. Illustrated. *Ebony*. 38: 27-30+ (Jul 83)

Results Of Ebony Reader Poll: Should A Black Run For President?. *Ebony*. 38: 76+ (Oct 83)

What Every Black Man Should Know About Black Women. Illustrated. *Ebony*. 38: 132+ (Aug 83)

Why Some Women Prefer Older Men. Illustrated. *Ebony*. 38: 132+ (Apr 83)

Norris, William C.

A New Role For Corporations: Linking Technology To Socioeconomic Development.. *The Urban League Review*. 08: 88-94 (Winter 83)

North Carolina

See Also College Integration—North Carolina Segregation In Education—North Carolina

Nosocomial Infections

Nosocomial Infection: Update. Tables, notes. Edwin T. Johnson. *National Medical Association Journal*. 75: 147-154 (Feb 83)

Novels

A Gathering Of Old Men [Excerpt]. Reviewed by Ernest Gaines. *Black Scholar*. 14: 42-49 (Summer 83)

Great Black Russian: Chapter Five - Part 5. Reviewed by John Oliver Killens. *Crisis*. 90: 44-49 (Oct 83)

Run Like Hell And Holler Fire! (Part I). Reviewed by John Oliver Killens. *Freedomways*. 23: No. 4: 244-256 (83)

Nowlin, T. A. (III) and Webster, G. Y.

Computerization Of Procedural Requests And Reports Of Clinical Laboratory Data: A Case Study. Tables. *National Medical Association Journal*. 75: 409-414 (Apr 83)

Numeration

The Yoruba Number System. Illustrated, tables. Claudia Zaslavsky. *Journal of African Civilizations*. 05: 110-126 (Apr-Nov 83)

Nunes, Maria Luisa

An Artist's Identity Versus The Social Role Of The Writer: The Case For Joaquim Maria Machado De Assis. Notes. *CLA Journal*. 27: 187-196 (Dec 83)

Nunez-Harrell, Elizabeth

Youngblood. Book review. *Crisis*. 90: 42-43 (Oct 83)

Nunley, Dorsey (about)

Dorsey Nunley: Creating Community Change. Illustrated. Robin Wilson. *about. . . time*. 11: 20-21 (Nov 83)

Nurses

The National Black Nurses' Association. Illustrated. E. Lorraine Baugh and Beryl Elyese Shorter. *Black Collegian*. 13: 62 (Apr-May 83)

Nursing

Emergency Service Nursing Staff: A Survey Of Knowledge, Attitudes, And Concerns. Tables, notes. F. M. Baker and Barbara Moynihan. *National Medical Association Journal*. 75: 417-421 (Apr 83)

The Nurse Practitioner's Role In Complex Patient Management: Hypertension. Tables, notes. Michael J. Reichgott and others. *National Medical Association Journal*. 75: 1197-1204 (Dec 83)

Nutrition Disorders

Interaction Of Nutrition And Infection: Effect Of Zinc Deficiency On Immunoglobulin Levels In Trypanosoma Musculi Infection. Tables, notes. Clarence Lee and others. *National Medical Association Journal*. 75: 677-682 (Jul 83)

Nyang, Sulayman S.

Reflections Of An African Nationalist. Book review. *Phylon*. 44: 164-168 (Jun 83)

Nyden, Philip W.

Evolution Of Black Political Influence In American Trade Unions. Notes. *Journal of Black Studies*. 13: 379-398 (Jun 83)

O'Daniel, Therman B.

In Memoriam: Nick Aaron Ford (1904-1982).. *Black American Literature Forum*. 17: 99 (Fall 83)

O'Dell, J. H.

The Silence Is Broken. Editorial. *Freedomways*. 23: No. 2: 66-69 (83)

Oakes, James

The Ruling Race: A History Of American Slaveholders. Book review. Joseph P. Reidy. *Journal of Negro History*. 68: 95-97 (Winter 83)

Oakland Tribune (Newspaper)

Maynard Buys Tribune. Illustrated. Rose Ragsdale. *Black Enterprise*. 13: 18 (Jul 83)

Oates, Stephen B.

Let The Trumpet Sound: The Life Of Martin Luther King, Jr.. Book review. Gereald C. Horne. *Freedomways*. 23: No. 4: 290-294 (83)

Oberlin College

The Antebellum "Talented Thousandth": Black College Students At Oberlin Before The Civil War. Notes, tables. Ellen N. Lawson and Marlene Merrill. *Journal of Negro Education*. 52: 142-155 (Spring 83)

Obesity

See Also Leanness

Obituaries

Adams, Betty A. *Jet*. 64: 18 (30 May 83)

Alexander, T. M. (Jr.). *Jet*. 64: 30 (23 May 83)

Allen, Moses. *The Black Perspective in Music*. 11: 223 (Fall 83)

Anderson, John. *Jet*. 65: 18 (14 Nov 83)

Andrew, Muriel R.
Jet. 64: 22 (27 Jun 83)

Armstrong, Lucille.
Jet. 65: 18 (24 Oct 83)

Bailey, Gonzelle.
Jet. 65: 16 (24 Oct 83)

Barrett, Audrey Mae.
Jet. 65: 15 (12 Dec 83)

Barrett, Emma.
Jet. 63: 53 (21 Feb 83)

Barrett, Sweet Emma.
The Black Perspective in Music. 11: 223 (Fall 83)

Barrow, Keith E.
Jet. 65: 18 (14 Nov 83)

Basie, Catherine.
Jet. 64: 58 (2 May 83)

Bentley, Lemuel E.
Jet. 65: 16 (24 Oct 83)

Best, Mike Clotee.
Jet. 65: 30 (3 Oct 83)

Beverly, Lillian S.
Jet. 64: 22 (27 Jun 83)

Bishop, Maurice.
Jet. 65: 55 (7 Nov 83)

Blackburn, Leo.
Jet. 63: 18 (3 Jan 83)

Blake, Eubie (1883-1983).
Jet. 63: 17-18 (28 Feb 83)

Blake, Eubie (1883-1983).
The Black Perspective in Music. 11: 223+ (Fall 83)

Boatner, Clifford L.
Jet. 65: 16 (24 Oct 83)

Bobbitt, Charles (Jr.).
Jet. 63: 6 (7 Mar 83)

Bobo, Willie.
Jet. 65: 63 (3 Oct 83)

Booker, James (III).
Jet. 65: 18 (5 Dec 83)

Boulware, Harold R.
Jet. 63: 53 (21 Feb 83)

Bowser, John A.
Jet. 65: 30 (3 Oct 83)

Braggs, Arthur.
Jet. 63: 18 (10 Jan 83)

Brown, Leatha J.
Jet. 63: 53 (21 Feb 83)

Brown, Malcolm.
Jet. 64: 15 (15 Aug 83)

Brown, Nelson.
Jet. 64: 16 (28 Mar 83)

Bryant, Arthur.
Jet. 63: 59 (17 Jan 83)

Bryant, Hazel J.
Jet. 65: 15 (12 Dec 83)

Burton, Freddie G.
Jet. 64: 31 (23 May 83)

Butler, Benjamin L.
Jet. 64: 31 (22 Aug 83)

Butler, Kid Twat.
The Black Perspective in Music. 11: 225 (Fall 83)

Cabell, Clarence E.
Jet. 63: 53 (21 Feb 83)

Carroll, Bebop.
The Black Perspective in Music. 11: 225 (Fall 83)

Chatmon, Sam.
The Black Perspective in Music. 11: 225 (Fall 83)

Christian, Robert.
Jet. 63: 16 (28 Feb 83)

Clark, Mamie Phipps.
Jet. 64: 18 (28 Aug 83)

Clark, Maud Allen.
Jet. 64: 22 (18 Jul 83)

Cobbs, Eugene D. (Sr.).
Jet. 64: 31 (23 May 83)

Cofield, Bill.
Jet. 64: 50 (11 Jul 83)

Cole, Frances Elaine.
The Black Perspective in Music. 11: 225 (Fall 83)

Collins, M. L. (Jr.).
Jet. 64: 8 (1 Aug 83)

Cook, Jesse W.
Jet. 65: 30 (3 Oct 83)

Cooper, Jean Ollie.
Jet. 64: 15 (1 Aug 83)

Darden, Lillian Allen.
The Black Perspective in Music. 11: 225 (Fall 83)

Davis, Allison.
Jet. 65: 15 (12 Dec 83)

DeFeaster, Trohelious Phillips.
Jet. 64: 53 (9 May 83)

Dent, Meta.
Jet. 64: 58 (21 Mar 83)

DePriest, Oscar S.
Jet. 65: 18 (5 Dec 83)

Dodson, Owen.
Jet. 64: 54 (11 Jul 83)

Donald, Leo Edward.
Jet. 64: 15 (15 Aug 83)

Draper, Raymond Allen.
The Black Perspective in Music. 11: 226 (Fall 83)

Duckworth, Mary.
Jet. 64: 53 (9 May 83)

Dunn, Tracy.
Jet. 63: 53 (21 Feb 83)

Dunnigan, Alice.
Jet. 64: 42 (30 May 83)

Dunnigan, Alice A.
Crisis. 90: 48 (Aug-Sep 83)

Duster, Alfreda B.
Jet. 64: 18 (25 Apr 83)

Edwards, Robert.
Jet. 65: 18 (5 Dec 83)

Elliott, Bill.
Jet. 65: 63 (10 Oct 83)

Ellison, Coleman Wesley.
Jet. 63: 22 (7 Mar 83)

Eversley, Frederick W. (Jr.).
Jet. 63: 24 (7 Feb 83)

Fisher, Peter William (Sr.).
Jet. 64: 18 (11 Apr 83)

Fitzpatrick, Cynthia.
Jet. 64: 58 (21 Mar 83)

Flowers, Johnnie.
Jet. 64: 15 (15 Aug 83)

Frisby, Herbert M.
Jet. 64: 15 (15 Aug 83)

Gould, William Benjamin (III).
Jet. 65: 30 (3 Oct 83)

Granderson, John Lee.
The Black Perspective in Music. 11: 226 (Fall 83)

Greene, W. Henry.
Jet. 65: 17 (24 Oct 83)

Griffin, Clarence.
Jet. 64: 53 (9 May 83)

Gryce, Gigi.
The Black Perspective in Music. 11: 226 (Fall 83)

Hadley, Hattie Bunion.
Jet. 64: 58 (21 Mar 83)

Hall, Frederick Douglass.
Jet. 64: 18 (4 Apr 83)

Hall, Frederick Douglass.
The Black Perspective in Music. 11: 226 (Fall 83)

Hall, Louise V.
Jet. 65: 15 (12 Dec 83)

Hankins, Emma A.
Crisis. 90: 36 (Apr 83)

Hardmon, Berdine McGlaun.
Jet. 63: 18 (3 Jan 83)

Hartman, Johnny.
Jet. 65: 63 (3 Oct 83)

Haywood, William H. (Sr.).
Jet. 64: 57 (20 Jun 83)

Henry, Charles F. (II).
Jet. 63: 24 (7 Feb 83)

Hill, Julius.
Jet. 65: 55 (7 Nov 83)

Hines, Earl "Fatha".
Jet. 64: 62 (9 May 83)

Hines, Earl Fatha (1905-1983).
The Black Perspective in Music. 11: 226-227 (Fall 83)

Hutto, Joseph Benjamin.
Jet. 64: 22 (18 Jul 83)

Ivy, Bessie Partee.
Jet. 64: 18 (11 Apr 83)

Jackson, Earl.
Jet. 63: 53 (21 Feb 83)

Jackson, Graham W.
The Black Perspective in Music. 11: 227 (Fall 83)

Jackson, Graham Washington.
Jet. 63: 24 (7 Feb 83)

Jackson, Preston.
Jet. 65: 15 (12 Dec 83)

Jackson, Walter.
The Black Perspective in Music. 11: 227 (Fall 83)

Jackson, Yoshiko.
Jet. 64: 18 (30 May 83)

Jamerson, James.
Jet. 65: 18 (5 Dec 83)

Jemison, James H.
Jet. 64: 31 (23 May 83)

Jenkins, Joseph H. (Jr.).
Jet. 63: 53 (21 Feb 83)

Johnson, Adrian Winslow.
Crisis. 90: 48 (Feb 83)

Jones, Charles V.
Jet. 63: 22 (7 Mar 83)

Jones, Edith A.
Jet. 64: 22 (18 Jul 83)

Jones, James.
The Black Perspective in Music. 11: 227 (Fall 83)

Jordan, James Taft.
The Black Perspective in Music. 11: 227 (Fall 83)

Kearney, Joe.
Jet. 63: 22 (7 Mar 83)

Kemp, James.
Crisis. 90: 47 (Dec 83)

Kemp, James.
Jet. 65: 18 (26 Dec 83)

Kersey, Joseph A.
Jet. 63: 18 (10 Jan 83)

King, W. Calvin.
Jet. 64: 58 (21 Mar 83)

Kirkendoll, Mattie D.
Jet. 65: 16 (24 Oct 83)

Landry, Kenneth C.
Jet. 64: 31 (23 May 83)

Laster, Clarence (Jr.).
Jet. 63: 24 (7 Feb 83)

Lawrence, George.
Jet. 65: 14 (26 Dec 83)

LeCesne, Archibald T.
Jet. 64: 18 (25 Apr 83)

Lee, Edith B. Spurlock.
Jet. 63: 22 (7 Mar 83)

Lei, Jon.
Jet. 63: 24 (7 Feb 83)

Lewis, Milton D.
Jet. 65: 15 (12 Dec 83)

Lewis, Ramsey (Sr.).
Jet. 65: 63 (24 Oct 83)

Lewis, Raymond C.
Jet. 65: 18 (5 Dec 83)

Lindsay, Inable Burns.
Jet. 65: 16 (24 Oct 83)

Smith, Rosie Lee.
Jet. 64: 18 (30 May 83)

Stackhouse, Houston.
The Black Perspective in Music. 11: 228 (Fall 83)

Stamps, George.
Jet. 64: 53 (9 May 83)

Stewart, Marcus C. (Sr.).
Jet. 64: 18 (25 Apr 83)

Stokes, William McKinley.
Jet. 64: 31 (22 Aug 83)

Stroger, Hans Eric.
Jet. 63: 18 (3 Jan 83)

Sutton, Myron.
The Black Perspective in Music. 11: 228 (Fall 83)

Sutton, Oliver C.
Jet. 64: 15 (15 Aug 83)

Sykes, Roosevelt.
Jet. 64: 15 (1 Aug 83)

Sykes, Roosevelt.
The Black Perspective in Music. 11: 228 (Fall 83)

Tandy, Opal L.
Jet. 64: 15 (15 Aug 83)

Taylor, Guy Russell.
Jet. 63: 18 (10 Jan 83)

Teamer, Eddie L.
Jet. 64: 18 (25 Apr 83)

Theard, Spo-De-oDee.
The Black Perspective in Music. 11: 229 (Fall 83)

Thomas, Maxwell S.
Jet. 64: 18 (11 Apr 83)

Thompson, Leon Evanette.
The Black Perspective in Music. 11: 229 (Fall 83)

Thompson, Walter E.
Jet. 63: 24 (7 Feb 83)

Towles Caesar, Lois.
The Black Perspective in Music. 11: 230 (Fall 83)

Trenier, Cliff.
Jet. 64: 63 (21 Mar 83)

Tucker, Tommy.
The Black Perspective in Music. 11: 230 (Fall 83)

Turner, William R.
Jet. 65: 18 (14 Nov 83)

Van Der Zee, James.
Jet. 64: 14 (30 May 83)

Von Dickersohn, Elmer J.
Jet. 64: 58 (21 Mar 83)

Walker, Marion.
The Black Perspective in Music. 11: 230 (Fall 83)

Walker, Marion Dozier.
Jet. 64: 18 (25 Apr 83)

Walters, Albert.
The Black Perspective in Music. 11: 230 (Fall 83)

Ward, Theodore.
Jet. 64: 18 (30 May 83)

Washington, Bob.
Jet. 64: 15 (15 Aug 83)

Washington, Chester L.
Jet. 65: 30 (3 Oct 83)

Washington, George Leward.
Jet. 64: 22 (18 Jul 83)

Waters, Muddy.
The Black Perspective in Music. 11: 230-231 (Fall 83)

Watson, Barbara (1918-1983).
Jet. 63: 13 (7 Mar 83)

Westmoreland, John.
Jet. 64: 15 (15 Aug 83)

Williams, Arlene E.
Jet. 65: 15 (12 Dec 83)

Williams, Big Joe.
The Black Perspective in Music. 11: 231 (Fall 83)

Williams, Cenie J. (Jr.).
Jet. 64: 18 (11 Apr 83)

Williams, Fat Man.
The Black Perspective in Music. 11: 231 (Fall 83)

Williams, Francis.
Jet. 65: 63 (24 Oct 83)

Williams, Janice.
Jet. 64: 18 (25 Apr 83)

Williams, Maria L.
Jet. 64: 31 (22 Aug 83)

Williams, Nathaniel D.
Jet. 65: 18 (5 Dec 83)

Williams, Warren (Jr.) (1938-1983).
Journal of Religious Thought. 40: 8
(Spring-Summer 83)

Wilson, Harvey L.
Jet. 64: 53 (9 May 83)

Wood, Eugene.
Jet. 65: 18 (5 Dec 83)

Wright, Emanuel C.
Jet. 63: 22 (7 Mar 83)

Wright, Vassie Davis.
Negro History Bulletin. 46: 92 (Oct-Dec 83)

Yette, Sadie.
Jet. 65: 16 (26 Dec 83)

Young, Buddy.
Jet. 65: 52-53 (26 Sep 83)

Younge, Benjamin M.
Jet. 63: 22 (7 Mar 83)

Occupational Diseases

Do You Work At A Job That Could Be Making You Sick? Jan Solet. *Essence.* 13: 58+ (Mar 83)

Video Terminals And Your Health. James Harney. *Essence.* 14: 50 (Oct 83)

Occupational Mobility

Making That Move: Relocating For A Better Job. Lloyd Gite. *Essence.* 13: 32+ (Jan 83)

Occupational Training

Tracking Down A Technical School. Janice L. Greene. *Black Enterprise.* 13: 71-72 (Feb 83)

Occupations

Built To Last! Illustrated, tables. Linda D. Addison. *Essence.* 14: 35 (Dec 83)

Career Niches In The Comming Era: An Interview With Alvin Toffler. Interview, Illustrated. Alvin Toffler and James Borders. *Black Collegian.* 14: 112-114+ (Sep-Oct 83)

Get Somewhere In Travel. Marcia McNair. *Essence.* 13: 29 (Apr 83)

Glamour Careers Without A Sheepskin. Illustrated. Edmund Newton. *Black Enterprise.* 13: 66-68+ (Feb 83)

Hot Careers In The Eighties. Beatryce Nivens. *Essence.* 14: 32 (Aug 83)

How To Get The Job You Want. John William Zehring. *Black Collegian.* 13: 50-54+ (Feb-Mar 83)

Keys To The Future. Illustrated. Harriet Jackson Scarupa and Marcia McNair. *Essence.* 14: 46 (Oct 83)

Night People. Illustrated. *Ebony.* 39: 44+ (Dec 83)

Ready Or Not, Here Comes The Computer Future. Rosemary L. Bray. *Essence.* 14: 99-100+ (Oct 83)

A Streak Of Ebony In The Ivory Tower. Illustrated. Shcila Sinclair. *Black Enterprise.* 13: 84-86+ (Feb 83)

You Can Count On Mathematics! Harriet Jackson Scarupa. *Essence.* 13: 30 (Feb 83)

1983 Job Index.. *Black Collegian.* 13: 88+ (Feb-Mar 83)

See Also Vocational Interests

Occupations And Race

Occupational Cancer In The Black Population: The Health Effects Of Job Discrimination. Notes. David Michaels. *National Medical Association Journal.* 75: 1014-1018 (Oct 83)

Occupations, Choice Of

See Vocational Guidance

Ocean Travel

Cruising Into The Sun. Illustrated. Ben F. Carruthers. *Black Enterprise.* 14: 119 (Dec 83)

Oceanography—Vocational Guidance

Careers In Oceanography. Illustrated. Otha Richard Sullivan. *Black Collegian.* 14: 123-125+ (Sep-Oct 83)

Charting Your Course In Oceanography. Illustrated. Barbara Price. *Black Collegian.* 14: 124-125 (Sep-Oct 83)

Odetta (about)

Odetta-A Citzen Of the World. Illustrated. Don Armstrong. *Crisis.* 90: 51-52 (Jun-Jul 83)

Odom, Antonia (about)

Where There's A Will: Antonia's Incredible Triumph. Illustrated. Roger Witherspoon and Claudia Huff. *Essence.* 14: 69-70+ (Dec 83)

Oestreich, Alan E. (joint author)

See Lumpkins, Lola

Offices

When Your Office Is At Home. Illustrated. Ann Arnott. *Black Enterprise.* 14: 132 (Oct 83)

Offices—Location

House Work. Illustrated. Udayan Gupta. *Black Enterprise.* 13: 59-60+ (Apr 83)

Ogbaa, Kalu

The Literary Half-Yearly. Book review. *Research in African Literatures.* 14: 126-128 (Spring 83)

Ogungbesan, Kolawole

The Writing Of Peter Abrahams. Book review. Clive Leeman. *Research in African Literatures.* 14: 245-248 (Summer 83)

Ogunyemi, Chikwenye Okonjo

Helping With Literature. Book review. *Research in African Literatures.* 14: 254-255 (Summer 83)

Ohio

See Also Elections—Ohio
Legislators—United States—Ohio
Public Contracts—Ohio

Ojaide, Tanure

The Voice And Viewpoint Of The Poet In Wole Soyinka's "Four Archetypes". Notes. *Research in African Literatures.* 14: 58-67 (Spring 83)

Okeahialam, Theodore C.

Growth Of Nigerian Children With Marasmus After Hospital Treatment. Tables. *National Medical Association Journal.* 75: 75-80 (Jan 83)

Okihiro, Gary Y. and Sly, Julie

The Press, Japanese Americans, And The Concentration Camps. Notes. *Phylon.* 44: 66-83 (Mar 83)

Oklahoma

See Also Petroleum Industry And Trade—Oklahoma

Okonkwo, Rina L.

Orishatukeh Faduma: A Man Of Two Worlds. Notes. *Journal of Negro History.* 68: 24-36 (Winter 83)

Olajubu, Oludare

Yoruba Myths. Book review. *Research in African Literatures.* 14: 538-543 (Winter 83)

Older Persons

See Aged

Olion, LaDelle and Gillis-Olion, Marion

Improving The Assessment Of Black Students. Notes. *Negro Educational Review.* 34: 52-60 (Apr 83)

Oliva, Sergio (about)

Pounding Pavement And Pumping Iron. Illustrated. *Ebony.* 38: 57-58+ (Jul 83)

Olivas, Michael A.

The Dilemma Of Access: Minorities In Two Year Colleges. Book review. Obra V. Hackett. *Journal of Negro History*. 68: 130-131 (Winter 83)

Oliver, Jennifer

How To Put The Zip Back In Love. Illustrated. *Essence*. 14: 91+ (Sep 83)

Oliver, Kitty

Essence Women: Eleanor Workman. Illustrated. *Essence*. 14: 54 (Dec 83)

Oliver, Stephanie Stokes

Maya Angelou: The Heart Of The Woman. Illustrated. *Essence*. 14: 112-114+ (May 83)

The New Choice: Single Motherhood After 30.. *Essence*. 14: 131-132+ (Oct 83)

Peggy Dillard: A Model Life Of Health And Beauty. Illustrated. *Essence*. 13: 100-101 (Jan 83)

The Private Side Of Julian Bond. Illustrated. *Essence*. 14: 103-104+ (Nov 83)

Oliver, Stephanie Stokes and Gallman, Vanessa J.

Should You Buy Your Own Phone?. *Essence*. 13: 124 (Mar 83)

Oluwole, Soji F. and others

Retroperitoneal Abscess. Tables, illustrated, notes. *National Medical Association Journal*. 75: 693-700 (Jul 83)

Olympic Games

Relections On Olympic Sportpolitics: History And Prospects, 1968-1984. Illustrated. Harry Edwards. *Crisis*. 90: 20-24 (May 83)

Olympic Games, Los Angeles, 1984

Going For The Gold. Illustrated. Janet Clayton. *Black Enterprise*. 13: 65-66+ (Apr 83)

Omotoso, Kole

Al-Drama Al-Afriqia. Book review. *Research in African Literatures*. 14: 108-110 (Spring 83)

Opa-Locka, Florida

See Also Police Chiefs—Florida—Opa-Locka

Opera

National Opera Ebony Is Alive And Doing Well. Helen R. Williams. *Crisis*. 90: 25 (Apr 83)

Operation Fair Share

Demanding A Fair Share. Interview, Illustrated. Benjamin L. Hooks and S. Lee Hilliard. *Black Enterprise*. 14: 40-42 (Aug 83)

"Fair Share Approach Is Fourfold". Benjamin L. Hooks. *Crisis*. 90: 4 (Oct 83)

Fair Share Points The Way. . . "We Are Laying A Foundation To Change The Face Of America". Benjamin L. Hooks. *Crisis*. 90: 10-11 (Oct 83)

An Interview With Benjamin L. Hooks. . . Demanding A Fair Share. Interview, Illustrated. Benjamin L. Hooks. *Crisis*. 90: 6-7 (Oct 83)

Oral Contraceptives

Urinary Estrogen And Serum Gonadotropin Profiles In Women Ingesting Oral Contraceptive Steroid Formulations With Variable Estrogen Content. Tables, notes. Elwyn M. Grimes and others. *National Medical Association Journal*. 75: 575-580 (Jun 83)

Oral Literature

See Folk Literature

Oral Tradition—Africa

Oral Tradition In African Societies. Bibliography, notes. Grace C. Cooper. *Negro History Bulletin*. 46: 101-103 (Oct-Dec 83)

Oral Tradition—Nigeria

The Audience In Gullah And Igbo: A Comparison Of Oral Traditions. Notes. Patricia Jones-Jackson. *CLA Journal*. 27: 197-209 (Dec 83)

Oral Tradition—Sea Islands

The Audience In Gullah And Igbo: A Comparison Of Oral Traditions. Notes. Patricia Jones-Jackson. *CLA Journal*. 27: 197-209 (Dec 83)

Organ, Brian C. (joint author)

See Organ, Claude H. (Jr.)

Organ, Claude H. (Jr.) and Organ, Brian C.

Fibroadenoma Of The Female Breast: A Critical Clinical Assessment. Tables, notes. *National Medical Association Journal*. 75: 701-704 (Jul 83)

Osa, Osayimwense

Children's Fiction About Africa In English. Book review. *Research in African Literatures*. 14: 257-261 (Summer 83)

Osbey, Brenda Marie

Mama Sitting. Poem. *Essence*. 14: 137 (Aug 83)

Osborne, Alfred E. (Jr.)

A Flat-Rate Tax Will Hurt The Middle Class.. *Black Enterprise*. 14: 31 (Sep 83)

Othow, Helen Chavis

Roots And The Heroic Search For Identity. Notes. *CLA Journal*. 26: 311-324 (Mar 83)

Otto, John Solomon and Burns, Augustus Marion (III)

Black Folks And Poor Buckras: Archeological Evidence Of Slave And Overseer Living Conditions On An Antebellum Plantation. Notes. *Journal of Black Studies*. 14: 185-200 (Dec 83)

Ovaries—Surgery

Salpingo-Oophorectomy In Women With Previous Hysterectomy. Illustrated. Enrique Hernandez and Neil B. Rosenshein. *National Medical Association Journal*. 75: 106-107 (Jan 83)

Owens, Diana Valdes (about)

Essence Women: Diana Valdes Owens. Illustrated. Ken Smikle. *Essence*. 13: 29-30 (Mar 83)

Owens, Jesse (about)

Jesse Owens' Olympic Triumph Over Time And Hitlerism. Illustrated. Lerone (Jr.) Bennett. *Ebony*. 39: 140+ (Dec 83)

Owens, Major R. (about)

New Faces On Capitol Hill. Illustrated. *Ebony*. 38: 36-38+ (Feb 83)

P.L.O.

See Palestinian Liberation Organization

Pain

Psychological Aspects Of Chronic Pain. Notes. Rosevelt Jacobs. *National Medical Association Journal*. 75: 387-391 (Apr 83)

See Also Backache

Palestinian Arabs—Israel

Inside The Camps.. *Freedomways*. 23: No. 2: 140-144 (83)

Liberation Theology And The Middle East Conflict. Wyatt Tee Walker. *Freedomways*. 23: No. 3: 147-152 (83)

Middle East Crossroads. Yael Lotan. *Freedomways*. 23: No. 3: 165-170 (83)

Palestinian Identity And The Land Of Palestine. James Zogby. *Freedomways*. 23: No. 2: 118-125 (83)

Palestinian Liberation Organization

Palestinian Prisoners: Are They Prisoners Of War? Notes. Gay J. McDougall. *Freedomways*. 23: No. 2: 126-139 (83)

Palmer, Debra D.

Confessions-Evidence Obtained Pursuant To An Illegal Arrest Is Inadmissible At Trial Taylor Vs Alabama. Notes. *Black Law Journal*. 08: 348-360 (Fall 83)

Palmer, John (joint author)

See Bell, Carl C.

Pamphile, Leon D.

Emigration Of Black Americans To Haiti, 1821-1863.. *Crisis*. 90: 43-44 (Nov 83)

Pan African News Agency

African News Agency Opens. Jennifer Beaumont. *Black Enterprise*. 14: 18 (Aug 83)

Pan-Africanism

Orishatukeh Faduma: A Man Of Two Worlds. Notes. Rina L. Okonkwo. *Journal of Negro History*. 68: 24-36 (Winter 83)

The Pan African Movement, 1900-1945: A Study In Leadership Conflicts Among The Disciples Of Pan Africanism. Notes. Alexandre Mboukou. *Journal of Black Studies*. 13: 275-287 (Mar 83)

Pancreas—Tumors

Traumatic Pancreatic Pseudocysts. Notes. Dapo Popoola and others. *National Medical Association Journal*. 75: 515-517 (May 83)

Pappademos, John

An Outline OF Africa's Role In The History Of Physics. Illustrated, notes, bibliography. *Journal of African Civilizations*. 05: 177-196 (Apr-Nov 83)

Parachuting

. . . Must Come Down. Illustrated. Roger Witherspoon. *Black Enterprise*. 13: 64-65 (Jul 83)

Paraplegics

Darryl Stingley: Happy To Be Alive. Illustrated. Darryl Stingley. *Ebony*. 38: 68+ (Oct 83)

Parent And Child

My Father, My Mother, Myself. Illustrated. Marita Golden. *Essence*. 14: 72-74+ (May 83)

Parenthood

"Selecting A Mate And Having Children Means Commitment And An End To Self-Indulgence". Illustrated. Brock Garland. *Essence*. 14: 27 (Dec 83)

Parenting

"This Culture Fosters The View That Men Are Supposed To Leave Children, Not Assume Responsibility For Them". Illustrated. Wesley Brown. *Essence*. 14: 22 (Jun 83)

Parents In Action On Special Education

IQ And The Courts: Larry P. Vs. Wilson Riles And PASE Vs Hann. Notes. Asa G. (III) Hillard. *Journal of Black Psychology*. 10: 1-18 (Aug 83)

Parents, Single

See Single Parents

Paris, Arthur E.

Black Pentecostalism: Southern Religion In An Urban World. Book review. Robert E. Moran. *Journal of Negro History*. 68: 122-124 (Winter 83)

Parties

See Also Entertaining

Partnership

Is The Strategy For You?. *Black Enterprise*. 13: 198 (Jun 83)

Joint Ventures: A Marriage Of Convenience. Udayan Gupta. *Black Enterprise*. 13: 191-192+ (Jun 83)

Pasteur, Alfred B.

Roots Of Soul. Book review. Charles A. Asbury. *Journal of Negro Education*. 52: 176-177 (Spring 83)

Patchen, Martin

Black-White Contact In Schools: Its Social And Academic Effects. Book review. Paul-Albert Emoungu. *Journal of Negro Education*. 52: 182-184 (Spring 83)

Patient And Physician

See Physician And Patient

Paton, Alan

Towards The Mountain: An Autobiography. Book review. Martin Rubin. *Research in African Literatures*. 14: 261-266 (Summer 83)

Patterson, Beeman C.

The Three Rs Revisited: Redistricting, Race And Representation In North Carolina. Notes, tables. *Phylon*. 44: 232-243 (Sep 83)

Patterson, Orlando

Slavery And Social Death: A Comparative Study. Book review. Howard Ross. *Phylon*. 44: 332-333 (Dec 83)

Patterson, Tiffany R. and Gilliam, Angela M.

Out Of Egypt: A Talk With Nawal El Saadawi.. *Freedomways*. 23: No. 3: 186-194 (83)

Patterson, Willis C.

Art Songs By Black American Composers. Record review. Josephine Wright. *The Black Perspective in Music*. 11: 93-95 (Spring 83)

Patton, Gerald W.

War And Race: The Black Officer In The American Military, 1915-1941. Book review. Phillip McGuire. *Journal of Negro History*. 68: 114-116 (Winter 83)

Patton, Sharon F.

Development Of Culture By Black Artisans. Notes. *Negro History Bulletin*. 46: 43-45 (Apr-Jun 83)

Paul, Saint

Paul's Reinterpretation Of Jewish Apocalypticism: A Faculty Response To J. Christian Beker. Notes. Cain H. Felder. *Journal of Religious Thought*. 40: 18-22 (Spring-Summer 83)

Paul, Saint (about)

The Challenge Of Paul's Apocalyptic Gospel For The Church Today. J. Christiaan Beker. *Journal of Religious Thought*. 40: 9-15 (Spring-Summer 83)

Paul's Apocalyptic In The Key Of Beker: A Student Response. Notes. Frank E. (Jr.) Drumwright. *Journal of Religious Thought*. 40: 16-17 (Spring-Summer 83)

Paulson, Darryl

Mainstreaming Outsiders: The Production Of Black Professionals. Book review. *Journal of Negro History*. 68: 99-101 (Winter 83)

Payne, Freda (about)

Freda Payne: Keeping Fit For Show Biz. Illustrated. *Ebony*. 39: 104-106 (Nov 83)

Payne, Kay T. (joint author)

See Taylor, Orlando L.

Payne, Les

If We Are Not For Ourselves. Illustrated. *Essence*. 13: 130 (Feb 83)

Payne, William

Race, Racism And American Law. Book review, Notes. *Black Law Journal*. 08: 361-366 (Fall 83)

Peace

Education For Peace And The Prevention Of War.. *Black Scholar*. 14: 64-66 (Nov-Dec 83)

Peace—Societies, Etc.

The U.S. Peace Movement And The Middle East. Notes. Damu Smith. *Freedomways*. 23: No. 2: 70-80 (83)

   See Also Anti-Nuclear Movement

Pearson, Edna

Ancient Civilization: Africa. Tables. *Negro History Bulletin*. 46: 97-98 (Oct-Dec 83)

Pearson, Kim

Lincoln Hawkins: A Black Engineering Pioneer. Illustrated. *Black Collegian*. 13: 48-50+ (Dec-Jan 83)

Pearson, Kim E.

Pioneering Black Bell Labs Engineer Still At Work At 71. Illustrated. *Crisis*. 90: 40-41 (Apr 83)

Pearson, Starr (joint author)

   See Reichgott, Michael J.
Reichgott, Michael J.

Peete, Calvin (about)

Golfing With Calvin Peete. Illustrated. John Putnam Ross. *Black Enterprise*. 13: 70 (Jul 83)

Pelton, Robert D.

The Trickster In West Africa: A Study Of Mythic Irony And Sacred Delight. Book review. Richard K. Priebe. *Research in African Literatures*. 14: 401-405 (Fall 83)

Pendergrass, Teddy (about)

Teddy Pendergrass Cheered At First Public Appearance Since Paralyzing Accident. Illustrated. Barbara Faggins. *Jet*. 63: 62-64 (28 Feb 83)

Penick, Benson E.

Ten Steps To Success: How To Succeed In Engineering School.. *Black Collegian*. 13: 70+ (Dec-Jan 83)

Penn, William H. (Sr.) and Johnson, Janice

A New Special Project. . . NAACP Regional Membership Coordinators. Illustrated. *Crisis*. 90: 18-19 (Apr 83)

Stand Up! Be Counted In '83! Join The NAACP!. . . The 74th NAACP Annual Convention. Illustrated. *Crisis*. 90: 6-13 (Aug-Sep 83)

Pension Trusts—Investments

The Hidden Power Of Pension Funds. Illustrated. Steve Askin. *Black Enterprise*. 13: 35-37 (Jan 83)

People United To Save Humanity (Organization)

Comedian Bill Cosby Is Honored At Annual PUSH Grande Reception. Illustrated. *Jet*. 64: 12-14 (23 May 83)

Fighting For Economic Parity. Joanne Ball. *Black Enterprise*. 14: 50 (Nov 83)

Trade And Unity Mark 12th Annual Convention Of PUSH In Atlanta, Ga. Illustrated. *Jet.* 64: 13-14 (15 Aug 83)

$500 Million Trade Agreement Signed By PUSH And Burger King. Illustrated. *Jet.* 64: 26-29 (9 May 83)

Peoples' College Of Law

Peoples' College Of Law.. *Black Law Journal.* 08: 456-458 (Winter 83)

Performing Arts And Youth

Nurturing And Refining Communications Skills. Illustrated. Madeline Sulaiman. *about. . . time.* 11: 10-12 (Apr 83)

Perfumes

The Ebony Man: Simply Scent-Sational! Illustrated. *Ebony.* 39: 115 (Dec 83)

Fragrance: The Perfect Holiday Gift. Illustrated. Alfred Fornay. *Ebony.* 39: 126-128 + (Nov 83)

Periodicals

"Border Operators": Black Orpheus And The Genesis Of Modern African Art And Literature. Notes. Peter Benson. *Research in African Literatures.* 14: 431-473 (Winter 83)

Breaking Out Of The Ghetto. Editorial. *Black Collegian.* 13: 10 (Feb-Mar 83)

The "Bulletin" In The Eighties: The Legacy And The Challenge. Illustrated. *Negro History Bulletin.* 46: 69 (Jul-Sep 83)

Origin; First Quarter Of A Century. Illustrated. *Negro History Bulletin.* 46: 74-77 (Jul-Sep 83)

A Year Of Awards, Achievements And Changes. Editorial, Illustrated. *Black Collegian.* 14: 14 + (Sep-Oct 83)

Periodicals, Juvenile

See Children's Periodicals

Periodicals, Scholarly

See Scholarly Periodicals

Perry, Dwight D. and Merritt, John C.

Congenital Ocular Toxoplasmosis. Illustrated, notes. *National Medical Association Journal.* 75: 169-174 (Feb 83)

Perry, Harmon

Howard Rollins, Irene Cara Star In Medgar Evers Story On TV. Illustrated. *Jet.* 64: 62-65 (28 Mar 83)

Lena Horne Finds Roots In Atlanta During Visit. Illustrated. *Jet.* 64: 28-30 (18 Jul 83)

Selma Amputee-Burn Victim Is Married To Hometown Policeman. Illustrated. *Jet.* 63: 22-25 (24 Jan 83)

Perry, Huey L.

The Impact Of Black Political Participation On Public Sector Employment And Representation On Municipal Boards And Commissions. Notes, tables. *Review of Black Political Economy.* 12: 203-217 (Winter 83)

Perry, Jean

Pregnancy Update.. *Essence.* 14: 34 (Aug 83)

See Gite, Lloyd

Perry, Louis (about)

An Actor Trades Pounds For Jobs! Illustrated. Ruth Dolores Manuel. *Essence.* 14: 116 (Nov 83)

Personal Finance

See Finance, Personal

Personal Growth

See Self-Actualization (Psychology)

Petersen, Kirsten Holst

A Critical View On John Pepper Clark's Selected Poems. Book review. Robert M. Wren. *Research in African Literatures.* 14: 110-112 (Spring 83)

Peterson, Manning Carlyle

The Struggle That Must Be. Book review. *Journal of Black Studies.* 14: 99-102 (Sep 83)

Petrie, Phil W.

Bankruptcy: Is It The Answer To Your Money Problems?. *Essence.* 14: 24 + (Jun 83)

Keeping Pace In The Computer Age. Illustrated. *Black Enterprise.* 13: 46-50 + (Feb 83)

New Orleans: Rich In Tradition. Illustrated. *Essence.* 14: 46 + (Dec 83)

"Where Is The Person Who Embodies My Needs?"- Men Too Ask That Question. Illustrated. *Essence.* 14: 18 (May 83)

Petroleum Industry And Trade—Connecticut —New Haven

Fueling His Way To The Top. Illustrated. Sondra Liburd-Jordan. *Black Enterprise.* 13: 169-170 + (Jun 83)

Petroleum Industry And Trade—Nigeria

The Lagos/Muskogee Connection. Illustrated. Frank (III) White. *Ebony.* 38: 69-70 + (May 83)

Petroleum Industry And Trade—Oklahoma

The Lagos/Muskogee Connection. Illustrated. Frank (III) White. *Ebony.* 38: 69-70 + (May 83)

Pets

Celebrities And Their Unusual Pets. Illustrated. *Ebony.* 39: 52 + (Nov 83)

Phencyclidine

Phencyclidine In An East Harlem Psychiatric Population. Tables, notes. Giovanni Caracci and others. *National Medical Association Journal.* 75: 869-874 (Sep 83)

Phillips, Glenn O.

Between Black And White: Race, Politics, And The Free Colored In Jamaica. Book review. *Afro-Americans in New York Life and History.* 07: 73-74 (Jul 83)

Phillips, Lloyd G. (Jr.) and others

A Nonclassifiable Anaplastic Tumor Of The Esophagus. Illustrated, notes. *National Medical Association Journal.* 75: 205-207 (Feb 83)

Phonorecords—Industry And Trade

Music Business Myths-And Truths. Illustrated. LeBaron Taylor. *Crisis*. 90: 33-35 (Nov 83)

Phonorecords—Preservation And Storage

Caring For Records And Tapes. Illustrated. Nelson George. *Essence*. 14: 54 (Jun 83)

Photographers

A Great Artist Passes. Illustrated. C. Gerald Fraser. *Black Enterprise*. 14: 22 (Aug 83)

Physical Fitness For Children

Fitness Fun And Healthful Habits For Kids. Illustrated. Angela Kinamore. *Essence*. 13: 108 + (Jan 83)

Physician And Patient

Talking To Your Doctor. Illustrated. Jane Brody. *Essence*. 14: 38 + (Jun 83)

Physicians

Dawson Receives NMA's 1982 Distinguished Service Award.. *National Medical Association Journal*. 75: 321 (Mar 83)

In Memoriam Frederic C. Bartter, MD 1914-1983. Melvin E. Jenkins. *National Medical Association Journal*. 75: 1111 (Nov 83)

Juggling Careers In Medicine And Music. Illustrated. Frank (III) White. *Ebony*. 38: 156-158 (Oct 83)

Message From The Class Of 1963. Lucius C. (III) Earles. *National Medical Association Journal*. 75: 1125-1129 (Dec 83)

A Physician Becomes An Historian. Illustrated. Leonidas H. Berry. *Negro History Bulletin*. 46: 22-23 (Jan-Mar 83)

President's Farewell Address "So Short The Season". Robert L. M. Hilliard. *National Medical Association Journal*. 75: 1049-1050 (Nov 83)

Prevention Began Early: Charles Edwin Bentley, DDS 1859-1926. Clifton O. Dummett. *National Medical Association Journal*. 75: 1235-1236 (Dec 83)

See Also Women Physicians

Physicians—Legal Status, Laws, Etc.

The Legal Status Of Physicians On Hospital Staffs. Arthur T. Davidson and Arthur H. Coleman. *National Medical Association Journal*. 75: 87-88 (Jan 83)

Physicians—Supply And Demand

Will There Be A Physician Glut OR An Exaggeration Of The Present Maldistribution Of Physicians? Another View. Illustrated. Robert L. M. Hilliard. *National Medical Association Journal*. 75: 855-859 (Sep 83)

Physics—History—Africa

An Outline OF Africa's Role In The History Of Physics. Illustrated, notes, bibliography. John Pappademos. *Journal of African Civilizations*. 05: 177-196 (Apr-Nov 83)

Pianists

Farewell To Ragtime's Apostle Of Happiness. Illustrated. Lynn Norment. *Ebony*. 38: 27-28 + (May 83)

Piazza, Thomas

The Anatomy Of Racial Attitudes. Book review. Keith A. Winsell. *Phylon*. 44: 246-248 (Sep 83)

Pickering, Kareem (about)

Young Wilma Rudolph Admirer Holds U.S. Record For 8-Year-Olds. Illustrated. *Jet*. 65: 47-48 (12 Dec 83)

Pickhardt, Irene

Coping With First-Baby Blues.. *Essence*. 13: 112 (Feb 83)

Pieces Of A Dream (Musical Group)

Pieces Of A Dream: A Young College Trio Puts It Together. Illustrated. Kalamu Ya Salaam. *Black Collegian*. 13: 122-124 (Feb-Mar 83)

Pierce, Samuel R. (Jr.) (about)

Sam Pierce Hangs Tough. Illustrated. *Black Enterprise*. 13: 43 (Mar 83)

Pinderhughes, Dianne M.

Collective Goods And Black Interest Groups. Notes , tables. *Review of Black Political Economy*. 12: 219-236 (Winter 83)

Pinkney, Jerry

Count On Your Fingers African Style. Book review. Jane Califf. *Interracial Books for Children*. 14: No. 5: 27 (83)

Pinnock, Thomas

Money Is Power In America. My Lady Was Out Earning It. I Was At Home Not Earning It. Illustrated. *Essence*. 14: 20 (Jul 83)

Pisano, Joseph C. and Epps, Anne Cherrie

The Impact Of A Medical-School-Based Summer Program On The Acceptance Of Minority Undergraduate Students Into Health Professional Schools. Tables. *National Medical Association Journal*. 75: 17-23 (Jan 83)

The Impact Of MCAT Intervention Efforts on Medical Student Acceptance Rates. Tables, notes. *National Medical Association Journal*. 75: 773-777 (Aug 83)

Pitre, Merline

Frederick Douglass And American Diplomacy In The Caribbean. Notes, bibliography. *Journal of Black Studies*. 13: 457-475 (Jun 83)

Pitts, Bill

What Effects Will Computer Technology Have On You?. *The Urban League Review*. 08: 68-76 (Winter 83)

Placksin, Sally

American Women In Jazz: 1900 To The Present. Book review. D. Antoinette Handy. *The Black Perspective in Music*. 11: 83-85 (Spring 83)

Plumpp, Sterling D.

The Mojo Hands Call/I Must Go. Book review. Doris Davenport. *Black American Literature Forum*. 17: 177-179 (Winter 83)

Poems

After Farewell. Reviewed by Sybil Dunbar. *Essence*. 14: 89 (Oct 83)

The Agony Of Cape Town. Reviewed by Winnie Williams. *Crisis*. 90: 43 (Apr 83)

All The Way Home. Reviewed by Gail Alexis. *Black American Literature Forum*. 17: 153 (Winter 83)

Alone. Reviewed by Sylvia Louise Balkum. *about. . . time*. 11: 24 (Jun 83)

And A Child Shall. . . . Reviewed by Richard V. Rice. *about. . . time*. 11: 43 (Nov 83)

The Anesthesia Is Taking Effect. Reviewed by Toi Derricotte. *Black American Literature Forum*. 17: 155 (Winter 83)

Another Ecclesiastical Morning. Reviewed by James C. Kilgore. *Black American Literature Forum*. 17: 172 (Winter 83)

April. Reviewed by Nancy Morejon. *Black Scholar*. 14: 51 (Summer 83)

Athlete. Reviewed by Gail Alexis. *Black American Literature Forum*. 17: 153 (Winter 83)

An Autumn Memoir: Of Adam And Sunday Strolls In Mid-Century Harlem. Reviewed by Winnie Williams. *Crisis*. 90: 34-36 (Feb 83)

Be Kind To Me. Reviewed by Dudley Randall. *Black American Literature Forum*. 17: 168 (Winter 83)

Beau Monde. Reviewed by Toi Derricotte. *Black American Literature Forum*. 17: 155 (Winter 83)

Beauty That Is Never Old. Reviewed by James Weldon (1871-1938) Johnson. *Ebony*. 38: 48 (Feb 83)

Behind A Black Face. Reviewed by Richard V. Rice. *about. . . time*. 11: 27 (Oct 83)

Benny's Place. Reviewed by Richard V. Rice. *about. . . time*. 11: 27 (Oct 83)

The Black Messiah. Reviewed by Mbembe Milton Smith. *Black American Literature Forum*. 17: 151 (Winter 83)

Black Woman. Reviewed by Nancy Morejon. *Black Scholar*. 14: 50-51 (Summer 83)

Black Woman. Reviewed by Charles (Sr.) Jackson. *about. . . time*. 11: 24 (May 83)

Black Woman. Reviewed by Catherine Felix. *Black American Literature Forum*. 17: 170-171 (Winter 83)

The Broken Church Window. Reviewed by Mbembe Milton Smith. *Black American Literature Forum*. 17: 151 (Winter 83)

A Brown Girl Dead. Reviewed by Countee (1903-1946) Cullen. *Ebony*. 38: 154 (Oct 83)

But I Say. Reviewed by Jill Witherspoon Boyer. *Essence*. 14: 140 (Dec 83)

The Centrifugal Force Of Orez. Reviewed by Stephen Todd Booker. *Black American Literature Forum*. 17: 171 (Winter 83)

Claudie Mae. Reviewed by Paulette Childress White. *Essence*. 14: 125 (Jul 83)

Cloistered In High School. Reviewed by Thadious Davis. *Black American Literature Forum*. 17: 148 (Winter 83)

Communication. Reviewed by Nikki Giovanni. *Ebony*. 38: 48 (Feb 83)

Contradiction. Reviewed by Richard V. Rice. *about. . . time*. 11: 27 (Oct 83)

DeLiza Spend The Day In The City. Reviewed by June Jordan. *Freedomways*. 23: No. 4: 234-235 (83)

Dream. Reviewed by Milton L. Cofield. *about. . . time*. 11: 22 (Sep 83)

The Duty Of Love. Reviewed by Richard V. Rice. *about. . . time*. 11: 23 (Sep 83)

El Hajj Malik El-Shabazz. Reviewed by Wanda Coleman. *Black American Literature Forum*. 17: 175 (Winter 83)

Ethiopian In The Fuel Supplies. Reviewed by Wanda Coleman. *Black American Literature Forum*. 17: 176 (Winter 83)

The Eyes Of The Ancestors. Reviewed by Mbembe Milton Smith. *Black American Literature Forum*. 17: 150 (Winter 83)

Fathers. Reviewed by Jerry W. (Jr.) Ward. *Freedomways*. 23: No. 4: 256-257 (83)

For A Lady I Know. Reviewed by Countee (1903-1946) Cullen. *Ebony*. 38: 154 (Oct 83)

For Kim. Reviewed by Dudley Randall. *Black American Literature Forum*. 17: 169 (Winter 83)

For Lincoln Perry. Reviewed by William M. Clements. *Black American Literature Forum*. 17: 174 (Winter 83)

For Robeson (From New Orleans). Reviewed by Tom Dent. *Freedomways*. 23: No. 4: 243 (83)

For Robin H, Upon Seven Years Of Motherhood, At Age 21. Reviewed by Gail Alexis. *Black American Literature Forum*. 17: 152 (Winter 83)

For Some Black Men. Reviewed by Carolyn M. Rodgers. *Essence*. 14: 20 (Sep 83)

For Vivian. Reviewed by Dudley Randall. *Black American Literature Forum*. 17: 170 (Winter 83)

From The Dark Tower. Reviewed by Countee (1903-1946) Cullen. *Ebony*. 38: 154 (Oct 83)

Frost Came Too Early This Year. Reviewed by Alice Jones-Miller. *Essence*. 13: 22 (Mar 83)

GIGO (Garbage In, Garbage Out). Reviewed by Mbembe Milton Smith. *Black American Literature Forum*. 17: 150 (Winter 83)

The Girls In Booths. Reviewed by Dudley Randall. *Black American Literature Forum*. 17: 170 (Winter 83)

Grace. Reviewed by June Jordan. *Essence*. 14: 124 (Aug 83)

Greensboro: North Carolina: Reviewed by June Jordan. *Freedomways*. 23: No. 4: 235 (83)

He Looked At Me. Reviewed by Sylvia Louise Balkum. *about. . . time*. 11: 24 (Jun 83)

Heritage (For Harold Jackman). Reviewed by Countee (1903-1946) Cullen. *Ebony*. 38: 154 (Oct 83)

The Highest Bidder. Reviewed by Richard V. Rice. *about. . . time*. 11: 43 (Nov 83)

The House Is The Enemy. Reviewed by Toi Derricotte. *Black American Literature Forum*. 17: 155 (Winter 83)

I Am. Reviewed by Sylvia Louise Balkum. *about. . . time*. 11: 24 (Jun 83)

I Am. Reviewed by Trena T. Marsh-Joiner. *Essence*. 14: 142 (Nov 83)

I Hear You. Reviewed by Richard V. Rice. *about. . . time*. 11: 23 (Sep 83)

I Know A Lady (For My Aunt Corine Coffey). Reviewed by Joyce Carol Thomas. *Essence*. 14: 131 (Jul 83)

I Like Me. Reviewed by Sylvia Louise Balkum. *about. . . time*. 11: 24 (Jun 83)

I Smile Just A Little. Reviewed by J. E. M. Jones. *about. . . time*. 11: 22 (Sep 83)

I've Reached For You. Reviewed by Richard V. Rice. *about. . . time*. 11: 23 (Sep 83)

I Wrote A Good Omelet. Reviewed by Nikki Giovanni. *Essence*. 14: 88 (Oct 83)

Identity Card. Reviewed by Mahmoud Darwish. *Freedomways*. 23: No. 2: 112-113 (83)

Incident (For Eric Walrond). Reviewed by Countee (1903-1946) Cullen. *Ebony*. 38: 155 (Oct 83)

Jealousy. Reviewed by Richard V. Rice. *about. . . time*. 11: 23 (Sep 83)

Like The Drunk. Reviewed by James C. Kilgore. *Black American Literature Forum*. 17: 173 (Winter 83)

Limited Vision. Reviewed by Richard V. Rice. *about. . . time*. 11: 23 (Sep 83)

Listen Children. Reviewed by Lucille Clifton. *Essence*. 14: 88 (Oct 83)

Loss/Angel-Less/Blue. Reviewed by Houston A. (Jr.) Baker. *Black American Literature Forum*. 17: 174 (Winter 83)

Love. Reviewed by Carolyn M. Rodgers. *Ebony*. 38: 48 (Feb 83)

Love After Love. Reviewed by Derek Walcott. *Essence*. 14: 137 (Aug 83)

Love (For Diane). Reviewed by Harold McDougall. *Essence*. 14: 108 (Nov 83)

Love Poem. Reviewed by Imogunla Alakoye. *Essence*. 13: 16 (Feb 83)

Love Rising. Reviewed by Geraldine L. Wilson. *Essence*. 14: 88 (Oct 83)

Loyalty. Reviewed by Richard V. Rice. *about. . . time*. 11: 23 (Sep 83)

Mama Sitting. Reviewed by Brenda Marie Osbey. *Essence*. 14: 137 (Aug 83)

Maya-2. Reviewed by Norman Jordan. *Essence*. 14: 20 (Sep 83)

Meditation 83/US. Reviewed by Jerry W (Jr.) Ward. *Freedomways*. 23: No. 4: 257 (83)

Miracles Of Ministry. Reviewed by Mildred Elizabeth Nero Drinkard. *Journal of Religious Thought*. 40: 72 (Spring-Summer 83)

Moments. Hamilton Bobb. *Essence*. 13: 16 (Apr 83)

A Mother's Day Message. Reviewed by Gary Badi. *about. . . time*. 11: 24 (May 83)

Motown Polka. Reviewed by Dudley Randall. *Black American Literature Forum*. 17: 168 (Winter 83)

My Best Friend. Reviewed by Sylvia Louise Balkum. *about. . . time*. 11: 24 (Jun 83)

My Side. Reviewed by Sylvia Louise Balkum. *about. . . time*. 11: 24 (Jun 83)

Mythologies. Reviewed by Nancy Morejon. *Black Scholar*. 14: 53 (Summer 83)

New Face. Reviewed by Alice Walker. *Essence*. 14: 122 (Nov 83)

New World Griot. Reviewed by Thadious Davis. *Black American Literature Forum*. 17: 149 (Winter 83)

The Night She Dreamed She Was Mad. Reviewed by Toi Derricotte. *Black American Literature Forum*. 17: 155 (Winter 83)

Nobody Says Baby. Reviewed by B. Wiggins Wells. *Essence*. 14: 140 (Nov 83)

Not Without Love. Reviewed by Jon C. Randall. *Essence*. 14: 17 (Dec 83)

An Oakland Apple Tree. Reviewed by Nancy Morejon. *Black Scholar*. 14: 52 (Summer 83)

Old Detroit. Reviewed by Dudley Randall. *Black American Literature Forum*. 17: 168 (Winter 83)

Once A Man Twice A Child. Reviewed by Barbara A. Childs. *about. . . time*. 11: 22 (Sep 83)

Page 3. Reviewed by James C. Kilgore. *Black American Literature Forum*. 17: 173 (Winter 83)

Pennsiveness. Reviewed by Gary Badi. *about. . . time*. 11: 17 (Mar 83)

The Phone Call. Reviewed by Sylvia Louise Balkum. *about. . . time*. 11: 24 (Jun 83)

A Picture Of Bird. Reviewed by Herm Beavers. *Black American Literature Forum*. 17: 154 (Winter 83)

The Question. Reviewed by Richard V. Rice. *about. . . time*. 11: 23 (Sep 83)

A Question For Our Time. Reviewed by Richard V. Rice. *about. . . time*. 11: 43 (Nov 83)

Rallies (For Michael). Reviewed by Reggie Henson. *Black American Literature Forum*. 17: 175 (Winter 83)

Reprobate. Reviewed by Elma Stuckey. *Black American Literature Forum*. 17: 171 (Winter 83)

Reunion. Reviewed by Thadious Davis. *Black American Literature Forum.* 17: 149 (Winter 83)

Rush Hour. Reviewed by Thylias Moss. *Essence.* 14: 134 (Dec 83)

The Sculpture At Night. Reviewed by Toi Derricotte. *Black American Literature Forum.* 17: 155 (Winter 83)

The Seventh Sense. Reviewed by Audre Lorde. *Essence.* 14: 17 (Dec 83)

Silly Jim. Reviewed by Dudley Randall. *Black American Literature Forum.* 17: 169 (Winter 83)

Simon The Cyrenian Speaks. Reviewed by Countee (1903-1946) Cullen. *Ebony.* 38: 155 (Oct 83)

Sin Of Omission. Reviewed by Richard V. Rice. *about. . . time.* 11: 43 (Nov 83)

Some Days. Reviewed by Sylvia Louise Balkum. *about. . . time.* 11: 24 (Jun 83)

The Song. Reviewed by June Gatlin. *Essence.* 13: 17 (Jan 83)

Straight Talk From Plain Women. Reviewed by Sherley Anne Williams. *Essence.* 14: 89 (Oct 83)

A Subliminal Trait. Reviewed by Richard V. Rice. *about. . . time.* 11: 43 (Nov 83)

Talking Horse. Reviewed by Gail Alexis. *Black American Literature Forum.* 17: 152 (Winter 83)

Telephone Conversations. Reviewed by Gwendolyn Brooks. *Black American Literature Forum.* 17: 148 (Winter 83)

Ten Years (1983). Reviewed by Andrew Salkey. *Black Scholar.* 14: 46-47 (Sep-Oct 83)

That Undying Spirit. Reviewed by Gary Badi. *about. . . time.* 11: 17 (Mar 83)

Time Is More Than Money. Reviewed by James C. Kilgore. *Black American Literature Forum.* 17: 173 (Winter 83)

To A Man. Reviewed by Maya Angelou. *Ebony.* 38: 50 (Feb 83)

To Mareta. Reviewed by Herschel Johnson. *Ebony.* 38: 50 (Feb 83)

To Poets Who Preach In Prose. Reviewed by Dudley Randall. *Black American Literature Forum.* 17: 169 (Winter 83)

To Women. Reviewed by Richard V. Rice. *about. . . time.* 11: 23 (Sep 83)

The Touching Of Hands. Reviewed by Richard V. Rice. *about. . . time.* 11: 23 (Sep 83)

The Tryouts. Reviewed by Sylvia Louise Balkum. *about. . . time.* 11: 24 (Jun 83)

Untitled. Reviewed by Herm Beavers. *Black American Literature Forum.* 17: 154 (Winter 83)

Untitled. Reviewed by Ruth Dolores Manuel. *Essence.* 13: 16 (Apr 83)

Untitled. Reviewed by C. Tillery Banks. *Essence.* 14: 88 (Oct 83)

The Warrior. Reviewed by Guy Johnson. *Essence.* 14: 122 (Aug 83)

Weaponed Woman. Reviewed by Gwendolyn Brooks. *Essence.* 14: 147 (Oct 83)

Well, After All What Is There To Say? Reviewed by Sandra Jackson-Opoku. *Essence.* 14: 89 (Oct 83)

A Wellness Has Spoken. Reviewed by Mariah Britton. *Essence.* 14: 89 (Oct 83)

What Has The NAACP Done For Me? Reviewed by Jonathan Mark McCoy. *Crisis.* 90: 46 (May 83)

What I'm Talking About. Reviewed by Mbembe Milton Smith. *Black American Literature Forum.* 17: 151 (Winter 83)

Where We Belong, A Duet. Reviewed by Maya Angelou. *Ebony.* 38: 46 (Feb 83)

Why. Reviewed by Richard V. Rice. *about. . . time.* 11: 23 (Sep 83)

Woman Of Ghana. Reviewed by Dudley Randall. *Black American Literature Forum.* 17: 169 (Winter 83)

Yet Do I Marvel. Reviewed by Countee (1903-1946) Cullen. *Ebony.* 38: 152 (Oct 83)

Young Being. Reviewed by Reggie Henson. *Black American Literature Forum.* 17: 175 (Winter 83)

Yourself Fulfilling History. Reviewed by Mbembe Milton Smith. *Black American Literature Forum.* 17: 151 (Winter 83)

Youth Sings A Song Of Rosebuds (To Roberta). Reviewed by Countee (1903-1946) Cullen. *Ebony.* 38: 155 (Oct 83)

Poetry

A Black Poet's Vision: An Interview With Lance Jeffers. Interview. Lance Jeffers and Doris L. Laryea. *CLA Journal.* 26: 422-433 (Jun 83)

Poetic Encounters: An Interview With Jean F. Brierre. Notes. Jean Brierre and Herman F. Bostick. *CLA Journal.* 26: 277-287 (Mar 83)

See Also Bards and Bardism
Epic Poetry
Nigerian Poetry

Poetry—History And Criticism

Dudley Randall: A Humanist View. Illustrated, notes. D. H. Melhem. *Black American Literature Forum.* 17: 157-167 (Winter 83)

Jean Toomer: A Cubist Poet. Illustrated, notes. Ann Marie Bush and Louis D. Mitchell. *Black American Literature Forum.* 17: 106-108 (Fall 83)

Point And Counterpoint In Harlem Gallery. Notes. Patricia R. Schroeder. *CLA Journal.* 27: 152-168 (Dec 83)

Poetry—Themes, Motives

New Light On Tennyson's Blackness. Notes. Robert F. Fleissner. *CLA Journal.* 26: 334-340 (Mar 83)

Poets

A Black Poet's Vision: An Interview With Lance Jeffers. Interview. Lance Jeffers and Doris L. Laryea. *CLA Journal.* 26: 422-433 (Jun 83)

Paul Laurence Dunbar: Master Player In A Fixed Game. Notes. Ralph Story. *CLA Journal*. 27: 30-55 (Sep 83)

Poets, South African

Dennis Brutus Fights Deportation. Illustrated. *Black Scholar*. 14: 72 (Mar-Apr 83)

Police

See Also Arrest (Police Methods)

Police Chiefs

Chicago Mayor Names City's First Black Police Supt. First facts, illustrated. *Jet*. 65: 8 (12 Sep 83)

Police Chiefs—Florida—Opa-Locka

Man Of God And Gun. Illustrated. Raymond Lang. *Ebony*. 38: 102-104 (Sep 83)

Police Chiefs—Missouri—Columbia

Columbia, Mo., Gets First Black Police Chief. Illustrated, first facts. *Jet*. 63: 57 (10 Jan 83)

Police Chiefs—New York (State)—New York (City)

Veteran New York Cop Is Named City's First Black Commissioner Of Police. First facts, illustrated. *Jet*. 65: 12 (28 Nov 83)

Police Chiefs—Texas—Houston

Report From Houston. . . Community Involvement Is Key To Future Success. Illustrated. Lee P. Brown. *Crisis*. 90: 38-39 (Feb 83)

Police—Complaints Against

Arthur McDuffee's Ghost Still Haunts. . . Racial Injustice In Miami. Illustrated. Kevin Moss. *Crisis*. 90: 48-49 (Jan 83)

Many U.S. Cities Need A Visit From Conyers Committee. Illustrated. Chester A. (Sr.) Higgins. *Crisis*. 90: 23-24 (Nov 83)

"The People Have Spoken". Charles E. Cobb. *Crisis*. 90: 28 (Nov 83)

"Who Can We Turn To For Justice?" Illustrated. Don Armstrong. *Crisis*. 90: 20-21 (Nov 83)

Police—Complaints Against—New Orleans

New Orleans Cops On Trial. Illustrated. Keith M. Woods. *Black Enterprise*. 13: 23 (Mar 83)

Policewomen

Essence Women: Dorothy Cousins. Illustrated. Margo Walker Williams. *Essence*. 13: 25 (Feb 83)

Political Parties

Black Political Insurgency In Louisville, Kentucky: The Lincoln Independent Party Of 1921. Notes. George C. Wright. *Journal of Negro History*. 68: 8-23 (Winter 83)

Political Parties—Great Britain

Race And Political Parties In Britain, 1954-1965. Notes. Fred R. Van Hartesveldt. *Phylon*. 44: 126-134 (Jun 83)

Political Science

See Also Conservatism
Power (Social Sciences)

Politicians

See Also Women In Politics

Politics And Christianity

See Christianity And Politics

Politics And Labor Unions

See Trade-Unions—Political Activity

Politics, Practical

Beyond The Ballot Box. Illustrated. Bebe Moore Campbell and Elliott D. Lee. *Black Enterprise*. 13: 40-42 + (Mar 83)

A Black Presidential Candidacy? Bayard Rustin. *about. . . time*. 11: 19 (Jun 83)

The Black Vote: The New Power In Politics. Illustrated. Harold Washington. *Ebony*. 39: 108-110 (Nov 83)

Blacks Exhibit Clout At The Ballot Box. Illustrated. Earl G. Graves. *Black Enterprise*. 13: 11 (Feb 83)

The Business Of Getting Elected. Illustrated. S. Lee Hilliard. *Black Enterprise*. 14: 57-58 + (Nov 83)

A Candidate Of Our Own. Michael Thelwell. *Essence*. 14: 144 (Nov 83)

A Coalition With Clout. Barbara A. Reynolds. *Essence*. 14: 56 (Jul 83)

The Coming Of Age Of Black Political Power. Tables. Joseph E. Madison. *Crisis*. 90: 30 (Aug-Sep 83)

Jesse Jackson's Push For Power. Illustrated. Frank Dexter Brown. *Black Enterprise*. 14: 44-46 + (Nov 83)

Understanding The Political Process. James M. Blount. *about. . . time*. 11: 4 (Oct 83)

What's Next? Illustrated. Julian Bond. *Negro History Bulletin*. 46: 72-73 + (Jul-Sep 83)

Pollard, William E.

A Letter To The Justice Department.. *Crisis*. 90: 41 (Oct 83)

Polski, Harry A.

The Negro Almanac: A Reference Work On The Afro-American. Book review. Earle H. West. *Journal of Negro Education*. 52: 455-457 (Fall 83)

Poma, Pedro A.

Hispanic Cultural Influences On Medical Practice. Notes. *National Medical Association Journal*. 75: 941-946 (Oct 83)

Poole, Isaiah

The Disappearing Civil Servant. Illustrated. *Black Enterprise*. 13: 91-92 + (Feb 83)

Poole, Isaiah J.

Are The Promises Being Kept? Illustrated. *Black Enterprise*. 14: 117-118 + (Oct 83)

Poor

Freedom From Want. William Clay. *about. . . time*. 11: 8 (Jul 83)

Hunger In Detroit. Illustrated. Lloyd Gite. *Black Enterprise*. 13: 19 (Apr 83)

Ministers As Apocalyptic Advocates For The Poor. Jesse L. Jackson. *Journal of Religious Thought*. 40: 23-28 (Spring-Summer 83)

Task Force Probes Hunger.. *Black Enterprise*. 14: 22 (Nov 83)

White N.Y. Suburbanite Lives With Poor Family To Study The 'Other Side'. Illustrated. D. Michael Cheers. *Jet*. 63: 30-33 (31 Jan 83)

See Also Unemployed

Poor—Medical Care—United States

Children And Federal Health Care Cuts. Sara Rosenbaum and Judith Weitz. *Freedomways*. 23: No. 01: 17-22 (83)

Popoola, Dapo and others

Traumatic Pancreatic Pseudocysts. Notes. *National Medical Association Journal*. 75: 515-517 (May 83)

Population—Statistics

America's Black Population: 1970 To 1982 - A Statistical View. Tables. William C. (Jr.) Mathey and Dwight L. Johnson. *Crisis*. 90: 10-18 (Dec 83)

Porter, David D. and Porter, Rosalyn Gist

The Changing Profile Of Charlotte. Illustrated. *Black Enterprise*. 13: 178-180+ (Jun 83)

Porter, Lewis

Jazzforschung/Jazz Research. Book review. *The Black Perspective in Music*. 11: 85-86 (Spring 83)

Teddy Wilson. Time-Life Giants Of Jazz STL-j20. Record review. *The Black Perspective in Music*. 11: 95-96 (Spring 83)

Porter, Rosalyn Gist (joint author)

See Porter, David D.

Posivitism

See Also Legal Posivitism

Post, Robert M.

Journey Toward Light: Athol Fugard's Tsotsi . Notes. *CLA Journal*. 26: 415-421 (Jun 83)

Postage Stamps—Topics—Henson, Josiah

New Canadian Stamp. Illustrated. *Jet*. 65: 20 (3 Oct 83)

Postal Service—Employees

Perils Of Black Postal Workers In A Technological Age: Some Strategies For Survival. Tables, notes. Lenneal J. Henderson and Charles Murphy. *The Urban League Review*. 07: 33-43 (Summer 83)

Postal Service—Postmasters

Essense Women: Mary Brown. Illustrated. Margo Walker Williams. *Essence*. 13: 24 (Apr 83)

Postmasters

See Postal Service—Postmasters

Potatoes

See Also Cookery (Potatoes)

Potholm, Christian P.

Integration And Disintegration In East Africa. Book review. Frank M. Chiteji. *Review of Black Political Economy*. 12: 243-245 (Winter 83)

Poussaint, Alvin F.

The Black Male-White Female: An Update. Illustrated. *Ebony*. 38: 124+ (Aug 83)

Poverty

See Also Poor

Power, Jane

The Longest War: Israel In Lebanon. Book review. *Freedomways*. 23: No. 3: 202-205 (83)

Yol. Record review. *Freedomways*. 23: No. 3: 195-198 (83)

Power (Social Sciences)

Money Power! Editorial. Susan L. Taylor. *Essence*. 14: 71 (Jun 83)

Practice Of Medicine

See Medicine—Practice

Prakash, T. V.

Critical Perspectives On Wole Soyinka. Book review. *Research in African Literatures*. 14: 102-107 (Spring 83)

Prather, H. Leon (Sr.)

From The Old South To The New: Essays On The Transitional South. Book review. *Journal of Negro History*. 68: 120-122 (Winter 83)

Preer, Jean L.

Lawyers V. Educators: Black Colleges And Desegregation In Public Higher Education. Book review. Yvette Chancellor. *Black Law Journal*. 08: 160-161 (Spring 83)

Pregnancy

Expecting? Illustrated. *Essence*. 14: 72 (Oct 83)

Isoenzymes Of Lactate Dehydrogenase In Amnionic Fluid In Early Pregnancy. Tables, notes. Joseph M. Miller and others. *National Medical Association Journal*. 75: 687-689 (Jul 83)

Sex During Pregnancy: Common Questions And Practical Answers. Notes. Malikha V. Rogers. *National Medical Association Journal*. 75: 1087-1088+ (Nov 83)

Pregnancy, Complications Of

Pregnancy Update. Jean Perry. *Essence*. 14: 34 (Aug 83)

Ritodrine Use In Placenta Previa. Notes. William K. Flowers. *National Medical Association Journal*. 75: 427-428 (Apr 83)

Prejudice In Textbooks

See Text-Book Bias

Prejudices And Antipathies

Homophobia: Why Bring It Up? Barbara Smith. *Interracial Books for Children*. 14: No. 3: 7-8 (83)

See Also Ethocentrism

Presbyterian Church In The U.S.A.

Woman At The Helm Of Philadelphia Presbytery. Illustrated. Marilyn Marshall. *Ebony*. 38: 51-52 + (Jul 83)

Presenile Dementia

A Letter To Mama. Illustrated. Peggy Taylor. *Essence*. 14: 38 + (Dec 83)

Presidents, College

See College Presidents

Presidents—United States—Election

Democratic Presidential Hopefuls. Bebe Moore Campbell. *Black Enterprise*. 14: 35 (Oct 83)

Excerpts From. . . What Presidential Candidates Told NAACP Convention Delegates. Walter F. Mondale and others. *Crisis*. 90: 32-35 (Aug-Sep 83)

Results Of Ebony Reader Poll: Should A Black Run For President? Lynn Norment. *Ebony*. 38: 76 + (Oct 83)

What's Next? Illustrated. Julian Bond. *Negro History Bulletin*. 46: 72-73 + (Jul-Sep 83)

Price, Barbara

Charting Your Course In Oceanography. Illustrated. *Black Collegian*. 14: 124-125 (Sep-Oct 83)

Price, Leontyne (about)

Leontyne Price-Still The Diva. Illustrated. *Crisis*. 90: 32-33 (Jun-Jul 83)

Price, Paul W.

Who's Supporting The Kids? Why Men Leave Their Children: One Man's Story.. *Essence*. 14: 74 + (Jul 83)

Priebe, Richard K.

The Trickster In West Africa: A Study Of Mythic Irony And Sacred Delight. Book review. *Research in African Literatures*. 14: 401-405 (Fall 83)

Principals, School

See School Superintendents And Principals

Prisoners

Battling Illiteracy Among Prisoners. Latique Adrian Jamel. *Crisis*. 90: 40-41 + (Nov 83)

School Of Religion For Men Behind Bars. Illustrated. Frank (III) White. *Ebony*. 38: 154 + (Apr 83)

Two Innocents Who Suffered On Death Row. Illustrated. Raymond Lang. *Ebony*. 38: 29-30 + (Sep 83)

See Also Ex-convicts

Prisoners' Families

Why Women Marry Men In Prison. Illustrated. *Ebony*. 38: 150 + (Jun 83)

Prisoners—Legal Status, Laws, Etc.

Access To The Courts: Prisoners' Right To A Law Library. Notes. Wayne Ryan. *Howard Law Journal*. 26: No. 1: 91-117 (83)

State Prisoners' Rights To Medical Treatment: Merely Elusive Or Wholly Illusory? Notes. Damon Martin. *Black Law Journal*. 08: 427-455 (Winter 83)

Prisoners Of War—Israel

Inside The Camps.. *Freedomways*. 23: No. 2: 140-144 (83)

Palestinian Prisoners: Are They Prisoners Of War? Notes. Gay J. McDougall. *Freedomways*. 23: No. 2: 126-139 (83)

Prisons—Law And Legislation

Challenging Cruel And Unusual Conditions Of Prison Confinement: Refining The Totality Of Conditions Approach. Notes. Deborah A. Montick. *Howard Law Journal*. 26: No. 1: 227-266 (83)

Private Schools—Michigan—Detroit

Essence Women: Carmen N'Namdi. Illustrated. Bethany L. Spotts. *Essence*. 13: 22 + (Feb 83)

Prize Contests In Advertising

Contests And Sweepstakes: Can you Ever Win? Illustrated. *Essence*. 14: 118 + (Jun 83)

Procainamide

Low-Dose Procainamide: Low Risk Of Complications With Long-Term Use. Tables, notes. Cao Van Pham and others. *National Medical Association Journal*. 75: 705-708 (Jul 83)

Proctor, Samuel D.

How To Believe If The Worst Should Come.. *Journal of Religious Thought*. 40: 34-44 (Spring-Summer 83)

Producers, Television

See Television Producers And Directors

Producers, Theatrical

See Theatrical Producers And Directors

Professions

See Also Occupations

Progeria

Aging Disease Makes 6-Year-Old Boy Look Like 60. Illustrated. Trudy S. Moore and James Mitchell. *Jet*. 65: 22-26 (5 Dec 83)

Programs, Television

See Television Programs

Prophecies

Psychic June Gatlin Looks 1984. Patrice Miles. *Essence*. 14: 79 + (Dec 83)

Protests, Demonstrations, Etc.

A Call To The Nation For A New Coalition Of Conscience For Jobs, Peace And Freedom.. *Freedomways*. 23: No. 01: 6-9 (83)

"Coalition Of Conscience". Illustrated. William Clay. *about. . . time*. 11: 23 (Oct 83)

Jobs, Peace, Freedom: A Political Assessment Of The August 27 March On Washington. Notes. Marable Manning. *Black Scholar*. 14: 2-20 (Nov-Dec 83)

March On Washington '83. Illustrated. Lloyd Dennis. *Black Collegian*. 14: 35-37 (Nov-Dec 83)

Minister Louis Farrakhan's Stirring Address. Illustrated. Louis Farrakhan. *Black Collegian*. 14: 36-37 (Nov-Dec 83)

The Overground Railroad. Illustrated. Chauncey Bailey. *Crisis*. 90: 6-9+ (Nov 83)

A Tale Of Two Marches. Illustrated. Bebe Moore Campbell. *Black Enterprise*. 14: 27 (Aug 83)

Twentieth Anniversary Mobilization Jobs, Peace, And Freedom. Illustrated. Benjamin L. Hooks. *Crisis*. 90: 22-23 (Oct 83)

We Still Have A Dream. Illustrated. Lerone (Jr.) Bennett. *Ebony*. 39: 152-153+ (Nov 83)

1963-A Rochester Perspective. Illustrated. W. Cooper and others. *about. . . time*. 11: 21-23 (Oct 83)

1983 March Reflections. Illustrated. Talik Aboul Basheer. *about. . . time*. 11: 20-21 (Oct 83)

Pryor, Aaron (about)

Aaron Pryor: His Own Boss Inside And Outside The Ring. Illustrated. Walter Leavy. *Ebony*. 38: 35-36+ (May 83)

Pryor, Richard (about)

Comic Richard Pryor Puts All Jokes Aside To Give King Tribute. Illustrated. *Jet*. 63: 7-9 (31 Jan 83)

Pryor Forms Production Co. Signs $40Mil. Film Pact With Columbia Pictures. Illustrated. *Jet*. 64: 54-55 (6 Jun 83)

Richard, Pryor, Jackie Gleason Team For Laughs And Lesson In 'The Toy'. Illustrated. Trudy S. Moore. *Jet*. 63: 60-62 (10 Jan 83)

Richard Pryor's Movie Company Releases First Film, 'Here And Now'. Illustrated. *Jet*. 65: 56-58 (28 Nov 83)

Richard Pryor: 'Superman III' And Hollywood's New $40 Million Man. Illustrated. *Jet*. 64: 60-63 (11 Jul 83)

Psychiatric Hospitals—Emergency Services

Survey Of The Demographic Characteristics Of Patients Requiring Restraints In A Psychiatric Emergency Service. Tables, notes. Carl C. Bell and John Palmer. *National Medical Association Journal*. 75: 981-987 (Oct 83)

Psychiatric Research

An Empirical And Theoretical Review Of Articles In The Journal Of Black Psychology: 1974-1980. Tables, notes. Robert E. Steele and Sherry E. Davis. *Journal of Black Psychology*. 10: 29-42 (Aug 83)

Psychological Stress

See Stress (Psychology)

Psychology

See Also Adolescent Psychology

Psychosomatic Medicine

See Medicine, Psychosomatic

Psychotherapy

A Theoretical Model For The Practice Of Psychotherapy With Black Populations. Tables, notes. Anna Mitchell Jackson. *Journal of Black Psychology*. 10: 19-27 (Aug 83)

Public Contracts—Ohio

Ohio Law Challenged. Britt Robson. *Black Enterprise*. 13: 20+ (May 83)

Public Contracts—United States

Five Cents Gas Tax Promises Business Opportunities For Blacks. Illustrated. Bebe Moore Campbell. *Black Enterprise*. 13: 21 (Jul 83)

Maxima's 8a Dilemma. Illustrated. Harold J. Logan. *Black Enterprise*. 13: 42-45 (Jan 83)

Public Defenders—Massachusetts—Roxbury

"Call My Lawyer": Styling A Community Based Defender Program. Notes. Harold R. Washington and Geraldine S. Hines. *Black Law Journal*. 08: 186-197 (Fall 83)

Public Health—United States

Is The United States Entering A Period Of Retrogression In Public Health? Editorial, Tables, notes. Richard Cooper. *National Medical Association Journal*. 75: 741-744 (Aug 83)

Public Policy

See Social Policy

Public Schools

NAACP Preliminary Report On Public School Education.. *Crisis*. 90: 28-29 (Aug-Sep 83)

Public Schools—Finance—Virginia

Public School Bonds And Virginia's Massive Resistance. Notes, tables. James H. (Jr.) Hershman. *Journal of Negro Education*. 52: 398-409 (Fall 83)

Public Schools—New York (State)—Brooklyn —History

Did Brooklyn (N.Y.) Blacks Have Unusual Control Over Their Schools? Period I: 1815-1845. Notes. Robert J. Swan. *Afro-Americans in New York Life and History*. 07: 25-46 (Jul 83)

Public Speaking

Giving That Winning Presentation. Illustrated. Lloyd Gite. *Black Enterprise*. 14: 49-50+ (Sep 83)

Speak Easy: Making Presentations Without Falling Apart. Constance Garcia-Barrio. *Essence*. 13: 34+ (Apr 83)

Publishers And Publishing

Give The Man A Hand. Illustrated. Elaine C. Ray. *Essence*. 14: 50 (Aug 83)

Puerto Ricans In Children's Literature

A Decade Of Progress? Byron Williams. *Interracial Books for Children*. 14: No. 1: 4-5 (83)

Puerto Rico

See Also Education—Puerto Rico—History
   Racism—Puerto Rico
   Women—Puerto Rico

Puerto Rico—Description And Travel

Puerto Rico's Cerromar Beach. Illustrated. Felipe Luciano. *Black Enterprise*. 13: 67 (May 83)

Pulitzer Prizes

Author Alice Walker Wins Pulitzer Prize For Novel. First facts, Illustrated. *Jet*. 64: 9 (9 May 83)

Punishment

Constitutional Law- A 40-Year Sentence of Imprisonment Within The Limits Of A Statute Does Not Amount To Cruel And Unusual Punishment. Notes. Anita Eve. *Howard Law Journal*. 26: No. 1: 305-325 (83)

Push For Excellence, Inc.

Black College Leaders Tackle Issues At First PUSH/EXCEL Conference. Illustrated, first facts. *Jet*. 63: 40-41 (24 Jan 83)

Pyramids—Egypt

The Pyramids: Ancient Showcase Of African Science And Technology. Illustrated, notes, tables. Beatrice Lumpkin. *Journal of African Civilizations*. 05: 67-83 (Apr-Nov 83)

Quarterman, Lloyd and Van Sertima, Ivan

Dr. Lloyd Quarterman-Nuclear Scientist. Interview. *Journal of African Civilizations*. 05: 266-274 (Apr-Nov 83)

Quintuplets

Quints Are 'Gift From God' Proud 'Pop' Gaither Says. Illustrated. *Jet*. 64: 14-15 (28 Aug 83)

Quintuplets Born To Black Indiana Couple.. *Jet*. 64: 7 (22 Aug 83)

Race

What Makes You Black? Illustrated. *Ebony*. 38: 115-116+ (Jan 83)

Race And Occupations

See Occupations And Race

Race Awareness

Brown France Vs. Black Africa: The Tide Turned In 1932. Notes. Martin Steins. *Research in African Literatures*. 14: 474-497 (Winter 83)

The Color Crutch. Illustrated. Marlene Hodge Martin. *Essence*. 14: 140 (Aug 83)

My Father, My Mother, Myself. Illustrated. Marita Golden. *Essence*. 14: 72-74+ (May 83)

The Price Of Integration. Illustrated. Patrice Gaines-Carter. *Essence*. 14: 150 (Jul 83)

Race Awareness In Literature

Les Négres: A Look At Genet's Excursion Into Black Consciousnes. Notes. Keith Q. Warner. *CLA Journal*. 26: 397-414 (Jun 83)

Psychic Duality Of Afro-Americans In The Novels Of W. E. B. DuBois. Notes. James B. Stewart. *Phylon*. 44: 93-107 (Jun 83)

Race Identity

Black Families In White Suburbs Retain Positive Image - Study Shows.. *Crisis*. 90: 39 (Dec 83)

Minority Identity Development And Preference For Counselor Race. Notes, tables. George Morten and Donald R. Atkinson. *Journal of Negro Education*. 52: 156-161 (Spring 83)

Race Relations

See Also Church And Race Relations
Intercultural Education

Racism

Black Women, White Women: Separate Paths To Liberation. Notes. Elizabeth F. Hood. *Black Scholar*. 14: 26-37 (Sep-Oct 83)

Childcare Shapes The Future: Racism, Related Problems, Research And Strategies. Illustrated. *Interracial Books for Children*. 14: No. 7: 6+ (83)

A Conversation With Dr. Charles H. King Jr. Interview, Illustrated. Charles H. (Jr.) King and Linda Horton. *Essence*. 14: 15+ (Dec 83)

Inside The Klan. Illustrated. Jerry Thompson. *Ebony*. 38: 100-102+ (Jun 83)

Interconnections. James S. Tinney. *Interracial Books for Children*. 14: No. 3: 4-6+ (83)

The Politics Of The Living: A Case Study In Scientific Neo-Racism. Notes. Alan Davies. *Journal of Religious Thought*. 39: 26-40 (Fall-Winter 83)

Racism And Anti-Feminism.Chisholm Shirley. *Black Scholar*. 14: 2-7 (Sep-Oct 83)

Racism Toward Black African Diplomats During The Kennedy Administration. Notes. Calvin B. Holder. *Journal of Black Studies*. 14: 31-48 (Sep 83)

There Is No Hierarchy Of Oppressions. Aundre Lorde. *Interracial Books for Children*. 14: No. 3: (83)

See Also Antisemitism
Genocide

Racism—Great Britain

Race And Political Parties In Britain, 1954-1965. Notes. Fred R. Van Hartesveldt. *Phylon*. 44: 126-134 (Jun 83)

Racism—Puerto Rico

Racism No Longer Denied. Notes. Samuel Betances and Virginia Copeland. *Interracial Books for Children*. 14: No. 1: 24 (83)

Rackow, Sylvia

Mixing Business With Pleasure. Illustrated. *Black Enterprise*. 14: 84 (Aug 83)

Radio—Apparatus And Supplies

Do You Need A Beeper? Ruth Dolores Manuel. *Essence*. 14: 35 (Nov 83)

Radio Stations—Kentucky—Louisville

Publisher John H. Johnson Wins Praise As New Owner Of Station WLOU. Illustrated. *Jet*. 63: 10-15 (10 Jan 83)

Radio Stations—New York (State)—Rochester

Andrew Langston: Mighty Like A River. Illustrated. Adolph Dupree. *about. . . time*. 11: 14-21 (Apr 83)

A Commitment And Sacrifice To Goals. James M.
Blount. *about. . . time*. 11: 4 (Apr 83)

Radiotherapy

Radiotherapy In Tanzania. Illustrated, tables.
George A. Alexander. *National Medical Association
Journal*. 75: 289-295 (Mar 83)

Ragsdale, Rose

Maynard Buys Tribune. Illustrated. *Black
Enterprise*. 13: 18 (Jul 83)

Rahming, Melvin B.

Complacency And Community: Psychocultural
Patterns In The West Indian Novel. Notes. *CLA
Journal*. 26: 288-302 (Mar 83)

Railroad Travel

Coasting Down California By Rail. Illustrated. Dale
Wright. *Black Enterprise*. 13: 270 + (Jun 83)

Ralph-Bowman, Mark

"Leaders And Left-Overs": A Reading Of
Soyinka's: Death And The King's Horseman.
Notes. *Research in African Literatures*. 14: 81-97
(Spring 83)

Randall, Dudley

Be Kind To Me. Poem. *Black American Literature
Forum*. 17: 168 (Winter 83)

For Kim. Poem. *Black American Literature Forum*.
17: 169 (Winter 83)

For Vivian. Poem. *Black American Literature
Forum*. 17: 170 (Winter 83)

The Girls In Booths. Poem. *Black American
Literature Forum*. 17: 170 (Winter 83)

Motown Polka. Poem. *Black American Literature
Forum*. 17: 168 (Winter 83)

Old Detroit. Poem. *Black American Literature
Forum*. 17: 168 (Winter 83)

Silly Jim. Poem. *Black American Literature Forum*.
17: 169 (Winter 83)

To Poets Who Preach In Prose. Poem. *Black
American Literature Forum*. 17: 169 (Winter 83)

Woman Of Ghana. Poem. *Black American
Literature Forum*. 17: 169 (Winter 83)

Randall, Dudley—Criticism And Interpretation

Dudley Randall: A Humanist View. Illustrated,
notes. D. H. Melhem. *Black American Literature
Forum*. 17: 157-167 (Winter 83)

Randall, James H.

This Was Harlem: A Cultural Portrait, 1900-1950.
Book review. *Journal of Negro History*. 68:
105-107 (Winter 83)

Randall, Jon C.

Not Without Love. Poem. *Essence*. 14: 17 (Dec 83)

Randall, Margaret

Sandino's Daughters: Testimonies Of Nicaraguan
Women In Struggle. Book review. Janice Bevien.
Black Scholar. 14: 74-75 (Mar-Apr 83)

Sandino's Daughters. Excerpt, Illustrated. *Black
Scholar*. 14: 48-57 (Mar-Apr 83)

Randall-Tsuruta, Dorothy

Ain't I A Woman: Black Women And Feminism.
Book review. *Black Scholar*. 14: 46-52 (Jan-Feb
83)

The Color Purple. Book review. *Black Scholar*. 14:
54-55 (Summer 83)

Randolph, Laura B.

Jayne Kennedy: Portrait Of A Woman Who Lost
Her Husband And Found Herself. Illustrated.
Ebony. 38: 107-108 + (Jul 83)

Randolph, Marc L. and Wade, Robert E.

Global Telecommunications: Transborder Data Flow
And The Role For Blacks. Tables, notes. *The
Urban League Review*. 08: 55-67 (Winter 83)

See Kweli, Kujaatele

Rangel, Charles B. (about)

Federal Budget: Charles B. Rangel (D. N. Y.).
Illustrated. Bebe Moore Campbell. *Black
Enterprise*. 14: 56 (Oct 83)

Rasheed, Fred H.

Alternative Economic Strategies For Blacks.
Illustrated. *Crisis*. 90: 8-9 (Oct 83)

Ravell-Pinto, Thelma

Un Fusil Dans La Main, Un Poème Dans La
Poche. Book review. *Journal of Black Studies*. 13:
369-371 (Mar 83)

Ray, Elaine C.

Give The Man A Hand. Illustrated. *Essence*. 14: 50
(Aug 83)

How To Find Money For College. Illustrated.
Essence. 14: 50 (May 83)
Jones-Miller, Alice

Read, Danny L.

The Literature Of Jazz: A Critical Guide. Book
review. George L. Starks. *The Black Perspective in
Music*. 11: 215-218 (Fall 83)

Reading (Elementary)

Influence OF Parent Practices Upon Reading
Achievement Of Good And Poor Readers. Notes,
tables. Portia H. Shields and others. *Journal of
Negro Education*. 52: 436-445 (Fall 83)

Reagan, Ronald (about)

Are The Promises Being Kept? Illustrated. Isaiah J.
Poole. *Black Enterprise*. 14: 117-118 + (Oct 83)

Black Americans In Reagan's America. Notes. John
E. Jacob. *Black Law Journal*. 08: 417-426 (Winter
83)

Black GOP Warns Reagan. Derek T. Dingle. *Black
Enterprise*. 14: 20 (Nov 83)

The Keynote. . . "Take Up This Crusade".
Illustrated. Kelly M. (Sr.) Alexander. *Crisis*. 90:
16-18 (Aug-Sep 83)

NAACP Civil Rights Report. . . President Ronald
Reagan-The First Two Years. Althea T. L.
Simmons. *Crisis*. 90: 30-33 (Jan 83)

Reagan Civil Rights: The First Twenty Months.
Notes. *Black Law Journal*. 08: 68-94 (Spring 83)

Reagan Foreign Policy: War On The Doorstep? Illustrated. George W. (Jr.) Crockett. *Crisis*. 90: 48-49 (Dec 83)

Turning Back The Clock On Women And Minority Rights: The Regan Record. Illustrated. Mary Frances Berry. *Negro History Bulletin*. 46: 82-84 (Jul-Sep 83)

Reagins, Ann L.

Juanita Jewel Craft: Just Look At Her "Kids". Illustrated. *Crisis*. 90: 36-37 (Jun-Jul 83)

Record Reviews

Art Songs By Black American Composers. By Willis C. Patterson. Reviewed by Josephine Wright. *The Black Perspective in Music*. 11: 93-95 (Spring 83)

Spirituals. By A. Grace Lee Mims. Reviewed by Josephine Wright. *The Black Perspective in Music*. 11: 93-95 (Spring 83)

Teddy Wilson. Time-Life Giants Of Jazz STL-j20. By Teddy Wilson. Reviewed by Lewis Porter. *The Black Perspective in Music*. 11: 95-96 (Spring 83)

Yol. Reviewed by Jane Power. *Freedomways*. 23: No. 3: 195-198 (83)

Records, Phonograph

See Phonorecords

Redd, Lawrence N.

The Use Of Two-Way Television To Solve Problems Of Inequality In Education: A Comment. Notes, tables. *Journal of Negro Education*. 52: 446-453 (Fall 83)

Reducing

Be A Diet-Wise Dieter.. *Essence*. 14: 127 (May 83)

Determination Diet. Illustrated. *Ebony*. 38: 81+ (May 83)

Diet Right. Illustrated. Wista Johnson. *Essence*. 13: 107 (Jan 83)

Diet Right: You Can Keep It Off! Karen Kreps. *Essence*. 13: 131 (Apr 83)

How Full-Figured Women Can Handle Their Weight Problem. Illustrated. *Jet*. 64: 22-24+ (11 Apr 83)

'Loving Myself Came Hard'. Illustrated. Maxine Anderson Moffett. *Essence*. 13: 116 (Feb 83)

The Man Who Lost 385 Lbs. Illustrated. *Ebony*. 38: 66+ (Jan 83)

The $100 Bet I Won By Losing Weight. Illustrated. Beverly Alford. *Essence*. 14: 130 (Jun 83)

Reducing Diets

Diet Right! Losing Weight Soulfully. Illustrated. Lloyd Gite and Jean Perry. *Essence*. 14: 117-118 (Aug 83)

Working On Your Diet. Illustrated. Marcia McNair. *Essence*. 13: 135 (Mar 83)

Reed, Ishamel

God Made Alaska For The Indians: Selected Essays. Book review. Jerome Klinkowitz. *Black American Literature Forum*. 17: 137-139 (Fall 83)

The Terrible Twos. Book review. Henry Louis (Jr.) Gates. *Black Enterprise*. 13: 16 (Apr 83)

The Terrible Twos. Book review. Carole Bovoso. *Essence*. 13: 19 (Jan 83)

Reed, Rodney J.

Affirmative Action In Higher Education: Is It Necessary? Notes, tables. *Journal of Negro Education*. 52: 332-349 (Summer 83)

Refugees, Ethiopian

Are Black Refugees Getting A Dirty Deal? Illustrated. Lynn Norment. *Ebony*. 38: 132-134+ (Oct 83)

Refugees, Haitian

Are Black Refugees Getting A Dirty Deal? Illustrated. Lynn Norment. *Ebony*. 38: 132-134+ (Oct 83)

Blood Ties. Illustrated. Alexis DeVeaux. *Essence*. 13: 62-64+ (Jan 83)

Refugees, South African

Dennis Brutus Fights Deportation. Illustrated. *Black Scholar*. 14: 72 (Mar-Apr 83)

Reggae Music

Jamming In Jamaica. Illustrated. Nelson George and Isaac Fergusson. *Black Enterprise*. 13: 59-60+ (May 83)

Registration Of Voters

See Voters, Registration Of

Reichgott, Michael J. and others

The Nurse Practitioner's Role In Complex Patient Management: Hypertension. Tables, notes. *National Medical Association Journal*. 75: 1197-1204 (Dec 83)

Reid, Craig

Showstopper: Kim Fields. Illustrated. *Essence*. 14: 47 (Aug 83)

Reid, Craig W.

Marla Gibbs. Illustrated. *Essence*. 13: 15 (Mar 83)

Reid, G. W.

A Black Odyssey: John Lewis Waller And The Promise Of American Life, 1878-1900. Book review. *Journal of Negro History*. 68: 119-120 (Winter 83)

Reid, Herbert O. (Sr.) and Foster-Davis, Frankie

State Of The Art: The Law And Education Since 1954. Notes. *Journal of Negro Education*. 52: 234-249 (Summer 83)

Reid, Ira DeA. (about)

On Reconsidering Park, Johnson, DuBois, Frazier And Reid: Reply To Benjamin Bowser's "The Contribution Of Blacks To Sociological Knowledge.". Notes. Jerry G. Watts. *Phylon*. 44: 273-291 (Dec 83)

Reidy, Joseph P.

The Ruling Race: A History Of American Slaveholders. Book review. *Journal of Negro History*. 68: 95-97 (Winter 83)

Relaxation

Relaxation Therapy: Adjunctive Therapy For The Physician. Tables, notes. Dorothy D. Harrison. *National Medical Association Journal*. 75: 193-198 (Feb 83)

Religion In Literature

Towards A View Of The Influence Of Religion On Black Literature. Notes. Ernest Bradford. *CLA Journal*. 27: 18-29 (Sep 83)

Religion, Primitive

See Also Voodooism

Religions

See Also Cults

Republican Party

Black GOP Warns Reagan. Derek T. Dingle. *Black Enterprise*. 14: 20 (Nov 83)

Vice President Bush Says He'll Continue To 'Plug' For GOP Among Blacks. Illustrated. Simeon Booker. *Jet*. 64: 16-17 (22 Aug 83)

Republican Party—History

Frederick Douglass And American Diplomacy In The Caribbean. Notes, bibliography. Merline Pitre. *Journal of Black Studies*. 13: 457-475 (Jun 83)

Republican Party. Kentucky

Black Political Insurgency In Louisville, Kentucky: The Lincoln Independent Party Of 1921. Notes. George C. Wright. *Journal of Negro History*. 68: 8-23 (Winter 83)

Research

See Also Literary Research

Resumes (Employment)

A Basic Guide To Resumes. Tables. Marilyn Kern-Foxworth. *Black Collegian*. 14: 84-88 (Sep-Oct 83)

How To Write A Winning Resume. Jeff Davidson. *Black Collegian*. 13: 62+ (Feb-Mar 83)

Retail Franchises

See Franchises (Retail Trade)

Retail Trade

See Also Wholesale Trade

Retirement Income

Planning For Your Retirement. Illustrated. Edmund Newton. *Black Enterprise*. 14: 89-92+ (Oct 83)

Revlon, Inc.

Johnson Publishing Company Sues Revlon, Inc; Charges Infringement Of Trademarks. Illustrated. *Jet*. 65: 14-15 (7 Nov 83)

Revolution, American

See United States—History—Revolution, 1775-1783

Revolutionists

The Black Scholar Interviews: Mirna Cunningham. Interview. Mirna Cunningham and Robert Chrisman. *Black Scholar*. 14: 17-27 (Mar-Apr 83)

Mandela: Man Of The Resistance. Illustrated. *Crisis*. 90: 42-43 (Feb 83)

Sandino's Daughters. Excerpt, Illustrated. Margaret Randall. *Black Scholar*. 14: 48-57 (Mar-Apr 83)

Revolutionists—South Africa

The South African Freedom Movement: Factors Influencing Its Ideological Development, 1912-1980s. Notes. Elaine A. Friedland. *Journal of Black Studies*. 13: 337-354 (Mar 83)

Revolutions—Nicaragua

The War Of Terror Against Nicaragua. Illustrated. Hector Frances. *Black Scholar*. 14: 2-16 (Mar-Apr 83)

Rewards (Prizes, Etc.)

Debbie Allen, Michael Warren Host American Black Achievement Awards Annual TV Show. Illustrated. *Jet*. 63: 54-57+ (28 Feb 83)

A Tribute To Black Excellence. Illustrated. *Ebony*. 38: 42-44+ (Apr 83)

Reyes, Angelita

Echos Du Commonwealth. Book review. *Research in African Literatures*. 14: 123-126 (Spring 83)

Reynolds, Barbara A.

Another Blow For Affirmative Action.. *Essence*. 14: 54 (Jul 83)

A Coalition With Clout.. *Essence*. 14: 56 (Jul 83)

Potshots At Apartheid.. *Essence*. 14: 58 (Jun 83)

Rhetoric

The Evolution Of The Attitude Of Malcolm X Toward Whites. Notes. Raymond Rodgers and Jimmie N. Rogers. *Phylon*. 44: 108-115 (Jun 83)

Rhodes, Crystal V.

From Ragtime To Realtime: A Profile Of Howard Rollins. Illustrated. *Black Collegian*. 14: 134-135+ (Sep-Oct 83)

Rhodesia

See Zimbabwe

Rice, Fred (about)

Chicago Mayor Names City's First Black Police Supt. First facts, illustrated. *Jet*. 65: 8 (12 Sep 83)

Rice, Herbert W.

Repeated Images In Part One Of Cane. Notes. *Black American Literature Forum*. 17: 100-105 (Fall 83)

Rice, Richard V.

And A Child Shall. . . . Poem. *about. . . time*. 11: 43 (Nov 83)

Behind A Black Face. Poem. *about. . . time*. 11: 27 (Oct 83)

Benny's Place. Poem. *about. . . time*. 11: 27 (Oct 83)

Ohio Law Challenged.. *Black Enterprise*. 13: 20 + (May 83)

The Rebirth Of Avondale. Illustrated. *Black Enterprise*. 13: 35 (Jun 83)

Robson, Clifford B.

Ngugi Wa' Thiong'o. Book review. Govind Narain Sharma. *Research in African Literatures*. 14: 238-242 (Summer 83)

Rochester, New York

See Also Community Development—New York (State)—Rochester
Radio Stations—New York (State)—Rochester
Theater—New York (State)—New York (City)

Rochester, New York—Economic Conditions

The Industrial Management Council. Interview, Illustrated. John D. Hostutler and Carolyne S. Blount. *about. . . time*. 11: 12-13 + (Aug 83)

Rodgers, Carolyn M.

For Some Black Men. Poem. *Essence*. 14: 20 (Sep 83)

Love. Poem, Illustrated. *Ebony*. 38: 48 (Feb 83)

Rodgers, Curtis E.

So You Want To Be In The Movies? Illustrated. *Crisis*. 90: 6-10 (Jan 83)

Rodgers, Raymond and Rogers, Jimmie N.

The Evolution Of The Attitude Of Malcolm X Toward Whites. Notes. *Phylon*. 44: 108-115 (Jun 83)

Rodman, Harvey M. (joint author)

See Lederman, Michael M.
Lederman, Michael M.

Rogers, Jimmie N. (joint author)

See Rodgers, Raymond

Rogers, Malikha V.

Sex During Pregnancy: Common Questions And Practical Answers. Notes. *National Medical Association Journal*. 75: 1087-1088 + (Nov 83)

Rogers, Philip

No Longer At Ease: Chinua Achebe's "Heart Of Whiteness". Notes. *Research in African Literatures*. 14: 165-183 (Summer 83)

Rollins, Howard (about)

From Ragtime To Realtime: A Profile Of Howard Rollins. Illustrated. Crystal V. Rhodes. *Black Collegian*. 14: 134-135 + (Sep-Oct 83)

Roscoe, A. A.

Twelve African Writers. Book review. *Research in African Literatures*. 14: 232-236 (Summer 83)

Rosenbaum, Sara and Weitz, Judith

Children And Federal Health Care Cuts.. *Freedomways*. 23: No. 01: 17-22 (83)

Rosenshein, Neil B. (joint author)

See Hernandez, Enrique

Rosner, Fred (joint author)

See Blum, Lawrence

Ross, Diana (about)

Diana and Michael: They Are Undisputed King And Queen Of Entertainment. Illustrated. Charles L. Sanders. *Ebony*. 39: 29-30 + (Nov 83)

Ross, Howard

Slavery And Social Death: A Comparative Study. Book review. *Phylon*. 44: 332-333 (Dec 83)

Ross, John Putnam

Golfing With Calvin Peete. Illustrated. *Black Enterprise*. 13: 70 (Jul 83)

Rosser, Pearl L. (joint author)

See Washington, Anita C.

Rothschild, Mary Aickin

A Case Of Black And White: Northern Volunteers And The Southern Freedom Summers, 1964-65. Book review. Gerald Horne. *Journal of Negro History*. 68: 107-109 (Winter 83)

Rouselle, William and Borders, James

Black Engineering Schools. Illustrated. *Black Collegian*. 13: 96 + (Dec-Jan 83)

See Dole, Elizabeth
Francis, Norman
Franklin, Yvette
Newsom, Lionel

Roxbury, Massachusetts

See Also Public
Defenders—Massachusetts—Roxbury

Rozier, Mike (about)

Rozier Gets Early Xmas, 10th Straight Black To Win Coveted Heisman Trophy. Illustrated. *Jet*. 65: 48 (26 Dec 83)

Rubenstein, Roberta

Doris Lessing: The Problem Of Alienation And The Form Of The Novel. Book review. *Research in African Literatures*. 14: 242-244 (Summer 83)

Rubin, Martin

Towards The Mountain: An Autobiography. Book review. *Research in African Literatures*. 14: 261-266 (Summer 83)

Ruderman, Judith

Miltons's Choices: Styron's Use Of Robert Frost's Poetry In Lie Down In Darkness. Notes. *CLA Journal*. 27: 141-151 (Dec 83)

Ruffin, Frances E.

Baby, It's Cold Outside: 10 Ways To Take The B-r-r-r Out Of Winter. Illustrated. *Black Enterprise* 13: 57-58 (Jan 83)

Ruffin, James

Disney Epcot Center: A Family Experience. Illustrated. *Black Enterprise*. 13: 105-106 + (Feb 83)

Sarroca, Manuel V. (joint author)

See Phillips, Lloyd G. (Jr.)

Satcher, David (about)

Satcher Inaugurated Meharry's Eighth President. Illustrated. *National Medical Association Journal.* 75: 210+ (Feb 83)

Satiafa

For Dark Women And Others. Book review. Alene Barnes-Harden. *Journal of Black Studies.* 14: 261-262 (Dec 83)

Satterfield, Ben

Facing The Abyss: The Floating Opera And End Of The Road. Notes. *CLA Journal.* 26: 341-352 (Mar 83)

Saunders, Doris E.

Black Women As Clergy And The Black Religious Experience. Illustrated. *Crisis.* 90: 16+ (Jun-Jul 83)

Saunders, Mari P.

Fathers And Daughters.. *Essence.* 14: 85-86+ (Aug 83)

Savage, Gus

America In The Wrong.. *Freedomways.* 23: No. 3: 171-175 (83)

Sayin, Afife

Fair Representation In Employment: A Historical Look. Notes. *The Urban League Review.* 07: 19-32 (Summer 83)

Scarupa, Harriet Jackson and McNair, Marcia

Keys To The Future. Illustrated. *Essence.* 14: 46 (Oct 83)

You Can Count On Mathematics!. *Essence.* 13: 30 (Feb 83)

Schart-Hyman, Trina

Big Sixteen. Book review. Geraldine L. Wilson. *Interracial Books for Children.* 14: No. 5: 25 (83)

Schild, Romuald (joint author)

See Wendorf, Fred

Schizophrenia

An Evaluation Of The Cost Effectiveness Of Day Hospitalization For Black Male Schizophrenics. Tables. Patricia A. Newton. *National Medical Association Journal.* 75: 273-285 (Mar 83)

Schmidt, Nancy J.

Children's Fiction About Africa In English. Book review. Osayimwense Osa. *Research in African Literatures.* 14: 257-261 (Summer 83)

Commonwealth Children's Literature. Book review. *Research in African Literatures.* 14: 255-257 (Summer 83)

Schneider, William H.

An Empire For The Masses: The French Popular Image Of Africa, 1870-1900. Book review. Sylvia M. Jacobs. *Journal of Negro History.* 68: 116-117 (Winter 83)

Scholarly Periodicals

The CLA Journal As A Mirror Of Changing Ethnic And Academic Perspectives. Notes. A. Russell Brooks. *CLA Journal.* 26: 265-276 (Mar 83)

Scholars

Baccalaureate College Of Origin Of Black Doctorate Recipients. Notes, tables. William F. Brazziel. *Journal of Negro Education.* 52: 102-109 (Spring 83)

Scholarships

Graduate School: CIC Fellowships. John A. (Jr.) McCluskey. *Black Collegian.* 14: 124-127 (Nov-Dec 83)

How To Find Money For College. Illustrated. Elaine C. Ray. *Essence.* 14: 50 (May 83)

Scholtz, Merwe

Leipolot 100. Book review. Ampie Coetzee. *Research in African Literatures.* 14: 248-251 (Summer 83)

Schomburg Center For Research In Black Culture

The New Schomburg Center For Research In Black Culture. Illustrated. *Crisis.* 90: 28-29 (Feb 83)

The Schomburg Library Then And Now. Yusef A. Salaam. *Freedomways.* 23: No. 01: 29-36 (83)

School Boards

Politics And Education. Illustrated. Till Nelson. *Black Enterprise.* 13: 17 (Jul 83)

School Discipline

The Color Of Misbehaving: Two Case Studies Of Deviant Boys. Notes. Catherine A. Emihovich. *Journal of Black Studies.* 13: 259-273 (Mar 83)

School Integration

Court-Ordered School Desegregation: One Community's Attitude. Notes. Frank Brown and Waithira Muigai. *Journal of Black Studies.* 13: 355-368 (Mar 83)

Fostering Constructive Intergroup Contact In Desegregated Schools: Suggestions For Future Research. Notes. William B. Lacy and others. *Journal of Negro Education.* 52: 130-141 (Spring 83)

The Impact Of The Desegregation Process On The Education Of Black Students: Key Variables. Notes, tables. Russell W. Irvine. *Journal of Negro Education.* 52: 410-422 (Fall 83)

The Price Of Integration. Illustrated. Patrice Gaines-Carter. *Essence.* 14: 150 (Jul 83)

State Of The Art: The Law And Education Since 1954. Notes. Herbert O. (Sr.) Reid and Frankie Foster-Davis. *Journal of Negro Education.* 52: 234-249 (Summer 83)

Time For The Teachers: Putting Educators Back Into The Brown Remedy. Notes. Derrick Bell. *Journal of Negro Education.* 52: 290-301 (Summer 83)

Views Of Black School Superintendents On School Desegregation. Tables, notes. Hugh J. Scott. *Journal of Negro Education*. 52: 378-382 (Fall 83)

See Also Segregation In Education

School Integration—Arkansas—Little Rock

Little Rock Revisited: Desegregation To Resegregation. Notes. Wiley A. Branton. *Journal of Negro Education*. 52: 250-269 (Summer 83)

School Integration—Bibliography

School Desegregation In The United States, 1973-1982: An Annotated Bibliography. William J. Holloway. *Negro Educational Review*. 34: 115-138 (Jul-Oct 83)

School Integration—Dayton, Ohio

Reflections On Desegregation: Columbus, Ohio - A Case In Point. Notes. Beverly M. Gordon. *Negro Educational Review*. 34: 12-19 (Jan 83)

School Integration—Duval County, Florida

The Major Problems And Concerns Of Black Students In The Duval County Public Schools. Tables, notes. R. Grann Lloyd. *Negro Educational Review*. 34: 92-114 (Jul-Oct 83)

School Integration—Milwaukee, Wisconsin

Criteria For Evaluating School Desegregation In Milwaukee. Notes, tables. Ian M. Harris. *Journal of Negro Education*. 52: 423-435 (Fall 83)

Desegregation In Milwaukee: Attitudes May Be A Factor. Notes, tables. Gary C. Benedict and Robert J. Gerardi. *Negro Educational Review*. 34: 20-26 (Jan 83)

School Integration—United States

Without Justice. NotesLeadership Conference On Civil Rights. *Black Law Journal*. 08: 24-59 (Spring 83)

School Integration—Virginia

Public School Bonds And Virginia's Massive Resistance. Notes, tables. James H. (Jr.) Hershman. *Journal of Negro Education*. 52: 398-409 (Fall 83)

School Superintendents And Principals

On Becoming A Superintendent: Contest Or Sponsored Mobility? Notes. Charles D. (Sr.) Moody. *Journal of Negro Education*. 52: 383-397 (Fall 83)

School Superintendents And Principals —Attitudes

Views Of Black School Superintendents On School Desegregation. Tables, notes. Hugh J. Scott. *Journal of Negro Education*. 52: 378-382 (Fall 83)

Schools

See Also Private Schools
Public Schools

Schools Of Engineering

See Engineering Schools

Schroeder, Patricia R.

Point And Counterpoint In Harlem Gallery. Notes. *CLA Journal*. 27: 152-168 (Dec 83)

Schubert, Daniel S. P.

Primary Physicians' Care And Referral Of Patients With Psychiatric Problems. Editorial, Notes. *National Medical Association Journal*. 75: 13-14 (Jan 83)

Schwartz, David J.

Make It Happen! How To Put Action Behind Your Ideas.. *Essence*. 13: 93 + (Mar 83)

Science

See Also Physics

Science—Africa

The Lost Sciences Of Africa: An Overview. Ivan Van Sertima. *Journal of African Civilizations*. 05: 7-26 (Apr-Nov 83)

Science, Applied

See Technology

Scientists

African-American Contributions To Information Technology. Illustrated. Kirstie Gentleman. *Journal of African Civilizations*. 05: 273-292 (Apr-Nov 83)

Bibliographical Guide [To Black Scientists]. Bibliography. John Henrik Clarke. *Journal of African Civilizations*. 05: 295-302 (Apr-Nov 83)

The Black American: A Vision For The Future With Special Emphasis On Science. John B. Slaughter. *Negro History Bulletin*. 46: 24-25 (Jan-Mar 83)

Blackspace. Illustrated, notes. James G. Spady. *Journal of African Civilizations*. 05: 258-265 (Apr-Nov 83)

Dr. Lloyd Quarterman-Nuclear Scientist. Interview. Lloyd Quarterman and Ivan Van Sertima. *Journal of African Civilizations*. 05: 266-274 (Apr-Nov 83)

In Memoriam: Robert A. Thornton. Asa (III) Hilliard. *Journal of Negro History*. 68: 142-143 (Winter 83)

Space Science: The African-American Contribution. Illustrated. Curtis M. Graves and Ivan Van Sertima. *Journal of African Civilizations*. 05: 238-257 (Apr-Nov 83)

Scott, Gary A. (1945-1968) (about)

The Quality Of Leadership: Gary A. Scott (July 11, 1945-March 29, 1968). Illustrated. Adolph Dupree. *about. . . time*. 11: 22-26 (Nov 83)

Scott, Hugh J.

Views Of Black School Superintendents On School Desegregation. Tables, notes. *Journal of Negro Education*. 52: 378-382 (Fall 83)

Scott, Patricia Bell

But Some Of Us Are Brave. Book review. Hortense D. Lloyd. *Negro Educational Review*. 34: 45-46 (Jan 83)

Scott, Ruth

Implementing The MBE Program.. *about. . . time*. 11: 1 (Sep 83)

Scott, Samuel Fisher

The President That Time Forgot. Marvin Leon Lake. *Negro History Bulletin*. 46: 51-52 (Apr-Jun 83)

Scripps Institution Of Oceanography

Charting Your Course In Oceanography. Illustrated. Barbara Price. *Black Collegian*. 14: 124-125 (Sep-Oct 83)

Scruggs, Otey M.

Garveyism As A Religious Movement: The Institutionalization Of A Black Civil Religion. Book review. *Afro-Americans in New York Life and History*. 07: 71-72 (Jul 83)

Sea Islands

See Also Oral Tradition—Sea Islands

Sea Islands, Georgia—Social Life And Customs

Alive: African Traditions On The Sea Islands. Illustrated. Patricia Jones-Jackson. *Negro History Bulletin*. 46: 95-96+ (Oct-Dec 83)

Searches And Seizures—California

Constitutional Reflections On California's Request For Identification Law. Notes. Alexander (Jr.) Williams. *Black Law Journal*. 08: 177-185 (Fall 83)

Searches And Seizures—United States

United States Vs Ross: Final Obliteration Of Fourth Amendment Protection From Warrantless Searches Of Cars And Their Contents. Notes. Michael A. Jeter. *Black Law Journal*. 08: 306-321 (Fall 83)

Sears, Priscilla F.

A Piller Of Fire To Follow: American Indian Dramas, 1808-1859. Book review. Ola B. Criss. *Phylon*. 44: 90-91 (Mar 83)

Segregation In Education—Law And Legislation

Formula For Failure: A Critique Of The Intent Requirement In School Segregation Litigation. Notes. Harold J. Sullivan. *Journal of Negro Education*. 52: 270-289 (Summer 83)

Segregation In Education—North Carolina

North Carolina's Rationale For Mandating Separate Schools: A Legal History. Notes. Bruce Beezer. *Journal of Negro Education*. 52: 213-226 (Summer 83)

Segregation In Sports

The Black Athlete In Big-Time Intercollegiate Sports, 1941-1968. Notes. Donald Spivey. *Phylon*. 44: 116-125 (Jun 83)

Sekoni, 'Ropo

Metaphor As Basis Of Form In Soyinka's Drama. Notes. *Research in African Literatures*. 14: 45-57 (Spring 83)

Sekora, John

The Art Of Slave Narrative: Original Essays In Criticism And Theory. Book review. Henry-Louis (Jr.) Gates. *Black American Literature Forum*. 17: 131-134 (Fall 83)

Self-Actualization (Psychology)

Make It Happen! How To Put Action Behind Your Ideas. David J. Schwartz. *Essence*. 13: 93+ (Mar 83)

Moving Your Life Forward. Editorial. Susan L. Taylor. *Essence*. 13: 57 (Jan 83)

Self-Confidence

Getting Confident. Editorial. Susan L. Taylor. *Essence*. 14: 61 (Aug 83)

Self-Perception

Acknowledge Your Truth. Editorial. Susan L. Taylor. *Essence*. 14: 77 (Oct 83)

Insist On Being You! Editorial. Susan L. Taylor. *Essence*. 14: 69 (Jul 83)

Self-Realization

Make The Rest Of Your Life The Best Of Your Life. Carla A. Mikell. *Essence*. 14: 67-68 (May 83)

There Is A Way! Editorial. Susan L. Taylor. *Essence*. 13: 71 (Apr 83)

You've Got The Power! Editorial. Susan L. Taylor. *Essence*. 14: 65 (May 83)

Self-Respect

Don't Beg To Be Loved. Terry McMillan. *Essence*. 14: 172 (Oct 83)

'Loving Myself Came Hard'. Illustrated. Maxine Anderson Moffett. *Essence*. 13: 116 (Feb 83)

Senior Citizens

See Aged

Seniority, Employee

Seniority And Layoffs: A Dilemma In The Workplace. Phyllis A. Wallace. *Black Enterprise*. 14: 37-38 (Nov 83)

Senkamanisken, King Of Egypt

African King In Confederate Capital. Illustrated, bibliography. V. Spottswood Simon. *Negro History Bulletin*. 46: 9-10 (Jan-Mar 83)

Seraile, William

Henrietta Vinton Davis And The Garvey Movement. Notes. *Afro-Americans in New York Life and History*. 07: 7-24 (Jul 83)

Sermons

I Heard A Child Crying. Notes. Frank Williams. *Journal of Religious Thought*. 40: 65-71 (Spring-Summer 83)

Sex

See Also Homosexuality
Lesbianism

Sex Change

See Change Of Sex

Sex Crimes

See Also Incest

Sex In Marriage

How To Put The Zip Back In Love. Illustrated. Jennifer Oliver. *Essence*. 14: 91+ (Sep 83)

Sex Role

Of Men And Money. Illustrated. Bonnie Allen. *Essence*. 14: 89+ (Jun 83)

"A Woman's Place": The Attitudes Of Middle-Class Black Men. Notes, tables. Noel A. Cazenave. *Phylon*. 44: 12-32 (Mar 83)

Sex Therapists

Dr. June Dobbs Butts: How Did A Nice Lady Like Her Get To Be An Expert On Sex? Illustrated. Charles L. Sanders. *Ebony*. 38: 143-144+ (May 83)

Sexism

Black Women, White Women: Separate Paths To Liberation. Notes. Elizabeth F. Hood. *Black Scholar*. 14: 26-37 (Sep-Oct 83)

Interconnections. James S. Tinney. *Interracial Books for Children*. 14: No. 3: 4-6+ (83)

Seydou, Christiane

A Few Reflections On Narrative Structures Of Epic Texts: A Case Example Of Bambara And Fulani Epics. Notes. *Research in African Literatures*. 14: 312-331 (Fall 83)

Shackford, Kate

All The Colors Of The Race. Book review. *Interracial Books for Children*. 14: No. 1: 35 (83)

Shade, Barbara J.

The Social Success Of Black Youth: The Impact Of Significant Others. Notes. *Journal of Black Studies*. 14: 137-150 (Dec 83)

Shahak, Israel

Is Israel On The Road To Nazism?. *Freedomways*. 23: No. 3: 153-164 (83)

Shaik, Fatima

Execution By Injection. Illustrated. *Black Enterprise*. 13: 25 (Mar 83)

New President At Universal. Illustrated. *Black Enterprise*. 13: 36 (Jun 83)

Shakespeare, William (1564-1616)—Characters

Shakespeare's Paulina: Characterization And Craftsmanship In the Winter's Tale. Notes. Myles Hurd. *CLA Journal*. 26: 303-310 (Mar 83)

Shakespeare, William (1564-1616)—Political And Social Views

The Orchard And The Street: The Political Mirror Of The Tragic In Julius Caesar And Coriolanus. Notes. H. George Hahn. *CLA Journal*. 27: 169-186 (Dec 83)

Shalash, Ali

Al-Drama Al-Afriqia. Book review. Kole Omotoso. *Research in African Literatures*. 14: 108-110 (Spring 83)

Shange, Ntozake

Sassafrass, Cypress And Indigo. Book review. Kuumba Na Kazi. *Black Collegian*. 13: 132+ (Feb-Mar 83)

Shange, Ntozake—Criticism And Interpretation

Conflicting Impulses In The Plays Of Ntozake Shange. Illustrated, notes. Sandra L. Richards. *Black American Literature Forum*. 17: 73-78 (Summer 83)

Shangi, Lennard M.

Racial Stratification, Sex, And Mental Ability: A Comparison Of Five Groups In Trinidad. Tables, notes. *Journal of Black Studies*. 14: 69-82 (Sep 83)

Sharma, Govind Narain

An Introduction To The Writings Of Ngugi. Book review. *Research in African Literatures*. 14: 238-242 (Summer 83)

Ngugi Wa Thiong'o. Book review. *Research in African Literatures*. 14: 238-242 (Summer 83)

Sharp, Curtis (Jr.) (about)

Learning To Live With $5 Million. Illustrated. Trudy S. Moore. *Ebony*. 38: 52+ (Apr 83)

$5 Million Lottery Winner Has $50,000 Wedding To Remember. Illustrated. Trudy S. Moore and Moneta (Jr.) Sleet. *Jet*. 64: 14-16+ (18 Jul 83)

$5 Million Man To Take Bride. Illustrated. Trudy S. Moore. *Jet*. 63: 20-27 (31 Jan 83)

Sharpeville-Langa Massacre, 1960

Reflections On The Sharpville-Langa Massacres Of 1960. Illustrated. Boji Jordon. *Crisis*. 90: 44-45 (Apr 83)

Shaw, Leander J. (Jr.) (about)

Fla. Gov. Appoints Black To State Supreme Court.. *Jet*. 63: 4 (17 Jan 83)

Shaw, Patricia Walker (about)

A Family Affair: Patricia Shaw Succeeds Father As President Of Universal Life. Illustrated. Lynn Norment. *Ebony*. 38: 75-76+ (May 83)

New President At Universal. Illustrated. Fatima Shaik. *Black Enterprise*. 13: 36 (Jun 83)

Shaw, Valerie (about)

Essence Women: Valerie Shaw. Illustrated. Retha Camp. *Essence*. 13: 25 (Jan 83)

Sheehy, Bill

The Illustrated Encyclopedia Of Black Music. Book review. Doris Evans McGinty. *The Black Perspective in Music*. 11: 212-214 (Fall 83)

Sherwin, Sally

Grocery-Shopping Make-Over. Illustrated. *Essence*. 13: 98 (Jan 83)

Shields, Audrey

Attorney's Expanding Right To Advertise Under The First Amendment. Notes. *Howard Law Journal*. 26: No. 1: 281-304 (83)

Shields, Portia H. and others

Influence OF Parent Practices Upon Reading Achievement Of Good And Poor Readers. Notes, tables. *Journal of Negro Education*. 52: 436-445 (Fall 83)

Shore, Debra

Steel-Making In Ancient Africa. Illustrated, tables. *Journal of African Civilizations*. 05: 157-162 (Apr-Nov 83)

Short Stories

All That Glitters May Not Be Gold! Reviewed by Fran Norman. *about. . . time*. 11: 35 (Nov 83)

The Cut Of The Vest. Reviewed by Lizandro Chavez Alfaro. *Black Scholar*. 14: 58-71 (Mar-Apr 83)

The Envelope. Reviewed by Michele Wallace. *Essence*. 14: 93-94 (Aug 83)

One Of These Days. Reviewed by Fran Norman. *about. . . time*. 11: 21 (Sep 83)

The Story Teller. Reviewed by Michele Wallace. *Essence*. 14: 72-74 + (Dec 83)

Unrecognized Musicians. Reviewed by Fran Norman. *about. . . time*. 11: 12-13 (Feb 83)

Shorter, Beryl Elyese (joint author)

See Baugh, E. Lorraine

Shurney, Robert E. (about)

Space Science: The African-American Contribution. Illustrated. Curtis M. Graves and Ivan Van Sertima. *Journal of African Civilizations*. 05: 238-257 (Apr-Nov 83)

Sick

See Also Cardiacs

Sick—Psychology

Munchausen's Syndrome Or Chronic Factitious Illness: A Review And Case Presentation. Tables, notes. Gary L. Howe and others. *National Medical Association Journal*. 75: 175-181 (Feb 83)

Sickle Cell Anemia

The Black Enterprise Guide To Good Health. Illustrated. Sandra R. Gregg. *Black Enterprise*. 13: 39-43 (May 83)

Evaluation Of Clinical Severity In Sickle Cell Disease. Tables, notes. Bruce F. Cameron and others. *National Medical Association Journal*. 75: 483-487 (May 83)

Sickled Hypochromic Red Blood Cells. Illustrated, notes. Theresa B. Haddy and Oswaldo L. Castro. *National Medical Association Journal*. 75: 423 + (Apr 83)

Studies Of The Kallikrein-Kinin System In Patients With Sickle Cell Anemia. Tables, notes. Russell L. Miller and others. *National Medical Association Journal*. 75: 551-556 (Jun 83)

Siegel, Ellen

The Road To Jerusalem: Beirut September. Illustrated. *Freedomways*. 23: No. 2: 90-98 (83)

Silber, Leonard (joint author)

See Chawla, Kiran

Silverman, Jason H.

Revisiting Black Canada: Notes On Recent Literature.. *Journal of Negro History*. 68: 93-94 (Winter 83)

Slaves No More: Letters From Liberia, 1833-1869. Book review, Notes. *Negro History Bulletin*. 46: 105 (Oct-Dec 83)

Simmons, Althea T. L.

The Black Woman-Overcoming The Odds.. *Crisis*. 90: 14-15 (Jun-Jul 83)

NAACP Civil Rights Report. . . President Ronald Reagan-The First Two Years.. *Crisis*. 90: 30-33 (Jan 83)

NAACP Membership- Your Fight For Freedom Insurance. Illustrated. *Crisis*. 90: 20-21 (Apr 83)

Simmons, Donald (about)

The Lagos/Muskogee Connection. Illustrated. Frank (III) White. *Ebony*. 38: 69-70 + (May 83)

Simmons, Judy

Great Expectations. Illustrated. *Essence*. 13: 64 + (Feb 83)

Simmons, Rocky (about)

"Rocky" Simmons: A Bedrock Of Community Involvement. Illustrated. Richard Walton and Robin Wilson. *about. . . time*. 11: 24-25 (Oct 83)

Simon, Roger

Lives Of Their Own: Blacks, Italians, And Poles In Pittsburgh, 1900-1960. Book review. Clayborne Carson. *Journal of Negro History*. 68: 98-99 (Winter 83)

Simon, V. Spottswood

African King In Confederate Capital. Illustrated, bibliography. *Negro History Bulletin*. 46: 9-10 (Jan-Mar 83)

Sims, Edward G.

Hypothyroidism Causing Macrocytic Anemia Unresponsive To B_{12} And Folate. Notes. *National Medical Association Journal*. 75: 429-431 (Apr 83)

Sims, Naomi

All About Success For The Black Woman. Book review. Elza Teresa Dinwiddie. *Black Enterprise*. 13: 31 (Jun 83)

Sims, Rudine

Shadow And Substance: Afro-American Experience In Contemporary Children's Fiction. Book review. Charlotte K. Brooks. *Black American Literature Forum*. 17: 136-137 (Fall 83)

Shadow & Substance: Afro-American Experience In Contemporary Children's Fiction. Book review. Minnie Finch. *Journal of Negro Education*. 52: 184-185 (Spring 83)

Sims, William E.

Perspectives In Multicultural Education. Book review. Geneva Gay. *Journal of Negro Education*. 52: 461-463 (Fall 83)

Sims-Wood, Janet L.

Marian Anderson: A Catalog Of The Collection At University Of Pennsylvania Library. Book review. *The Black Perspective in Music*. 11: 221-222 (Fall 83)

Music, Printed And Manuscript, In The James Weldon Johnson Memorial Collection Of Negro Arts And Letters: An Annotated Catalog. Book review. *The Black Perspective in Music*. 11: 221-222 (Fall 83)

Sinclair, Sheila

A Streak Of Ebony In The Ivory Tower. Illustrated. *Black Enterprise*. 13: 84-86+ (Feb 83)

Singers

Diana and Michael: They Are Undisputed King And Queen Of Entertainment. Illustrated. Charles L. Sanders. *Ebony*. 39: 29-30+ (Nov 83)

Dionne Warwick: Speaks Out For Strong Black Women. Illustrated. Dennis Hunt. *Ebony*. 38: 95-96+ (May 83)

'Dreamgirls' A Smash Hit In Hollywood. Illustrated. *Jet*. 64: 28-31 (27 Jun 83)

Evelyn King. Frederick D. Murphy. *Essence*. 13: 13 (Apr 83)

Freda Payne: Keeping Fit For Show Biz. Illustrated. *Ebony*. 39: 104-106 (Nov 83)

Gladys Knight Talks About Her Family And Career. Illustrated. Robert E. Johnson. *Jet*. 64: 54-57 (18 Apr 83)

Gospel Star Shirley Caesar Weds Bishop In Durham, N.C. Illustrated. *Jet*. 64: 13 (18 Jul 83)

Jazz Great Ella Fitzgerald Performs In-Flight Concert. Illustrated. Clarence Waldron. *Jet*. 63: 62+ (31 Jan 83)

Joan Armatrading. Illustrated. Eric Copage. *Essence*. 14: 51 (Dec 83)

Juggling Careers In Medicine And Music. Illustrated. Frank (III) White. *Ebony*. 38: 156-158 (Oct 83)

Lena Horne Finds Roots In Atlanta During Visit. Illustrated. Harmon Perry. *Jet*. 64: 28-30 (18 Jul 83)

Leona Mitchell: An All-American Opera Star. Illustrated. Aldore Collier. *Ebony*. 38: 37-38+ (Sep 83)

Leontyne Price-Still The Diva. Illustrated. *Crisis*. 90: 32-33 (Jun-Jul 83)

Lionel Richie Tells Why He Really Quit The Commodores. Illustrated. *Jet*. 63: 36-38 (21 Feb 83)

Louis Gossett, Natalie Cole Tell Of Changes In Their Lives. Illustrated. *Jet*. 64: 60-63 (23 May 83)

Marilyn McCoo: How She Keeps Fit. Illustrated. *Ebony*. 38: 80-82+ (Feb 83)

Marvin Gaye: Talks About His Troubled Life. Illustrated. Robert E. Johnson. *Jet*. 64: 56-60 (15 Aug 83)

Natalie Cole. Illustrated. Jack Slater. *Essence*. 14: 86-87+ (Oct 83)

Nona! Illustrated. Michele Wallace. *Essence*. 14: 78-79 (Jul 83)

Odetta-A Citzen Of the World. Illustrated. Don Armstrong. *Crisis*. 90: 51-52 (Jun-Jul 83)

Patrice Rushen. Illustrated. Gerrie E. Summers. *Essence*. 13: 15 (Feb 83)

Remembering Dinah, Queen Of The Blues. Illustrated. Betty DeRamus and Leslie Gourse. *Essence*. 14: 76-78+ (May 83)

Rhapsody In Black. Illustrated. *Essence*. 14: 80-92 (Dec 83)

Rick James Talks About Life With Fast Women And Hot Cars. Illustrated. Aldore D. Collier. *Jet*. 65: 58-61 (26 Sep 83)

Rita Marley: Showstopper. Illustrated. Isaac Fergusson. *Essence*. 14: 51 (Jul 83)

Shari And Harry. Illustrated. Michele Wallace. *Essence*. 14: 82-83 (Aug 83)

Spingarn Medal Presentation To. . . Lena Horne-A Living Legend. Vernon E. (Jr.) Jordan. *Crisis*. 90: 36 (Aug-Sep 83)

Spingarn Medalist's Acceptance Recalls. . . A Measure Of What Has Gone Before. Illustrated. Lena Horne. *Crisis*. 90: 38-40 (Aug-Sep 83)

Teddy Pendergrass Cheered At First Public Appearance Since Paralyzing Accident. Illustrated. Barbara Faggins. *Jet*. 63: 62-64 (28 Feb 83)

What's Going On With Marvin Gaye? Illustrated. David Ritz. *Essence*. 13: 58-60+ (Jan 83)

Singing Groups

Taste Of Honey Sees Success In The New Year. Illustrated. Aldore D. Collier. *Jet*. 63: 60-62 (3 Jan 83)

Vanity 6 Lives Out Daring Fantasies On Stage. Illustrated. *Jet*. 63: 58-62 (24 Jan 83)

Single Men

Bachelors For 1983. Illustrated. *Ebony*. 38: 76+ (Jun 83)

Single-Parent Family

Single-Parent Black Families. James P. Comer. *Crisis*. 90: 42-47 (Dec 83)

Who's Supporting The Kids? Women And Children Left Behind. Illustrated. Bebe Moore Campbell. *Essence*. 14: 75+ (Jul 83)

Single Parents

The New Choice: Single Motherhood After 30. Stephanie Stokes Oliver. *Essence*. 14: 131-132+ (Oct 83)

Single Parents—Sexual Behavior

Single Mothers: Taking Time Out For Love. Illustrated. *Essence*. 13: 108+ (Feb 83)

Single Women

Bachelorettes: Choices For '83. Illustrated. *Ebony*. 38: 117-118+ (Jul 83)

Singleton, Alice Faye (joint author)

See Wachsman, Laura

Singleton, Alvin and Wyatt, Lucius

Conversation With. . . Alvin Singleton, Composer. Interview, Illustrated. *The Black Perspective in Music*. 11: 178-189 (Fall 83)

Sirius

African Observers Of The Universe: The Sirius
Question. Illustrated, notes, tables. Hunter Havelin
(III) Adams. *Journal of African Civilizations*. 05:
27-46 (Apr-Nov 83)

A Further Note On Sirius B. Laurie Ryan. *Journal
of African Civilizations*. 05: 50 (Apr-Nov 83)

New Light On The Dogon And Sirius. Notes.
Hunter Havelin (III) Adams. *Journal of African
Civilizations*. 05: 47-49 (Apr-Nov 83)

Sisters And Brothers

See Brothers And Sisters

Skiis And Skiing

Black Skiers-Push Youths Toward '88 Winter
Olympics. Illustrated. D. Michael Cheers. *Jet*. 64:
46-48+ (18 Apr 83)

Skis And Skiing—Montana

Big Sky's The Limit. Illustrated. Pam Conklin.
Black Enterprise. 13: 46-48 (Jan 83)

Skowronski, JoAnn

Black Music In America: A Bibliography. Book
review. Dominique-Rene DeLerma. *Negro History
Bulletin*. 46: 85-86 (Jul-Sep 83)

Black Music In America: A Bibliography. Book
review. Lucius R. Wyatt. *The Black Perspective in
Music*. 11: 219-220 (Fall 83)

Slater, Jack

Natalie Cole. Illustrated. *Essence*. 14: 86-87+ (Oct
83)

Slater, Shirley

Traveling Light.. *Essence*. 14: 22-23 (Nov 83)

Slaughter, John B.

The Black American: A Vision For The Future
With Special Emphasis On Science.. *Negro History
Bulletin*. 46: 24-25 (Jan-Mar 83)

**Slavery In The United States—Anti-Slavery
Movements**

Abolitionism And Wooden Nutmegs: Repealing The
Gag Rule. Notes. Karen Williams Biestman. *Black
Law Journal*. 08: 408-416 (Winter 83)

See Also Abolitionists

**Slavery In The United States—Condition Of
Slaves**

Black Folks And Poor Buckras: Archeological
Evidence Of Slave And Overseer Living Conditions
On An Antebellum Plantation. Notes. John
Solomon Otto and Augustus Marion (III) Burns.
Journal of Black Studies. 14: 185-200 (Dec 83)

"We Slipped And Learned To Read:" Slave
Accounts Of The Literacy Process, 1830-1865.
Notes, tables. Janet Cornelius. *Phylon*. 44: 171-186
(Sep 83)

Slavery In The United States—Law

Black Americans vs. Citizenship: The Dred Scott
Decision. Gossie Harold Hudson. *Negro History
Bulletin*. 46: 26-28 (Jan-Mar 83)

Slaves

Chronicles Of Black Courage. Illustrated. Lerone
(Jr.) Bennett. *Ebony*. 38: 147-148+ (Oct 83)

Sleet, Moneta (Jr.) (joint author)

See Bailey, Peter
Moore, Trudy S.

Sly, Julie (joint author)

See Okihiro, Gary Y.

Smalls, Robert (about)

Chronicles Of Black Courage. Illustrated. Lerone
(Jr.) Bennett. *Ebony*. 38: 147-148+ (Oct 83)

Smallwood-Murchison Catherine (about)

Essence Women: Catherine Smallwood-Murchison.
Illustrated. Earl Anthony. *Essence*. 14: 62 (Oct 83)

Smart-Grosvenor, Vertamae

'When In Rome. . . ' Why Travel If You're Just
Going To Act Ugly?. *Essence*. 14: 46+ (Jun 83)

Smart, Ian I.

The Life And Poems Of A Cuban Slave: Juan
Francisco Manzano, 1797-1854. Book review.
Research in African Literatures. 14: 414-417 (Fall
83)

Smikle, Ken

Essence Women: Barbara Murray. Illustrated.
Essence. 14: 56 (Jun 83)

Essence Women: Diana Valdes Owens. Illustrated.
Essence. 13: 29-30 (Mar 83)

Essence Women: Sylvia H. Williams. Illustrated.
Essence. 14: 52 (Aug 83)

Smith, A. Wade

The N.A.A.C.P. Crusade Against Lynching,
1909-1950. Book review. *Phylon*. 44: 169 (Jun 83)

**Smith, Ada Beatrice Queen Victoria Louise
Virginia**

Bricktop. Excerpt. *Ebony*. 39: 59-60+ (Dec 83)

Bricktop. Excerpt. *Ebony*. 39: 59-60+ (Dec 83)

Smith, Archie (Jr.)

The Relational Self Ethics And Therapy From A
Black Church Perspective. Book review. John B.
Eubanks. *Journal of Religious Thought*. 40: 73-74
(Spring-Summer 83)

Smith, Barbara

But Some Of Us Are Brave. Book review.
Hortense D. Lloyd. *Negro Educational Review*. 34:
45-46 (Jan 83)

Ain't I A Woman: Black Women And Feminism.
Book review. *Black Scholar*. 14: 38-45 (Jan-Feb
83)

Homophobia: Why Bring It Up?. *Interracial Books
for Children*. 14: No. 3: 7-8 (83)

Smith, Damu

The U.S. Peace Movement And The Middle East.
Notes. *Freedomways*. 23: No. 2: 70-80 (83)

Smith, Earl (joint author)

See Green, Dan S.

Smith, Earl Belle

Synchronous Cancers Of The Gastrointestinal Tract: Results, Diagnosis, And Treatment. Tables, notes. *National Medical Association Journal.* 75: 311-313 (Mar 83)

Smith, Frederick, F.

Race Attacks On The Rise.. *Black Enterprise.* 13: 40 (Jun 83)

Smith, J. Clay (Jr.)

A Black Lawyer's Response To The Fairmont Papers. Notes. *Howard Law Journal.* 26: No. 1: 195-225 (83)

Louis Rothschild Mehlinger: The First One Hundred Years. Notes. *Howard Law Journal.* 26: No. 2: 359-441 (83)

The Marion County Lawyers CLub: 1932 And The Black Lawyer. Notes. *Black Law Journal.* 08: 170-176 (Fall 83)

The Role Of Primary And Secondary Teachers In The Motivation Of Black Youth To Become Lawyers. Notes. *Journal of Negro Education.* 52: 302-313 (Summer 83)

Smith, Joshua I. (about)

Maxima's 8a Dilemma. Illustrated. Harold J. Logan. *Black Enterprise.* 13: 42-45 (Jan 83)

Smith, Mary F.

Baba Of Karo: A Woman Of The Muslim Hausa. Book review. Margaret M. Knipp. *Research in African Literatures.* 14: 407-409 (Fall 83)

Smith, Mbembe Milton

The Black Messiah. Poem. *Black American Literature Forum.* 17: 151 (Winter 83)

The Broken Church Window. Poem. *Black American Literature Forum.* 17: 151 (Winter 83)

The Eyes Of The Ancestors. Poem. *Black American Literature Forum.* 17: 150 (Winter 83)

GIGO (Garbage In, Garbage Out). Poem. *Black American Literature Forum.* 17: 150 (Winter 83)

What I'm Talking About. Poem. *Black American Literature Forum.* 17: 151 (Winter 83)

Yourself Fulfilling History. Poem. *Black American Literature Forum.* 17: 151 (Winter 83)

Smith, Robert J.

Volvulus Of The Stomach. Illustrated, notes. *National Medical Association Journal.* 75: 393-397 (Apr 83)

Smitherman, Geneva

Language And Liberation. Notes. *Journal of Negro Education.* 52: 15-23 (Winter 83)

Snipes, Peedie (about)

Aging Disease Makes 6-Year-Old Boy Look Like 50. Illustrated. Trudy S. Moore and James Mitchell. *Jet.* 65: 22-26 (5 Dec 83)

Snorgrass, J. William

America's Ten Oldest Black Newspapers. Illustrated, notes. *Negro History Bulletin.* 46: 11-14 (Jan-Mar 83)

Sobo, Steven and others

Intrathoracic Thyroid. Illustrated, notes. *National Medical Association Journal.* 75: 522-524 (May 83)

Social Change

The Time Is Now. Editorial. *Freedomways.* 23: No. 01: 3-5 (83)

Social Classes

W. E. B. DuBois And The Concepts Of Race And Class. Notes. Dan S. Green and Earl Smith. *Phylon.* 44: 262-272 (Dec 83)

See Also Middle Classes

Social Policy—United States

An Act of War. William Clay. *about. . . time.* 11: 8 (May 83)

Social Role

See Also Sex Role

Social Security—United States

Blacks And Social Security Reform. Illustrated. Bebe Moore Campbell. *Black Enterprise.* 13: 25 (May 83)

Social Security Reform: What Has Been Accomplished? Barber A. (Jr.) Conable. *about. . . time.* 11: 22 (Apr 83)

Society And Literature

See Literature And Society

Society And Theater

See Theater And Society

Sociologists

Oliver C. Cox: A Biographical Sketch Of His Life And Work. Notes. Herbert M. Hunter. *Phylon.* 44: 249-261 (Dec 83)

On Reconsidering Park, Johnson, DuBois, Frazier And Reid: Reply To Benjamin Bowser's "The Contribution Of Blacks To Sociological Knowledge.". Notes. Jerry G. Watts. *Phylon.* 44: 273-291 (Dec 83)

Role Relations Of Black Sociologists With The Black Community: Perceptions Of Sociologists. Tables, notes. Arthur S. Evans. *Journal of Black Studies.* 13: 477-487 (Jun 83)

W. E. B. DuBois And The First Scientific Study Of Afro-America. Notes, tables. Werner J. Lange. *Phylon.* 44: 135-146 (Jun 83)

Sofola, J. A.

The Onyenualagu (Godparent) In Traditional And Modern African Communities: Implications For Juvenile Delinquency. Notes. *Journal of Black Studies.* 14: 21-30 (Sep 83)

Sola, Peter

Just Schools: The Ideal Of Racial Equality In American Education. Book review. *Journal of Negro Education.* 52: 457-459 (Fall 83)

Solet, Jan

Do You Work At A Job That Could Be Making You Sick?. *Essence*. 13: 58+ (Mar 83)

Sons And Fathers

See Fathers And Sons

Sons And Mothers

See Mothers And Sons

South Africa

See Also Boycott—South Africa
Massacres-South Africa
Middle Classes—South Africa
Sports And State—South Africa
Theater—South Africa
Visitors, Foreign—South Africa

South Africa—Foreign Economic Relations —United States

Potshots At Apartheid. Barbara A. Reynolds. *Essence*. 14: 58 (Jun 83)

South Africa And Its Firm Foundations. Reggie Major. *Black Scholar*. 14: 12-20 (Jan-Feb 83)

Southern African Issues In United States Courts. Notes. Goler Teal Butcher. *Howard Law Journal*. 26: No. 2: 601-643 (83)

Testimony Before The House Foreign Affairs Subcommittcs On Africa And International Economic Policy And Trade U.S. House Of Representatives. Notes. Goler Teal Butcher. *Howard Law Journal*. 26: No. 1: 153-193 (83)

South Africa—Foreign Relations—Namibia

No Progress On Namibia. Illustrated. Jeanne M. Woods. *Black Enterprise*. 14: 22 (Nov 83)

South Africa—Foreign Relations—United States

American Policy In Southern Africa. Illustrated. George W. (Jr.) Crockett. *Negro History Bulletin*. 46: 104-105 (Oct-Dec 83)

Apartheid's Ally: Reagan's Southern Africa Policy. Illustrated. Bebe Moore Campbell. *Black Enterprise*. 13: 29 (Apr 83)

South Africa—Politics And Government

The Road Ahead. . . South Africa Faces Bloody Future. Illustrated. Robert S. McNamara. *Crisis*. 90: 46-49 (Apr 83)

South Africa—Race Relations

Black South Africa: One Day Soon. Illustrated. Alexis DeVeaux. *Essence*. 14: 80-81+ (Jul 83)

The Impact Of Multinational Corporations On Power Relations In South Africa. Notes. Timothy Bates. *Review of Black Political Economy*. 12: 133-143 (Winter 83)

South Africans speak Out In America. Robert McNatt. *Black Enterprise*. 13: 54 (Apr 83)

South Africa—Race Relations—Foreign Opinion

The People Vs. Apartheid. Illustrated. Chuck Sutton and Frank Dexter Brown. *Black Enterprise*. 13: 15 (Jul 83)

States Versus Apartheid. Illustrated. Frank Dexter Brown. *Black Enterprise*. 13: 22 (Apr 83)

We Say "No" To Apartheid Sport. Illustrated. Richard Lapchick and Franklin H. Williams. *Crisis*. 90: 42-45 (Jan 83)

South African Literature—History And Criticism

The Motif Of The Ancestor In The Conservationist . Notes. Michael Thorpe. *Research in African Literatures*. 14: 184-192 (Summer 83)

South African Poets

See Poets, South African

South African Refugees

See Refugees, South African

South Central Legal Services Program, Los Angeles

South Central Legal Services Program. Elaine Mallette. *Black Law Journal*. 08: 147-149 (Spring 83)

Southern, Eileen

Biographical Dictionary Of Afro-American And African Musicians. Book review. Doris Evans McGinty. *The Black Perspective in Music*. 11: 79-82 (Spring 83)

Southern Negro Youth Congress

Louis Rothschild Mehlinger: The First One Hundred Years. Notes. J. Clay (Jr.) Smith. *Howard Law Journal*. 26: No. 2: 359-441 (83)

Southern States—History

Black Folks And Poor Buckras: Archeological Evidence Of Slave And Overseer Living Conditions On An Antebellum Plantation. Notes. John Solomon Otto and Augustus Marion (III) Burns. *Journal of Black Studies*. 14: 185-200 (Dec 83)

Sowell, Thomas (about)

Sowell's Knowledge And Decisions: Can Black Conservatism Establish Its Intellectual Credibility? Notes. Alex Willingham. *Review of Black Political Economy*. 12: 179-187 (Winter 83)

Markets And Minorities. Book review. Bernadette P. Chachere. *Review of Black Political Economy*. 12: 163-177 (Winter 83)

Soyinka, Wole

Aké: The Years Of Childhood. Book review. Carole Bovoso. *Essence*. 13: 20 (Mar 83)

Ake, The Years Of Childhood. Book review. James Gibbs. *Research in African Literatures*. 14: 98-102 (Spring 83)

Opera Wonyosi. Book review. A. Rasheed Yesufu. *Journal of Black Studies*. 13: 496-499 (Jun 83)

Soyinka, Wole—Criticism And Interpretation

"Leaders And Left-Overs": A Reading Of Soyinka's: Death And The King's Horseman. Notes. Mark Ralph-Bowman. *Research in African Literatures*. 14: 81-97 (Spring 83)

Metaphor As Basis Of Form In Soyinka's Drama. Notes. 'Ropo Sekoni. *Research in African Literatures*. 14: 45-57 (Spring 83)

A Nigerian Version Of A Greek Classic: Soyinka's Transformation Of The Bacchae. Notes. Norma Bishop. *Research in African Literatures*. 14: 68-80 (Spring 83)

Tear The Painted Masks; Join The Poison Stains: A Preliminary Study Of Wole Soyinka's Writings For The Nigerian Press. Notes. James Gibbs. *Research in African Literatures*. 14: 3-44 (Spring 83)

The Voice And Viewpoint Of The Poet In Wole Soyinka's "Four Archetypes". Notes. Tanure Ojaide. *Research in African Literatures*. 14: 58-67 (Spring 83)

Space Flight—Shuttle Missions

Ants In Space. Illustrated. *Ebony*. 38: 83-84 + (Sep 83)

Spady, James G.

Blackspace. Illustrated, notes. *Journal of African Civilizations*. 05: 258-265 (Apr-Nov 83)

Speaking

See Also Rhetoric

Special Education

See Exceptional Children—Education

Speculation

Wall Street's Biggest Gamblers. Illustrated. Roger Witherspoon. *Black Enterprise*. 14: 103-104 + (Dec 83)

Spencer, Ray

Art Tatum: A Guide To His Recorded Music. Book review. James Remel Burden. *The Black Perspective in Music*. 11: 86-88 (Spring 83)

Spiegel, Rotraut

Doris Lessing: The Problem Of Alienation And The Form Of The Novel. Book review. Roberta Rubenstein. *Research in African Literatures*. 14: 242-244 (Summer 83)

Spigner, Nieda

Honey, I Love. Book review. *Freedomways*. 23: No. 01: 55-56 (83)

Langston Hughes: Before And Beyond Harlem. Book review. *Freedomways*. 23: No. 4: 285-286 (83)

Spikes, Lerah A. (joint author)

See Spikes, W. Curtis

Spikes, W. Curtis and Spikes, Lerah A.

Development Of A College Curriculum To Enhance Essay Writing Skills At A Predominantly Black College. Notes, tables. *Journal of Negro Education*. 52: 110-117 (Spring 83)

Spine—Diseases—Diagnosis

The Radiographic Evaluation Of Infections Of The Spine. Illustrated, notes. Sharon E. Byrd and others. *National Medical Association Journal*. 75: 969-977 (Oct 83)

Spingarn Medalists, 1983

NAACP's Spingarn Medal To Lena Horne Climaxes 75th Annual Convention. Illustrated. *Jet*. 64: 12-14 (1 Aug 83)

Spingarn Medal Presentation To. . . Lena Horne-A Living Legend. Vernon E. (Jr.) Jordan. *Crisis*. 90: 36 (Aug-Sep 83)

Spingarn Medalist's Acceptance Recalls. . . A Measure Of What Has Gone Before. Illustrated. Lena Horne. *Crisis*. 90: 38-40 (Aug-Sep 83)

Spinks, Michael (about)

$4 Million Makes Foes Of Friends. Illustrated. Norman O. Unger. *Jet*. 63: 46-48 (14 Mar 83)

Spitzer, Carlton E.

Raising The Bottom Line: Business Leadership In A Changing Society. Book review. Elza Teresa Dinwiddie. *Black Enterprise*. 13: 30 (Jun 83)

Spivey, Donald

The Black Athlete In Big-Time Intercollegiate Sports, 1941-1968. Notes. *Phylon*. 44: 116-125 (Jun 83)

Sponsors

The Onyenualagu (Godparent) In Traditional And Modern African Communities: Implications For Juvenile Delinquency. Notes. J. A. Sofola. *Journal of Black Studies*. 14: 21-30 (Sep 83)

Sports

. . . Must Come Down. Illustrated. Roger Witherspoon. *Black Enterprise*. 13: 64-65 (Jul 83)

What A Racquet! Illustrated. Joyce White. *Black Enterprise*. 13: 274 + (Jun 83)

What Goes Up. . . . Illustrated. Janice L. Greene. *Black Enterprise*. 13: 64-65 (Jul 83)

See Also College Sports
Discrimination In Sports
Football
Golf
Olympic Games
Skiis And Skiing
Track-Athletics

Sports—Accidents And Injuries

Darryl Stingley: Happy To Be Alive. Illustrated. Darryl Stingley. *Ebony*. 38: 68 + (Oct 83)

Sports And State

Relections On Olympic Sportpolitics: History And Prospects, 1968-1984. Illustrated. Harry Edwards. *Crisis*. 90: 20-24 (May 83)

Sports And State—South Africa

We Say "No" To Apartheid Sport. Illustrated. Richard Lapchick and Franklin H. Williams. *Crisis*. 90: 42-45 (Jan 83)

Sports—Economic Aspects

The New Bidding Game In Sports. Illustrated. Nelson George. *Black Enterprise*. 13: 28-32 (Jan 83)

Scandal In The Sports Business. Illustrated. Earl G. Graves. *Black Enterprise*. 13: 7 (Jan 83)

Sports For Children

Keeping Your Child Afloat. Illustrated. Patrice Gaines-Carter. *Black Enterprise*. 13: 272 + (Jun 83)

Sports—Political Aspects

See Sports And State

Sports—Social Aspects

The Challenge To Black Supremacy In Sports. Illustrated. *Ebony*. 38: 49-50+ (Aug 83)

Spotts, Bethany L.

Essence Women: Carmen N'Namdi. Illustrated. *Essence*. 13: 22+ (Feb 83)

Stop The Banning Of Books. Illustrated. *Essence*. 13: 122 (Jan 83)

Super Interviewing Tips From A Corporate Recruiter. Illustrated. *Black Collegian*. 14: 92+ (Nov-Dec 83)

Spritzer, Lorrain Nelson

The Belle Of Ashby Street: Helen Douglas Mankin And Georgia Politics. Book review. Margaret L. Dwight. *Journal of Negro History*. 68: 102-104 (Winter 83)

Squash (Game)

What A Racquet! Illustrated. Joyce White. *Black Enterprise*. 13: 274+ (Jun 83)

Squire, Madelyn C.

Good Intentions Gone Wrong: 8(A)(3) Supreme Court And Circuit Round-Up/With A Look At Wright Line. Notes. *Howard Law Journal*. 26: No. 1: 9-52 (83)

St. Pierre Roger

The Illustrated Encyclopedia Of Black Music. Book review. Doris Evans McGinty. *The Black Perspective in Music*. 11: 212-214 (Fall 83)

Standards And Standardization In Education

See Education—Standards

Staples, Robert

Black Male Sexuality: Has It Changed? Illustrated. *Ebony*. 38: 104+ (Aug 83)

Stargell, Willie (about)

Willie Stargell: The Rare Combination Of Athlete And Humanitarian. Illustrated. Madeline Sulaiman. *about... time*. 11: 8-11 (Jan 83)

Starks, George L.

The Jazz Book: From Ragtime To Fusion And Beyond. Book review. *The Black Perspective in Music*. 11: 215-218 (Fall 83)

Jazz Piano: A Jazz History. Book review. *The Black Perspective in Music*. 11: 215-218 (Fall 83)

The Jazz Tradition. Book review. *The Black Perspective in Music*. 11: 215-218 (Fall 83)

Jelly Roll, Jabbo & Fats: 19 Portraits In Jazz. Book review. *The Black Perspective in Music*. 11: 215-218 (Fall 83)

The Literature Of Jazz: A Critical Guide. Book review. *The Black Perspective in Music*. 11: 215-218 (Fall 83)

Starvation

Fasting: The Myths And The Facts. Illustrated. Pamela Noel. *Ebony*. 38: 36+ (Jan 83)

State And Education

See Education And State

State And Industry

See Industry And State

State And Sports

See Sports And State

Steel Industry And Trade

The Threat To American Steel Independence. Norman Hill. *about... time*. 11: 11 (Aug 83)

Steele, Robert E. and Davis, Sherry E.

An Empirical And Theoretical Review Of Articles In The Journal Of Black Psychology: 1974-1980. Tables, notes. *Journal of Black Psychology*. 10: 29-42 (Aug 83)

Steen, Ivan D.

Education To What End? An Englishman Comments On The Plight Of Blacks In The "Free" States, 1830. Notes. *Afro-Americans in New York Life and History*. 07: 55-57 (Jan 83)

Stein, Ruthe

Making Sense Of Your Dreams. Illustrated. *Ebony*. 38: 51+ (Oct 83)

Steins, Martin

Brown France Vs. Black Africa: The Tide Turned In 1932. Notes. *Research in African Literatures*. 14: 474-497 (Winter 83)

Imaginaire, Langage-Identité Culturelle, Négritude. Book review. *Research in African Literatures*. 14: 553-554 (Winter 83)

Stephens, Alonzo T.

Ethnocultural Processes And National Problems In The Modern World. Book review. *Journal of Negro History*. 68: 128-129 (Winter 83)

Stereotype

The Ten Biggest Myths About Black Men. Illustrated. *Ebony*. 38: 96+ (Aug 83)

Stetson, Erlene

Black Feminism In Indiana, 1893-1933. Notes. *Phylon*. 44: 292-298 (Dec 83)

Stevens, Arena L.

Music, Printed And Manuscript, In The James Weldon Johnson Memorial Collection Of Negro Arts And Letters: An Annotated Catalog. Book review. *Journal of Negro History*. 68: 101-102 (Winter 83)

Stewart, James B.

Psychic Duality Of Afro-Americans In The Novels Of W. E. B. DuBois. Notes. *Phylon*. 44: 93-107 (Jun 83)

Stice, Carole F.

Reading, Dialect, And The Low-Achieving Black College Student. Notes. *Negro Educational Review*. 34: 84-87 (Apr 83)

Stingley, Darryl

Darryl Stingley: Happy To Be Alive. Illustrated. *Ebony*. 38: 68+ (Oct 83)

Stinnett, T. M.

America's Public Schools In Transition: Future Trends And Issues. Book review. Wilfred A. Johnson. *Journal of Negro Education*. 52: 459-461 (Fall 83)

Stinson, Patricia

Making The Right Moves.. *Black Enterprise*. 14: 55-56+ (Sep 83)

Stitt, Van J. (Jr.)

Root Doctors As Providers Of Primary Care. Notes. *National Medical Association Journal*. 75: 719-721 (Jul 83)

Stockard, Bessie

The Black Female Athlete - Past And Present. Illustrated. *Crisis*. 90: 16-18 (May 83)

Stokes, Louis (about)

The Election Of An Ohio Congressman. Notes. Philip A. (Jr.) Grant. *Negro History Bulletin*. 46: 60-62 (Apr-Jun 83)

Stomach—Cancer

Gastric Cancer In An Urban Hospital: A 25-Year Review. Notes. Patrick Kola Fadahunsi. *National Medical Association Journal*. 75: 623-625 (Jun 83)

Stomach—Diseases

Volvulus Of The Stomach. Illustrated, notes. Robert J. Smith. *National Medical Association Journal*. 75: 393-397 (Apr 83)

Stone, Elizabeth Walker

A Plan For The Special Preparation Of Attorneys In Effective Writing Skills. Notes. *Journal of Negro Education*. 52: 314-331 (Summer 83)

Story, Ralph

Paul Laurence Dunbar: Master Player In A Fixed Game. Notes. *CLA Journal*. 27: 30-55 (Sep 83)

Stovall, Joyce Moore

Pneumatosis Coli: A Case Presentation And Review Of The Literature. Illustrated, notes. *National Medical Association Journal*. 75: 626-629 (Jun 83)

Strayhorne, Pauline (about)

Pauline Strayhorne Is Major Federal's Prime Asset. Illustrated, tables. Sharron Kornegay. *Black Enterprise*. 13: 129-130+ (Jun 83)

Stress (Psychology)

How To Tame The Stress In Your Life. Wista Johnson. *Essence*. 13: 82-83 (Apr 83)

Stress And The Black Medical Family. Illustrated. Leonard E. Lawrence. *National Medical Association Journal*. 75: 749-753 (Aug 83)

Strict Liability

Strict Legal Liability, Upper Class Criminality, And The Model Penal Code. Notes. Walter Gordon. *Howard Law Journal*. 26: No. 2: 781-797 (83)

Stuckey, Elma

Reprobate. Poem. *Black American Literature Forum*. 17: 171 (Winter 83)

Student Aid

Going To College On Uncle Sam. Illustrated. Patrice Gaines-Carter. *Black Enterprise*. 13: 79-80+ (Feb 83)

Student National Medical Association

Strengthening Our Ties. Illustrated. Alexis A. Thompson. *National Medical Association Journal*. 75: 459-460 (May 83)

Student-Teacher Relationships

See Teacher-Student Relationships

Students

See Also Engineering Students
High School Students
Medical Students

Study, Method Of

Take Note! Stephanie Renfrow Hamilton. *Essence*. 14: 49 (Oct 83)

Styron, William—Criticism And Interpretation

Miltons's Choices: Styron's Use Of Robert Frost's Poetry In Lie Down In Darkness. Notes. Judith Ruderman. *CLA Journal*. 27: 141-151 (Dec 83)

Success

Aspire To Excellence: Don't Let Others Limit Your Ambition. Illustrated. Walter Cooper. *about. . . time*. 11: 4 (Jun 83)

Get Ready! Editorial. Susan L. Taylor. *Essence*. 14: 53 (Sep 83)

How You Can Get What You Want. Betty DeRamus. *Essence*. 13: 67+ (Jan 83)

Make It Happen! How To Put Action Behind Your Ideas. David J. Schwartz. *Essence*. 13: 93+ (Mar 83)

Strategy Sessions For Corporate Success. Illustrated. Jan Alexander. *Black Enterprise*. 14: 61-62+ (Aug 83)

Winning At Office Politics. Illustrated. Bea Keith. *Essence*. 14: 79-80+ (Sep 83)

See Also Academic Achievement

Suelzle, Marijean

The Anatomy Of Racial Attitudes. Book review. Keith A. Winsell. *Phylon*. 44: 246-248 (Sep 83)

Suicide

Why Are Blacks Less Suicide Prone Than Whites? Joseph Williams. *Crisis*. 90: 29 (Dec 83)

Sulaiman, Madeline

The Black Eagles: Story Of The Tuskegee Airmen. Illustrated. *about. . . time*. 11: 14-17 (Feb 83)

Community Action Works. Illustrated. *about. . . time*. 11: 14-19 (Jul 83)

Maximizing Youth: With A Canteen Full Of Skills, Plans, Aspirations And Hope. Illustrated. *about. . . time*. 11: 14-18 (Jun 83)

No More Tapioca. . . Please! Illustrated. *about. . . time.* 11: 8-9 (Apr 83)

Nurturing And Refining Communications Skills. Illustrated. *about. . . time.* 11: 10-12 (Apr 83)

An Open Letter To Mommie. Illustrated. *about. . . time.* 11: 22-23 (May 83)

Pack Your Parachute Carefully (Collect Skills And Contacts While Employed). Illustrated. *about. . . time.* 11: 18-20 (Mar 83)

When All Else Fails. . . Substitute!. *about. . . time.* 11: 22-23 (Mar 83)

Willie Stargell: The Rare Combination Of Athlete And Humanitarian. Illustrated. *about. . . time.* 11: 8-11 (Jan 83)

Sullivan, Harold J.

Formula For Failure: A Critique Of The Intent Requirement In School Segregation Litigation. Notes. *Journal of Negro Education.* 52: 270-289 (Summer 83)

Sullivan, Leon H.

"Dreams Of The Future". Illustrated. *Negro History Bulletin.* 46: 6-8 (Jan-Mar 83)

Sullivan, Louis W. (about)

Sullivan Inaugurated As First President Of Morehouse School Of Medicine. Illustrated. Virgie S. Heffernan. *National Medical Association Journal.* 75: 826+ (Aug 83)

The Morehouse School Of Medicine: A State Of Mind, Of Mission, And Of Commitment.. *National Medical Association Journal.* 75: 837-839 (Aug 83)

Sullivan, Otha Richard

Careers In Oceanography. Illustrated. *Black Collegian.* 14: 123-125+ (Sep-Oct 83)

Sulzer, Peter

Preisgedichte Und Verse Aus Südwestafrika-Namibia. Book review. Dieter Riemenschneider. *Research in African Literatures.* 14: 412-413 (Fall 83)

Sumler-Lewis, Janice

The Free Black In Urban America: 1800-1850. Book review. *Black Law Journal.* 08: 162-163 (Spring 83)

Summer Employment

Summer Job Opportunities For Engineering Students. Illustrated. Kuumba Na Kazi. *Black Collegian.* 13: 85-88 (Dec-Jan 83)

Summer Homes

Tips On Renting A Vacation Home. Evalyn Kaufman. *Black Enterprise.* 13: 236 (Jun 83)

Summers, Gerrie E.

Patrice Rushen. Illustrated. *Essence.* 13: 15 (Feb 83)

Sundquist, Eric J.

Faulkner: The House Divided. Book review. Elizabeth J. Higgens. *CLA Journal.* 27: 97-101 (Sep 83)

Superintendents, School

See School Superintendents And Principals

Supply And Demand

Supply-Side Economics: The Rise To Prominence. Notes. Ronald Johnson. *Review of Black Political Economy.* 12: 189-202 (Winter 83)

Supreme Courts

See Also United States. Supreme Court

Surgeons

See Also Women Surgeons

Sutton, Chuck

Blacks Fight TV Censoring. Illustrated. *Black Enterprise.* 13: 25-26 (Mar 83)

Sutton, Chuck and Brown, Frank Dexter

The People Vs. Apartheid. Illustrated. *Black Enterprise.* 13: 15 (Jul 83)

Sutton, Isaac (joint author)

See Collier, Aldore
Johnson, Robert E.

Swan, Robert J.

Did Brooklyn (N.Y.) Blacks Have Unusual Control Over Their Schools? Period I: 1815-1845. Notes. *Afro-Americans in New York Life and History.* 07: 25-46 (Jul 83)

Sweezer, William P. (Jr.) and others

Clinical Experience With Carotid Stump Pressure And EEG Monitoring To Determine Shunt Placement During Carotid Endarterectomy. Tables, notes. *National Medical Association Journal.* 75: 583-587 (Jun 83)

Swimsuits

See Bathing Suits

Swinton, David H.

Orthodox And Systemic Explanations For Unemployment And Racial Inequality: Implications For Policy. Notes. *Review of Black Political Economy.* 12: 9-25 (Spring 83)

Sydnor, Norris W. (Jr.) (about)

Sydnor To Serve As U.S. Ambassador To Mauritius. Illustrated. *Jet.* 63: 4 (7 Mar 83)

Symbolism In Literature

Flying As Symbol And Legend In Toni Morrison's The Bluest Eye, Sula, And Song Of Solomon. Notes. Grace Ann Hovet and Barbara Loansberry. *CLA Journal.* 27: 119-140 (Dec 83)

No Longer At Ease: Chinua Achebe's "Heart Of Whiteness". Notes. Philip Rogers. *Research in African Literatures.* 14: 165-183 (Summer 83)

Syracuse University

Black Alumni Return To Foster Racial Liberation Of Syracuse University. Illustrated. *Jet.* 65: 6-7 (24 Oct 83)

T'Shaka, Oba Simba

Make The Past Serve The Present: Strategies For Black Liberation. Notes. *Black Scholar*. 14: 21-37 (Jan-Feb 83)

Taliaferro, Beverley Seawright

Celebrating Kwanza: One Family's Story. Illustrated. *Essence*. 14: 103+ (Dec 83)

Tamarkin, Civia

Marva Collins' Way. Book review. Carole Bovoso. *Essence*. 13: 19 (Jan 83)

Tanzania

See Also Cancer—Tanzania
      Medical Care—Tanzania

Tanzanian Epic Poetry

See Epic Poetry, Tanzanian

Taste Of Honey (Singing Group)

Taste Of Honey Sees Success In The New Year. Illustrated. Aldore D. Collier. *Jet*. 63: 60-62 (3 Jan 83)

Tate, Charles E.

Technology As A Means Of Promoting Black Development.. *The Urban League Review*. 08: 9-13 (Winter 83)

Tate, Claudia

Black Women Writers At Work. Book review. Carole E. Gregory. *Freedomways*. 23: No. 4: 287-289 (83)

Tate, Claudia and others

In Their Own Write. Illustrated. *Essence*. 14: 24+ (Oct 83)

Tax Auditing

Surviving A Tax Audit. Illustrated. Udayan Gupta. *Black Enterprise*. 14: 29 (Sep 83)

Tax Planning

Countdown To Tax Time. Flora Johnson. *Black Enterprise*. 14: 67-68+ (Nov 83)

Individual Retirement Accounts: Everyman's Tax Shelter. Tables. Udayan Gupta. *Black Enterprise*. 13: 22 (Jan 83)

Last-Minute Tax Saving. Julianne Malveaux. *Essence*. 14: 28-29 (Dec 83)

Taxation

Proposition 13 And 1/2 (A No-Taxation Fantasy). William Clay. *about. . . time*. 11: 37 (Nov 83)

Taxation, Exemption From

See Also Church Property—Taxation

Taxation—United States

Income And Taxes. Illustrated. Andrew F. Brimmer. *Black Enterprise*. 14: 43-44 (Dec 83)

Taxoplasmosis, Ocular

Congenital Ocular Toxoplasmosis. Illustrated, notes. Dwight D. Perry and John C. Merritt. *National Medical Association Journal*. 75: 169-174 (Feb 83)

Taylor, Billy

Jazz Piano: A Jazz History. Book review. George L. Starks. *The Black Perspective in Music*. 11: 215-218 (Fall 83)

Taylor, Clyde

Black Films In Search Of A Home. Notes. *Freedomways*. 23: No. 4: 226-233 (83)

Taylor, Edward F.

Le Harlem De Chester Himes. Book review. *CLA Journal*. 27: 224-225 (Dec 83)

Taylor, Estelle W.

This Was Harlem: A Cultural Portrait, 1900-1950. Book review. *Journal of Negro Education*. 52: 178-182 (Spring 83)

Taylor, Henry and Dozier, Carol

Television Violence, African-Americans, And Social Control 1950-1976. Tables, notes. *Journal of Black Studies*. 14: 107-136 (Dec 83)

Taylor, Howard F.

The IQ Game: A Methodological Inquiry Into The Heredity-Environment Controversy. Book review. Sandra E. Taylor. *Phylon*. 44: 244-245 (Sep 83)

Taylor, LeBaron

Music Business Myths-And Truths. Illustrated. *Crisis*. 90: 33-35 (Nov 83)

Taylor, Orlando L. and others

A Survey OF Bidialectal Language Arts Programs In The United States. Notes, tables. *Journal of Negro Education*. 52: 35-45 (Winter 83)

Taylor, Pamela A.

Neighborhoods Reach For The Stars. Illustrated, notes. *The Urban League Review*. 08: 77-81 (Winter 83)

Taylor, Peggy

A Letter To Mama. Illustrated. *Essence*. 14: 38+ (Dec 83)

Taylor, Sandra E.

The IQ Game: A Methodological Inquiry Into The Heredity-Environment Controversy. Book review. *Phylon*. 44: 244-245 (Sep 83)

Taylor, Susan L.

About Men. Editorial. *Essence*. 14: 51 (Nov 83)

Acknowledge Your Truth. Editorial. *Essence*. 14: 77 (Oct 83)

Get Ready! Editorial. *Essence*. 14: 53 (Sep 83)

Getting Confident. Editorial. *Essence*. 14: 61 (Aug 83)

Insist On Being You! Editorial. *Essence*. 14: 69 (Jul 83)

Making Love Work. Editorial. *Essence*. 13: 59 (Feb 83)

Money Power! Editorial. *Essence*. 14: 71 (Jun 83)

Moving Your Life Forward. Editorial. *Essence*. 13: 57 (Jan 83)

Reach For It! Editorial. *Essence*. 13: 65 (Mar 83)

There Is A Way! Editorial. *Essence*. 13: 71 (Apr 83)

You've Got The Power! Editorial. *Essence*. 14: 65 (May 83)

You've Got To Believe. Editorial. *Essence*. 14: 67 (Dec 83)

Taylor, Susie King (about)

From Slavery To Achievement: Keep On A Goin'. Illustrated. Robert L. (Jr.) Harris. *Black Collegian*. 13: 142-147 (Feb-Mar 83)

Teacher-Student Realtionships

The Role Of Primary And Secondary Teachers In The Motivation Of Black Youth To Become Lawyers. Notes. J. Clay (Jr.) Smith. *Journal of Negro Education*. 52: 302-313 (Summer 83)

Teachers

See Also Educators

Teachers Of Exceptional Children, Training Of

Affective Attributes Of Special Education And Regular Class Preprofessionals. Notes. Wilfred A. Johnson and Brenda A. Caple. *Negro Educational Review*. 34: 73-78 (Apr 83)

Teachers Of Handicapped Children, Training Of —Ghana

A Comparison Of Personnel Training Needs And Program Priorities For The Disabled In Ghana And Nigeria. Notes, tables. Sylvia Walker. *Journal of Negro Education*. 52: 162-169 (Spring 83)

Teachers Of Handicapped Children, Training Of —Nigeria

A Comparison Of Personnel Training Needs And Program Priorities For The Disabled In Ghana And Nigeria. Notes, tables. Sylvia Walker. *Journal of Negro Education*. 52: 162-169 (Spring 83)

Teaching—Data Processing

See Computer-Assisted Instruction

Teague, Bob

Live And Off-Color: News Biz. Book review. Gerald C. Horne. *Freedomways*. 23: No. 01: 51-54 (83)

Technology

Coming To Terms With The Information Age: A Glossary. Notes. *The Urban League Review*. 08: 107-119 (Winter 83)

The Information Revolution: A Declaration For Survival. John P. (Jr.) Imlay. *The Urban League Review*. 08: 82-87 (Winter 83)

Perils Of Black Postal Workers In A Technological Age: Some Strategies For Survival. Tables, notes. Lenneal J. Henderson and Charles Murphy. *The Urban League Review*. 07: 33-43 (Summer 83)

Technology As A Means Of Promoting Black Development. Charles E. Tate. *The Urban League Review*. 08: 9-13 (Winter 83)

Trends In High Technology. James Borders. *Black Collegian*. 14: 100-104+ (Sep-Oct 83)

What Effects Will Computer Technology Have On You? Bill Pitts. *The Urban League Review*. 08: 68-76 (Winter 83)

Technology—Social Aspects

The Information Age: Promise Or Nightmare? Editorial. Kujaatele Kweli. *The Urban League Review*. 08: 5-8 (Winter 83)

Teen-Age Mothers

See Adolescent Mothers

Teeth—Care And Hygiene

Keeping A Winning Smile. Illustrated. Sandra Gregg. *Black Enterprise*. 13: 82 (Mar 83)

Telecommunication

Neighborhoods Reach For The Stars. Illustrated, notes. Pamela A. Taylor. *The Urban League Review*. 08: 77-81 (Winter 83)

Selected Funding Sources For Telecommunications Projects. Notes. *The Urban League Review*. 08: 120-123 (Winter 83)

Telecommunication Systems

Understanding Telecommunications Systems. Notes. Early D. Monroe. *The Urban League Review*. 08: 95-106 (Winter 83)

Telephone Systems

Are Discount Long-Distance Services All They're Wired Up To Be? Illustrated. Vanessa Gallman. *Essence*. 14: 120 (May 83)

Pick The Right Telephone Service For Your Personal Needs. Illustrated, tables. Sandra Jackson-Opoku. *Black Enterprise*. 14: 56-58 (Aug 83)

Television

See Also Cable Television
Violence In Television

Television And Community Development

Satellite Teleconferencing: A New Tool For Community And Economic Development. Illustrated, notes. Kujaatele Kweli and Marc L. Randolph. *The Urban League Review*. 08: 40-54 (Winter 83)

Television And Youth

Nurturing And Refining Communications Skills. Illustrated. Madeline Sulaiman. *about. . . time*. 11: 10-12 (Apr 83)

TV And The Black Child: What Black Children Say About The Shows They Watch. Notes, tables. William H. (Jr.) Anderson and BIshetta Merritt Williams. *Journal of Black Psychology*. 09: 27-42 (Feb 83)

Television Broadcasting Of News

No More Tapioca. . . Please! Illustrated. Madeline Sulaiman. *about. . . time*. 11: 8-9 (Apr 83)

Television In Education

The Use Of Two-Way Television To Solve Problems Of Inequality In Education: A Comment. Notes, tables. Lawrence N. Redd. *Journal of Negro Education*. 52: 446-453 (Fall 83)

Television—Law And Legislation

Now You See It, Now You Don't: Federal Policy And Minority Ownership In The Video Industry. Notes. Allen S. (IV) Hammond. *The Urban League Review*. 08: 26-39 (Winter 83)

Television Producers And Directors

Essence Women: Barbara Murray. Illustrated. Ken Smikle. *Essence*. 14: 56 (Jun 83)

Lights! Camera! Action! Illustrated. S. Lee Hilliard and Nelson George. *Black Enterprise*. 14: 48-50+ (Dec 83)

Television Programs

Black History Month Specials. Illustrated. Mary Aladj. *about. . . time*. 11: 22-23 (Feb 83)

Blacks Fight TV Censoring. Illustrated. Chuck Sutton. *Black Enterprise*. 13: 25-26 (Mar 83)

Celebrate 10th Season Of 'The Jeffersons'. Illustrated. Aldore D. Collier. *Jet*. 65: 58-61 (3 Oct 83)

The Ebony/Jet Celebrity Showcase. Illustrated. *Ebony*. 38: 150-151+ (May 83)

Howard Rollins, Irene Cara Star In Medgar Evers Story On TV. Illustrated. Harmon Perry. *Jet*. 64: 62-65 (28 Mar 83)

Michael Jackson Discusses Career On Ebony/Jet Television Show. Illustrated. *Jet*. 64: 60-63 (25 Apr 83)

Moving Right Along. Illustrated. *Crisis*. 90: 27-30 (Oct 83)

TV's New Season: What's Ahead For Blacks? Illustrated. Aldore Collier. *Ebony*. 38: 58+ (Oct 83)

Temporary Employment

Working Temp: Temporary Jobs Now Offer Full-Time Benefits And Other Options. Illustrated. Vanessa J. Gallman. *Essence*. 14: 36 (Jun 83)

Tenant And Landlord

See Landlord And Tenant

Tennessee

See Also Education, Higher—Tennessee—History Legislators—United States—Tennessee

Tennis Players

See Also Women Tennis Players

Tennyson, Alfred Tennyson (1809-1892) —Criticism And Interpretation

New Light On Tennyson's Blackness. Notes. Robert F. Fleissner. *CLA Journal*. 26: 334-340 (Mar 83)

Terrell, Mary Church (1863-1954)

The Justice Of Woman Suffrage [September, 1912].. *Crisis*. 90: 6 (Jun-Jul 83)

Terrorist Bombings

See Bombings—Texas—Dallas

Tests And Measurements In Education

See Educational Tests And Measurements

Texas

See Also Text-Books—Texas

Text-Book Bias

U.S. History Texts: Any Change In Ten Years? Illustrated, notes. Sharon Wigutoff and Iris Santos-Rivera. *Interracial Books for Children*. 14: No. 1: 17-20 (83)

Text-Books

Basal Readers: Paltry Progress Pervades. Tables, notes. Gwyneth Britton and Margaret Lumpkin. *Interracial Books for Children*. 14: No. 6: 4-7 (83)

Text-Books—Texas

The Textbook Selection Process In Texas. Illustrated. *Interracial Books for Children*. 14: No. 5: 14-20 (83)

Theater

A Look At. . . The Contemporary Black Theatre Movement. Illustrated. A. Peter Bailey. *Crisis*. 90: 22-25 (Feb 83)

A Look At The Contemporary Black Theatre Movement. Notes. A. Peter Bailey. *Black American Literature Forum*. 17: 19-21 (Spring 83)

See Also Drama

Theater—Africa

Traditional African Theatre. Ethel Pitts Walker. *Black American Literature Forum*. 17: 14 (Spring 83)

Theater And Society

Theatre And The Afro-American Rite Of Being. Notes. George Houston Bass. *Black American Literature Forum*. 17: 60-64 (Summer 83)

Theater Audiences

AUDELCO, An Organization Of Theatre True Believers. Illustrated. A. Peter Bailey. *Black Collegian*. 13: 140 (Feb-Mar 83)

The First Ten Years Of AUDELCO. Vivian Robinson. *Black American Literature Forum*. 17: 79-81 (Summer 83)

Theater—Directories

Black Theaters And Theater Organizations In America, 1961-1982: A Research List. Andrzej Ceynowa. *Black American Literature Forum*. 17: 84-93 (Summer 83)

Theater—Finance

Risky Business Of Broadway. Illustrated. Robert McNatt. *Black Enterprise*. 14: 69-70+ (Dec 83)

See Also Federal Aid To The Theater

Theater For The Deaf

See Deaf, Theater For

Theater—Indexes

An Index Of Proper Nouns For "The Place Of The Negro In The Evolution Of The American THeatre, 1767 To 1940," A Dissertation By Fannin Saffore Belcher, Jr. (Yale University, 1945). Neil Conboy and James V. Hatch. *Black American Literature Forum*. 17: 38-47 (Spring 83)

Theater—Mississippi

The Free Southern Theatre, 1963-1979. Notes. Genevieve Fabre. *Black American Literature Forum*. 17: 55-59 (Summer 83)

Theater—New York (State)—New York (City)

The Magic Of Technical Theatre. Illustrated. A. Peter Bailey. *Black Collegian*. 14: 75+ (Sep-Oct 83)

Rituals At The New Lafayette Theatre. Notes. Anthony D. Hill. *Black American Literature Forum*. 17: 31-35 (Spring 83)

Rosetta LeNoire: The Lady And Her Theatre. Notes. Linda Kerr Norflett. *Black American Literature Forum*. 17: 69-72 (Summer 83)

Theater—New York (State)—Rochester

Black Theatre In Rochester-A Coming Of Age. Illustrated. Bruce Jacobs. *about. . . time*. 11: 20-23 (Jun 83)

Theater—South Africa

Black Theater In South Africa (Links With The United States Of America?). Notes. Cedric Callaghan. *Black American Literature Forum*. 17: 82-83 (Summer 83)

Theater—Washington, D.C.

A Slender Thread Of Hope: The Kennedy Center Black Theatre Project. Notes. Winona L. Fletcher. *Black American Literature Forum*. 17: 65-68 (Summer 83)

Witnesses To A Possibility: The Black Theater Movement In Wasington, D. C., 1968-1976. Illustrated, notes. Taquiena Boston and Vera J. Katz. *Black American Literature Forum*. 17: 22-26 (Spring 83)

Theaters—New York (State)—New York (City)

Stars To Shine At The Apollo. Illustrated. Ken Jones. *Black Enterprise*. 14: 18 (Sep 83)

Theatrical Producers And Directors

Risky Business Of Broadway. Illustrated. Robert McNatt. *Black Enterprise*. 14: 69-70+ (Dec 83)

Thelwell, Michael

A Candidate Of Our Own.. *Essence*. 14: 144 (Nov 83)

Thelwell, Raphael

An Assessment Of Minority Income Differences And Governmental Policies. Notes. *Black Law Journal*. 08: 387-398 (Winter 83)

Theology Of Liberation

See Liberation Theology

Theology—Philosophy

See Christianity—Philosophy

Theses

See Dissertations, Academic

Third World

See Underdeveloped Areas

Thomas, Alfred Jack (1884-1962) (about)

In Retrospect: Alfred Jack Thomas: Performer, Composer, Educator. Notes. James Nathan Jones. *The Black Perspective in Music*. 11: 62-75 (Spring 83)

Thomas, Arthur E. (cited)

Black College Leaders Tackle Issues At First PUSH/EXCEL Conference. Illustrated, first facts. *Jet*. 63: 40-41 (24 Jan 83)

Thomas, Clarence (about)

"We Are Going To Enforce The Law.". Illustrated. Chester A. (Sr.) Higgins. *Crisis*. 90: 50-52+ (Feb 83)

The Challenge For Black Students: Confronting New Forms Of Discrimination. Illustrated. *Black Collegian*. 13: 44-46+ (Feb-Mar 83)

Thomas, Doris Mossie (1917-1983) (about)

In Memoriam: Doris Mossie Thomas. Bethel Dukes. *Journal of Negro History*. 68: 144-145 (Winter 83)

Thomas, Franklin (about)

Essense Man: Franklin Thomas. Illustrated. Eric Copage. *Essence*. 14: 40 (Nov 83)

Thomas, Gail E.

Black Students In Higher Education: Conditions And Experiences In The 1970's. Book review. Vanneise A. Collins. *Afro-Americans in New York Life and History*. 07: 70-71 (Jan 83)

Thomas, John and others

Precursors Of Hypertension: A Review. Notes. *National Medical Association Journal*. 75: 359-369 (Apr 83)

Thomas, John Charles (about)

First Black Appointed To Virginia Supreme Court. First facts. *Jet*. 64: 30 (2 May 83)

Thomas, Joyce Carol

Marked By Fire. Book review. Geraldine L. Wilson. *Freedomways*. 23: No. 4: 289-290 (83)

I Know A Lady (For My Aunt Corine Coffey). Poem. *Essence*. 14: 131 (Jul 83)

Thompsom, Robert Farris

Flash Of The Spirit: African And Afro-American Art And Philosophy. Book review. Beth Brown. *CLA Journal*. 27: 230-234 (Dec 83)

Thompson, Alexis A.

Strengthening Our Ties. Illustrated. *National Medical Association Journal*. 75: 459-460 (May 83)

Thompson, Edward (III)

Race And The 1983 Chicago Election. Illustrated. *Crisis*. 90: 14-15 (Oct 83)

Thompson, Garland

The Nuclear Controversy: The Black Point Of View. Illustrated. *Black Enterprise*. 13: 215-216+ (Jun 83)

Thompson, Irwin E. (joint author)

See Grimes, Elwyn M.

Gene Upshaw: Gridders Union's New Boss. Illustrated. *Ebony.* 39: 76+ (Dec 83)

Trade-Unions—Political Activity

Black Trade Unionists' Forum Presents Outstanding Experts. Illustrated. *Crisis.* 90: 26 (Oct 83)

Trade-Unions—United States—Afro-American Membership

Evolution Of Black Political Influence In American Trade Unions. Notes. Philip W. Nyden. *Journal of Black Studies.* 13: 379-398 (Jun 83)

Tran, Ruc Manh (joint author)

See Madison, L. Keith

Transplantation Of Organs, Tissues, Etc.

Human Histocompatibility Antigens And Organ Transplantation. Notes. Arthur T. Davidson. *National Medical Association Journal.* 75: 526-527+ (May 83)

Travel

Avoid Foreign Faux Pas. Illustrated. Sandra Jackson-Opoku. *Black Enterprise.* 13: 241-245 (Jun 83)

Barbados Happenings. Illustrated. *Essence.* 13: 118-119+ (Apr 83)

Bay Area: California Dreamin'. Illustrated. Gerri Lange. *Essence.* 14: 38+ (May 83)

Bermuda: More Than A Honeymoon Haven. Illustrated. Ben F. Carruthers. *Black Enterprise.* 14: 72-73 (Sep 83)

Carnival In Trinidad And Tobago. Illustrated. Misani Gayle. *Black Enterprise.* 13: 78 (Mar 83)

Cruising Into The Sun. Illustrated. Ben F. Carruthers. *Black Enterprise.* 14: 119 (Dec 83)

Dominica: A Lush And Inviting Wilderness. Illustrated. Emile Milne. *Black Enterprise.* 13: 68+ (May 83)

Follow The Sun For Vacation Fun. Illustrated. *Ebony.* 38: 120+ (Jan 83)

How To Make Traveling For Business A Breeze. Sandra Jackson-Opoku. *Essence.* 13: 42+ (Mar 83)

How Travel Agents Can Smooth Out Your Trip. Estelle Whiting. *Essence.* 13: 38+ (Jan 83)

Life On The Nile: One Woman's Travels Through Egypt-Land Of The Pharaohs. Illustrated. Kathleen Wyer Lane. *Essence.* 14: 38+ (Jul 83)

Maui: A Hawaiian Adventure. Roger Witherspoon. *Black Enterprise.* 14: 153 (Oct 83)

New Orleans: Rich In Tradition. Illustrated. Phil W. Petrie. *Essence.* 14: 46+ (Dec 83)

Off-season Bargains; On-season Fun. Illustrated. Marcia Wallace. *Black Enterprise.* 13: 82+ (May 83)

Puerto Rico's Cerromar Beach. Illustrated. Felipe Luciano. *Black Enterprise.* 13: 67 (May 83)

Settings Sights For India. Illustrated. Mira Nair. *Essence.* 14: 22+ (Sep 83)

Summer Vacation: Border Base Will Give You Chance To Spend Some Time 'Abroad'. Illustrated. *Ebony.* 38: 157-158+ (May 83)

A Tale Of Three Islands. Illustrated. Sandra Jackson-Opoku. *Essence.* 13: 41-42+ (Apr 83)

Three Isles Of Diversity. Illustrated. Sandra Jackson-Opoku. *Essence.* 14: 38+ (Oct 83)

Touring Kenya's Fabulous Coast. Illustrated. Joan Harris. *Black Enterprise.* 13: 80 (Apr 83)

A Train Trip Through History. Illustrated. Omonike Weusi-Puryear. *Essence.* 14: 41-42+ (Aug 83)

Traveling Light. Shirley Slater. *Essence.* 14: 22-23 (Nov 83)

The Unexpected Pleasures Of A Quiet Island. Illustrated. Frank Dexter Brown. *Black Enterprise.* 13: 66+ (May 83)

Weekend Getaways For You And Your Man. Illustrated. Stephanie Bialick. *Essence.* 13: 36+ (Feb 83)

Travel Etiquette

'When In Rome. . . ' Why Travel If You're Just Going To Act Ugly? Vertamae Smart-Grosvenor. *Essence.* 14: 46+ (Jun 83)

Travel—Hygienic Aspects

Good Health Guide For Travelers. Illustrated. Evalyn Kaufman. *Black Enterprise.* 13: 80 (Mar 83)

Trefousse, Hans L.

Carl Schurz: A Biography. Book review. Daniel C. Vogt. *Journal of Negro History.* 68: 124-125 (Winter 83)

Trengove, Chris

The Illustrated Encyclopedia Of Black Music. Book review. Doris Evans McGinty. *The Black Perspective in Music.* 11: 212-214 (Fall 83)

Trenz, Günter

Die Funktion Englischsprachiger Westafrikanischer Literatur: Eine Studie Zur Gesellschaftlichen Bedeutung Des Romans In Nigeria. Book review. Eckhard Breitinger. *Research in African Literatures.* 14: 212-215 (Summer 83)

Trichinosis

Growth Of Trichinella Spiralis Larvae In Rats Receiving Folic-Acid-Deficient Diet. Tables, notes. Mohamed A. Elhelu and others. *National Medical Association Journal.* 75: 501-502 (May 83)

Immunobiology Of Trichinosis. Notes. Clarence M. Lee and Yvette Best. *National Medical Association Journal.* 75: 565-570 (Jun 83)

Trinidad And Tobago

See Also Cults—Trinidad And Tobago

Trinidad And Tobago—Carnival

Carnival In Trinidad And Tobago. Illustrated. Misani Gayle. *Black Enterprise.* 13: 78 (Mar 83)

Trinidad And Tobago—Description And Travel

Carnival In Trinidad And Tobago. Illustrated. Misani Gayle. *Black Enterprise.* 13: 78 (Mar 83)

Truth, Sojourner (1797-1883) (about)

Two Suffrage Movements [September, 1912]. Tables. Martha Gruening. *Crisis*. 90: 6-8 (Jun-Jul 83)

Tsukashima, Ronald Tadao

Chronological, Cognitive And Political Effects In The Study Of Interminority Group Prejudice. Notes, tables. *Phylon*. 44: 217-231 (Sep 83)

Tuberculosis

Therapy Of Tuberculosis. Tables, notes. Earl M. Armstrong. *National Medical Association Journal*. 75: 714-716+ (Jul 83)

Tucker, Barbara E.

Why You Should Buckle Up Baby. Illustrated. *Essence*. 14: 120+ (Jul 83)

Tucker, M. Belinda (joint author)

See Mitchell-Kernan, Claudia

Tucker, Martin

Kipling And Conrad: The Colonial Fiction. Book review. *Research in African Literatures*. 14: 228-232 (Summer 83)

Turner, Darwin T.

The Art Of Slave Narrative: Original Essays In Criticism And Theory. Book review. Henry-Louis (Jr.) Gates. *Black American Literature Forum*. 17: 131-134 (Fall 83)

Turner, Gladys

Papa Babe's Stamp Collection. Book review. Nancy L. Arnez. *Crisis*. 90: 50 (Aug-Sep 83)

Turner, William H.

Blacks In Appalachian America: Reflections On Biracial Education And Unionism. Notes. *Phylon*. 44: 198-208 (Sep 83)

Tuskegee Institute—History

Chronicles Of Black Courage (Part IV). Illustrated. Lerone (Jr.) Bennett. *Ebony*. 38: 131-134 (Sep 83)

Twins

Black Twins Search And Find Their White Mother After 34 Years. Illustrated. Clarence Waldron. *Jet*. 64: 24-30 (6 Jun 83)

New Jersey Mother Gives Birth To Third Set Of Twins In 10 Years. Illustrated. Clarence Waldron. *Jet*. 65: 38-40 (31 Oct 83)

Twins Find Mother After 34 Years. Illustrated. Clarence Waldron. *Ebony*. 38: 95-96+ (Sep 83)

World's Most Unusual Twins: One Is Black, The Other Is White. Illustrated. D. Michael Cheers. *Jet*. 65: 21-24 (12 Dec 83)

U.N.C.F.

See United Negro College Fund

U.N.I.A.

See United Negro Improvement Association

U.S.F.L.

See United States Football League

Underdeveloped Areas

The Role Of The Non-Aligned Movement For Peace And Life.. *Black Scholar*. 14: 58-59 (Nov-Dec 83)

See Also Administrative Law—Underdeveloped Areas

Underdeveloped Areas—Foreign Economic Conditions

Nuclear Policy, Social Justice, And The Third World. Tables. Robert Chrisman. *Black Scholar*. 14: 26-43 (Nov-Dec 83)

Unemployed

Avoiding After-College Panic. Curtia James. *Essence*. 14: 20+ (Aug 83)

Boycotting For Jobs. Illustrated. David J. Dent. *Black Enterprise*. 13: 28 (Mar 83)

Bracing For Hard Times. Illustrated. Thad Martin. *Ebony*. 38: 78+ (Aug 83)

Economic Recovery And Black Employment. Illustrated. Bernard E. Anderson. *Black Enterprise*. 13: 29 (Jul 83)

In Pursuit Of Affirmative Action. Robert L. White. *The Urban League Review*. 07: 6-7 (Summer 83)

Joblessness In Detroit Is "Devastating". Illustrated. Kevin Moss. *Crisis*. 90: 14 (Apr 83)

No Prospects For Work. Illustrated. Lloyd Gite. *Black Enterprise*. 14: 17 (Aug 83)

Pack Your Parachute Carefully (Collect Skills And Contacts While Employed). Illustrated. Madeline Sulaiman. *about. . . time*. 11: 18-20 (Mar 83)

The Shame Of Unemployment? Illustrated. William Clay. *about. . . time*. 11: 8 (Mar 83)

The Unemployed Tell What Should Be Done About Their Plight. Illustrated. D. Michael Cheers and Clarence Waldron. *Jet*. 63: 12-15 (07 Feb 83)

Unemployment: How To Bounce Back. Rosemary L. Bray. *Essence*. 14: 121-122+ (Jun 83)

Unemployment Is Not Leisure. Martha Falconer-Blake. *Crisis*. 90: 41 (Jan 83)

Victims Of Unemployment: Coping With Stress. Illustrated. Willis Anderson. *about. . . time*. 11: 10-13+ (Mar 83)

See Also Full Employment Policies—United States

Unemployment

See Also Labor Supply

Unger, Norman O.

Football's Controversial Multimillion Dollar Man. Illustrated. *Jet*. 64: 46-48+ (4 Apr 83)

Reggie Jackson Admits Second Love Is For His 50 Cars. Illustrated. *Jet*. 63: 46-49 (17 Jan 83)

Sugar Ray Leonard Replaces Boxing With Family, TV Show And New $2 Million Home. Illustrated. *Jet*. 65: 20-23 (14 Nov 83)

$4 Million Makes Foes Of Friends. Illustrated. *Jet*. 63: 46-48 (14 Mar 83)

United Mine Workers—History

Blacks In Appalachian America: Reflections On Biracial Education And Unionism. Notes. William H. Turner. *Phylon*. 44: 198-208 (Sep 83)

United Nations

The Role Of The United Nations For Peace And Disarmament.. *Black Scholar*. 14: 50-52 (Nov-Dec 83)

United Negro College Fund

Educator Benjamin E. Mays, Publisher John H. Johnson Honored At UNCF Dinner. Illustrated. *Jet*. 65: 13-14 (31 Oct 83)

UNCF Schools In Crisis. David J. Dent. *Black Enterprise*. 13: 20 (May 83)

UNCF Starts D.C. Drive For $9.9 Million, R.J. Reynolds Makes Gift Of $1 Million. Illustrated. *Jet*. 64: 14-16 (11 Jul 83)

United Negro Improvement Association

Henrietta Vinton Davis And The Garvey Movement. Notes. William Seraile. *Afro-Americans in New York Life and History*. 07: 7-24 (Jul 83)

United States

See Also Administrative Law—United States
   Budget—United States
   Due Process Of Law—United States
   Emigration And Immigration—United States
   Evidence (Law)—United States
   Full Employment Policies—United States
   Income—United States
   Legislators—United States
   Medical Care—United States
   Middle Classes—United States
   Money Supply—United States

United States. Air Force—History

The Black Eagles: Story Of The Tuskegee Airmen. Illustrated. Madeline Sulaiman. *about. . . time*. 11: 14-17 (Feb 83)

United States. Air Force—Officers

Air Force Graduates First Black Woman Pilot. Illustrated, first facts. *Ebony*. 38: 46 + (Jan 83)

United States—Air National Guard

Air Guard Appoints First Black General. Illustrated, first facts. *Jet*. 63: 53 (24 Jan 83)

United States—Armed Forces

Going To College On Uncle Sam. Illustrated. Patrice Gaines-Carter. *Black Enterprise*. 13: 79-80 + (Feb 83)

United States—Civil Rights Commission

Packing Of Rights Body Reagan's "Most Severe Attack". Charles E. Cobb. *Crisis*. 90: 5 (Oct 83)

United States. Coast Guard Academy

Women Cadets Make Coast Guard History. Illustrated, first facts. Marilyn Marshall. *Ebony*. 38: 138 + (Apr 83)

United States. Congress—Freedom Of Debate

Abolitionism And Wooden Nutmegs: Repealing The Gag Rule. Notes. Karen Williams Biestman. *Black Law Journal*. 08: 408-416 (Winter 83)

United States. Constitution—Amendments

What The ERA Means To Us. Illustrated. Carmen Carter. *Essence*. 13: 1154 (Mar 83)

United States. Constitution. 1st-10th Amendments

The Black Muslim Movement And The American Constitutional System. Tables, notes. Oliver (Jr.) Jones. *Journal of Black Studies*. 13: 417-437 (Jun 83)

United States. Constitution—13th Amendment

Exclusion Zoning - City Of Memphis V. Greene. Notes. Julie E. Hall. *Black Law Journal*. 08: 138-143 (Spring 83)

United States. Department Of Defense

Bombs Or Bread: Black Unemployment And The Pentagon Budget. Tables. Marion Anderson. *Black Scholar*. 14: 2-11 (Jan-Feb 83)

United States. Department Of Education

An Interview With The Secretary Of Education: Terrell Bell. Interview, Illustrated. Terrel Bell and Hughes Jones. *Black Collegian*. 13: 51-53 (Apr-May 83)

United States. Department Of Housing And Urban Development

Sam Pierce Hangs Tough. Illustrated. *Black Enterprise*. 13: 43 (Mar 83)

United States. Department Of Justice

Civil Rights Enforcement Activity Of The Department Of Justice. Notes. Jack Greenberg. *Black Law Journal*. 08: 60-67 (Spring 83)

Without Justice. NotesLeadership Conference On Civil Rights. *Black Law Journal*. 08: 24-59 (Spring 83)

United States—Economic Conditions

Black Economic Plight - A Look Into The Past Forecasts Challenge To The Present. Illustrated. William C. (Jr.) Matney. *Crisis*. 90: 6-7 (Dec 83)

Black/White Equality: The Socioeconomic Conditions Of Blacks In America, Part II. Notes. Sidney M. Willhelm. *Journal of Black Studies*. 14: 151-184 (Dec 83)

The Economic Outlook For Blacks In 1983. Illustrated. Andrew F. Brimmer. *Black Enterprise*. 13: 37 (Feb 83)

Economics, Politics, And Blacks. Notes. Glenn C. Loury. *Review of Black Political Economy*. 12: 43-54 (Spring 83)

Twentieth Anniversary Mobilization Jobs, Peace, And Freedom. Illustrated. Benjamin L. Hooks. *Crisis*. 90: 22-23 (Oct 83)

United States—Economic Policy

An Assessment Of Minority Income Differences And Governmental Policies. Notes. Raphael Thelwell. *Black Law Journal*. 08: 387-398 (Winter 83)

United States—Equal Employment Opportunity Commission

Civil Rights Challenges For The 1980's. Illustrated. Paul A. Fisher and Ralph G. Neas. *about. . . time.* 11: 10-13+ (May 83)

"We Are Going To Enforce The Law.". Illustrated. Chester A. (Sr.) Higgins. *Crisis.* 90: 50-52+ (Feb 83)

United States—Federal Bureau Of Investigation

FBI Liable In Freedom Rider Attack. Illustrated. *Jet.* 64: 7 (20 Jun 83)

The FBI's Top-Ranking Black. Illustrated. *Ebony.* 38: 108+ (Apr 83)

United States Football League

The USFL: A Whole New Ball Game. Illustrated. *Ebony.* 38: 33-34+ (Jun 83)

United States—Foreign Economic Relations —South Africa

Potshots At Apartheid. Barbara A. Reynolds. *Essence.* 14: 58 (Jun 83)

South Africa And Its Firm Foundations. Reggie Major. *Black Scholar.* 14: 12-20 (Jan-Feb 83)

Southern African Issues In United States Courts. Notes. Goler Teal Butcher. *Howard Law Journal.* 26: No. 2: 601-643 (83)

Testimony Before The House Foreign Affairs Subcommitties On Africa And International Economic Policy And Trade U.S. House Of Representatives. Notes. Goler Teal Butcher. *Howard Law Journal.* 26: No. 1: 153-193 (83)

United States—Foreign Relations

Black Folks And Foreign Policy. Illustrated. June Jordan. *Essence.* 14: 162 (Jun 83)

Reagan Foreign Policy: War On The Doorstep? Illustrated. George W. (Jr.) Crockett. *Crisis.* 90: 48-49 (Dec 83)

The Silence Is Broken. Editorial. J. H. O'Dell. *Freedomways.* 23: No. 2: 66-69 (83)

United States—Foreign Relations—Israel

America In The Wrong. Gus Savage. *Freedomways.* 23: No. 3: 171-175 (83)

An Open Letter On The Middle East. George W. (Jr.) Crockett. *Freedomways.* 23: No. 3: 176-178 (83)

United States—Foreign Relations—Latin America

Opening Speech In The Meeting Of Intellectuals For The Sovereignty Of The Peoples Of Our America. Armando Hart. *Black Scholar.* 14: 2-12 (Summer 83)

United States—Foreign Relations—Middle East

An Afro-American Perspective On The Middle East. Bibliography. Angela M. Gilliam. *Freedomways.* 23: No. 2: 81-89 (83)

The U.S. Peace Movement And The Middle East. Notes. Damu Smith. *Freedomways.* 23: No. 2: 70-80 (83)

United States—Foreign Relations—Nicaragua

The War Of Terror Against Nicaragua. Illustrated. Hector Frances. *Black Scholar.* 14: 2-16 (Mar-Apr 83)

United States—Foreign Relations—South Africa

American Policy In Southern Africa. Illustrated. George W. (Jr.) Crockett. *Negro History Bulletin.* 46: 104-105 (Oct-Dec 83)

Apartheid's Ally: Reagan's Southern Africa Policy. Illustrated. Bebe Moore Campbell. *Black Enterprise.* 13: 29 (Apr 83)

United States—Full Employment Policies

Perspectives On Unemployment And Policy. Notes. Nancy S. Barrett. *Review of Black Political Economy.* 12: 55-61 (Spring 83)

United States—History

The Pride And Passion - Introduction To Black History. Illustrated. Graham Berry. *Negro History Bulletin.* 46: 47-50 (Apr-Jun 83)

United States—History—Revolution, 1775-1783 —Polish Participation

Tadeusz Kosciuszko And The Black Connection. E. P. Kulawiec. *Negro History Bulletin.* 46: 46 (Apr-Jun 83)

United States. Military Academy

A Family Affair At West Point. Illustrated. Pamela Noel. *Ebony.* 39: 45-46+ (Nov 83)

United States. National Aeronautics And Space Administration

Careers Behind The Launchpad. Illustrated. *Black Enterprise.* 13: 59-60+ (Feb 83)

United States—National Foundation On The Arts And The Humanities

The National Endowment For The Humanities: A Selected Bibliography For Two Years Of Funded Projects On The Black Experience 1977-1978. Notes. M. Sammye Miller. *Journal of Negro History.* 68: 59-79 (Winter 83)

United States—National Institute On Aging

Aging Research, Black Americans, And The National Institute On Aging. Daniel D. Cowell. *National Medical Association Journal.* 75: 99+ (Jan 83)

United States. Navy

The Navy's Black Professionals: In Fields From Nuclear Propulsion To Computerized Electronics. Illustrated. Mike McGougan. *about. . . time.* 11: 18-20 (Feb 83)

United States—Officials And Employees

Armstrong Gets Personnel Position At White House.. *Jet.* 64: 6 (5 Sep 83)

Bradley Gets Upgraded Position On Reagan Staff. Illustrated. *Jet.* 63: 4 (21 Feb 83)

Food Stamp Administrator Named Aide To Head Of Department Of Agriculture. First facts, Illustrated. *Jet.* 63: 4 (7 Feb 83)

Sam Pierce Hangs Tough. Illustrated. *Black Enterprise.* 13: 43 (Mar 83)

United States—Politics And Government

Jesse Jackson Begins Run For U.S. President. Illustrated. *Jet*. 65: 14-16 (21 Nov 83)

United States—Race Relations

"Dreams Of The Future". Illustrated. Leon H. Sullivan. *Negro History Bulletin*. 46: 6-8 (Jan-Mar 83)

The Lincoln Day Call February 12, 1909.. *Crisis*. 90: 5 (Feb 83)

United States—Social Conditions

Black/White Equality: The Socioeconomic Conditions Of Blacks In America, Part II. Notes. Sidney M. Willhelm. *Journal of Black Studies*. 14: 151-184 (Dec 83)

United States—Social Policy

Black Americans In Reagan's America. Notes. John E. Jacob. *Black Law Journal*. 08: 417-426 (Winter 83)

Federalism, "Civil Rights" And Black Progress. Notes. Ronald W. Walters. *Black Law Journal*. 08: 220-234 (Fall 83)

The New Federalism And The Unfinished Civil Rights Agenda. Notes. Marguerite Ross Barnett. *Black Law Journal*. 08: 375-386 (Winter 83)

United States. Supreme Court

Black And The Supreme Court. Diane Camper. *Black Enterprise*. 13: 48 (Mar 83)

Foreword [To Volume 8 Number 3]. Reginald H. (Jr.) Alleyne. *Black Law Journal*. 08: 370-372 (Winter 83)

Supreme Court Challenge: Laying Off Affirmative Action. Illustrated. Bebe Moore Campbell. *Black Enterprise*. 13: 31 (Feb 83)

United States. Supreme Court—Decisions

Black Americans vs. Citizenship: The Dred Scott Decision. Gossie Harold Hudson. *Negro History Bulletin*. 46: 26-28 (Jan-Mar 83)

Supreme Court Rules: Coleman Wins Case To Deny Biased School Tax Exemptions. Illustrated. *Jet*. 64: 21-22 (13 Jun 83)

United Steelworkers Of America

Evolution Of Black Political Influence In American Trade Unions. Notes. Philip W. Nyden. *Journal of Black Studies*. 13: 379-398 (Jun 83)

Universal Life Insurance Co.

A Family Affair: Patricia Shaw Succeeds Father As President Of Universal Life. Illustrated. Lynn Norment. *Ebony*. 38: 75-76+ (May 83)

New President At Universal. Illustrated. Fatima Shaik. *Black Enterprise*. 13: 36 (Jun 83)

Universities And Colleges

Baccalaureate College Of Origin Of Black Doctorate Recipients. Notes, tables. William F. Brazziel. *Journal of Negro Education*. 52: 102-109 (Spring 83)

The Black College Initiative: A Conversation With Elizabeth Dole. Interview, Illustrated. Elizabeth Dole and William Rouselle. *Black Collegian*. 14: 44-46 (Nov-Dec 83)

Can Black Public Colleges Be Saved? Illustrated. Thad Martin. *Ebony*. 38: 130+ (Feb 83)

Private Back Colleges: Struggle Against The Odds. Illustrated. Thad Martin. *Ebony*. 38: 84+ (Oct 83)

The Role Of The Historic Black Colleges In The Training Of Black Professionals. Notes. Arthur T. Davidson. *National Medical Association Journal*. 75: 1019-1022 (Oct 83)

The Struggle To Save A Black School: An Interview With Central State President Newsom. Interview, Illustrated. Lionel Newsom and William Rouselle. *Black Collegian*. 13: 38+ (Apr-May 83)

See Also Education, Higher
Medical Colleges

Universities And Colleges—Administration

See Also College Presidents

Universities And Colleges—Admission

Affirmative Action In Higher Education: Is It Necessary? Notes, tables. Rodney J. Reed. *Journal of Negro Education*. 52: 332-349 (Summer 83)

Universities And Colleges—Curricula

Development Of A College Curriculum To Enhance Essay Writing Skills At A Predominantly Black College. Notes, tables. W. Curtis Spikes and Lerah A. Spikes. *Journal of Negro Education*. 52: 110-117 (Spring 83)

Universities And Colleges—Employees

A Streak Of Ebony In The Ivory Tower. Illustrated. Sheila Sinclair. *Black Enterprise*. 13: 84-86+ (Feb 83)

Universities And Colleges—Finance

UNCF Schools In Crisis. David J. Dent. *Black Enterprise*. 13: 20 (May 83)

Universities And Colleges—Graduate Work

Graduate School: Minority Admissions Recruitment Network: Taking Care Of Business. Norm Campbell and others. *Black Collegian*. 14: 128-131 (Nov-Dec 83)

How To Get Into Grad School And Survive. Illustrated. Marilyn Kern-Foxworth. *Black Collegian*. 14: 110+ (Nov-Dec 83)

Universities And Colleges—Selection

See College, Choice Of

University Students

See College Students

Upshaw, Gene (about)

Gene Upshaw: Gridders Union's New Boss. Illustrated. *Ebony*. 39: 76+ (Dec 83)

Urban Churches

See City Churches

Urban Economics

The Fate Of America's Cities. James M. Blount. *about. . . time*. 11: 4 (Jul 83)

Urban Life

See City And Town Life

Urology

Urological Emergency Admissions To A Community Hospital: A Review. Tables, notes. Sam O. Atkins. *National Medical Association Journal*. 75: 557-559 (Jun 83)

Uzzell, Odell

Black Decision Makers: An Exploratory Study In Role Perception And Role Performances. Tables, notes. *Journal of Black Studies*. 14: 83-98 (Sep 83)

Vacations

Camping. Illustrated. Catherine Kerr. *Black Enterprise*. 13: 260-262 (Jun 83)

Van Der Zee, James (about)

A Great Artist Passes. Illustrated. C. Gerald Fraser. *Black Enterprise*. 14: 22 (Aug 83)

Van Hartesveldt, Fred R.

Race And Political Parties In Britain, 1954-1965. Notes. *Phylon*. 44: 126-134 (Jun 83)

Van Pham, Cao and others

Low-Dose Procainamide: Low Risk Of Complications With Long-Term Use. Tables, notes. *National Medical Association Journal*. 75: 705-708 (Jul 83)

Van Sertima, Ivan

The Lost Sciences Of Africa: An Overview.. *Journal of African Civilizations*. 05: 7-26 (Apr-Nov 83)

See Graves, Curtis M.
Quarterman, Lloyd

Vanbrugh, John—Criticism And Interpretation

Comic Irony In Vanbrugh's The Relapse: Worthy's Repentance. Notes. James S. Malek. *CLA Journal*. 26: 353-361 (Mar 83)

Vanity 6 (Singing Group)

Vanity 6 Lives Out Daring Fantasies On Stage. Illustrated. *Jet*. 63: 58-62 (24 Jan 83)

Vaughn-Cooke, Denys

Blacks In Labor Markets: A Historical Assessment. Notes. *The Urban League Review*. 07: 8-18 (Summer 83)

Vegetables

See Also Cookery (Vegetables)

Vegetarianism

Eating Less Meat? Know Your Nutrients. Lucinda Moore. *Essence*. 14: 144+ (Oct 83)

Vei (African Tribe)

The Conceptual Nature Of Music Among The Vai Of Liberia. Illustrated, notes. Lester P. Monts. *The Black Perspective in Music*. 11: 143-156 (Fall 83)

Vena, John E.

Lung Cancer Incidence Among Nonwhites In Erie County, New York. Notes, tables. *National Medical Association Journal*. 75: 1229-1231 (Dec 83)

Verly, Gerard P. (joint author)

See Lim, Sook K.

Verma, Pritam S. (joint author)

See Miller, Russell L.

Victims Of Crimes

Where There's A Will. . . This Woman Should Not Be Alive: The Miracle Of Merri Dee. Illustrated. Roger Witherspoon. *Essence*. 13: 72-74+ (Apr 83)

Vietnamese War, 1957-1975

A Percussion of Finality: Vietnam Flashback. Illustrated. Phillip L. Woodall. *about. . . time*. 11: 28-32 (Nov 83)

Villarosa, Linda

Body Alive: Getting Stronger With Weights. Illustrated. *Essence*. 14: 120 (Aug 83)

Hypertension: Controlling It May Save Your Life.. *Essence*. 14: 30+ (Sep 83)

Violence

The Malady Of Violent Crime. Illustrated. Earl G. Graves. *Black Enterprise*. 13: 11 (Apr 83)

Race Attacks On The Rise. Frederick F. Smith. *Black Enterprise*. 13: 40 (Jun 83)

Violence In Television

Television Violence, African-Americans, And Social Control 1950-1976. Tables, notes. Henry Taylor and Carol Dozier. *Journal of Black Studies*. 14: 107-136 (Dec 83)

Violent Deaths

Black Doctor Killed Under "Suspicious Circumstances". Illustrated. *Crisis*. 90: 23 (Apr 83)

See Also Murder
Suicide

Virgin Islands

See British Virgin Islands

Virginia

See Also Judges—Virginia
Public Schools—Finance—Virginia
School Integration—Virginia

Visitors, Foreign—South Africa

My South African Odyssey. Illustrated. William A. Brown. *The Black Perspective in Music*. 11: 3-21 (Spring 83)

Vocational Guidance

From Part Time To Full Time. Illustrated. Sandra Roberts. *Black Enterprise*. 13: 61-62 (Jul 83)

Keys To The Future. Illustrated. Harriet Jackson Scarupa and Marcia McNair. *Essence*. 14: 46 (Oct 83)

Outlook For Liberal Arts Majors. Illustrated. Yvette Franklin and William Rouselle. *Black Collegian.* 13: 20-22 (Dec-Jan 83)

Planning A Successful Career: Taking It One Step At A Time. Illustrated. Monica C. Jones. *Black Collegian.* 14: 78-80 (Sep-Oct 83)

Vocational Interests

The Role Of Primary And Secondary Teachers In The Motivation Of Black Youth To Become Lawyers. Notes. J. Clay (Jr.) Smith. *Journal of Negro Education.* 52: 302-313 (Summer 83)

Vogt, Daniel C.

Carl Schurz: A Biography. Book review. *Journal of Negro History.* 68: 124-125 (Winter 83)

Voodooism

Root Doctors As Providers Of Primary Care. Notes. Van J. (Jr.) Stitt. *National Medical Association Journal.* 75: 719-721 (Jul 83)

Voters, Registration Of

Essence Man: Joe Madison. Illustrated. Lloyd Gite. *Essence.* 14: 38 (Nov 83)

"God Will Not Do For Us What We Can Do For Ourselves. . . ''. Benjamin L. Hooks. *Crisis.* 90: 4 (Nov 83)

Jesse Jackson Goes South With Crusade To Register Voters. Illustrated. Charles Sanders. *Jet.* 64: 6-8 + (13 Jun 83)

NBA To Boost Voting Ranks. Janice Green. *Black Enterprise.* 14: 24 (Dec 83)

The Overground Railroad. Illustrated. Chauncey Bailey. *Crisis.* 90: 6-9 + (Nov 83)

Voters, Registration Of—Illinois—Chicago

Give The Man A Hand. Illustrated. Ruth Dolores Manuel. *Essence.* 14: 54 (Jul 83)

Voting

Attorneys Aim For Greater Black Voter Participation In '80s. Illustrated. *Jet.* 64: 17-18 (9 May 83)

The 1984 Elections: A Checklist For Black Voters. Norman Hill. *Crisis.* 90: 31-32 (Nov 83)

Voting—Alabama—Birmingham

The Impact Of Black Political Participation On Public Sector Employment And Representation On Municipal Boards And Commissions. Notes, tables. Huey L. Perry. *Review of Black Political Economy.* 12: 203-217 (Winter 83)

Voting Rights Act Of 1965

How Ronald Reagan, Henry Hyde, And William French Smith Became Voting Rights Heroes: Political Actors And The Press Fool The Public. Michael Goldstein. *CAAS Newsletter.* 07: 1 + (May 83)

Voting Rights: The Symbol And The Substance. Bebe Moore Campbell. *Black Enterprise.* 14: 25 (Sep 83)

Voting—United States

Beyond The Ballot Box. Illustrated. Bebe Moore Campbell and Elliott D. Lee. *Black Enterprise.* 13: 40-42 + (Mar 83)

Wachsman, Laura and Singleton, Alice Faye

Assessing The Quality Of Care Provided To Pediatric Patients By Emergency Room Physicians. Tables, notes. *National Medical Association Journal.* 75: 31-35 (Jan 83)

Wade, Carlson

Body Alive.. *Essence.* 13: 132 + (Apr 83)

Wade, Robert E. (joint author)

See Randolph, Marc L.

Wages

Bargaining: For What You're Worth. Illustrated. Janice L. Greene. *Black Enterprise.* 13: 47-49 (May 83)

How To Get Paid What You're Worth. Illustrated. Shirley Sloan Fader. *Essence.* 14: 81 + (Jun 83)

Wakefield, J. Alvin

Black Life In Corporate America: Swimming In The Mainstream. Book review. *The Urban League Review.* 07: 113 115 (Summer 83)

Walcott, Derek

Love After Love. Poem. *Essence.* 14: 137 (Aug 83)

Walden, Oscar (Jr.) (about)

Preacher Wages 30-Year Fight To Clear Name Of Rape Charge Against Him. Illustrated. D. Michael Cheers. *Jet.* 63: 14-16 (7 Mar 83)

Waldron, Clarence and Mitchell, James

Adopted Dwarf, 10, Has Happy Childhood With A Dwarf Father And An Average-Sized Mother. Illustrated. *Jet.* 65: 20-24 (12 Sep 83)

Black Twins Search And Find Their White Mother After 34 Years. Illustrated. *Jet.* 64: 24-30 (6 Jun 83)

Body Buried For Six Years Unearthed, Skull Removed; Suspect Cult Ritualists. Illustrated. *Jet.* 64: 28-31 (11 Jul 83)

Dorothy Donegan: Bouncy As Ever At Age 61. Illustrated. *Ebony.* 39: 87-88 + (Dec 83)

Eddie Murphy: Hot Comic Sizzles In '48 Hrs.' Film. Illustrated. *Jet.* 63: 28-31 (14 Feb 83)

Guy Bluford: Black Astronaut Makes First Space Mission. First facts, illustrated. *Jet.* 64: 20-22 + (5 Sep 83)

Jazz Great Ella Fitzgerald Performs In-Flight Concert. Illustrated. *Jet.* 63: 62 + (31 Jan 83)

Kennedy Leads Democrats To Back Washington As Mayor Byrne Quits Race. Illustrated. *Jet.* 64: 6-8 (11 Apr 83)

New Jersey Mother Gives Birth To Third Set Of Twins In 10 Years. Illustrated. *Jet.* 65: 38-40 (31 Oct 83)

Twins Find Mother After 34 Years. Illustrated. *Ebony*. 38: 95-96+ (Sep 83)

Cheers, D. Michael

Walker, Alice (about)

Author Alice Walker Wins Pulitzer Prize For Novel. First facts, Illustrated. *Jet*. 64: 9 (9 May 83)

The Color Purple. Book review. Dorothy Randall-Tsuruta. *Black Scholar*. 14: 54-55 (Summer 83)

The Color Purple. Book review, Illustrated. Chester A. (Sr.) Higgins. *Crisis*. 90: 49 (Jun-Jul 83)

The Color Purple. Book review. Maryemma Graham. *Freedomways*. 23: No. 4: 278-280 (83)

The Color Purple: A Moral Tale. Book review. Ernece B. Kelley. *CLA Journal*. 27: 91-96 (Sep 83)

'But Yet And Still The Cotton Gin Kept On Working. . .'.. *Black Scholar*. 14: 13-17 (Sep-Oct 83)

New Face. Poem. *Essence*. 14: 122 (Nov 83)

Walker, Annette

Grenada's Women Move Forward With The Revolution.. *Freedomways*. 23: No. 01: 23-28 (83)

Walker, Cheryl Lynn

Am I My Brother's Keeper? Editorial. *National Medical Association Journal*. 75: 867-868 (Sep 83)

Walker, Ethel Pitts

Traditional African Theatre.. *Black American Literature Forum*. 17: 14 (Spring 83)

Walker, Herschel (about)

Football's Controversial Multimillion Dollar Man. Illustrated. Norman O. Unger. *Jet*. 64: 46-48+ (4 Apr 83)

Running For The Money. Illustrated. Roger Witherspoon. *Black Enterprise*. 13: 18 (May 83)

Walker, Madame C. J.

See Walker, Sarah McWilliams (1837-1919)

Walker, Mark and Hall, Macy (Jr.)

Necrotizing Fasciitis: The Howard University Hospital Experience. Tables, illustrated, notes. *National Medical Association Journal*. 75: 159-163 (Feb 83)

Walker, S. Jay

Frederick Douglass And Woman Suffrage. Notes. *Black Scholar*. 14: 18-25 (Sep-Oct 83)

Walker, Sarah McWilliams (1867-1919) (about)

The Fortune That Madame Built. Illustrated. Jill Nelson. *Essence*. 14: 84-86+ (Jun 83)

Walker, Solomon W. (II) (about)

Pilgrim's Progress. Illustrated, tables. Linda Horton. *Black Enterprise*. 13: 145-146+ (Jun 83)

Walker, Sylvia

A Comparison Of Personnel Training Needs And Program Priorities For The Disabled In Ghana And Nigeria. Notes, tables. *Journal of Negro Education*. 52: 162-169 (Spring 83)

Walker, Wyatt Tee

Liberation Theology And The Middle East Conflict.. *Freedomways*. 23: No. 3: 147-152 (83)

Walking

Body Alive. Carlson Wade. *Essence*. 13: 132+ (Apr 83)

Wallace, George C. and Sanders, Charles L.

Has Gov. George Wallace Really Changed? Interview, Illustrated. *Ebony*. 38: 44-46+ (Sep 83)

Wallace, Marcia

Dining Caribbean: From Callaloo Soup To Coconut Bread. Illustrated. *Black Enterprise*. 13: 70+ (May 83)

Off-season Bargains; On-season Fun. Illustrated. *Black Enterprise*. 13: 82+ (May 83)

Wallace, Michele

Ed Bradley At Ease. Illustrated. *Essence*. 14: 66-67 (Nov 83)

The Envelope. Short story, Illustrated. *Essence*. 14: 93-94 (Aug 83)

Iman! Illustrated. *Essence*. 14: 64-65+ (Sep 83)

Nona! Illustrated. *Essence*. 14: 78-79 (Jul 83)

Shari And Harry. Illustrated. *Essence*. 14: 82-83 (Aug 83)

The Story Teller. Short story, Illustrated. *Essence*. 14: 72-74+ (Dec 83)

Wallace, Phyllis A.

Seniority And Layoffs: A Dilemma In The Workplace.. *Black Enterprise*. 14: 37-38 (Nov 83)

Walter, John C.

Frank R. Crosswaith And Labor Unionization In Harlem, 1939 - 1945. Notes. *Afro-Americans in New York Life and History*. 07: 47-58 (Jul 83)

Walter, Mildred Pitts

My Mama Needs Me. Book review. Geraldine L. Wilson. *Interracial Books for Children*. 14: No. 5: 26-27 (83)

Walters, Ronald W.

Federalism, "Civil Rights" And Black Progress. Notes. *Black Law Journal*. 08: 220-234 (Fall 83)

Walton, Hanes (Jr.) and others

Henry Highland Garnet Revisited Via His Diplomatic Correspondence: The Correction Of Misconceptions And Errors. Notes. *Journal of Negro History*. 68: 80-92 (Winter 83)

Walton, Richard and Wilson, Robin

"Rocky" Simmons: A Bedrock Of Community Involvement. Illustrated. *about. . . time*. 11: 24-25 (Oct 83)

Wanakee (about)

Wanakee. Illustrated. Paula S. White. *Essence*. 14: 62 (Dec 83)

War

The Danger Of War And The Problems Of The
Middle East, Asia, Africa And Latin America..
Black Scholar. 14: 59-64 (Nov-Dec 83)

Ward, Benjamin (about)

Veteran New York Cop Is Named City's First
Black Commissioner Of Police. First facts,
illustrated. *Jet*. 65: 12 (28 Nov 83)

Ward, Jerry W. (Jr.)

Fathers. Poem. *Freedomways*. 23: No. 4: 256-257
(83)

Meditation 83/US. Poem. *Freedomways*. 23: No. 4:
257 (83)

Wardlaw, Larry (about)

Fueling His Way To The Top. Illustrated. Sondra
Liburd-Jordan. *Black Enterprise*. 13: 169-170 +
(Jun 83)

Wardoco, Inc.

Fueling His Way To The Top. Illustrated. Sondra
Liburd-Jordan. *Black Enterprise*. 13: 169-170 +
(Jun 83)

Ware, Gilbert

Hocutt: Genesis Of Brown. Notes. *Journal of
Negro Education*. 52: 227-233 (Summer 83)

Warner, Keith Q.

Kaiso! The Trinidad Calypso. Book review. Wilson
Harris. *Research in African Literatures*. 14:
417-421 (Fall 83)

African Literature In French: A History Of Creative
Writing In French From West And Equatorial
Africa. Book review. *Research in African
Literatures*. 14: 202-203 (Summer 83)

Les Négres: A Look At Genet's Excursion Into
Black Consciousnes. Notes. *CLA Journal*. 26:
397-414 (Jun 83)

Warren, Reuben C. (about)

Meharry Med School Gets New Dental School
Dean. Illustrated. *Jet*. 63: 39 (24 Jan 83)

Warwick, Dionne (about)

Dionne Warwick: Speaks Out For Strong Black
Women. Illustrated. Dennis Hunt. *Ebony*. 38:
95-96 + (May 83)

Washington, Anita C. and others

Contraceptive Practices Of Teenage Mothers.
Tables, notes. *National Medical Association
Journal*. 75: 1059-1063 (Nov 83)

Washington, Booker Taliaferro (1856-1915)
(about)

Private Consequences Of A Public Controversy. . .
Grandmother, Grandfather, W.E.B. Du Bois And
Booker T. Washington. Illustrated. Adele Logan
Alexander. *Crisis*. 90: 8-11 (Feb 83)

Washington, D.C.

See Also Theater—Washington, D.C.

Washington, Dinah (about)

Remembering Dinah, Queen Of The Blues.
Illustrated. Betty DeRamus and Leslie Gourse.
Essence. 14: 76-78 + (May 83)

Washington, Harold

Washington Upsets Foes To Win Democratic Bid In
Chicago Mayoral Race. Illustrated. Robert E.
Johnson. *Jet*. 63: 6-7 + (14 Mar 83)

Washington, Harold (about)

Black Power At The Polls. Illustrated. Frank
McRae. *Black Enterprise*. 13: 17 (May 83)

Democratic Party Leaders To Stick By Washington
Despite Byrne Write-In. Illustrated. D. Michael
Cheers. *Jet*. 64: 6-8 (4 Apr 83)

Harold Washington: Makes Bold Bid To Become
Chicago's First Black Mayor. Illustrated. Robert E.
Johnson. *Jet*. 64: 12-16 + (21 Mar 83)

Harold Washington Wins Hot Race To Become
First Black Mayor Of Chicago. Illustrated, first
facts. *Jet*. 64: 4-6 + (2 May 83)

Kennedy Leads Democrats To Back Washington As
Mayor Byrne Quits Race. Illustrated. Clarence
Waldron. *Jet*. 64: 6-8 (11 Apr 83)

Mayor Harold Washington: Changing Of The Guard
In Chicago. Illustrated. Lynn Norment. *Ebony*. 38:
27-30 + (Jul 83)

Unity Banquet Draws 5,500: Washington
Supporters Told Beware Of 'False Security'.
Illustrated. *Jet*. 64: 6-8 (18 Apr 83)

The Black Vote: The New Power In Politics.
Illustrated. *Ebony*. 39: 108-110 (Nov 83)

Washington, Harold R. and Hines, Geraldine S.

"Call My Lawyer": Styling A Community Based
Defender Program. Notes. *Black Law Journal*. 08:
186-197 (Fall 83)

Watkins, Levi (Jr.) and others

Coronary Heart Disease And Bypass Surgery In
Urban Blacks. Tables, notes. *National Medical
Association Journal*. 75: 381-383 (Apr 83)

Watson, Glegg

Black Life In Corporate America: Swimming In
The Mainstream. Book review. Elza Teresa
Dinwiddie. *Black Enterprise*. 13: 27 + (Jun 83)

Black Life In Corporate America: Swimming In
The Mainstream. Book review. Gerald C. Horne.
Freedomways. 23: No. 01: 51-54 (83)

Black Life In Corporate America: Swimming In
The Mainstream. Book review. J. Alvin Wakefield.
The Urban League Review. 07: 113-115 (Summer
83)
Davis, George

Watts, Jerry G.

On Reconsidering Park, Johnson, DuBois, Frazier
And Reid: Reply To Benjamin Bowser's "The
Contribution Of Blacks To Sociological
Knowledge.". Notes. *Phylon*. 44: 273-291 (Dec
83)

Watts, Velma Gibson

New Government Proposals: The Effect On Minority Medical Education.. *National Medical Association Journal*. 75: 247-249 (Mar 83)

Wealth

See Also Millionaires

Wealth, Ethics of

Money Is The Root Of All Evil. . . And Other Bad Ideas That Keep Us Poor. Audrey Edwards. *Essence*. 14: 72-73 (Jun 83)

Of Men And Money. Illustrated. Bonnie Allen. *Essence*. 14: 89+ (Jun 83)

Weathers, Diane

His Mama!. *Essence*. 14: 57+ (Nov 83)

Webb, Joan

15th Annual Image Awards: An Historic Event. Illustrated. *Crisis*. 90: 22-27 (Jan 83)

Webb, Margot (about)

Dancing In The Dark: The Life And Times Or Margot Webb In AfrAmerican Vaudeville Of The Swing Era. Illustrated, notes. Brenda Dixon-Stowell. *Black American Literature Forum*. 17: 3-7 (Spring 83)

Weber, Michael P.

Lives Of Their Own: Blacks, Italians, And Poles In Pittsburgh, 1900-1960. Book review. Clayborne Carson. *Journal of Negro History*. 68: 98-99 (Winter 83)

Webster, Bayard

African Cattle Bones Stir Scientific Debate.. *Journal of African Civilizations*. 05: 65-66 (Apr-Nov 83)

Webster, G. Y. (joint author)

See Nowlin, T. A. (III)

Weekes, Leroy R.

Cesarean Section: A Seven-Year Study. Tables, notes. *National Medical Association Journal*. 75: 465-476 (May 83)

Weight Lifters

Pounding Pavement And Pumping Iron. Illustrated. *Ebony*. 38: 57-58+ (Jul 83)

Weight Lifting

Body Alive: Getting Stronger With Weights. Illustrated. Linda Villarosa. *Essence*. 14: 120 (Aug 83)

Weitz, Judith (joint author)

See Rosenbaum, Sara

Weixlmann, Joe

The Afro-American Novel Since 1960. Book review. *Black American Literature Forum*. 17: 134-136 (Fall 83)

Natural Birth: Poems. Book review. *Black American Literature Forum*. 17: 180-182 (Winter 83)

Wells, B. Wiggins

Nobody Says Baby. Poem. *Essence*. 14: 140 (Nov 83)

Wells, Claudette (about)

New Faces In Hollywood. Illustrated. *Ebony*. 38: 62-64+ (Apr 83)

Wendorf, Fred and others

An Ancient Harvest On The Nile. Tables. *Journal of African Civilizations*. 05: 58-64 (Apr-Nov 83)

Wesker, Lindsay

The Illustrated Encylopedia Of Black Music. Book review. Doris Evans McGinty. *The Black Perspective in Music*. 11: 212-214 (Fall 83)

Wesley, Valerie Wilson

Cost Cutting For Parents.. *Essence*. 14: 22+ (Jul 83)

'She Hit Me First!': How To Combat Sibling Rivalry.. *Essence*. 14: 138 (Oct 83)

West, Earle H.

The Negro Almanac: A Reference Work On The Afro-American. Book review. *Journal of Negro Education*. 52: 455-457 (Fall 83)

West, Emory

Auto Trade Policy: What It Means For African-Americans. Notes. *The Urban League Review*. 07: 100-112 (Summer 83)

West Indian Fiction

See Fiction, West Indian

West Indians In The United States

Children Of The Caribbean: A Study Of Diversity. Alban Cummings and others. *Journal of Black Studies*. 13: 489-495 (Jun 83)

West Point Military Academy

See United States. Military Academy

Westking Construction Corp.

Trade Pact For Guinea. Jill Nelson. *Black Enterprise*. 13: 40 (Jun 83)

Westlake, Neda M.

Marian Anderson: A Catalog Of The Collection At University Of Pennsylvania Library. Book review. Janet L. Sims-Wood. *The Black Perspective in Music*. 11: 221-222 (Fall 83)

Weusi-Puryear, Omonike

A Train Trip Through History. Illustrated. *Essence*. 14: 41-42+ (Aug 83)

Wharton-Boyd, Linda F.

The Significance Of Black American Children's Singing Games In An Educational Setting. Notes. *Journal of Negro Education*. 52: 46-56 (Winter 83)

Wharton, Clifton R. (about)

Noted Educator Says. . . "Blacks Must Never Give Up Pursuit Of Equality". Illustrated. *Crisis*. 90: 38-39 (Oct 83)

Wheat, Alan D. (about)

New Faces On Capitol Hill. Illustrated. *Ebony*. 38: 36-38 + (Feb 83)

Wheeler, Elizabeth

Essence Women: Zina Garrison. Illustrated. *Essence*. 13: 30 (Mar 83)

Whiskey

What You'd Like To Know About Scotch. Illustrated. Eunice Fried. *Black Enterprise*. 14: 140 (Oct 83)

White, Barry (about)

Barry White & Glodean White: How He Divides His Love Between His Wife And His Music. Illustrated. *Jet*. 65: 58-59 (24 Oct 83)

White, Clarence (Jr.)

The Educational Panacea Of The Black Man: Black Americans Faith In America Education, 1954-1983. Notes. *Negro Educational Review*. 34: 61-73 (Apr 83)

White, Frank (III)

Black Architects: Shapers Of Urban America. Illustrated. *Ebony*. 38: 62-64 + (Jul 83)

Dallas: A "New Frontier" For Blacks. Illustrated. *Ebony*. 38: 52-54 + (Jan 83)

A Father For All Seasons. Illustrated. *Ebony*. 38: 112-114 + (Aug 83)

How Young Men Cope With Baldness. Illustrated. *Ebony*. 38: 54 + (Jun 83)

Juggling Careers In Medicine And Music. Illustrated. *Ebony*. 38: 156-158 (Oct 83)

The Lagos/Muskogee Connection. Illustrated. *Ebony*. 38: 69-70 + (May 83)

The Man Who Has Lived Ten Years With Someone Else's Heart. Illustrated. *Ebony*. 38: 90 + (Sep 83)

The New Soul Christmas. Illustrated. *Ebony*. 39: 29-30 + (Dec 83)

School Of Religion For Men Behind Bars. Illustrated. *Ebony*. 38: 154 + (Apr 83)

Widows Who Run The Family Business. Illustrated. *Ebony*. 39: 87-88 + (Nov 83)

White, Joyce

What A Racquet! Illustrated. *Black Enterprise*. 13: 274 + (Jun 83)

White, Paula S.

Betting It All Together. Book review. *Essence*. 14: 48 (Nov 83)

Leave The Styling To Us! Illustrated. *Essence*. 14: 18 (Nov 83)

Wanakee. Illustrated. *Essence*. 14: 62 (Dec 83) Garth-Taylor, Mikki

White, Paulette Childress

Claudie Mae. Poem. *Essence*. 14: 125 (Jul 83)

White, Rita (about)

How This Sister Turned A Winning Bid Into A Gold Mine! Illustrated. Lloyd Gite. *Essence*. 14: 31 (Jul 83)

White, Robert L.

In Pursuit Of Affirmative Action.. *The Urban League Review*. 07: 6-7 (Summer 83)

White, Terry L.

Havens Realty Corp. V. Coleman: Standing To Sue Under The Fair Housing Act. Notes. *Black Law Journal*. 08: 127-131 (Spring 83)

Whitehead, Tony L. (joint author)

See Gentemann, Karen M.

Whiting, Estelle

How Travel Agents Can Smooth Out Your Trip.. *Essence*. 13: 38 + (Jan 83)

Whitley, Elaine Brown

Can We Have It All? Illustrated. *Essence*. 13: 84-86 + (Mar 83)

Whitlow, Joan

Men's Health Watch.. *Essence*. 14: 25-26 (Nov 83)

Whitman, Daniel

Bio-Bibliographie Des Ecrivains Congolais: Belles Lettres - Littérature. Book review. *Research in African Literatures*. 14: 215-216 (Summer 83)

Wholesale Trade

Behind The Eight Ball In The Wholesale Industry. Illustrated. Andrew F. Brimmer. *Black Enterprise*. 13: 35 (Apr 83)

Wife Abuse

Why Women Stay With Men Who Beat Them And Why They Finally Leave. Illustrated. Beverly Mesch. *Essence*. 13: 84-87 + (Apr 83)

Wigutoff, Sharon and Santos-Rivera, Iris

U.S. History Texts: Any Change In Ten Years? Illustrated, notes. *Interracial Books for Children*. 14: No. 1: 17-20 (83)

Wiley, Bell I.

Slaves No More: Letters From Liberia, 1833-1869. Book review, Notes. Jason H. Silverman. *Negro History Bulletin*. 46: 105 (Oct-Dec 83)

Wilkerson, Margaret B.

The Sighted Eyes And Feeling Heart Of Lorraine Hansberry. Notes. *Black American Literature Forum*. 17: 8-13 (Spring 83)

Willhelm, Sidney M.

Black/White Equality: The Socioeconomic Conditions Of Blacks In America, Part II. Notes. *Journal of Black Studies*. 14: 151-184 (Dec 83)

Williams, Alexander (Jr.)

Constitutional Reflections On California's Request For Identification Law. Notes. *Black Law Journal*. 08: 177-185 (Fall 83)

The Impact Of Rule 48 Upon The Black Student Athlete: A Comment. Notes, tables. *Journal of Negro Education.* 52: 362-373 (Summer 83)

Williams, Alice Mae (about)

Super Mom, Super Kids. Illustrated. Pamela Noel. *Ebony.* 38: 44+ (Oct 83)

Williams, Billy Dee (about)

Billy Dee Williams: The Serious Side Of A Sex Symbol. Illustrated. Charles L. Sanders. *Ebony.* 38: 126-128+ (Jun 83)

Gladys Knight And Billy Dee Williams: Stars Of 'EbonysJet Celebrity Showcase'. Illustrated. *Jet.* 64: 54-56 (1 Aug 83)

Williams, Bishetta Merritt (joint author)

See Anderson, WIlliam H. (Jr.)

Williams, Byron

A Decade Of Progress?. *Interracial Books for Children.* 14: No. 1: 4-5 (83)

Williams, Darnell (about)

Showstopper: Darnell Williams. Illustrated. Ruth Dolores Manuel. *Essence.* 14: 35 (Nov 83)

Williams, David

Hit Hard. Book review. Chester A. (Sr.) Higgins. *Crisis.* 90: 44-47 (Nov 83)

Williams, Dennis

No Tax Breaks For Racism. Illustrated. *Black Enterprise.* 14: 17 (Sep 83)

When Your Child Is Young, Gifted And Black. Illustrated. *Black Enterprise.* 14: 68-69 (Sep 83)

Williams, Dennis A.

Gain The Competitive Edge. Illustrated. *Black Enterprise.* 14: 34-38+ (Sep 83)

Making The Best Deal For New Wheels. Illustrated. *Black Enterprise.* 14: 81-82+ (Nov 83)

Williams, Frank

I Heard A Child Crying. Notes. *Journal of Religious Thought.* 40: 65-71 (Spring-Summer 83)

Williams, Franklin H. (joint author)

See Lapchick, Richard

Williams, Helen R.

National Opera Ebony Is Alive And Doing Well.. *Crisis.* 90: 25 (Apr 83)

Williams, James

The Negro Almanac: A Reference Work On The Afro-American. Book review. Earle H. West. *Journal of Negro Education.* 52: 455-457 (Fall 83)

Williams, Joseph

Why Are Blacks Less Suicide Prone Than Whites?. *Crisis.* 90: 29 (Dec 83)

Williams, Margo Walker

Essence Women: Dorothy Cousins. Illustrated. *Essence.* 13: 25 (Feb 83)

Essense Women: Mary Brown. Illustrated. *Essence.* 13: 24 (Apr 83)

Williams, Martin

The Jazz Tradition. Book review. George L. Starks. *The Black Perspective in Music.* 11: 215-218 (Fall 83)

Williams-Myers, A. J.

Biological Differences, Social Inequality, And Distributive Goods: An Exploratory Argument. Notes. *Journal of Black Studies.* 13: 399-416 (Jun 83)

Williams, Sherley Anne

Straight Talk From Plain Women. Poem. *Essence.* 14: 89 (Oct 83)

Williams, Sylvia H. (about)

Essence Women: Sylvia H. Williams. Illustrated. Ken Smikle. *Essence.* 14: 52 (Aug 83)

Williams, Vanessa (about)

Here She Is. . . Miss America. Illustrated. Lynn Norment. *Ebony.* 39: 132-134+ (Dec 83)

Miss America Visits Chicago And Tells How She Copes With Her New Role. Illustrated. *Jet.* 65: 12-14 (24 Oct 83)

The New Miss America: Beauty, Brains And Blackness. Illustrated. Kuumba Kazi-Ferrouillet. *Black Collegian.* 14: 48-49+ (Nov-Dec 83)

Vanessa Williams: New Miss America Wants Character, Not Color To Count. Illustrated. *Jet.* 65: 12-16+ (10 Oct 83)

Williams, Winnie

The Agony Of Cape Town. Poem, Illustrated. *Crisis.* 90: 43 (Apr 83)

An Autumn Memoir: Of Adam And Sunday Strolls In Mid-Century Harlem. Poem, Illustrated. *Crisis.* 90: 34-36 (Feb 83)

Willie, Charles V.

Community Politics And Educational Change: Ten School Systems Under Court Order. Book review. George L. Mims. *Journal of Black Studies.* 13: 375-376 (Mar 83)

A Theory Of Liberation Leadership. Notes. *Journal of Negro History.* 68: 1-7 (Winter 83)

Willingham, Alex

Sowell's Knowledge And Decisions: Can Black Conservatism Establish Its Intellectual Credibility?. Notes. *Review of Black Political Economy.* 12: 179-187 (Winter 83)

Willis, Miriam DeCosta

Folklore And The Creative Artist: Lydia Cabrera And Zora Neale Hurston. Notes. *CLA Journal.* 27: 81-90 (Sep 83)

Wills

Will Power: Don't Leave Life Without It. David C. Larsen. *Essence.* 14: 35+ (Oct 83)

Wilson, Ernest J. (III)

Blacks And The Industrial Policy Debate. Illustrated. *about. . . time.* 11: 8-10 (Aug 83)

Wolf, Jacquelyn H. and others

Access Of The Black Urban Elderly To Medical Care. Tables, notes. *National Medical Association Journal*. 75: 41-46 (Jan 83)

Women

The Black Woman-Overcoming The Odds. Althea T. L. Simmons. *Crisis*. 90: 14-15 (Jun-Jul 83)

Black Women And Homeownership: The Financial Challenge Of The '80s. Tables, notes. Shirley Better. *Black Scholar*. 14: 38-45 (Sep-Oct 83)

Black Women-Meeting Today's Challenges. Illustrated. Jewell Jackson McCabe. *Crisis*. 90: 10-12 (Jun-Jul 83)

What To Say When Someone Tells You, 'It Pays To Be A Black Woman'. Vanessa J. Gallman. *Essence*. 13: 89-90 (Mar 83)

See Also Beauty Contestants
Mothers
Single Women

Women—Africa

The Role Of Women In The Revolution. Sekou Toure. *Black Scholar*. 14: 8-12 (Sep-Oct 83)

Women Air Pilots

Air Force Graduates First Black Woman Pilot. Illustrated, first facts. *Ebony*. 38: 46+ (Jan 83)

Women And Alcohol

See Alcohol And Women

Women And Men

About Men. Editorial. Susan L. Taylor. *Essence*. 14: 51 (Nov 83)

Any Man Won't Do! Carol Botwin and Jerome L. Fine. *Essence*. 13: 74-75+ (Feb 83)

Can Women And Men Be Friends? Illustrated. Rosemary L. Bray. *Essence*. 14: 71-72+ (Jul 83)

My 'Dream Girl' Is Beautiful, Smart, Ambitious, But Can I Deal With Her In Real Life? Illustrated. Nelson George. *Essence*. 14: 14 (Aug 83)

Of Men And Money. Illustrated. Bonnie Allen. *Essence*. 14: 89+ (Jun 83)

Women Artists

Varnette Honeywood: Art That Hits Home. Illustrated. Stephanie Honeywood. *Essence*. 14: 97+ (Aug 83)

Women Authors

Jessie Fauset Of The Crisis: Novelist, Feminist, Centenarian. Illustrated. Joseph J. Feeney. *Crisis*. 90: 20+ (Jun-Jul 83)

Maya Angelou: The Heart Of The Woman. Illustrated. Stephanie Stokes Oliver. *Essence*. 14: 112-114+ (May 83)

Women Automobile Racing Drivers

Essence Women: Cheryl Glass. Illustrated. Joy Duckett. *Essence*. 13: 29 (Mar 83)

Women Clergy

Baptist Church Appoints First Black Woman Pastor. Illustrated, first facts. *Jet*. 64: 25 (13 Jun 83)

Black Women As Clergy And The Black Religious Experience. Illustrated. Doris E. Saunders. *Crisis*. 90: 16+ (Jun-Jul 83)

Essence Women: Suzan D. Johnson. Illustrated. Mai Brown. *Essence*. 14: 42 (Sep 83)

Woman At The Helm Of Philadelphia Presbytery. Illustrated. Marilyn Marshall. *Ebony*. 38: 51-52+ (Jul 83)

Women College Presidents

New Jersey Gets First Black Woman President At Stockton State College. Illustrated, first facts. *Jet*. 64: 23 (20 Jun 83)

Women College Students

Campus Queens At Black Colleges. Illustrated. *Ebony*. 38: 40-42+ (May 83)

How To Speak Effectively: Tips For Coeds. Illustrated. Rosanne Kent. *Black Collegian*. 13: 30+ (Apr-May 83)

Women Cadets Make Coast Guard History. Illustrated, first facts. Marilyn Marshall. *Ebony*. 38: 138+ (Apr 83)

Women—Crimes Against

See Also Wife Abuse

Women—Employment

Are Black Women Taking Black Men's Jobs? Illustrated. Marilyn Marshall. *Ebony*. 38: 60+ (Aug 83)

Can We Have It All? Illustrated. Elaine Brown Whitley. *Essence*. 13: 84-86+ (Mar 83)

The Essence Working Woman's Guide: Take Charge! Illustrated. Alice Jones-Miller and Elaine C. Ray. *Essence*. 13: 75-82 (Mar 83)

Making That Move: Relocating For A Better Job. Lloyd Gite. *Essence*. 13: 32+ (Jan 83)

Women Executives

Beer Brewery Boss. Illustrated. Pamela Noel. *Ebony*. 38: 40+ (Jun 83)

Black Women In Corporate America: Managing The Game. Illustrated. Audrey Edwards. *Essence*. 13: 70-72+ (Mar 83)

Essence Women! Lenora T. Cartright. Illustrated. Angela Kinamore. *Essence*. 14: 40 (Sep 83)

Essence Women: Sylvia H. Williams. Illustrated. Ken Smikle. *Essence*. 14: 52 (Aug 83)

Essense Women: Mary Hatwood Futrell. Illustrated. Celeste Bullock. *Essence*. 14: 38 (Nov 83)

A Family Affair: Patricia Shaw Succeeds Father As President Of Universal Life. Illustrated. Lynn Norment. *Ebony*. 38: 75-76+ (May 83)

Mary Hatwood Futrell: Top Teacher. Illustrated. Steve Askin. *Black Enterprise*. 14: 124-126+ (Oct 83)

New President At Universal. Illustrated. Fatima Shaik. *Black Enterprise*. 13: 36 (Jun 83)

Pauline Strayhorne Is Major Federal's Prime Asset. Illustrated, tables. Sharron Kornegay. *Black Enterprise*. 13: 129-130+ (Jun 83)

Teachers Union Boss. Illustrated. *Ebony*. 38: 140+ (Oct 83)

Virna Canson: Fighting Fire With Fire. Illustrated. Elizabeth Fernandez. *Crisis*. 90: 26+ (Jun-Jul 83)

Women—Grenada

Grenada's Women Move Forward With The Revolution. Annette Walker. *Freedomways*. 23: No. 01: 23-28 (83)

Women—Health And Hygiene

See Also Beauty, Personal

Women—History

A Black Women's History Conference. Shirley B. Cathie and Willa Blackshear. *Crisis*. 90: 56-57 (Jun-Jul 83)

Women In Literature

Dilsey: Faulkner's Black Mammy In The Sound And The Fury. Notes. Sandra D. Milloy. *Negro History Bulletin*. 46: 70-71 (Jul-Sep 83)

"Tuh de Horizon And Back": The Female Quest In Their Eyes Were Watching God. Notes. Missy Dehn Kubitschek. *Black American Literature Forum*. 17: 109-115 (Fall 83)

Women In Caribbean Literature: The African Presence. Notes. Loeta S. Lawrence. *Phylon*. 44: 1-10 (Mar 83)

Women In Politics

Essence Women: Gloria Davis. Illustrated. Ruth Manuel. *Essence*. 14: 56 (Jul 83)

Women In Public Life

Dorsey Nunley: Creating Community Change. Illustrated. Robin Wilson. *about. . . time*. 11: 20-21 (Nov 83)

Essence Women: Barbara J. Mahone. Illustrated. Marcie Eanes. *Essence*. 14: 56 (Dec 83)

In Memoriam: Doris Mossie Thomas. Bethel Dukes. *Journal of Negro History*. 68: 144-145 (Winter 83)

Juanita Jewel Craft: Just Look At Her "Kids". Illustrated. Ann L. Reagins. *Crisis*. 90: 36-37 (Jun-Jul 83)

Women In The Mass Media Industry

Where There's A Will. . . This Woman Should Not Be Alive: The Miracle Of Merri Dee. Illustrated. Roger Witherspoon. *Essence*. 13: 72-74+ (Apr 83)

Women Journalists

Essence Women: Barbara Banks. Illustrated. Curtia James. *Essence*. 13: 20+ (Jan 83)

Women Judges

Black Woman Judge Is Named To Missouri Court. First facts. *Jet*. 64: 30 (2 May 83)

Black Women On The Bench: Wielding The Gavel Of Change. Illustrated. *Ebony*. 38: 110-112+ (Feb 83)

Profiles: LaDoris Hazzard Cordell. Portrait. Julie E. Hall. *Black Law Journal*. 08: 150-151 (Spring 83)

Women Lawyers

Profiles: Linda Taylor Ferguson. Portrait. Sandra K. Mitchell. *Black Law Journal*. 08: 144-146 (Spring 83)

Women Missionaries

See Missionaries, Women

Women-Owned Business Enterprises

A Dallas Paralegal Builds Her Own Lucrative Business. Illustrated. Lloyd Gite. *Essence*. 14: 22 (May 83)

Entrepreneurship: A Viable Alternative. Illustrated. Philip A. Loyd. *about. . . time*. 11: 14-16+ (Mar 83)

Essence Women: Jaki Hall. Illustrated. Sandra Harley. *Essence*. 14: 54 (Jun 83)

Essence Women: Valerie Shaw. Illustrated. Retha Camp. *Essence*. 13: 25 (Jan 83)

The Fortune That Madame Built. Illustrated. Jill Nelson. *Essence*. 14: 84-86+ (Jun 83)

How This Sister Turned A Winning Bid Into A Gold Mine! Illustrated. Lloyd Gite. *Essence*. 14: 31 (Jul 83)

In The Chips! Illustrated. Knolly Moses. *Essence*. 14: 30 (Aug 83)

Keeping It In The Family. Illustrated. Lloyd Gite. *Essence*. 14: 36 (Dec 83)

Leave The Styling To Us! Illustrated. Paula S. White. *Essence*. 14: 18 (Nov 83)

Star Teacher: Training Kids For TV Ads. Illustrated. Marcia McNair. *Essence*. 14: 18+ (Sep 83)

Taking Care Of Business. Illustrated. Lloyd Gite. *Essence*. 13: 28 (Jan 83)

Two Women In Houston Turn Their Dreams Of Owning A Bookstore Into A Successful Reality. Illustrated. Lloyd Gite. *Essence*. 13: 32+ (Mar 83)

Up, Up And Away. Illustrated. Lloyd Gite. *Essence*. 14: 44 (Oct 83)

Widows Who Run The Family Business. Illustrated. Frank (III) White. *Ebony*. 39: 87-88+ (Nov 83)

Women Physicians

The Black Female Physician: A Double Jeopardy. Robert L. M. Hilliard. *National Medical Association Journal*. 75: 253-254 (Mar 83)

Women Politicians

Her Honor, The Mayor. Illustrated. Julie Chenault. *Essence*. 14: 14+ (Jul 83)

Women—Psychology

Black Women's Anger. Illustrated. Audre Lorde. *Essence*. 14: 90-92+ (Oct 83)

Coping With First-Baby Blues. Irene Pickhardt. *Essence*. 13: 112 (Feb 83)

What Every Black Man Should Know About Black Women. Illustrated. Lynn Norment. *Ebony*. 38: 132+ (Aug 83)

Why Some Women Prefer Older Men. Illustrated. Lynn Norment. *Ebony*. 38: 132+ (Apr 83)

Women—Puerto Rico

The Roles Of Women In Puerto Rico. Iris Santos-Rivera. *Interracial Books for Children.* 14: No. 1: 21-22 (83)

Women's Liberation Movement

See Feminism

Women's Rights

What The ERA Means To Us. Illustrated. Carmen Carter. *Essence.* 13: 1154 (Mar 83)

Women—Sexual Behavior

The Price We Paid For 'Giving It Up'. Bonnie Allen. *Essence.* 13: 61-62+ (Feb 83)

Women—Social Conditions

Out Of Egypt: A Talk With Nawal El Saadawi. Tiffany R. Patterson and Angela M. Gilliam. *Freedomways.* 23: No. 3: 186-194 (83)

Women—Suffrage

Colored Women As Voters (September, 1912). Adella Hunt Logan. *Crisis.* 90: 11 (Feb 83)

Frederick Douglass And Woman Suffrage. Notes. S. Jay Walker. *Black Scholar.* 14: 18-25 (Sep-Oct 83)

The Justice Of Woman Suffrage [September, 1912]. Mary Church (1863-1954) Terrell. *Crisis.* 90: 6 (Jun-Jul 83)

Two Suffrage Movements [September, 1912]. Tables. Martha Gruening. *Crisis.* 90: 6-8 (Jun-Jul 83)

Women Surgeons

Neurosurgery: Two Black Women Surgeons Are Pioneers In Highly Specialized Medical Field. Illustrated. Marilyn Marshall. *Ebony.* 38: 72-74+ (Sep 83)

Women Tennis Players

Essence Women: Zina Garrison. Illustrated. Elizabeth Wheeler. *Essence.* 13: 30 (Mar 83)

Wonder, Stevie

A Message To Black College Students. Illustrated. *Black Collegian.* 13: 24-25 (Dec-Jan 83)

Woodall, Phillip L.

A Percussion of Finality: Vietnam Flashback. Illustrated. *about. . . time.* 11: 28-32 (Nov 83)

Woods, Jeanne M.

No Progress On Namibia. Illustrated. *Black Enterprise.* 14: 22 (Nov 83)

UN Debate On Namibia. Illustrated. *Black Enterprise.* 14: 18 (Aug 83)

Woods, Keith M.

New Orleans Cops On Trial. Illustrated. *Black Enterprise.* 13: 23 (Mar 83)

Woods, Randall Bennett

A Black Odyssey: John Lewis Waller And The Promise Of American Life, 1878-1900. Book review. G. W. Reid. *Journal of Negro History.* 68: 119-120 (Winter 83)

Woodson, Carter Godwin (1875-1950) (about)

Chronicles Of Black Courage (Part III): Father Of Black History Changed Vision Of Black America. Illustrated. Lerone (Jr.) Bennett. *Ebony.* 38: 31-32+ (Feb 83)

Wordsworth, William—Criticism And Interpretation

Wordsworth's Secular Imagination And "Spots On Time". Notes. Allen Chavkin. *CLA Journal.* 26: 452-464 (Jun 83)

Workman, Eleanor (about)

Essence Women: Eleanor Workman. Illustrated. Kitty Oliver. *Essence.* 14: 54 (Dec 83)

World Assembly For Peace And Life Against Nuclear War, 1983

Dialogues Of The World Assembly For Peace And Life, Against Nuclear War - Prague, Czechoslovakia June 21-26, 1983.. *Black Scholar.* 14: 44-46 (Nov-Dec 83)

Nuclear Policy, Social Justice, And The Third World. Tables. Robert Chrisman. *Black Scholar.* 14: 26-43 (Nov-Dec 83)

World's Fair

See New Orleans. Louisiana World's Exposition, 1984

Worry

Reach For It! Editorial. Susan L. Taylor. *Essence.* 13: 65 (Mar 83)

Wren, Robert M.

A Critical View On Elechi Amadi's. Book review. *Research in African Literatures.* 14: 110-111 (Spring 83)

A Critical View On John Pepper Clark's Selected Poems. Book review. *Research in African Literatures.* 14: 110-112 (Spring 83)

A Critical View On Wole Soyinka's The Lion And The Jewel. Book review. *Research in African Literatures.* 14: 110-111 (Spring 83)

The Hero As A Villain. Book review. *Research in African Literatures.* 14: 112-113 (Spring 83)

Wright, Charles H.

The Active Management Of Prolonged Labor. Illustrated, notes. *National Medical Association Journal.* 75: 223-226 (Feb 83)

Wright, Dale

Coasting Down California By Rail. Illustrated. *Black Enterprise.* 13: 270+ (Jun 83)

Wright, George C.

Black Political Insurgency In Louisville, Kentucky: The Lincoln Independent Party Of 1921. Notes. *Journal of Negro History.* 68: 8-23 (Winter 83)

Wright, Josephine

Art Songs By Black American Composers. Record review. *The Black Perspective in Music.* 11: 93-95 (Spring 83)

Spirituals. Record review. *The Black Perspective in Music.* 11: 93-95 (Spring 83)

Wright, Michael Frank

Grenada: The Events, The Future.. *Black Scholar.* 14: 21-25 (Nov-Dec 83)

Wright, Richard L.

Functional Language, Socialization, And Academic Achievement. Notes. *Journal of Negro Education.* 52: 3-14 (Winter 83)

Wright, Richard (1908-1960)—Criticism And Interpretation

Folkloric Aspects Of Wright's "The Man Who Killed A Shadow". Notes. Eugene E. Miller. *CLA Journal.* 27: 210-223 (Dec 83)

Wright, Sonny (about)

No Checks; Cash Only. Valerie J. Hill. *Black Enterprise.* 13: 22 (Apr 83)

Writing, Akan

The Ancient Akan Script: A Review Of Sankofa, By Niangoran-Bouah. Illustrated. Willard R. Johnson. *Journal of African Civilizations.* 05: 197-207 (Apr-Nov 83)

Writing (Authorship)

See Authorship

Writing, Mande

The Ancient Manding Script. Notes, illustrated. Clyde-Ahmad Winters. *Journal of African Civilizations.* 05: 208-214 (Apr-Nov 83)

Wyatt, Lucius (joint author)

See Singleton, Alvin

Wyatt, Lucius R.

Black Music In America: A Bibliography. Book review. *The Black Perspective in Music.* 11: 219-220 (Fall 83)

Fifteen Black American Composers: A Bibliography Of Their Works. Book review. *The Black Perspective in Music.* 11: 219-220 (Fall 83)

A Paul Robeson Research Guide: A Selected Annotated Bibliography. Book review. *The Black Perspective in Music.* 11: 219-220 (Fall 83)

Wynne, Darcel (about)

New Faces In Hollywood. Illustrated. *Ebony.* 38: 62-64 + (Apr 83)

Yancey, Elana

Becoming A Lawyer: A Humanistic Perspective On Legal Education And Professionalism. Book review. *Black Law Journal.* 08: 164-166 (Spring 83)

Yankah, Kwesi

To Praise Or Not To Praise The King: The Akan Apae In The Context Of Referential Poetry. Notes. *Research in African Literatures.* 14: 381-400 (Fall 83)

Yanz, Lynda

Sandino's Daughters: Testimonies Of Nicaraguan Women In Struggle. Book review. Janice Bevien. *Black Scholar.* 14: 74-75 (Mar-Apr 83)

Yeager, Peter C.

Corporate Crime. Book review, Notes. Walter L. (III) Gordon. *Black Law Journal.* 08: 152-159 (Spring 83)

Yesufu, A. Rasheed

Opera Wonyosi. Book review. *Journal of Black Studies.* 13: 496-499 (Jun 83)

Yorubas

The Yoruba Number System. Illustrated, tables. Claudia Zaslavsky. *Journal of African Civilizations.* 05: 110-126 (Apr-Nov 83)

Young, Andrew S.

Major Issues Facing Black Youth. Illustrated. *Black Collegian.* 14: 54-56 + (Sep-Oct 83)

Youth

Major Issues Facing Black Youth. Illustrated. Andrew S. Young. *Black Collegian.* 14: 54-56 + (Sep-Oct 83)

See Also Adolescence
Handicapped Youth

Youth And Drugs

See Drugs And Youth

Youth And Television

See Television And Youth

Youth And The Performing Arts

See Performing Arts And Youth

Youth—Attitudes

Psychopolitical Orientations Of White And Black Youth: A Test Of Five Models. Tables, notes. Samuel Long. *Journal of Black Studies.* 13: 439-456 (Jun 83)

Youth—Employment

Black Teenage Unemployment. Frank (III) Harris. *Crisis.* 90: 38-39 (Jan 83)

Boycotting For Jobs. Illustrated. David J. Dent. *Black Enterprise.* 13: 28 (Mar 83)

Eighteen-Year-Old Financial Whiz. Illustrated. *Ebony.* 38: 121-122 (Oct 83)

How To Plan A Productive Summer. Illustrated. Doris Clarke. *Black Collegian.* 13: 27-28 + (Dec-Jan 83)

The Implications Of Labor Market Orientation Programs For Black Teenage Job Entry: A Response To Nelms And Pentecoste. Notes. Ruppert L. Evans. *Negro Educational Review.* 34: 79-82 (Apr 83)

Zangrando, Robert L.

The N.A.A.C.P. Crusade Against Lynching, 1909-1950. Book review. A. Wade Smith. *Phylon.* 44: 169 (Jun 83)

Zaslavsky, Claudia

Count On Your Fingers African Style. Book review. Jane Califf. *Interracial Books for Children.* 14: No. 5: 27 (83)

Tic Tac Toe And Other Three-In-A-Row Games From Ancient Egypt To The Modern Computer. Book review. Marian Borenstein. *Freedomways*. 23: No. 01: 54-55 (83)

Senefer And Hatshepsut. Book review. *Freedomways*. 23: No. 4: 294-296 (83)

The Yoruba Number System. Illustrated, tables. *Journal of African Civilizations*. 05: 110-126 (Apr-Nov 83)

Zehring, John William

How To Get The Job You Want.. *Black Collegian*. 13: 50-54 + (Feb-Mar 83)

Zemach, Margot

Jake And Honeybunch Go To Heaven. Book review. Beryle Banfield. *Interracial Books for Children*. 14: No. 1: 32-33 (83)

Zimbabwe

   See Also Cities And Towns, Ancient—Zimbabwe

Zogby, James

Palestinian Identity And The Land Of Palestine.. *Freedomways*. 23: No. 2: 118-125 (83)

Zoning Law—United States

Exclusion Zoning - City Of Memphis V. Greene. Notes. Julie E. Hall. *Black Law Journal*. 08: 138-143 (Spring 83)